THE PARIS COMMUNE

THE PARIS COMMUNE

An Episode in the History of the
Socialist Movement

EDWARD S. MASON

NEW YORK

Howard Fertig

1967

First published in 1930 by The Macmillan Company

HOWARD FERTIG, INC. EDITION 1967
Published by arrangement with the author

Library of Congress Catalog Card Number: 67-24588

PRINTED IN THE UNITED STATES OF AMERICA
BY NOBLE OFFSET PRINTERS, INC.

PREFACE

The history of an event, a movement, or a situation is never and can never be a completed task, for we bring to the study of history a series of questions which change continually with our changing interests. As we ask different questions and select our materials with respect to these questions, we arrive at a story of the past which may indeed approach nearer than before to our ideal of historical accuracy but which never, by the very nature of the process, can attain it.

This history of the Commune of Paris had its origin in the socialist and communist interpretation of the revolution formulated by Karl Marx and embellished by his disciples. It examines the material and considers the issues very largely from the point of view of that interpretation. Since, to the socialists, the Commune is not merely an incident in the history of France, but an epoch-making event in the world struggle between proletariat and bourgeoisie, the questions it suggests and attempts to answer must conform to this conception.

Such a history is not and does not pretend to be inclusive. I have purposely neglected such important matters as the contemporary communal uprising in the provinces, the organizations which developed for conciliation between Paris and Versailles, and others, and have avoided a description of the details of the civil war. The primary thesis of the socialist interpretation is that the revolution was proletarian and socialist, and, in consequence, the origins and development of the Commune have been interrogated with this in mind. This explains the long chapter assigned to the socialism of the period in France and to the events

v

which immediately preceded the revolution. Furthermore, attention has been focussed on those things which the socialists emphasize, in an attempt to compare their interpretation with the reality as I see it.

The legend of the Commune has had, and will have, far more influence upon events than the fact. In order to understand the legend it is necessary to know the fact. In consequence I have attempted in the following pages to achieve two objects; first, to present an account of the Commune, and, second, of the socialist and communist interpretation of the Commune. My chief concern throughout has been to assign to the revolution its place in the history of the socialist movement.

I am greatly indebted to Professor C. C. Brinton and Professor W. L. Langer of Harvard, who have read the manuscript, and to my former student, Mr. C. Klepinin, who has given me invaluable aid on the section dealing with the communist interpretation of the Commune. I wish also to express my gratitude to the Harvard Bureau of International Research for a grant which has enabled me to carry on a study of material available only in Paris.

INTRODUCTION

THE HISTORICAL SIGNIFICANCE OF THE PARIS COMMUNE

THE close of the Franco-Prussian war, foreshadowed by the capitulation of Paris on January 28th, 1871, after four months of heroic resistance, was quickly followed by an uprising which has long ago taken its place beside the revolutions of 1830 and 1848. The radical republicans of Paris, among whom were mingled socialists of all shades of opinion, established a government which for two months ruled the capital and gave battle to established authority in France. This government collapsed during the last week of May in the bloodiest bit of street fighting of the century.

The Commune is often lost sight of in the larger panorama of the Franco-Prussian War. Despite the profound impression which it made upon contemporaries with its bombardment of Paris, its summary executions, the massacres in the streets, and the eccentricities of its revolutionary government, it quickly lost its separate identity. For a while conservatives in France and in Europe saw in the revolution of March 18th the hand of socialism. The Commune made the reputation of Karl Marx in France and generated in Europe a remarkable fear of the First International. But soon, as the real weakness of this organization became evident, opinion turned the other way and students of the Commune were inclined to regard it as a regrettable but inevitable by-product of the war. Its socialist origins were vague and its socialist intentions, dubious. Fifteen thousand men were dead, another fifteen thousand imprisoned, and a considerable part of the most beautiful city in Europe destroyed for apparently indefinable reasons and with inappreciable results. The Commune disappeared, leaving scarcely a trace on the institutional life or development of France.

It has been rescued, however, from its somewhat insignificant position as an incident in the history of France, by the activity of the socialists and the communists. In their hands it has become an event of world-shaking importance, a proletarian and socialist revolution par excellence, and the first real government of the working class. The Commune of Paris is, in the opinion of the communists, the immediate forbear of the Russian Soviet. The uprising of March 18th was more than a striking episode, a dramatic skirmish in the dawning world war of proletariat against bourgeoisie. It was, distinctly, a step toward the socialist world to come. From its achievements and its mistakes are to be learned lessons of indispensable importance in the strategy of the class struggle.

Marx, Engels, Lenin, Trotsky, Kautsky, to mention only the most eminent of socialist and communist leaders, have all studied the Commune. All have written accounts of this revolution and all have set down its lessons for the guidance of their parties. Marx finished his pamphlet, "Civil War in France" two days after the defeat of the Commune and cast it in the form of an address to the International Workingmen's Association, the First International. In this work, the classic socialist account of the Commune, the uprising appears as a revolution of the Paris proletariat; the Commune is a new achievement, the governmental instrument of the working class at last discovered.

The Russian communists recognize in the Paris Commune a true predecessor to the government of "Workers and Peasants." Lenin, who wrote voluminously on the Commune, was never tired of extolling its praises or pointing its moral. According to Zinoviev, on no other foreign proletarian movement did he lavish such attention.[1] "The soviet power," said Lenin, "is the second universal-historical step or stage in the development of the Dictatorship of the Proletariat. The first step was the Paris Commune." [2]

The leaders and the events of the revolution of 1871 have taken their place in socialist mythology. The 18th of March was the first recognized socialist celebration and is a holiday at the present time in Russia. The horrors of "bloody week," the "white terror of 1871," supply many-told tales in socialist and communist circles. The famous "mur des Fédérés" in the Parisian cemetery of Père Lachaise, where one hundred and fifty of the defenders of the Commune were shot, is a sacred shrine to true believers, and a favorite place of pilgrimage. Streets and squares are named for the leaders of the Commune wherever socialist or communist influence is strong. The street of the "18th of March" graces many a Russian town.

The socialists have taken the Commune from the history of France and, by their interpretation, have made of it a momentous event in the history of socialism. Such treatment has required, perhaps, a certain distortion of the facts.

Marxian socialism, taking its stand on the economic interpretation of history, leads naturally to the creation of an historical mythology. Marx's great contribution to the socialist movement was the "scientific" demonstration that a socialistic order of society is historically inevitable. Since the forces which are so inexorably engaged in producing this desired end make themselves manifest in history, there exists for Marxian socialists a practically uncontrollable tendency to discover in every historical event the evidence of the operation of these beneficent forces. This is not to say, of course, that other definitely formulated philosophies

[1] From a speech at the 5th Congress of the Komintern in celebration of the Paris Commune. See Gambarov, *Parizhskaia Kommuna* (Moscow, 1925).
[2] *Uroky Kommuny.*

of history do not have the same effect upon their votaries. But, in the Marxian interpretation, the evolution of history leads to results so eminently desirable to socialists that an extraordinary incentive to misrepresentation is unavoidable.[3] The Commune of Paris has been a subject peculiarly favored with such treatment.

The revolution of March 18th, thus resuscitated and properly clothed, has become a living force of very considerable moment in the socialist and particularly the communist movement. As so often happens, the living myth has supplanted the dead fact. The interpretation of the Commune, sponsored by Marx and Lenin, is now spread wide in communist Russia by agitators, propagandists, popular brochures, and anniversary celebrations. Its dramatic incidents have given birth to a dozen plays, and revolutionary poetry draws copious inspiration from this source. The Commune is now as much a part of the history of the socialist movement as is the American revolution a part of the history of the United States.

In the light of this fact the history of the revolution of 1871 must be reconsidered. Was it proletarian and was it socialist? Was it a revolutionary class struggle or something quite other than this? The Marxian version has it that the Commune was socialist because proletarian, "for the proletariat can fight for no other cause than socialism." But this is a complete *non sequitur* to any other than a believer in the Marxian theory of an economically determined class struggle in which the participants are a class-conscious proletariat and a class-conscious bourgeoisie.

The Commune of Paris, as a matter of fact, sprang from an exceedingly complicated historical situation. Irritation and disgust at the loss of the war, the misery of the four-month siege of Paris, the struggle of republicanism against

[3] Of course all "optimistic" philosophies of history, all philosophies embodying the conception of historical progress, are subject to the same dangers.

monarchy, socialist desires and aspirations clothed in the
ideas of Proudhon and Blanqui, all mingled inextricably in
the causes of the revolution. No simple explanation such
as that implied in the socialist theory of the class struggle
can be accepted.

CONTENTS

THE PARIS COMMUNE

CHAPTER I

SOCIALISM IN FRANCE IN THE 1860's

THE coup d'état of Napoleon III put the final quietus on the Utopianism of 1848. Commentators spoke of the death of socialism, held up to eternal obloquy in the national workshops of Louis Blanc.[1] As a matter of fact socialism was being reborn. At this very time Marx and Engels were drafting the manifesto of the Communist Party and were writing, "a spectre hovers over Europe—the spectre of communism."

In France, it is true, the eager, romantic socialism of the 1830's and 1840's appeared to have expired. Louis Blanc, exiled, was writing his history of the revolution, in London. Blanqui, the only true leader of the proletariat in 1848, as Marx called him, was serving another of his interminable prison sentences. Étienne Cabet was experiencing the tribulation of Icaria in the cold and hostile environment of Illinois. The school of Fourier was perpetuated only in the person of the compromising Victor Considérant, and the St. Simonians had long since ceased to follow the wanderings of Père Enfantin and had turned themselves to banking and engineering. After all, was not Napoleon himself an old follower of Fourier and professedly sympathetic with socialism? It was better to settle comfortably into the régime of a benign and far-sighted emperor interested in the welfare of the oppressed than to

[1] Reybaud, *Étude sur les Réformations,* Edition of 1856.

1

follow the crazy meanderings of the prophets of 1848. Then too the repression which spread over Europe after the revolutions made the profession of socialism difficult in France as elsewhere.

Nevertheless, neither in France nor in Europe was socialism dead, however soundly it may have been sleeping. After 1860 the proletarian and bohemian centers of Paris and the other large cities of France were alive and stirring with socialist propaganda. Proudhon and his followers taught his anarchist-federalism; Blanqui, moving shadow-like between Paris and Brussels, organized his communist revolutionaries among the students and *déclassés* of the "left bank"; the mutualists began in Paris a political movement among the working class. In 1864 the First International was established in London and quickly organized its sections throughout France. The latter part of the 60's witnessed a recrudescence of Jacobinism in Paris with the growth of the cult of the Commune of 1793. Hébert, Réal, Pache, Chaumette, the most violent of the Jacobin element in the great revolution were held up to the admiration of their decadent descendants suffering passively under the despotism of Napoleon III. All of these movements had their followers and these followers were among the makers of the Commune of 1871.

It does not follow from this that the Commune must be considered the product of socialist ideas or of the socialist movement. There was no socialist movement, in the proper sense of the word, at that time in France. The closest approximation to it, the International, was drawn into the communal revolution, but in no sense was important in its initiation. The currents and cross-currents of French socialism had not yet fused into a political organization. Every leader had his followers, every radical newspaper its own program and clientèle, every group its individual organization. French socialism has always been marked by its plethora of personalities and its lack of regimentation, and this was never more pronounced than in the 1860's. Marx had not yet overwhelmed his contemporaries and made of socialism a movement.

The Commune was not the product of the socialist movement. Yet socialist ideas flourished in the revolution, were actively present in the minds of the leaders, and to some extent shaped their policies. In the Commune assembly itself the reformist, socialist ideas of the International and the Proudhonians, battled against the communist and revolutionary policy of Blanqui and the Jacobins. The two great socialists of the period in France, Proudhon and Blanqui, met and, in a certain sense, struggled for command of the revolution of Paris.

The Communards were revolting against that government which had led France into defeat and signed a shameful peace. In the events of the siege of Paris, when the populace, half-starved and cold, saw its suffering go for naught, was created the spirit of revolution, encouraged later by the mistakes of the monarchical assembly sitting at Bordeaux. At the same time, large numbers of the revolutionists were socialists; and the direction which the Commune took was influenced by this, among other things. To measure the importance of socialism as a cause of the revolution, or as an influence on the course of its events, is impossible. It is, nevertheless, important to consider that socialist milieu out of which the Commune sprang.

The last few years of the life of the Second Empire were marked by the rapid growth of a revolutionary and socialist milieu in Paris. The repressive policy of the coup d'état which had muffled the voice of the press and prevented free speech and assembly was continued in the 1860's but never entirely succeeded in stifling the republican opposition. Now to this growing republican opposition was added a radical left wing which not only fulminated against Napoleon and the empire, but sneered at the cautious tactics followed by those moderate republicans, Jules Favre, Simon and Ollivier.

This new socialist movement sprang from the bohemian, the literary, and artistic quarters of the capital. Its leaders were journalists, writers of the feuilletons of the Paris press, students from the left bank, and *déclassés* of various or no professions. Their gathering places were the cafés of the Latin quarter and Montmartre. Radically different in temper from the reformist and somewhat Utopian socialism of 1848, this new movement was revolutionary and Jacobin.

The renaissance of socialist activity made itself conspicuous in 1865, the year of the death of Proudhon. Blanqui completed at that time a four-year prison sentence [2] and proceeded to the organization of a revolutionary secret society which united a number of the radical students of the Latin Quarter with some of the more active of the proletariat. The First International, organized in 1864, was multiplying its branches in Paris. In the newly established "Rive Gauche" edited by Longuet, a disciple of Proudhon, Rogeard published an attack upon the empire which aroused to literary activity the revolutionary youth of the city. [3] The same year witnessed the appearance of "Le Candide" edited by Tridon, a youthful disciple of Blanqui and a worshipper of the Commune of '93. [4]

Gustave Geffroy, the literary critic, and a member of this same political milieu, has described the awakening of revolutionary Paris. "Underneath this visible Paris, devoted to merrymaking, glittering with light, clamorous with shouting

[2] During these four years in the St. Pélagie prison, Blanqui had come in contact with a large number of the more active of the Paris revolutionaries incarcerated for their opposition to the Empire. Émile Villeneuve, later his friend and co-operator, Jules Miot, prominent in the future Commune, Tridon. Germain Casse, Vermorel and others. See Charles Da Costa, *Les Blanquistes*, p. 7.

[3] A. Rogeard, *Les Propos de Labiénus*.

[4] The program of this paper was announced as "Atheism, Communism and Revolution."

and bombast, another Paris, that one believed dead, was
quietly resuscitated, repaired its losses of blood, recreated
its organism. It was the Paris of the Revolution and of the
Republic which was reborn, which found itself and became
again self-conscious. It required fifteen years from the disaster of June, 1848, to awaken new generations of workers,
not to the hope of, but to the desire for a social
transformation." [5]

This new generation gathered at the Café de Madrid,
the Café de la Renaissance, on the river bank, the Café
d'Harcourt on the Boulevard Saint-Michel, at the Café Voltaire and the innumerable brasseries of bohemian Paris. It
mixed its politics with its literary activity and talked loudly
of revolution over innumerable "chopes." Journalists who
professed various brands of revolutionary socialism and
were later prominent in the Commune composed the bulk
of the leaders. But the revolutionary movement, as often
in Paris, was also recruited largely from the ranks of the
students of the Latin Quarter. Élisée Reclus, the eminent
geographer and philosophical anarchist, and his brother
Élie, soon to be director of the Bibliothèque Nationale
under the Commune, were students at this time and active
in the movement. The Blanquists were heavily represented
in the schools.

This radical bohemia had its own vehement, if somewhat
ephemeral, press. "Le Candide," "La Rive Gauche," "Le
Barbare," "Le Démocrite," "La Jeunesse," "Le Travail"
and dozens of others survived for a few issues to dissem-
inate the favorite arguments for materialism, revolution
and communism and then disappeared under the hounding
of the imperial police or the indifference of the reading
public. None of them had, at most, a circulation of more
than a few hundred, but they performed the function of
midwife at the birth of that literary talent in the young
radicals of the Quarter which went unrecognized by the

[5] *L'Enfermé,* p. 266. This is a life of Blanqui.

more substantial journals of the city. These sporadic sheets contributed little to the organization of a radical party.

On the other hand, such a party was forming and it gained shape and substance in contact with the events, strikes, political trials, and conspiracies, which marked the last three or four years of the Empire. The Congress of Liège, the affair of the Café de la Renaissance Hellénique, the conspiracy of the "Revolutionary Commune of the Workers of Paris," now forgotten incidents, arrayed the radical element in opposition to the government and helped to consolidate it.[6]

The Baudin affair was of more importance. After seventeen years of oblivion the tomb of Alphonse Baudin, killed on the barricades December 2, 1851, in the coup d'état of Napoleon III, was discovered. This dramatic reminder of the unsavory origins of the empire was immediately seized upon by the radical press. Delescluze opened in his paper a subscription for a monument to the heroic Baudin, martyred for liberty. The government unwisely decided to prosecute. The editor of "Le Réveil" was charged with having "practised manœuvres in the interior in the design of troubling the public peace and exciting disdain and hatred of the government." As is usual in such affairs the recoil did more damage than the discharge. Baudin was rescued from oblivion, Delescluze achieved an easy heroism, and Gambetta, who defended him at law, became at one stroke a leader of the republican opposition.[7]

The prestige of the empire, damaged by the books of Ténot on the Coup d'État [8] and the prosecution of the defenders of Baudin, was being further menaced by Henri Rochefort and his "La Lanterne," the first number of which

[6] On these events see Taxile Delord, *Histoire du Second Empire,* Vol. 4 (Paris, 1873) ; Charles Da Costa, *Les Blanquistes* (Paris, 1912).
[7] On the Baudin affair see A. Darimon, *Histoire de Douze Ans* (Paris, 1883), p. 341, and Jules Rouquette, *Baudin* (Paris, 1869).
[8] Eugène Ténot, *La Province en Décembre 1851* (Paris, 1865) and *Paris en Décembre 1851* (Paris, 1866). Ténot was editor of "Le Siècle."

was published on May 1st, 1868. Rochefort was a curious figure. Uninterested in economic and social reform, he was the champion of the revolutionary socialists of Paris. His journal, "La Marseillaise," was, for a few months in 1870, the official organ of the International. After the outbreak of the revolution of March 18th, he espoused the cause of the Commune and yet was one of the Commune's bitterest critics. A genius at satire and criticism, he railed against all men and all causes. During the last years of the empire he was by far the most popular and influential of the radical journalists and dealt the government many a keen blow.

The emperor, who had cultivated the good-will and esteem of the working class, witnessed the disappearance in this quarter also of whatever popularity he may have possessed, at least among the Parisian proletariat. Posing as sympathetic with the cause of socialism, he had looked with some favor on the formation of the International. Under the leadership of the mild Proudhonians, Tolain, Fribourg, Limousin, the Parisian sections had been organized as study clubs in which the industrious laboring class might examine and discuss "La question sociale." But the International escaped the influence of its founders; it tended to fall into the hands of the revolutionaries. In view of this situation and, after a succession of strikes in which the hand of the International was visible, the emperor lost his early sympathy. The Parisian branches took an active part in the republican and political agitation at the time of the Baudin affair. In consequence the International was prosecuted in three trials running from 1868 to 1870 and all but disorganized. These prosecutions pretty well completed the transition, in what remained of the Parisian sections, from a mild economic reformism to a political and revolutionary attitude.

All elements in this left-wing opposition to the empire united in the demonstration which followed the murder of the radical, Victor Noir, by Prince Pierre Bonaparte on

December 16, 1870. The day of the funeral, the workers of Paris gathered in large numbers, joining the journalists of the left, friends of the murdered man, for the funeral procession. A battle with the police was imminent, and troops were ordered out in the capital. However Rochefort and Delescluze exerted themselves to temper the passion of the mob, and the demonstration proceeded without serious disturbance.

This radical opposition to the empire in the last years of its existence was composed of a group by no means homogeneous either in its political ideas or in its ideas of economic and social reform. Socialists of all brands were numerous and the apostles of political revolution even more numerous. But no dominant leader or set of ideas drew together the opposition and made of it a party or a movement.

Nevertheless all factions had certain characteristics in common. All were intensely patriotic, a characteristic of French socialism during the whole of the century. However much the existence of the class struggle might be recognized, the interests of France came before the interests of the proletariat. In 1870 this extreme left stood as one man for war "à l'outrance" and formed the most difficult obstacle to the attempts of the government to make peace.

All groups, too, were anticlerical. To Proudhon the great opponents were the Church and the Revolution. To Blanqui the Church and Capitalism were one and the same exploiter of the working class. The Jacobin tradition was steeped in anticlericalism and the French sections of the International embraced this attitude as naturally as its members inhaled the surrounding air. British socialism has never concerned itself with the religious question and to a large extent this is true of the American movement. But in France anticlericalism is a primary tenet of any radical group and at no time was this more true than in 1870.

Above all these currents of radical thought which flourished in Paris towards the end of the empire hung, too, the shadow of the great French Revolution. Though it took a different form, this was as true of the followers of Blanqui and Proudhon as it was of the Jacobins. The leaders of the Paris International were steeped if not in the history, at least in the mythology of the Revolution. The cult of the first Commune was as familiar to Blanqui as it was to the Jacobins; and if Proudhon eschewed terrorism and violence, his disciples of the Commune of 1871 were never tired of referring to the heroes of '93.

In other respects, however, these socialist groups fell widely apart; their sharp divisions and antagonisms were to rend the communal assembly and to accelerate the failure of the revolution.

JACOBINISM IN THE 1860's

A discussion of the Jacobinism of the period may perhaps seem to be out of place in an account of the socialism of the 1860's. The political philosophy of Rousseau filtered through the minds of Robespierre and Saint-Just was egalitarian but hardly socialist. The Jacobinism of 1793 and of 1870 was essentially political, and envisaged economic reconstruction, in so far as this matter was at all considered, as a possible by-product of revolution in a vague and shadowy future. Jacobinism, too, was not a class movement; although concerned with the interest of the laboring man, it was the laboring man as a member of society and not as a member of the proletariat. The general will, whatever else it might have been, was certainly not the will of an economically determined class.

Yet Jacobinism as a social theory is closely allied to socialism and, in the hands of those who follow out the economic implications of its egalitarianism, it tends to become socialism. If we consider the *differentia specifica* of socialism to be, first, the more or less complete elimination of private property and the substitution for it of ownership

by the state or some other social group, and, second, a concentration upon the political and economic interests of the
proletariat, then Jacobinism in the hands of Babeuf comes
perilously close to it. And babouvism, according to Espinas,
is but the natural conclusion and last expression of
Jacobinism.[9]

This statement is not quite true. Babeuf was something
more than a belated and intransigent Jacobin. What he had
to add was a step in the direction of socialism. His preoccupation with *economic* equality and his emphasis on the
evils of private property were not common to the Jacobins
of the great period. Blanqui took a step further and with
that step became distinctly socialist. Taking Babeuf as his
starting point he attempted to justify the attack on private
property by economic analysis, and, further, he specifically
and explicitly espoused the cause of the proletariat as a
class. Malon puts his finger on the truth when he describes
Blanqui as a synthesis of revolutionary babouvism and
scientific socialism.[10]

Jacobinism is not socialism, yet the road between them
is short. And the Jacobinism of the 1860's was closer to
socialism than that of 1793. Blanqui and his group yielded
to none in their admiration of Hébert, Pache and the first
Commune of Paris. On the other hand the contemporary
Jacobins found the revolutionary communism of Blanqui
congenial, and in the proper tradition. There was, of
course, an enormous cleavage between Blanquism and
Jacobinism on the one hand and the socialism of Proudhon
and Louis Blanc on the other. The cleavage between revolution and reform has always been prominent in the socialism
of France. Yet the socialist movement embraces both, and
to its revolutionary branch the Jacobins of 1870 were
closely allied.

[9] Alfred Espinas, *La Philosophie Sociale du XVIII* siècle et de la Révolution* (Paris, 1898), p. 196.
[10] Benoît Malon, "Revue Socialiste" (1885), 2:597.

The Jacobin tradition was very much alive in France in the 1860's. The general opinion of Robespierre and Saint-Just as assassins and of Marat and Hébert as fools was rapidly giving place to a more favorable one. The rehabilitation of Danton, begun by Thiers and Mignet, had been continued by Michelet. In 1861 Bougeart came out with an adulatory study of Danton which was followed in 1865 by that of Doctor Robinet, later one of the staunch Commune sympathizers. In 1865 Bougeart shocked his contemporaries with an admiring two volumes on Marat, universally esteemed an unmentionable knave. For this work, which a recent biographer of Marat declares is still the best on the subject extant,[11] the author received four months in prison. But interest in the more violent of the revolutionary figures was not to be stifled and a veritable cult of them developed around 1865. When Edgar Quinet, according to a contemporary, "in an admirable book, *La Révolution,* protested in the name of the human conscience against the stupid ferocities of the Terror, condemned its authors and actors, and drove those bloody blackguards from the ranks of liberal democracy, an enormous clamor of savage anger was raised against this eloquent cry of an indignant soul." [12]

The conservatives of the period, it is true, still refused to differentiate between Montagnards. Robespierre and Saint-Just, Marat, Hébert and Chaumette were all members of the bloody crew and equally to be condemned. Every reform movement, said Roosevelt, has its lunatic fringe; to the conservatives of the 1860's the Jacobins were all fringe and no movement. Even Taine, a few years later, pretty much lumped the Jacobins together in his blanket anathema.

The Blanquists and the advanced Jacobins, on the other hand, made a sharp division between their predecessors. Hébert, Marat and the most violent exponents of the

[11] L. R. Gottschalk, *Jean Paul Marat* (New York, 1927), p. 193.
[12] Hector Pessard, *Mes Petits Papiers,* I (1860-70) (Paris, 1887).

Terror were the heroes of the revolutionaries of the 1860's; Robespierre and Saint-Just were more or less ineffectual moderates. "Robespierre," said Blanqui, "wished in reality to turn the guillotine against the revolutionaries, and to rally around him the party of the past through the immolation of the Mountain. The law of the 22 Prairial was to be the instrument of this butchery. His triumph, in Thermidor, would have been the triumph of the counter-revolution." [13]

Tridon, one time left-wing journalist and agitator of the schools, later a prominent member of the Commune, expressed the same opinion in his book on the Hébertists, published in 1864. "Robespierre died, crucified, the 9th Thermidor and was resuscitated after 1830.[14]. In his heart he was an ambitious vulgarian, a man who wanted to dominate at any price, a dandy who paraded his puritan morality in the midst of two mistresses and three horses; his soul was hateful and jealous, his spirit low and spiteful." [15]

Rigault, another of the prodigies of violence of the Latin Quarter, disdained Robespierre and found Saint-Just feeble. According to a friend, Rigault spent his hours in the Bibliothèque Nationale reading the *Père Duchêne* of Hébert and *L'Ami du Peuple* of Marat.[16] He was fond of shocking the bourgeoisie, or at least those well enough versed in history to be shocked, by announcing himself a follower of Pache, the mayor of Paris at the time of the first Commune.[17] If moderation was a crime to Hébert and Marat, it was equally so to Rigault and his admirer Ferré. This adulation of terrorism might have been considered the forgivable, if futile effervescence of youth, had not Rigault and Ferré put their prejudices into practice at the Prefecture of Police during the Commune.

[13] Blanqui, *MSS., Liasse I, B.,*[3] p. 183.
[14] He refers to the work of Buonarroti and Buchez.
[15] G. Tridon, *Les Hébertistes* (Paris, 1864), p. 16. The introduction to this book was written by Blanqui.
[16] Maxime Vuillaume, *Mes Cahiers Rouges III. Cahiers de la Quinzaine, 9ᵉ Série. Cahier 12.*, p. 320.
[17] Jules Formi, *Raoul Rigault* (Paris, 1871), p. 88.

The cult of violence is well expressed in the opening sentence of Tridon's book on the Hébertists. "Hail, Hébert and Pache, pure and noble citizens; Chaumette whom the people loved as a father; Momoro, ardent of pen, generous of spirit; Ronsin, intrepid general; and thou, sweet and melancholy figure through whom German Pantheism extended its hand to French Naturalism, Anarcharsis Cloots." [18]

The particular admiration of Hébert manifested itself during the Commune in the publication of a new *Père Duchêne,* imitating in the grossness of its language and the violence of its opinions the original paper of Hébert. The journalists who established it, Vuillaume, Vermersch and Humbert, latter-day Jacobins, so well estimated the public taste that their journal rapidly became the most popular of the Commune publications.

The cultivation of the Jacobin tradition in the 1860's, with its radical Hébertist fringe, gives some indication of the movement of political opinion in the period. The writing of the serious historians was proceeding in the same direction and this was not entirely the result of a sudden passion on the part of Clio for scientific exactitude. The new light, the accumulation of facts on the position of the Montagnards during the French Revolution, was in part the product of contemporary interests and contemporary values. The ideas and policies of 1793 were considered in the light of the political situation of 1865-70.

The issues which dominated the period of the French Revolution continued to live in the 19th century. Anticlericalism, centralization vs. decentralization, the "people in revolution," the "despotism of liberty against tyranny";

[18] *Les Hébertistes,* p. 16. Also *ibid.,* p. 16. "The coming of the Hébertists was the advent of science and of reason in its most energetic and popular form, the form which alone could assure a definitive triumph. The science of the Girondins, of the doctrinaires, was cloistered in a lettered oligarchy; was drawn from the boudoir and exhibited on the market place. The Hébertists addressed themselves to the people and said, 'Science is your conquest, science belongs to you, come and take it.' "

the causes and the phrases of 1793 were by no means dead three generations later. The political thought of any period of French history in the 19th century is pretty well indicated by its treatment of the personalities and the issues of the revolution, and this was certainly true of the 1860's.

The history of the political and social ideas of Jacobinism has never been written. Nevertheless there are ideas, expressed in its policy and in its institutions, to be taken account of. The Jacobins of the Revolution, in common with their foes the Girondists, inherited the natural-rights philosophy of the 18th century and with them embodied this philosophy in the Declaration of Rights of 1791. The Jacobins gave to the common doctrine an interpretation and application which in many points was characteristic and their own; and we find in their 19th-century descendants a perpetuation of the tradition.

The key to the understanding of Jacobinism, according to Taine, lies in the social milieu from which the leaders sprang. They were the failures, the economically and professionally unsuccessful, the *déclassés* of Paris and of France. In a passage now become famous, he asserts that "To-day and formerly, in the attics of students, in the garrets of bohemia, in the deserted offices of doctors without patients and of lawyers without clients, there are Brissots, Dantons, Marats, Robespierres and Saint-Justs in bud." [19]

Mathiez, on the other hand, discovers the nature of Jacobinism very largely in the necessities imposed by war on the revolutionary rulers of France. Besieged by enemies on the frontier, surrounded by traitors and conspirators in the interior, the Revolution pursued the policy and devised the institutions demanded by the situation. Jacobinism was the Revolution at war with its enemies at home and abroad.

Whatever the validity of these generalizations as applied to the situation in 1793, they are both useful in understand-

[19] Taine, *Les Origines de la France Contemporaine*, Vol. V, p. 12.

ing the Jacobinism of 1870. These latter-day Montagnards were largely *déclassés* and intellectual bohemians and, at the same time, violent patriots, who sought in the war against Germany to resuscitate that revolutionary enthusiasm and those revolutionary institutions which had flung back the enemies of France in 1793.

Although subscribing thoroughly to the democratic implications of Rousseau's general will, Jacobinism habitually drew a distinction between the general will and the will of all, quite destructive of democratic practices and policies. However equal men might be at birth in their natural inheritance of reason and goodness, the environment provided by contemporary society was not universally conducive to the development of the qualities necessary to the free man and the citizen. Not only was the ruling class, the clergy and their servitors disqualified, but the peasantry was in large part so steeped in the tradition of servility as to be unfitted, immediately, for the performance of the functions of citizenship. Jacobinism tended to mean, therefore, a minority dictatorship of the elect.

And certainly this element of the Jacobin tradition was strongly represented in 1870. The Parisian proletariat, to a lesser extent the proletariat of the large towns, and their intellectual leaders springing largely from the *déclassés,* formed the natural source of regenerative revolution. Their disdain of the political capacity of the peasantry was intense. Blanqui, who in his political ideas was nothing but an advanced Jacobin, is illuminating on this point. "The cruelty of spiritualism and the tolerance of materialism. On the one hand ignorance, bestiality, brutishness, fierce egoism, the predominance of material appetites; on the other, intelligence, light, the elevation of the spirit and the heart. The lower-Brittany peasant and the worker of Paris, types." [20]

Paris was the city of revolutions and because of this the

[20] Blanqui, "Ni Dieu, Ni Maître." No. 14. December 3, 1880.

city of light. During the war against Prussia when Paris held out for four months against the besieging enemy, the radical element, all for war "à l'outrance," felt that the capital had been betrayed by the caitiff provinces. The election of a government for the making of the peace drawn very largely from rural France was a confirmation of this feeling. The "rustics of Bordeaux," (later Versailles), was the favorite term of reproach. Paris is paying too much attention to "the decisions of 600 cow peddlers," said Henri Maret, one of the editors of "La Marseillaise," speaking of the enactments of the Assembly at Bordeaux. During the Commune, Versailles was continually treated by the Parisian Jacobins as typical of the fierce ignorance and invincible unenlightenment of the provinces.

The Jacobinism of the Revolution advocated a policy of extreme governmental centralization and this policy was not abandoned by its descendants in 1870. The Communal revolution is often taken as a movement toward decentralization and federalism in France. This was the ideal of Proudhon, and his followers in the Commune lost no time in proclaiming the revolution as a stroke for municipal liberty as against the authoritarian despotism of a centralized monarchy. However the Jacobin and Blanquist majority did not share these hopes and aims. When Blanqui in his "La Patrie en Danger," Delescluze in his "Le Réveil" and Pyat in his "Le Combat" urged the establishment of the Commune during the siege of Paris, several months before the 18th of March, and joined in attempts to overthrow the Government of the National Defense, on behalf of the Commune, they had in mind something other than a municipal assembly charged with the administration of Paris.[21]

[21] In Blanqui's opinion decentralization was advocated by the reactionaries in order to escape from the revolutionary influence of Paris. "There is no such thing as a Montagnard federalism. In a new era, with the acceptance by the entire country of a life of reason, the Parisification of the whole of France, we shall see the voluntary abdication of Paris in favor of her children come to their majority; her maternal joy in the virility of her intellectual sons." *MSS., I Liasse, B.,*[3] p. 231.

The Commune was to assume the responsibility of the war and save France, the Commune was to supplant the government of the National Defense and become the government of France. Jacobinism meant the centralized control of the state by an enlightened revolutionary minority in 1870 as in 1798.

The faith in popular, republican armies animated by revolutionary enthusiasm, which had won battles in 1793, was shared by the Jacobins of 1870, though it won few battles. All during the empire, opposition to the standing army and support of the National Guard had been part of the republican program. This opposition to the standing army was based not so much on distrust of regular troops as instruments of defense against external attack as of their use as instruments of internal repression. When, after the declaration of the republic on September 4th, the new government was called upon to justify its confidence in popular levies, democratically led, it hesitated. Nevertheless, the Jacobins of Paris pushed it on. But the National Guard of the capital turned out to be more dangerous to the government of France than it was to the besieging Prussians. It was not dangerous enough, however, to cause history to repeat itself; within, to sweep the enemies of the revolution from power, and, without, the enemies of France from her territories.

The violent anticlericalism of the Jacobinism of 1793 was duplicated in 1870. During the siege the attack on the priests provided nightly entertainment at the revolutionary clubs, and during the Commune, this attack proceeded from words to deeds.

The outstanding figure of the Jacobinism of the 1860's was Charles Delescluze, a veteran of the revolutions of 1830 and 1848 and the nearest approach to an heroic figure that the Commune produced. A member of a number of secret societies of the 1830's and 1840's, he imbibed the admiration of Robespierre and Saint-Just current in these circles. Delescluze seems never to have been particularly interested in the growing socialist movement, either in its attacks on private property or its exclusive attention to the interests of the proletariat. He remained a Jacobin in the old tradition, passionately devoted to its abstract conception of political liberty and to revolution as the proper means of attaining it.

At the time of the Franco-Prussian war he was sixty-one years old. Nineteen years had been spent in prison for political offenses. Returning from confinement in French Guiana in 1860, his health ruined by long imprisonment, he had retired from political life until 1868 when he joined the group of revolutionary opponents of the empire with the publication of his paper "Le Réveil." After the capitulation of Paris, which he had opposed with all his strength, he was elected to the Assembly from which he resigned in disdain to join forces with the Commune.

He exerted an enormous influence over the young and untried members of the Commune by reason of the very length of his revolutionary experience.[22] Old, worn-out and ill, he was compelled to take the direction of the military forces of the Commune during the last stages of their defeat and disorganization. He ended his life appropriately enough, shot down on the barricades by the Versaillese during that bloody week of May, 1871.[23]

BLANQUI AND THE BLANQUISTS

"Two great educational and directive influences dominated the men of the Commune," says one of the ablest historians of the revolution, himself a Communard, "Blanqui and Proudhon."[24] These two were the ablest representatives and contemporary exponents of the currents into

[22] A. Arnould, *La Commune,* II:87.
[23] On Delescluze see C. Prolès, *Charles Delescluze* (Paris, 1898); with an appreciation of Delescluze by Millerand. And Delescluze, *De Paris à Cayenne* (Paris, 1869).
[24] Lepelletier, II:127.

which French socialism has continually divided, the revolutionary and the reformist.

Blanqui is an example of Jacobinism turned socialist. In his hands the economic egalitarianism of the French Revolution becomes an attack upon the institution of private property, and an attempt to demonstrate that property incomes, rent and interest, arise out of the exploitation of the laboring class. The proletariat to him is a well-demarcated class formed in the creation of capitalist society, and with interests diametrically opposed to those of the ruling bourgeoisie. Although completely unfamiliar with Marx and Marxian socialism, and an avowed opponent of a materialist interpretation of history, Blanqui is in accord with the founder of scientific socialism on these essential points.

Marx, who was familiar with Blanqui's activities during the Revolution of 1848, considered him the true leader of the Parisian proletariat.[25] To Engels, nevertheless, he was the exponent of an outworn type of socialism. This opinion, however, was expressed at a period when the Blanquists threatened Marx's control of the First International. "Blanqui is really a political revolutionary, socialist only in his emotions, sympathizing with the suffering of the people, but without a socialist theory or definite, practical proposals for social reform; in his political activities he is essentially a man of deeds, and of the opinion that a small, well-organized minority, which strikes at the right moment, can carry with it the mass of the population and thus consummate a successful revolution. One sees that Blanqui is a revolutionary of a past generation."[26]

Lenin, whose nature and revolutionary policy drew him close to Blanqui, was more sympathetic. To him Blanqui was an "undoubted revolutionary and a strong supporter of socialism."[27]   And Russian communism, which has

[25] Marx, *18th Brumaire*, p. 19.

[26] Engels, *Program der blanquistischen Kommune-Fluchtlinge* (Volkstaat, 1874), No. 73.

[27] Lenin, *Uroky Kommuny*, Works XI, p. 509.

always had a strong Blanquist element, is of this general opinion.[28]

The great and essential difference which separated Blanqui and Marx was the opposition between 18th-century rationalism and 19th-century romanticism. Blanqui was essentially unhistorical, a rationalist and an individualist. Human reason was the supreme instrument of progress; ideas and habits of thought were not determined by any such instrumentality as the "mode of production;" human institutions are the product of the human mind. To Blanqui the Marxian idea that socialism will be ushered in through the inevitable action of historical forces was completely untenable. The society of the future will be built by the unaided reason of man, its organizational relations and institutions deduced in a rigidly logical way from certain accepted postulates of justice and morality.

Eighteenth-century rationalism is a natural source of revolutionary radicalism. The Jacobins, Babeuf, Blanqui, Bakunin, and most of 19th-century anarchism drank from this spring. The obvious contrast between our existing social order and the natural or rational order was a constant theme of the natural rights philosophy. The contrast was equally obvious to 19th-century revolutionaries. Add to this the belief that the human reason can create a proper institutional organization upon demand, given a clean slate to work upon, and the case for revolution is established. Before the reason can build it is the duty of revolution to tear down. Put in its very simplest form, this was the philosophy of Blanqui and his followers. As one of these followers put it, "As socialism, the Blanquist theory can be summed up as follows: nihilism first; then at the mercy of evolution." [29]

Blanqui himself, however, attempted an analysis of the

[28] See for example Lukin, *Parizhskaia Kommuna*, p. 58. "In spite of his great difference from Marx in outlook, Blanqui was much nearer to scientific socialism than any of the other French schools."
[29] Gaston Da Costa, *La Commune Vécue*, III:73.

evils of existing society; its failure to conform to the principles of the natural or rational order.[30] He also put forward a few suggestions as to how a rationally ordered society might be expected to look.

His attack on the existing economic order took the form
of a criticism of private property and a commendation of
the principle of communism. His attack on current economic
theory condemned the orthodox explanation of the distrib-
utive incomes, interest, rent, and wages and attempted a
demonstration of the validity of a labor theory of value.
From this he passed directly to the right of labor to its
full product.

There is in his thought the confusion, so common among
the socialists, of ethics with economics. Economic theory,
whatever the economists might pretend, was not a simple
description of the normal and typical behavior of men in
the market. It was not a portrayal of economic activity and
economic institutions, but an attempted justification of these
institutions and this activity. It was a defense of private
property and the policy of laissez-faire. As such, bourgeois
and individualist economics was directly and exactly opposed
to proletarian and socialist economics. Both were ideal con-
structions, the one representing the individualist, selfish and
anti-social paradise of the exploiting class and the other an
egalitarian society organized on the principle of justice.

[30] The chief source of information on Blanqui's ideas is his own writings.
La Critique Sociale (Paris, 1885) is a collection in two volumes, which
appeared posthumously, of short essays and remarks. This and the twenty
cartons of manuscripts deposited at the Bibliothèque Nationale contain everything essential. He published a number of articles in "Le Candide," a
journal edited in 1865 by his disciple Tridon. His own papers, "La Patrie
en Danger," 1871, and "Ni Dieu, Ni Maître," 1881, are also important. On
his life, the best book is Gustave Geffroy's *L'Enfermé* (Paris, 1897); on his
ideas, Dommanget, *Blanqui* (Paris, 1924). The Blanquist party is described
by one of his disciples, Charles Da Costa, *Les Blanquistes* (Paris, 1912). In
the last few years a whole series of books has appeared in France and in
Russia on Blanqui. They add nothing, however, to the above-mentioned
sources. A very good treatment of the Blanquists during the Commune is
given by another disciple, Gaston Da Costa, *La Commune Vécue*, 3 vols.
(Paris, 1903-05).

"A single glance suffices to measure the abyss which separates socialism from political economy. They are two conceptions of society diametrically opposed. What is a virtue in the eyes of one is a crime to the other. Denial corresponds to affirmation, malediction to applause, panegyric to anathema." [31]

The social studies, far from being sciences concerned with certain types of human behavior, are really branches of ethics, according to Blanqui. The end of such studies is not exact description, but the determination of the just order of society. "Justice is the sole criterion to be applied in human affairs." [32] A reasonable interrogation of the nature of justice in society leads but to one conclusion, socialism. The indifference of existing political economy to questions of true morality deprives it of all value as a social study. [33]

Blanqui was more familiar with the economic thought of the 19th century than most contemporary socialists. In his youth he was a friend of the son of J. B. Say and acquainted with the father and his writings. His brother, Jérôme Blanqui, was one of the ablest of the not very able group of French economists who wrote in the middle of the century. Blanqui had read Garnier, Dunnoyer, and Bastiat, the chief of the contemporary exponents of this science.

However, his own thoughts on this subject could hardly be called profound. They merely serve to establish the fact that Blanqui was in the full current of 19th-century socialism and that his revolutionary attitude was accompanied by a theory, however ill supported, of the right of labor to its full product and of the unjustifiability of property incomes. He makes no distinction between rent and interest, lumping

[31] *Critique Sociale*, I:11.
[32] *Ibid.*, II:58.
[33] At times Blanqui criticizes political economy for being purely descriptive, for avoiding altogether the question of justice. At other times he condemns it because its conception of justice is inseparably connected with the interests of the capitalist class.

all property incomes together. All incomes other than wages and wages of management are only various forms of interest and, as such, represent theft from the laborer.

"Capital is neither accumulated labor, nor an instrument of production—capital is stolen labor." [34]

Throwing overboard the conception of capital as an instrument of production, Blanqui demonstrates to his own satisfaction that capital, which he identified with money, is essentially sterile and unproductive. In the course of an imaginary conversation between the worker and the capitalist, the worker concludes, "You give value to something which is really worth nothing. That, precisely, is the crime. The foundation of exchange is the equivalence between the objects exchanged. Money is only an intermediary between two equal values. It has no other function. You buy it with your product. You must sell it again, against a product, for the same price." [35] The appearance of interest upsets this equivalence in exchange. "Will the economists deign to explain," demands Blanqui, "why, after establishing in principle the equivalence of exchange, they destroy it by the loan at interest and construct this lovely equation, $100=105$, or 110, 112, etc." [36]

One might suppose that the remedy called for was a suppression of the use of money and the institution of a barter economy. Blanqui says nothing about this, however, and demands instead the elimination of private property. The essentially unintelligent mélange of bold assertions and indignant condemnations which make up Blanqui's writings on the subject of economics lead him to the following important conclusions. First, that the existing system of property ownership has led to the division of society into two classes, the exploited class of workers, and the exploiting class of proprietors. Second, the interests of the proletariat

[34] *Critique Sociale,* I:22.
[35] *Ibid.*
[36] *Ibid.,* p. 11.

and the cause of social justice will be furthered by the abolition of private property and the institution of a communist régime.

The movement of history has been continuously in this direction. Blanqui envisages historical change as the slow conquest by human reason of the institutional obstacles established by cupidity and greed in the interests of a ruling class. He shares none of the 18th-century belief in and admiration for a state of nature antedating civilization. He did not associate himself with Marx and Engels' belief in a primitive communism. Communism is the end rather than the beginning of the movement of history. Communism as the perfect society must be the final achievement of the reason of man.

"In every time and in every country, individualism formed the first cradle of society. Its reign was that of ignorance, of savagery and of bestiality. . . . All social progress is the consequence of its defeat, the encroachment of communism upon its domain." [37]

Throughout the preceding centuries the great obstacle to the march of reason, in Blanqui's opinion, had been the church. Its function was the obscuring of issues, the mystification of the intellect and the lulling of the mass of mankind into a state of indifference toward the pressing problems of society. Religion and capitalism were the main objects of Blanqui's attack. His professed program was "Atheism, Communism and Revolution." The anticlericalism of the Blanquist party equalled the most extreme opposition to the church of revolutionary Jacobinism, and found an opportunity to express itself in action during the Commune.

"There is no longer any other opposition," said Blanqui, "than that of Jesuits and socialists. Reduced to these terms the question will not be long in debate. The opposition was really of this nature from the beginning and it has required

[37] MSS., Liasse VII, March 13, 1869.

much blood and suffering to join the issue squarely. We have now the alliance of Thiers and Montalembert, the close union of the bank and the clergy. The industrialists of Elbeuf collect themselves under the banner of Loyola; they will go to mass every Sunday for the salvation of the social order and of their écus." [38]

The chief significance of Blanqui to his contemporaries, however, lay not in economic reasonings on the subject of private property and property incomes, nor in his anticlericalism. It lay in his revolutionary theory and his revolutionary practice. And Blanqui's practice was consistent with his theory. In the two decades between the Revolution of 1848 and the Commune he was the outstanding apostle of revolution in France.

The revolutionary theory of the Blanquists does not differ importantly from that of Babeuf and the conspiracy of the "Equals" of 1795. In 1828 appeared Buonarroti's *Conjuration des Égaux,* and through Buonarroti were transmitted the ideas of Babeuf to a whole group of radical republicans, Blanqui included. In the 1830's he came into close contact with Buonarroti in the various secret societies with which they were mutually connected, and he received from the lips of the sole survivor of the "Égaux" the revolutionary tradition of Babeuf. He was at this time the political conspirator par excellence.

He pinned his revolutionary faith on the capacities of a small, well-organized group ready to strike at the proper moment and to carry the mass of the proletariat with it. The members of this group, the revolutionary élite, must be drawn very largely from the bourgeoisie. For in this class are to be found men of ideas and education. "The bourgeoisie includes an élite minority, an indissoluble group, nervous, ardent and full of zeal; it is the essence, the soul, the life of the revolution. . . . Who has planted the flag of the proletariat? Who has rallied it after its defeats?

[38] *MSS., Liasse I, B.,*[3] p. 145.

Who are the promulgators, the apostles of the doctrines of equality? Who leads the people to battle against the bourgeoisie? The bourgeoisie itself. . . . But what is the device on its banner? Democracy? No. . . . The proletariat. For its soldiers are workers though the leaders are not." [39]

Sombart explains certain characteristics of French socialism by the presence in metropolitan areas of a "populace in all stages of decadence, possessed of an arrogant belief in its capacity to rule." [40] This is true of Blanquism. Its ranks were recruited largely from the *déclassés* of Paris. Blanqui himself recognized the significance of this element and welcomed it. "These '*déclassés*,' invisible agents of progress, are to-day the secret ferment which sustains the masses and prevents them from sinking to a condition of impotence. To-morrow, they will be the reserve force of the revolution." [41]

Blanqui's revolutionary activity never extended beyond the confines of Paris nor was he ever, except under compulsion, outside this city of revolutions. The Blanquist party at its height, in 1867 or 1868 when it consisted of from 2500 to 3000 members, [42] was a group entirely Parisian in its constitution. It was composed principally of members of the bourgeoisie, radical students of the schools and journalists, joined with the more revolutionary elements of the Parisian proletariat. The aim of this party was the "Parisification" of France, the dictatorship of a metropolitan and revolutionary élite in the interests of the proletariat.

Liberal and democratic institutions, based as they are on the assumption that the average man is intelligent enough and well enough informed to know his own interest and that of his class, are an impossibility in a society in which the vast mass of the population, the proletariat, is in ignorance.

[39] *MSS., Liasse II*, p. 150.
[40] *Proletarische Sozialismus*, II:378.
[41] *Critique Sociale*, I:219.
[42] *Enquête sur le 18 Mars*, p. 540. Evidence of Lagrange of the political police.

Those institutions which pass as liberal and democratic in modern society are simply creations, in its own interests, of a minority. It follows that a dictatorship of *déclassés* and the enlightened proletariat, working in the interest of the mass of the population, is the revolutionary method called for. Only as the spread of enlightenment is furthered by this dictatorship will the masses become capable of directing their own political destiny.[43]

Blanqui exhibited all Marx's scorn for French Utopian socialism. He advised his disciples to eschew all doctrinal disputes, all discussion as to whether this or that organization of society is preferable, and to concentrate their attention on the problem of revolution. It was time enough to talk of building a new order when the present one had been overthrown. The systems of both St. Simon and Fourier he regarded as the imaginings of "disordered brains." "Revolution, which alone can save humanity, is incompatible with the revelations of budding prophets." [44]

The contemporary socialism of the First International also left Blanqui cold. He directed his followers not to attend the Geneva Congress of 1866 and was severely critical of the ideas expressed in the Bâle Congress in 1867. Blanqui, after all, was nothing of an internationalist. He never travelled outside of France except when imprisoned by the government on the island of Corsica, and, on another occasion, after escaping from the Paris prisons to Brussels. He was a fervent nationalist convinced of the cultural and civilizing mission of the French revolutionary movement in the rest of the world. In 1870 he espoused

[43] During the Revolution of 1848 Blanqui condemned the appeal to popular suffrage, on the ground that sixty years of oppression had rendered the people incapable of self-government. See Dommanget, *Blanqui,* p. 70. As soon as the Commune of 1871 was established the Blanquist members planned to introduce a resolution which would suspend all democratic forms, appoint a committee of public safety and militarize the Commune, until the government of France had been overcome. See Gaston Da Costa, *La Commune Vécue,* I:327.

[44] *MSS., Liasse VII,* April 3, 1869.

the cause of his country without examination and devoted his newly established journal, "La Patrie en Danger," to the problem of winning the war. Marxian internationalism was totally foreign to his outlook.

Curiously enough Blanqui's opinion of Proudhon, his great socialist contemporary, was high. Although to Marx, Proudhon was nothing but a petty-bourgeois reformist, and although Proudhon was opposed to revolution and the use of force, Blanqui admired the author of *La Justice dans la Révolution and dans l'Église*. The latter's strong and outspoken anticlericalism and his worship of the French revolutionary tradition gave them a common cause. On one occasion he likened his own communism and Proudhonism to the combination of fife and drums. "The two instruments do not resemble one another in the least. But they marry together extremely well and could make society dance very agreeably." [45] In another place he urges the followers of the two movements to cease their disputes as to what lies on the other side of the river and to unite their energies in the task of crossing over. [46]

As one would expect, Blanqui was bitterly opposed to all socialist reform schemes, such as co-operative ventures, mutual credit societies and the like. Since they appeal only to the upper level of the working class and are entirely outside the range of possibility for the lower, they have the effect of dividing the proletariat against itself. Not only that, but it deprives this class of its natural leaders who become possessed with the interests, habits and customs of thought of the bourgeoisie. With the strike, on the other hand, he was in entire sympathy. The organization of the working class into fighting units imbued with determination to resist the aggression of its natural enemy, the capitalists, is a plan which reaches the masses, and will strengthen the class consciousness of the proletariat. "The strike is intelligible to

[45] *La Critique Sociale,* II:316.
[46] *Ibid.,* II:314.

everyone; it is a simple idea, resistance to opression. Everyone will rally to it." [47]

Blanqui grasped the familiar socialist dilemma of the
correct attitude toward schemes for improving the condition
of the laboring class in true communist fashion. Should the
socialist favor such schemes if their result is, by raising the
standard of living of the working class, to soften the antagonism between capital and labor? Blanqui spoke out clearly
against any such amelioration.

This irreconcilable revolutionary communist was a person of almost legendary significance to the younger radicals
of 1870. He was known as "the old one" (*le vieux*) and
was rarely seen except in certain conspiratorial circles. He
flitted ghost-like about Paris, eluding the police by changing
his address frequently, by hairbreadth, rear-exit escapes,
and by getting himself up like a respectable bourgeois to
wander about with a copy of the Constitution under his arm.
At this time he had already spent 28 of his 65 years in
prison for political offenses and was looked at with awe by
the embryonic revolutionaries of the capital.

Blanqui was a man of some significance in the political
life of France, of more significance probably than any other
French socialist in the 19th century with the exception of
Louis Blanc. On two occasions, in 1848 and in 1871, there
was some possibility of his leading a temporarily successful
revolution. On both occasions his power was destroyed on
the eve of its fruition. In 1848 Blanqui was the leader and
organizer of the most influential radical club in Paris, La
Société Républicaine Centrale. The personnel of this club
was distinctly Blanquist: "by the side of sincere socialists,
were to be found intriguers who thought it useful to follow
Blanqui, suspicious characters, agents provocateurs, swin-
dlers, *déclassés*," etc.[48] It was the sole radical group of

[47] *MSS., Liasse VII*, October 17, 1867.
[48] Suzanne Wasserman, *Les Clubs de Barbès et Blanqui en 1848* (Paris,
1913), p. 10.

sufficient importance to inspire fear in the provisional government, and the power of Blanqui during February and March grew steadily. However, after the revelations of the Taschereau document, which made him out to be an ex-agent-provocateur, his influence with the masses collapsed like a pricked bubble.[49]

During the Paris Commune he could have occupied a position of power as leader of the strongest group in the Commune Assembly. But ironically enough he was arrested by the Thiers government on the day before the revolution broke out, and carried back to prison for another eight years.

The two attempts at revolution which Blanqui made with his own men failed rather ridiculously. In 1839, with eight or nine hundred followers, he attacked the Hôtel de Ville in an attempt to overthrow the government. Most of official Paris was at the Champ de Mars attending a demonstration, but sufficient troops were on the spot to make short work of Blanqui and his insurgents. In 1870, he sought to arouse the proletariat of Paris against the imperial government by an attempt made in Belleville, a working-class quarter. He was at the head of a hundred men who succeeded in killing a fireman but were unsuccessful in attracting a single recruit.

The Blanquism of the 1860's never appealed to considerable numbers, but in the compactness of its organization and in its willingness to act, it was a force to be reckoned with. During the Commune the Blanquist group formed a party of importance.

PROUDHON

THE influence of Proudhon upon contemporaries was immeasurably more wide-spread than that of Blanqui,

[49] On the question of the Taschereau document, the best case for the innocence of Blanqui is presented by Gustave Geffroy, his biographer, in *L'Enfermé*. However, M. Dommanget, himself a communist and a sincere admirer of Blanqui, is even more convincing on the other side. See his book on Blanqui (Paris, 1924).

though he possessed but few disciples and no party. By the end of the Second Empire, most of the laboring population, in Paris at least, had Socialist leanings.[50] Among the proletariat, as among the radical element of the schools, disputed the rival influences of Blanqui and Proudhon. But while the party of Blanqui was preponderantly bourgeois, Proudhon had his chief following in the upper levels of the proletariat.[51] The French founders of the First International were Proudhonians almost to a man and the working-class movement of the 60's, known as Mutualism, drew its main inspiration from the economic federalism of Proudhon.

"The masses do not read me, but, without reading me, they understand me," wrote Proudhon,[52] and this is, in a certain sense, true. No one read in its entirety the vast outpouring of words on religion, economics, philosophy and politics which were collected after his death in 37 volumes, not counting the 14 volumes of his published correspondence. Yet he was understood by his generation and he influenced those whom he wanted to influence. For in spite of the gigantic, sprawling, protean character of his work, he spoke out clearly on certain issues of the period, he suffered in prison for the frankness of his expression of opinion without abating that frankness, and he attempted sincerely to practice his preachings.

Proudhon sprang from the proletariat and remained of the proletariat in a fashion unusual among 19th-century socialists. The class struggle, a class-conscious proletariat, played no part in his system. Yet his sympathy for and understanding of the working man as an individual was profound. He pinned his faith in the regeneration of society on the innate capacity of the average man. The revolution must come from below, it must not be imposed from

---

[50] According to the *Enquête sur le 18 Mars*, p. 90.
[51] Georges Weill, *Le Parti Républicain 1814-1870*, p. 493.
[52] From a letter of May 21, 1858. Quoted by W. Harmel, *Proudhon et le Mouvement Ouvrier*, an essay in *Proudhon et Notre Temps* (Paris, 1920).

above. His doctrine is the complete antithesis of Blanqui's on this point. To Blanqui, man in the mass is a hopeless bit of inert material which must be guided and forced in its own interest by an intelligent and educated minority. Marxian socialism itself has always been inclined to lose sight of the individual in the class and of individual desires and motives in the inevitable action of externally determined forces. But Proudhon found the initiative of social change, of progress, in the sum of individual laborers and peasants, each possessed in his own right of the possibility of behavior consonant with the aims of the revolution.

The opinion of Proudhon held by Marx and the Marxians has always been decidedly low. From the time when Marx inverted Proudhon's "Philosophy of Poverty" to the "Poverty of Philosophy" until the present, he has been considered a petty-bourgeois socialist who possessed not even the merit of having dreamed great dreams. The fact is that Proudhon knew the material with which he was dealing; he recognized a proletarian when he saw one, instead of drawing him out of a series of concepts deduced from the materialistic interpretation of history.

To the Bolshevist and Blanquist ideal of coërcion by the class-conscious element of the proletariat, Proudhon opposed the ideal of self-determination or self-government. These opposing ideals have always divided the socialist movement and at no time more than under the Commune.[53] The Commune Assembly split roughly along these lines into a majority leaning toward Blanqui and a minority cleaving to the doctrines of Proudhon.

Authority in any form was anathema to Proudhon. In his classification of governmental forms his chief distinction is between the rôle of authority and the rôle of liberty.

---

[53] Henry de Man, *The Psychology of Socialism,* calls these ideals the eastern and the western, but he seems to identify his self-determination with democracy, which would be unacceptable to Proudhon.

"1. Régime of Authority.

A. The government of all by one; monarchy or patriarchy;

a. Government of all by all; Panarchy or Communism.

2. Régime of Liberty.

B. Government of all by each; Democracy;

b. Government of each by each; An-archy or self-government.

The essential characteristic of the second kind in both its forms, is the division of power." [54]

Proudhon's antagonism to the rôle of force and authority led him into frank opposition to revolutionary Jacobinism and its legitimate offspring, authoritarian communism. He viewed the contemporary Jacobinism of Paris with a jaundiced eye. Faithful to its principle of centralization it flourished but weakly in the provinces and throve only in the shadow of a despotic government from which it hoped to seize the reins.[55] Jacobinism, to him, represented a minority dictatorship skulking under the petticoats of democracy. "Defiant, hostile to ideas, partisan of the Raison d'État decorated now with the title of the public safety, living upon equivocations, Jacobinism turns easily to hypocrisy, and to Machiavellian tendencies; the Jacobins are the Jesuits of the Revolution."

Its every principle was opposed to his doctrines. Jacobinism favored centralization, Proudhon's ideal was anarchy or federalism; Jacobinism desired revolution by force, Proudhon preached revolution through enlightenment; Jacobinism stood for a minority dictatorship, Proudhon eulogized individual self-determination; Jacobinism destroyed the opposition by terrorism, Proudhon by reason; Jacobinism exalted the state and desired an extension of its

[54] *Du Principe Fédératif*, VIII:13, *Œuvres Complètes*.
[55] *La Justice dans la Révolution et dans l'Église*, VI:173, *Œuvres Complètes*, Vol. 26.

powers, Proudhon detested the state and wished to eliminate it.

The revolution will triumph when the idea of justice has become the common property of every man. But how, said the Jacobins and revolutionary communists, can the idea of justice make headway against the interested propaganda of the bourgeois-capitalist class? Must not the revolution strike sharply and surely, destroying the mass of superstition and untruth which serves to justify the present order, before the proletariat can be brought to see the light? "Such is," replied Proudhon, "the circle in which progress seems to turn, and which serves to-day as a pretext to those enterprisers dealing in purely political reforms. 'Make the revolution first,' they say, 'after which the light will dawn.' As if the revolution could be made without ideas. But let us reassure ourselves; just as the lack of ideas has lost the best-intentioned parties, so the war on ideas [which is Jacobinism] will only hasten the revolution." [56]

Proudhon made the mistake, for his own economic well-being, of taking the Declaration of Rights seriously. He was a man drunk with the idea of justice and feverish with the sense of injustice. "An illegitimate son of the Encyclopedia," Metternich called him; and this statement is correct except for the fact that the line of descent was in every sense legitimate. The Revolution was to him a living, pulsating force sprung from the egalitarian philosophy of the 18th century and bent on the bringing of justice into an unjust world. The statement "Man was born free and is everywhere in chains" was to Proudhon no merely elegant introduction to reflections on political philosophy, it was a confession of faith and a call to duty. His conception of justice was the center about which Proudhon's whole system of social reorganization turned.

The ideal order of society to Proudhon was anarchy.

[56] *La Justice dans la Révolution et dans l'Église,* II:133, *Œuvres Complètes,* Vol. 22.

From his earliest writings he contemplated an era in which men stripped of the prejudices and superstitions inculcated by religion and the state, would rationally and justly govern their own conduct and their relations with each other unguided and unmolested by authority in any form. From this conception of an ideal order proceeded his criticism of and attack on economic institutions and economic theory, on existing forms of government and the church.[57] In his later years, it is true, he was inclined to view anarchy as an unattainable ideal and to advocate a federalism based upon economic units, but it still remained the ideal.[58]

Anarchy, of course, is not to Proudhon a chaotic society without order or plan. On the contrary, it appears as the only society in which human conduct is ordered and regular, in which conflicts between individuals or groups or classes are impossible, and from which caprice and injustice are barred. "Anarchy may present the appearance of confusion and civil war; it might seem that the only thing which could induce people to govern themselves is their despair of all governments. One does not understand at first that as between man and man, between free being and free being, all inequality, all command, even when cloaked in the most pleasant mantle, is inadmissible, an offense to dignity. Pure justice, a mathematical equation, that is the whole plan of civilization."[59]

The possibility of a society from which force, restraint and authority are excluded lies in the undeveloped but potential capacities of human nature. Every man possesses within himself the ability to act reasonably and the will to do so. It is the task of the revolution to free his mind

[57] Karl Diehl, *Proudhon, seine Lehre und Leben* (Jena, 1888-96), 3 vols., the best study on the economics of Proudhon, sees his anarchism as a deduction from his economic analysis. This would seem, however, to be a reversal of the logic of Proudhon's thought.

[58] He develops his federalism as a *pis aller* in his *Du Principe Fédératif*, published in 1852.

[59] *La Justice dans la Révolution et dans l'Église*, III:227, *Œuvres Complètes*, Vol. 23.

from the superstitions disseminated by the church and the errors propagated in the interests of vested rights. The moral and the rational order is that order which will be spontaneously established by the educated intelligences of free men.

The sense of justice, or conscience, is innate in man; it requires only a proper environment for its development.[60] Equipped with a conscience and the ability to act reasonably, all that is required for a just order is the certainty, in all circumstances, of the distinction between right and wrong. This, according to Proudhon, exists. "Just as the mathematician is sure of not deceiving himself on the terms of his equation so long as he pursues his calculations; so is the moral being certain of not going astray on the question of good and evil, since this idea, which he bears engraven in his soul, is no other than that same equality." [61] That is to say, the innate equality of individuals provides us with the basis of the moral law. Proudhon's categorical imperative is a restatement of the golden rule: "Never do unto others what you would not have them do unto you, and do unto others always that which you would have them do unto you." [62]

It is not that Proudhon was a believer in equal human capacities. He was willing to recognize that individuals, regardless of environment, differ in physical strength, in intellectual power, and in natural aptitudes of various sorts. In common with most anarchists, he gloried in the prodigality of variation in the human species, though he was inclined to maintain that the range of variation between the highest and lowest individual capacities in any line was relatively slight. His doctrine of fundamental equality rested upon the absolute of human dignity, which is invariable and imponderable.

[60] *La Justice dans la Révolution et dans l'Église,* III:152.
[61] *Ibid.,* III:171.
[62] *De la Capacité Politique des Classes Ouvrières,* p. 64. Published posthumously. Taken from the Declaration of Rights.

"Man, by virtue of reason which is innate in him, has the power of appreciating the dignity of a fellow man as he does his own, and of affirming himself at the same time an individual and a member of the species.

"Justice is the product of this faculty; it is the respect spontaneously experienced and reciprocally guaranteed, by any person and in any circumstance, regardless of the risk or cost." [63]

From this conception may be deduced all rights and duties. In the ideal order the moral law provides its own sanction. Reasonable individuals possessed of conscience, which, according to Proudhon, is essentially a compound of a juridical sense or the will to justice with the clear certitude of the distinction between right and wrong, will act rightly because the consequences of wrong action are clearly present in their minds. The realization of the harm to society and consequently to themselves as members of society, is a sufficient deterrent to behavior contrary to the moral law. Just as the business man in modern society fulfills his promise without the threat of legal action, because he realizes the effect upon a sensitive credit structure of a failure to do so, just so would the enlightened anarchist obey the moral law. Intellectual awareness of the consequences of conduct plus the innate will to justice are the guarantees of order and stability in anarchy.

"What is the penal sanction connected with the law?" Proudhon asks himself, and he replies, "Everything flourishes and thrives in man, in society, and in nature when justice is observed; everything suffers and dies when it is violated.

"Does this sanction suffice, in every case, as the recompense of virtue, the expiation of crime and the rectification of error?" [64]

To which he replies emphatically yes.

[63] *La Justice dans la Révolution et dans l'Église,* I:224.
[64] *Ibid.,* IV:267.

In the ideal order, the laws of justice are at the same time descriptive generalizations regarding human behavior. Moral law is identical with scientific law. That is to say, in so far as right conduct is also typical conduct, the generalizations regarding typical human behavior which pass as the laws or principles of the social sciences might equally well be determined by observation or arrived at by deduction from more general moral laws. Proudhon was accustomed to make no distinction between the descriptive or explanatory generalizations of science and the evaluative generalizations of ethics.

"Reason tells us," he said, "and it is one of the most beautiful intuitions of modern philosophy, that human morality is part of the universal order, in such fashion that, in spite of a few dissonances, more apparent than real, which science must learn to reconcile, the laws of the one are also the laws of the other.

"From this superior point of view, man and nature, the world of liberty and the world of determinism (*fatalité*), form one harmonious whole; matter and spirit combine to constitute humanity and all which environs it, from the same elements obedient to the same laws." [65]

The materially determined behavior of natural phenomena and the rationally determined behavior of human beings may be described in laws which are at once just and true. This means (1) that the laws of the natural sciences, in addition to being generalized descriptions, are also evidences of an harmonious equilibrium in the physical universe; and (2) that the moral laws governing rational human conduct, in addition to being the *sine qua non* of an harmonious equilibrium in society, are also generalized descriptions of human behavior.

It is obvious to Proudhon that while the laws of the natural sciences are just as well as true, the laws of the so-called social sciences are neither just nor true. He takes

[65] *La Justice dans la Révolution et dans l'Église,* II:194.

the further step of asserting that they are untrue because they are unjust. In examining the errors of these social sciences, he is particularly struck by the ignorance of the economists.[66] They proclaim the most abysmal fallacies because they have excluded from their systems the idea of justice. "Under the pretext that such is the economic law, that thus is the ruling of events, they (the economists) sacrifice without remorse humanity to Mammon. It is this characteristic which has distinguished the economists in their struggle against socialism, this will be their crime and their shame before history." [67]

But if the economists of Proudhon's day were inclined to subscribe to the doctrine, "Whatever is, is just," he reversed the doctrine and proclaimed that "Whatever is just, is." For Proudhon was never able to distinguish between his economics as a description of human behavior in a just world and as a description of human behavior in the contemporary world. In consequence his economic analysis is a conglomeration in which logical errors, inconsistencies, and faulty observations mingle with a few keen and penetrating remarks. It was out of this analysis, however, that he drew his plans of economic reform, the plans upon which he built his scheme of economic federalism.

As has been mentioned, Proudhon was inclined to regard anarchy as an ideal perhaps never attainable. This does not deter him from occupying himself with reforms which tended in the direction of anarchism. He drew his Utopia a little nearer earth, though it remained, in all conscience, far enough removed from mundane experience.[68] The problem

[66] "I have attacked the economists with a pitiless criticism, for I must confess that, in general, I have no love for them. The haughtiness and inanity of their writings, their impertinent pride and their unqualifiable blunders have revolted me." *Qu'est-ce que la Propriété?* p. 4, *Œuvres Complètes,* Vol. 1.

[67] *La Justice dans la Révolution et dans l'Église,* I:294.

[68] Despite Proudhon's evident Utopianism, he was severe on the Utopias of his socialist predecessors. "Fallen into the hands of dreamers, of haranguers, professors of gastronomy and hermaphrodites, socialism, from occupying itself with justice according to the revolution, has become senti-

of social reform became to him one of how to maintain the
liberty of the individual and his right to the full product of
his labor while still preserving an irreducible minimum of
governmental authority. His solution was the division of
society into a large number of small, loosely-federated
groups in which government was restrained by an adequate
system of checks and balances; the maintenance of private
property among the peasantry and laboring class where the
ownership of property was associated with its utilization by
the owner; and the establishment of a system of gratuitous
or very cheap credit which was to suppress the "reign of
gold" and encourage the "subalternization of capital to
labor." [69]

He sums up the political aspects of his scheme in three
propositions: [70]

"1. The formation of small groups, respectively sovereign, and united to one another by a pact of federation.

"2. The organization of a government in each federated
unit, according to the principle of division of powers—
that is to say, the separation of all functions which can be
separated, the limitation of all that can be limited, distributing between the various organs or functionaries everything which has been separated and defined, leaving nothing
undetermined; the encirclement of the public administration
with all the conditions of publicity and control;

"3. Instead of absorbing the federated units or provincial authorities in a central authority, the reduction of the
attributes of this authority to the simple rôle of general
initiative, mutual guarantee and surveillance, according to
which decrees will be executed only after the consent of the
federated governments or their agents has been obtained,

mental, evangelical, theocratic, communist, erotico-bacchic and omnigamous;
it has been all that the reaction could have wished." *La Justice dans la
Révolution et dans l'Église,* I:79.

[69] See *Proudhon et Notre Temps,* p. xiii. Introduction by C. Bouglé.
[70] *Du Principe Fédératif,* p. 58.

just as, in a constitutional monarchy, all orders emanating from the king must, before being executed, receive the counter-signature of a minister."

Proudhon, in his *Idée Générale de la Révolution,* had explained the financial reforms which were to eliminate rent and interest in the new society.[71] In a posthumous work, *De la Capacité Politique des Classes Ouvrières,* he went ahead to explain his federalism as the direct consequence of the economic principle of mutualism, applied in the field of politics. Mutualism, so far as it meant anything definite to Proudhon, signified an economic order in which laborers, owning the instruments of production and the land, co-operate freely and without coërcion in the production, exchange, and distribution of commodities. Its institutions were mutual insurance agencies, associations of mutual credit, mutual assistance, instruction, and the like.[72]

This provided the basis of a popular socialist movement of some importance in the 1860's, a movement which throws light upon the influence of Proudhon with the Paris proletariat. Early in 1864 the "mutualists" published a program, the "Manifesto of the 60," which shows very clearly the influence of Proudhon. Albert Thomas, the socialist historian of the Second Empire, calls it "a capital document in our socialist history." [73] Although Proudhon had no hand in the drafting of it, and although he criticized it in certain details,[74] he was on the whole extremely sympathetic. He introduced his volume *De la Capacité Politique des Classes Ouvrières* with a eulogy of the 60 for their manifesto which represents a "reawakening of socialism." [75]

The mutualists were working for the abolition of the restrictions of the free association of laborers for purposes

[71] These schemes, which are discussed in any book on Proudhon—see for example Gide and Rist, *History of Economic Doctrines*—are summed up in the *Idée Générale,* pp. 182-214.

[72] See *De la Capacité Politique des Classes Ouvrières,* pp. 69-70.

[73] *Le Second Empire* (Paris, 1907), p. 215.

[74] See *Correspondance,* Vol. XIII, pp. 248, 256.

[75] P. iii.

of production, exchange, and consumption. Their program
had none of the violent and coërcive features of contemporary communism; they took no stock in the class struggle
nor was their ideal a forcible destruction of existing property rights. They looked toward a Proudhonian society of
cooperation among the workers in their economic activities,
an ownership of the instruments of production by small
groups of producers who used these instruments, and a system of gratuitous credit. The ideal of the revolution, political equality, could never be attained without economic and
social equality. Yet they were more vague, if possible, than
Proudhon, on the question of how these desirable ends were
to be attained.

The mutualists were strongly represented in the French
sections of the First International and disseminated the
ideas of Proudhon at the annual congresses. They were a
thorn in the side of Marx. After the Geneva Congress of
1866 he wrote, "Under the pretext of freedom and of anti-
governmentalism or anti-authoritarian individualism—these
gentlemen (from Paris) who have for the last 16 years so
peacefully endured the most miserable of despotisms, preach
in fact the ordinary bourgeois economy idealized by Proudhon! Proudhon has caused enormous harm. First his false
criticism and his false opposition to the Utopians (he himself is only a commonplace Utopian, while in the Utopias
of Fourier, Owen, etc., there appears the suggestion and
the fantastic expression of a new world) captured and cor-
rupted the 'jeunesse brillante,' the students, and then the
workers, particularly the Parisians, who as workers on luxury articles, without knowing it, belong very much in the
old rut." [76]

These Parisian mutualists brought their rather vague
Proudhonian socialism into the Commune. Beslay, one of
Proudhon's best friends, was the doyen of the Commune

[76] Letter to Kugelmann, October 9, 1866. Published in *Die Neue Zeit,*
XX,² 62.

Assembly. Longuet, the editor of the Commune's official journal, was another Proudhonian, as were Theisz, Avrial, Camelinat, A. Arnould and other significant figures in the revolution of March 18th. That the ideas of certain of them on social reconstruction were rather nebulous, can be seen from the definition of socialism given by Beslay in a work on the Commune.[77] "It is, in its largest sense, the application of all the ideas suggested for the reconstitution of labor upon new foundations, under those conditions of justice and truth which the conscience dictates." If we take this definition, says Beslay, there was a close connection between socialism and the Commune. Certainly the socialism of the Proudhonian group in the Commune reveals itself as a vague, though actively present, yearning.

Apart from his influence on the mutualists, Proudhon's chief imprint on the thought of his own generation was made through his attack on religion and the church. His great work, *De la Justice dans la Révolution et dans l'Église,* for which he was sentenced to three years' imprisonment, was much read in republican and anticlerical circles. Covering the whole field of the ethics of human behavior, it seeks to contrast the supernatural, mystical and outworn dogmas of the church with the rational, enlightened and tolerant ethics of the revolution.[78]

There can be little doubt that in the history of French and of European socialism Proudhon is a figure of first-rate importance. Despite the contempt of the founder of "Scientific Socialism," Marx drew heavily upon the ideas of his French contemporary. Proudhon influenced the French labor movement not only through mutualism; the proposals of economic reform of syndicalism bear a strong resemblance to his economic federalism. At the time of the Com-

[77] *La Vérité sur la Commune.*
[78] According to Weill, *Le Parti Républicain de 1814 à 1870,* p. 432, republican thought around 1860 received its best expression in three books: Proudhon, *De la Justice dans la Révolution et dans l'Église;* Vacherot, *La Démocratie;* and Jules Simon, *La Liberté.*

mune he was by all odds the outstanding representative of French socialism.[79]

THE FIRST INTERNATIONAL IN FRANCE

THE First International was in many important respects the creation of the French socialism of the 1860's. Although the General Council contained very few Frenchmen and maintained its headquarters in London; although the powerful hand of Karl Marx made itself felt at the outset and, with the passing of years, deflected the course of the International away from French socialism and its influence; still the initiative came largely from the French and the International spread more rapidly and waxed more powerful in France than elsewhere. With the continuously growing reputation of Marx and the importance of Marxian socialism it has become common to think of the First International as the creation of Marx. This is exaggerated. On the other hand it is inexact to think of Marx coming "like a cuckoo to lay his eggs in the nest" built largely by French socialism, as Guillaume, one of Marx's bitterest opponents, puts it.[80] Marx and his brand of authoritarian collectivism was represented in the International from the start, but during the first few years of its existence he was overshadowed by the Proudhonian mutualism of the French socialists. French socialism before the Commune never succeeded in swallowing Marx.

It was customary among the reactionaries immediately after the Commune to assign the responsibility for this

[79] Proudhon is usually regarded as an exponent of anarchism, which is, of course, in certain important respects the antithesis of socialism. I should prefer to regard him as a representative of that line of socialists which rests its emphasis on liberty and self-determination. In this, I agree with Karl Diehl, *Proudhon, seine Lehre und Leben,* I, p. vi and II, p. 311.

[80] James Guillaume, *Karl Marx, Pangermaniste* (Paris, 1915). Guillaume was a disciple of Bakunin, whose conflict with Marx led to the virtual dissolution of the First International at the Hague Congress. Both Guillaume and Bakunin were voted out of the International at this Congress, on the instigation of Marx.

bloody uprising to the Paris sections of the International, whose members, puppet-like, were agitated by strings manipulated by an "occult" power in London. The official "Enquiry on the 18th of March" devoted considerable space to the International and, despite the evidence of its most reliable witnesses to the contrary, came to the conclusion that this organization had assumed a major rôle.[81] The presence of large numbers of foreigners in the Commune, many of them occupying positions of importance, lent color to this belief. As the "Journal Officiel" of Versailles put it, "Paris wants to govern France. Who governs Paris? The American Cluseret, the Prussian Fränkel, the Russian Dombrowski, the Lithuanian Bruenschwick, the Italian Romanelli, Okolowitz, who is supposed to be a Pole; most of these creatures are denied or disavowed by their countrymen."[82]

The resources, both in men and money, of the International were wildly exaggerated. It was stated by the "Journal Officiel" that the organization included 8,000,000 members, although it is probable that the numbers in Europe and America never exceeded 1,200,000 in its most prosperous days.[83] While it was generally believed among conservatives that the International had at its disposal unlimited quantities of cash, the actual situation was quite the reverse. The total receipts of the General Council for the year 1867 were £63, or three hundred dollars, while the sources of income at the time for the Commune were limited to the dues of 10 centimes per week per member, which

---

[81] The evidence of Tolain, Fribourg, Corbon and Héligon, all former members of the International, who among the witnesses were best informed on the activities of this organization, was almost completely neglected by the committee. As the report put it: "The International, after having contributed to our disasters by its connection with the foreigner, organized in Paris the revolutionary army whose work we saw on March 18th. The fall of the Commune has not, unhappily, destroyed its forces or its aims; the enemy is there before us; it has the same aspirations, the same covetousness; it recruits every day its army" (p. 87).

[82] "Journal Officiel" (Versailles), April 22, 1871.

[83] Ibid., May 29, 1871.

remained generally unpaid.[84] Héligon, the treasurer of the
Paris sections of the International from 1865 to 1868,
states that never did he have in his possession more than
50 francs at one time.[85]

The belief in the power of the International and its responsibility for the Commune was confirmed in the minds
of conservatives by the attitude of internationalists all over
Europe toward the Commune. Everywhere they gloried
in this great struggle of the Paris proletariat against the
bourgeoisie. Marx expressed the opinion of the General
Council of the International in his pamphlet *The Civil War
in France* which appeared immediately after the Commune.
The identity of interests between the Commune and the
International was here proclaimed. The Communards fleeing from Paris to all parts of Europe were received by the
various sections of the International in Belgium, Switzerland, England, and elsewhere as brother proletarians and
brother socialists. The official committee on the 18th of
March felt that the willingness of the International to support and approve of the acts of the Commune and to take
the responsibility for them showed that the International
was strongly implicated.[86] It was this deep-rooted belief
which resulted in the Dufaure law of March 14, 1872, imposing severe penalties on any individual becoming a
member of the association.

Nevertheless, as we shall see, the International as an
organization had very little to do with the Commune
although individual members were influential in the Commune Assembly and in the Commune's economic and military organization. Marx, despite his later eulogy of this
"proletarian revolution," had been seriously opposed to

---

[84] M. G. Molinari, *Le Mouvement Socialiste* (Paris, 1872). Molinari was
well acquainted with the organization and work of the International, having
attended several of the annual congresses on behalf of his paper, "Le Journal des Débats." He was in close touch with the socialist movement in France.
[85] *Enquête sur le 18 Mars.* Evidence of Héligon, p. 832.
[86] *Ibid.*, Section 9, Chapter 9.

political action sponsored by the International destined to
overthrow the new republic in France.   On the 6th of September, 1870, two days after the revolution which established the Third Republic, Marx wrote to Engels complaining of the difficulties involved in moderating the plans of the
Federal Council in Paris.   "This is the more necessary since
at present the whole 'French section' of Paris is arising, in
order to perform stupidities in the name of the International.   They wish to overthrow the provisional government,
establish a commune of Paris, and recognize Pyat as the
French ambassador to England." [87]

Although the Paris sections played an active part in the
opposition to the government during the siege, the Federal
Council in Paris and the General Council in London were
as much surprised as anyone else by the revolution of March
18th.   During the Commune the "party of the International" was in a distinct minority and the Federal Council
seems to have had considerable difficulty in making up its
mind to side with the Communards. Its single act during the
Commune was the announcement of its support, after which
it appears to have ceased operations as a centralized
administrative organization.

The International did not make the revolution which
established the Commune of Paris nor did it shape in any
significant way the policy of the revolutionary government.
It is much more true to say that the Commune "made" the
First International.   Although it destroyed the association
in France it had the opposite effect elsewhere.   "The Commune's cannon awakened socialism throughout the whole
of Europe. After the 18th of March, the International
spread like a train of powder through Spain, Italy, Germany
and Austria; it established itself in Greece, Denmark, Hol-
land, Portugal, Poland and Russia." [88]   Conservative
Europe was inclined to take seriously the International's

[87] *Marx-Engels Briefwechsel*, IV:330.
[88] Benoît Malon, *L'Internationale*, "La Nouvelle Revue," 26:758.

opinion of the Commune as an opening skirmish in the approaching war between the proletariat and the bourgeoisie and to see in the association the initial organization of the proletarian armies.

Before the Communal revolution Marx was practically unknown outside of certain small groups in Germany and England. The Commune made him a figure of considerable magnitude. In France in the late 'sixties Marx was almost completely unknown.[89] His controversy with Proudhon had been ignored and was only brought to light by his later notoriety. French socialists were for the most part fluctuating between the extreme Jacobinism of Blanqui and the mutualism of Proudhon. "But the Commune came; one of the Versailles newspapers made of Marx the inspirer of the proletarian revolution of Paris, which he was not, and a principal founder of the International (which was true). Overnight the savant, the misunderstood philosopher, the unknown master of modern scientific socialism, was raised to the summit of universal celebrity." [90] If we make a small allowance for the exaggeration of Malon, a member of the International in little sympathy with Marx, the statement is substantially true.

Although the International did not make the revolution of March 18th it was a development of considerable importance in the French socialism of the 1860's and had a strong and direct influence upon a large number of individuals prominent in the Commune. French socialism in 1870-71 was conspicuously different from what it had been in 1864, and the International both caused and was affected by the change.

In 1862, Napoleon III, indulging himself in one of his tentative ventures in the direction of liberalism, took the

[89] A. Richard, *Les Propogateurs de l'Internationale en France,* "La Revue Socialiste," 23:643. Richard was a leading organizer of the International in Lyons and later a strong adherent of Bakunin's.

[90] Benoît Malon, *Karl Marx et Proudhon,* "La Revue Socialiste," 5:16 (1887).

occasion of the International Exposition in London to assist in the sending of seventy French workers for the purpose of conferring with their British fellows. "Quite naturally," as Malon delicately puts it, "the workers' delegates from the large republican cities spent their time upon other things than Bonapartist propaganda." [91] They agreed with the British laborers on the necessity of establishing an international association for the protection and furthering of the interests of the working class. The British representatives were the more eager to further this project in that recently British employers had shown an inclination to import strike breakers from the continent upon occasion. It was hoped that an international labor association might check this practice.[92]

The opportunity for the formation of the International Workingmen's Association, since known as the First International, came in 1864 when French and British laborers, who had been corresponding with each other, came together to protest against the Russian treatment of Poland. On this occasion the organization embodied in the provisional rules laid down by Karl Marx was adopted by the delegates and the association launched. The workers represented were of all colors and descriptions of socialist opinion and Marx found it necessary to cast his principles into a form fitting the circumstances. As he remarked in a letter to Engels, "It was very difficult to manage things in such a way that our views could secure expression in a form acceptable to the Labour movement in its present mood." [93]

At any rate the French delegates, who were Proudhonians and mutualists almost to a man, saw nothing in the address, preamble, and rules to object to and consequently affiliated

---

[91] Benoît Malon, *L'Internationale,* "La Nouvelle Revue," 26:733, February 15, 1884.
[92] G. M. Stekloff, *History of the First International.* English translation by Eden and Cedar Paul. New York, 1928, p. 61. Despite its Marxian bias, this is the best book on the First International.
[93] *Marx-Engels Briefwechsel,* III:191, November 4, 1864.

themselves with the International. In January of 1865 the Paris bureau was established and the association launched in France. Here it was well received by the liberal bourgeoisie and Napoleon himself. After all, as Laveleye remarks, John Stuart Mill and Michel Chevalier, who had both spoken of the principle of association as warmly as the Manifesto, might have signed the document.[94] In consequence a number of prominent French liberals joined the Paris branch, among them Jules Simon who later viewed the association with horror, and Gustave Chaudey who was shot by the Commune.

The leading socialists in France, on the other hand, outside of the Proudhonian group, regarded the International rather sourly. Louis Blanc preserved a hostile silence, Ledru-Rollin, an old republican socialist of 1848, found it too cold to political agitation against the Empire, while Blanqui saw in it nothing but a Bonapartist creation.[95] Nevertheless the little mutualist group managed to collect a following of some five or six hundred workers by 1866 and, in the Geneva Congress of that year, distinctly dominated the delegates from other countries. Six Blanquists from Paris who came to the Congress to denounce the French representatives as emissaries of Bonaparte were incontinently thrown out.

The history of the International in France, or rather Paris, falls pretty clearly into two parts. From its inception until the middle of 1868 the little group of Proudhonian mutualists, led by Fribourg, Tolain, Limousin, Murat and a few others, controlled the movement. This group eschewed political action, was entirely proletarian, and conceived the purpose of the International to be mainly educational. The workers were to learn by study the principles of cooperation and association. Whatever the brand of

[94] Émile de Laveleye, Le Socialisme Contemporain (Paris, 1883), 2nd ed., p. 175.
[95] Malon, L'Internationale, "La Nouvelle Revue," 26:736.

socialism favored by the International outside France, the Paris branches were originally, according to Tolain, nothing but study groups.[96] As Fribourg has it, "It was not a society formed for the purpose of action. When, at the London conference, we were confronted by a man named Karl Marx who had published a volume called *Capital* in which he had set himself the task of combatting the Proudhonian ideas which had been adopted by most of us, we knew well, in consequence, that we should not be in agreement. But we said that instead of fighting among ourselves and accusing one another, the different socialist schools ought to get together to study their problems, and to take the opportunity of exposing their ideas every year in a congress." [97]

It is noteworthy that scarcely any of the leaders of the International in Paris during this first period were later members of the Commune.

During the second period of its existence, which began roughly with the second trial of the International in 1868, the mutualists gradually lost their influence. Other leaders and other groups filled with plans of political action and more aggressive economic policy came to the fore. This alteration in the nature of the Paris branches corresponded with a change in the temper of the International, as a whole. At the Lausanne Congress in 1867, the swing towards the authoritarian collectivism of Karl Marx became obvious. The Paris group of Proudhonians who had led the way at Geneva were forced to take second place. This diversion of the movement became more and more pronounced with each successive congress until, by 1870, the influence of Proudhon had practically ceased to be effective.

The International in Paris became powerful when it accepted the notion of the class struggle and the idea that socialism must play an active part in the class struggle. It

[96] *Enquête sur le 18 Mars,* p. 844. Evidence of Tolain.
[97] *Ibid.,* p. 864. Evidence of Fribourg.

became powerful when it shed the anti-political policy of Proudhon and took up a position against the Empire. Tolain, Fribourg and their group sought to reconcile existing antagonisms in society, as one of their number put it, by peaceful means.[98] In general, they were opposed to strikes. Nevertheless it was the strike of the bronze workers in 1866 which brought notoriety to the International among the French working class. On that occasion Tolain was sent to London for funds and with the assistance of the association the bronze workers won their strike.

The popularity of the association was further enhanced by the trials of 1868. The rather rapid spread of the International in France alarmed the Empire. In March, 1868, the Paris Federal Council was prosecuted under a law of 1834 prohibiting the formation of unauthorized associations of more than twenty members. Although the association had existed for three years in France with the knowledge and tacit consent of the government, the fifteen members of the Federal Council were found guilty and sentenced to a fine of 100 francs each.[99] The Paris branches, two days after the arrest of the first bureau, appointed a second. The change in the policy of the International in France is obvious in the differences between these two bureaus.

The second bureau was headed by Malon and Varlin, both of whom were later active in the Commune. Although neither can be called a Marxin, their brand of socialism was distinctly more aggressive than that of the mutualists. Varlin, who was killed during the Commune, was a worker of great intelligence, an exceedingly able organizer of

[98] *Enquête sur le 18 Mars*, p. 833. Evidence of Héligon.
[99] The members of the bureau fined were Chemalé, Tolain, Héligon, Camelinat, Murat, Perrachon, Fournaise, Gautier, Dauthier, Bellamy, Gérardin, Bastien, Greyard, Delahaye, Delorme; all laborers. See *Le Procès de l'Association Internationale des Travailleurs*, published by the Communion de Propogande du Conseil Fédéral Parisien, 2nd edition (Paris, 1870).

workers' societies and a man who believed in the necessity and inevitability of the class struggle.[100] Malon, who escaped to Switzerland with great difficulty after the Commune, was as forceful a figure as Varlin and as able an organizer.[101]. Between them they managed greatly to extend the influence of the International through the proletarian centers of Paris.[102]

The Second Bureau had not been in existence two months before it was prosecuted on the same charge. This second trial saw both the prosecution and the defense in a different mood. The government had handled the First Bureau gently, even sympathetically. The nine members of the Second Bureau were sentenced to three months in prison. The public prosecutor denounced the International as a political society, and if, until this time, it had not been such, it now rapidly tended in this direction. Although the Federal Council was dissolved, the number of adherents of the association in France grew very rapidly. Radical republicans, revolutionaries, and a considerable number of Blanquists came to join the ranks. The old Proudhonist leaders were driven out by the newcomers. Fribourg and Héligon discontinued their connection in 1869 and although Tolain retained his membership until the war he ceased to be an important figure. Even Marx was alarmed at the rapid change in the nature of the Paris branches. "I promised you a long time ago," he says in a letter to Kugelmann, "to write you a couple of words about the 'French branch.' These ragamuffins are half or two thirds of them bullies and similar rabble, but all, hiding behind our people, pose as revolutionary heroes,

[100] See a twelve-page note on Varlin by Adolphe Clémence, "La Revue Socialiste" (1885), I:415.

[101] Malon, in spite of his proletarian origin, managed to acquire an education and made of himself something of a scholar. He mastered five languages and was the founder of "La Revue Socialiste."

[102] The members of the Second Bureau were Varlin, Malon, Humbert, Granjon, Bourdon, Charbonneau, Combault, Landrin and Molin. Five out of the nine later took an active part in the Commune.

who, from a safe distance, of course, would kill kings and emperors, and particularly Louis Napoleon." [103]

The law of June 6, 1868, which permitted public meetings was the signal for a rapid expansion of socialism in France and particularly in Paris. The free discussion of socialism, prohibited since 1851, brought the heroes of 1848 back into the field. But the socialism of 1848 was not the socialism of 1869. Cantagrel tried to preach the doctrines of Fourier, Cabet was referred to, one occasionally heard the names of Louis Blanc and Pierre Leroux. [104] However, Proudhon and Blanqui were the only leaders of 1848 who retained their influence on the masses, and the thoroughgoing Blanquists formed a comparatively small group. The socialists of 1869 appeared to fall into two groups, the mutualists, still expounding their master Proudhon and the exponents of the idea of class struggle; "la liquidation sociale." [105] The former were led, or at least represented, by Langlois, an early disciple of Proudhon later to relapse into the ranks of the bourgeoisie. The position of the latter group was expounded by those into whose hands the Paris branches of the International had recently fallen: Varlin, Malon, Vaillant, and, more particularly, Briosne, the admitted oratorical giant of the party.

The revival of the public discussion of socialism, together with certain events which marked the history of the last few years of the Second Empire, carried the membership of the International in France to around 200,000 by 1870. [106] Although branches were established in most of the industrial cities, although the association flourished particularly in Rouen, Lyons, and Marseilles, it is probable that a majority of these adherents belonged to the Paris sections. The representatives of the Paris sections at the general

[103] Marx, *Letters to Kugelmann*, December 5, 1868, "Neue Zeit," XX [2]:381.
[104] Molinari, *Le Mouvement Socialiste*, p. 9.
[105] *Ibid.*, p. 26.
[106] *Enquête sur le 18 Mars*, pp. 857-866. Evidence of Fribourg.

congresses were always twice as numerous as the representatives from the rest of France taken together.

Nevertheless, in spite of the numerical importance of the International in Paris, its strength as a party was relatively small and this fact is of considerable significance in connection with the history of the Commune. We have already mentioned the financial poverty of the Paris Federal Council and the variety of socialist opinion which divided the membership. In addition the nature of the relation between the individual member and his party representatives was not such as to promote a cohesive and close-knit organization. Most of the affiliations with the International came, not from individuals who thereby adhered to the International's program of socialist reconstruction, but from trade unions, cooperative associations and similar groups whose individual members might or might not take an interest in such a program.[107] "Unions (themselves bodies of uncertain composition) and whole localities would notify their adhesion to the International with the utmost lightheartedness, and would then, with the same levity, imperceptibly drift away from it."[108] The result, naturally, was that the International, even in Paris, never succeeded in building up a party. This fact should be remembered in connection with the position of the International during the Commune.

The rapid growth of the association in Paris and its activities during 1869 and 1870 alarmed the imperial government. Numerous members of the association had taken part in the political agitations which marked the rediscovery of the tomb of Baudin.[109]. At the funeral of Victor Noir, January, 1870, all the radical groups in Paris were temporarily united, the Paris sections playing a prominent part.[110] During the weeks which preceded the plebiscite of Napoleon III, the 8th of May, the International again interested itself

[107] Molinari, *Le Mouvement Socialiste*, p. 207.
[108] G. M. Stekloff, *History of the First International*, p. 147.
[109] See above, p. 6.
[110] *Enquête sur le 18 Mars*, p. 833. Evidence of Héligon.

in politics, urging abstention from the vote. In the numerous radical clubs founded in Paris after the passage of the law of June 6, 1868, representatives of the International did not always succeed in keeping off the forbidden subject of contemporary politics. The Paris sections accepted more and more completely the view of socialism as the theory and program of class struggle. As one of the now disgruntled founders put it, "Strikes, always strikes and more strikes; no more study or anything which resembled it. Under the influence of Varlin, the organization for fighting purposes grew every day; the foreign sections of the International, masters of the situation, supported the movement and founded violent journals; an epidemic of difficulties descended on France and paralyzed production." [111]

For these and other reasons the Empire brought the International to a third trial, this time on the charge of being a secret society. Nineteen were charged with being the founders or leaders of a secret society and nineteen with being members. Seven were sentenced to one year in prison and to 100 francs fine. Twenty-six were sentenced to two months in prison and 25 francs fine. [112] Among those brought to trial and sentenced were a number of later leaders in the Commune: Varlin, Malon, Murat, Johannard, Pindy, Combault, Avrial, Theisz, Fränkel and others. As it happened the Franco-Prussian War intervened and the condemned escaped their punishment.

The International in Paris had by 1870 changed pretty completely its program and its personnel in the five years following its formation. Among the rank and file the followers of Proudhon were still numerous and many of those

---

[111] E. E. Fribourg, *L'Association Internationale des Travailleurs* (Paris, 1871), p. 141. Fribourg's book, which is the best of the contemporary works on the First International, is, however, suspect in its handling of the later phase of the association's history. He dropped his membership in 1869 and was hostile to the element which supplanted the mutualists in the Paris sections.

[112] *Troisième Procès de L'Association Internationale des Travailleurs à Paris* (Paris, 1870).

who represented the International in the Commune were of this complexion. Beslay and Theisz were notable examples. Among the leaders, however, a more aggressive brand of socialism had found favor. The policies pursued by these leaders brought the association in Paris to a position of considerable numerical strength by the outbreak of the war. Nevertheless, for reasons we have given, the Paris sections did not form a closely welded organization. In consequence, although individual members took an active part both in the Communal revolution and in the determination of the Commune Assembly's policy, the International as a party was devoid of important influence.

CHAPTER II

THE PRELUDE TO REVOLUTION

THE Franco-Prussian War stripped the tinsel and decoration from a reign deeply devoted to surface ornamentation. The march of Prussian feet in the Champs-Élysées furnished the sad accompaniment to the burial of an imperial government whose chief had been imprisoned at the battle of Sedan and whose dissolution the fourth of September had pronounced. A lay figure whose false proportions had been set before the gaping nation by the clever finger of political stagecraft, Napoleon III had shown himself to be the most buoyant of fair-weather navigators. But the winds of adversity were not to be tamed by donning a startling uniform and appearing before the people with his hand in his coat, in the manner of his illustrious predecessor. He fell amid practically universal applause and the populace accepted with acclamation the designation prepared by that anti-court poet Victor Hugo, "Napoleon the Little."

The Germans marched into France and on to Paris glowing with moral satisfaction at the fall of "Babylon die Stolze," that cesspool of European civilization. The war had scarcely ended, and the German troops were still overlooking Paris, when the Commune came to confirm them in their certainty that this was the degenerate race. The Commune of 1871 capped the climax of the degradation of France and half of the bitterness of this sanguinary civil war is to be explained by its historical setting. Even France was convinced by the Commune of the moral degeneracy of Paris. The official report on this uprising finds its principal cause in the neglect of religion and true morality and the cultivation of a rationalistic attitude towards life. "In vain does our generation wish to efface God from its thought, to banish him from its activity. Social questions overshadow all others to-day and these questions raise primarily the problem of human destiny, that is to say, they lead back to the problems of the existence of God, of religion and of its dogmas." [1]

Whether or no the causes of the Commune are, in the last analysis, traceable to the decline of religion and morality in France, and particularly Paris, the events of the eight months which preceded the 18th of March, 1871, had something to do with it. Napoleon and France had entered upon the war with Germany too light-heartedly and with inadequate preparation. A series of disastrous encounters culminated in the battle of Sedan, which led to the capture of the emperor himself along with MacMahon and his army. Although this catastrophe occurred on September 1st, definite news was delayed in reaching Paris. Rather vague though ominous rumors emanating from Brussels and London circulated in the capital on the morning of the third but it was not until four o'clock in the afternoon that the full extent of the defeat was known. A telegram to the empress brought the information to Paris:

"The army has been defeated and captured; I myself am a prisoner.

"NAPOLEON."

This bombshell, bursting on the city of revolutions, led to the overthrow of the government. The legislative assembly, with a majority strongly conservative and allied to the Emperor, met to deliberate on the form of government demanded by the exigencies of the situation. While it deliberated, the Paris mob acted. Finding its leaders in the Republican minority of the legislature, the frenzied crowds,

[1] *Enquête sur l'Insurrection du 18 Mars, 1871: Annales de l'Assemblée Nationale* (1872), tome IX, p. 115.

after invading the special session of the legislative body itself, carried these leaders to the Hôtel de Ville, where the Republic was proclaimed. By six o'clock on the evening of September 4th the new Government of the National Defense was formed and announced to the rest of France. General Trochu, governor of Paris, was maintained in his functions and appointed Minister of War.

The Government of the National Defense, although the product of a spontaneous and unorganized revolutionary movement, found itself at the outset without opposition. It was more secure on its first day than at any other period in its history. The population of Paris and of France, stunned by the magnitude of the military disasters, closed its ranks silently behind the new government. The conservative majority of the Chamber of Deputies, reassembled after the invasion of the mob, faced the fact of the proclamation of the Republic and accepted it. In an able speech Thiers expressed the sense of the majority. "We have only a few moments to remain together; it is necessary to use them. Before recognizing the authority which has just been born, we have to establish certain questions of principle and of fact upon which it is not possible to speak out.

"To fight this authority would be unpatriotic. We can not oppose ourselves to it nor can we enter into collusion with it. I pray that God may assist it. Let us separate, let us conduct ourselves as good citizens, devoted to our country. As long as it demands of us nothing contrary to our conscience, or to the true principles of society, our position will be easy. We do not dissolve, but, in the presence of the terrible misfortunes of France, we return with dignity to our homes. It is impossible either to recognize a government born of an insurrection, or to oppose it when it fights against the enemy." [2]

The radical and revolutionary element in Paris, on the other hand, which was to be a thorn in the side of the new government during the siege, and which was later to make

[2] *Enquête sur le Gouvernement de la Défense Nationale,* 21:23.

the Commune of Paris, acquiesced in the events of September 4th, and in general lent its support. The future leaders of the Commune were present in the mob, rallying their cohorts and inciting the masses to action. There were demands on the part of the crowds surrounding the Hôtel de Ville that certain of these leaders, Delescluze, Millière, Blanqui and others, be taken into the government. But there is no evidence that the revolution of September 4th was planned or organized by any of the revolutionary groups prominent in Paris. In spite of the fact that Rochefort was the only radical included in the Government of the National Defense, the support of the radical as well as the conservative element in Paris was given to the newly constituted authority.

The enthusiasm for the Republic and the government which represented it in the streets of Paris was indescribable. "What a moral victory was this day in Paris," cried the liberal "L'Avenir National." [3] "It would console us for the defeat of Sedan, if anything could console us for such a disaster." Blanqui, the leader of the revolutionary communist party, with a dozen or fifteen of his followers signed a plea for united action in the defense of France, behind the new government.

> "In the presence of the enemy, no more parties, no more divisions.
>
> "With a government which betrayed the nation, cooperation was impossible.
>
> "The government created by the movement of September 4th represents republican thought and national defense.
>
> "That is sufficient.
>
> "All opposition, all contradiction must disappear to make way for national safety." [4]

But in spite of the enthusiasm of the radical element and

[3] September 6, 1870.
[4] Blanqui, "La Patrie en Danger," p. xxxvi.

the tacit support of the conservatives the position of the
Government of the National Defense was insecure. With
the fall of the emperor the custodian of national sovereignty became the National Assembly, duly elected by the
people. The new government supplanted the National
Assembly and yet was never given official recognition by it.
The Government of the National Defense was the work of
a Paris mob and in this mob the revolutionary element was
strong. A failure to satisfy the claims of radical groups
would mean opposition, more or less strong and more or
less organized, from the very people who felt themselves to
be, and with some justice, the creators of this government.
Falling between these two parties and facing the well-nigh
impossible task of fighting a superior force with the inadequate machinery of an incompetent empire, the Government
of the National Defense succeeded in making itself one of
the most unpopular régimes in the history of 19th century
France.

The opposition of the radical groups came first and the
next five months witnessed one long series of half-hearted
attempts on the part of the government to hold in check
insurrectionary movements in Paris. The final outcome of
this situation was the Commune of 1871. And the lack of
governmental success in repressing the revolutionary element was in large measure the result of its own revolutionary origin. The conservative opposition came later and
attributed to the Government of the National Defense not
only the responsibility of the disastrous conduct of the war
but that of the insurrectionary movements culminating in
the Commune of Paris which was but the logical outcome,
according to the conservatives, of the illegal assumption of
power on September 4th.

GROWTH OF THE RADICAL OPPOSITION

At the outset the new government enjoyed the support,
or at least was freed from the opposition, of the radical ele-

ment in Paris. Blanqui, Delescluze, Pyat and Rochefort, the most important leaders of revolutionary Paris, ostensibly united behind the régime in which Rochefort had become a member. But this attitude was short-lived. As early as September 9th, one of the editors of "La Marseillaise," Paschal Grousset, of whom we shall hear more during the Commune, avers that "most of the men who compose it (the government) are, with good right, more than suspect to the Socialist Democracy." On September 20th a liberal paper reproaches Delescluze, editor of "Le Réveil," for his attacks on Favre and Gambetta. "In the name of France, let us have no more quarrels. We have one aim and one alone: to repulse the enemy." [5]

Rochefort, released from prison by the mob on September 4th, had harangued the populace, demanding the election of a municipality which, placed near the central government, could oversee its actions in the manner of the Commune of 1793. He was placated by an appointment in the government. But Favre, Simon, Ferry, Trochu and Picard later avowed that almost from the outset they found themselves face to face with the Commune. "They felt that it was their adversary, they knew it, but they did not foresee then of what crimes the Commune was capable." [6]

Opinions differ on the part played by the International in this opposition which was later to lead to the Commune. It is impossible accurately to estimate its importance but the available evidence indicates that, directly or indirectly, it was considerable. With the outbreak of the war, the attention of the government being directed elsewhere, the association renewed its activities and recovered rather rapidly from the disorganization into which it had been thrown by the third trial.[7] Its membership in Paris on September 4th is unknown, but there seem to have been about twelve or

[5] *Moniteur de la Guerre,* September 20, 1870.
[6] *Enquête sur le Gouvernement,* Vol. XXI, p. 36. Report of Daru.
[7] See Chaper II, p. 56. Also O. Testut, *L'Internationale et le Jacobinisme* (Paris, 1872), I:195.

thirteen active sections, whose fortunes varied with the events of the siege.[8] By May 8th of the next year there were thirty sections,[9] and the temper of the association had changed as extensively as its numbers.

The seat of the Federal Council of the Paris sections was 6, Place de la Corderie, a location made famous by the events of the coming months. At the same *local* were situated at the time of the Commune nine of the thirty-odd labor unions existing in Paris.[10] To No. 6 came the representatives of the radical clubs established in great profusion during the months of the siege.[11] Also at the same address were located the headquarters of a number of the revolutionary republican committees organized by the International in conjunction with the representatives of the clubs.[12] In one way or another "La Corderie" served as a central clearing house for the ideas and plans of radical Paris and contributed most of the cohesiveness which existed in a rather haphazard and unorganized opposition.

The International Association at the outset was as patriotic as the other radical groups in Paris but feared reaction and viewed with some suspicion the members of the new Government. On the evening of September 4th, meeting at the Place de la Corderie, it drew up a proclamation supporting the government, but with reservations. Its support amounted to a statement that it would not attack, "because of the existing state of war, and the continued

[8] From a letter of Varlin, quoted in *Le Troisième Procès de l'Internationale*, p. 53.

[9] "La Révolution Politique et Sociale," May 8, 1871. One of the organs of the International during the Commune. The list of names and addresses is given.

[10] A list of the "Chambres Syndicales" in Paris was published during the Commune. A copy of this list is to be found at the Archives de la Seine. See for this list also, *l'Ouvrier de l'Avenir* (*Organe des Chambres Syndicales et des Associations Ouvrières*), March 12, 1871.

[11] Benoît Malon, *La Troisième Défaite du Prolétariat Français* (Neuchâtel, 1871), p. 41. Malon was undoubtedly one of the ablest members of the International in Paris at this time.

[12] J. Guillaume, *L'Internationale* (Paris, 1907), II:89.

disorganization of the popular forces." [13] One of the most
prominent leaders of the association, Malon, saw before it
"two great duties, the surveillance of the forces of reaction,
within, and the defense of Paris against the enemy, without." [14] On the whole it must be held that the International,
during the siege, performed its first duty with more éclat
than its second. Nevertheless the Paris sections initiated
their attack on the external enemy with a summons to their
German brethren to desist. In this dispatch to the Social
Democracy of Germany the French branch of the Internationale "invites it to withdraw its armies; if not it will be
necessary to fight to the last man." [15] Less impassioned
than the letter to the Germans of Victor Hugo, who appealed to the common ancestors, Vercingetorix and
Arminius, it had about the same effect.

The task of harassing the reaction lay more closely at
hand. Before separating, on the evening of September 4th,
the members of the Paris Federal Council had voted for the
establishment of a committee with members in every arrondissement, whose function it should be to supervise, or at
least investigate, the action of government officials. On the
following day the International joined forces to this end
with representatives of other radical groups, and by September 11th the "Comité Central des Vingt Arrondissements"
was established with delegates from fifteen arrondissements
represented.[16] From this time forward, until the end of the
Commune, the Committee was very much in evidence. Each
arrondissement was invited to form a committee and each
committee requested to select four delegates to represent

[13] This proclamation is reprinted in the evidence included with Daru's
report. *Enquête sur le Gouvernement: Annales,* Vol. 21, p. 206.
[14] "La Marseillaise," September 9.
[15] Published in "La Marseillaise," September 9.
[16] *Enquête sur le Gouvernement,* 21:207. From notes seized in the
possession of Chalain, second president of the "Comité," on November 2.
See also on the "Comité Central des Vingt Arrondissements," Georges
Bourgin, *La Commune de Paris et le Comité Central,* "Revue Historique,"
1925, 150:2. This is a very careful study.

the arrondissement in the Central Committee. The personnel of the local and Central Committee was pretty well divided between the International and the representatives of the clubs.[17]

The purpose of the committees according to Malon, one of the founders, was "to stimulate the municipal governments and to aid in the work of the defense. The Central Committee assumed the same task with respect to the central government."[18] But it met with little encouragement.[19]

However, it could, at least organize opposition to the administration. In the first two months of its existence, the Government of the National Defense was forced time and again to defend its policies before popular delegations which appeared, with and without arms, before the Hôtel de Ville. In these demonstrations the Committee played a prominent part. On September 17th it published its program, the chief demands of which were, (1) the abolition of the Prefecture of Police and the performance of this service by the National Guard, (2) the popular election of National Guard officers by the members of each military unit, (3) immediate municipal elections, and, (4) the establishment of the "levée en masse."[20] After a meeting of thirty delegates on September 20, at which similar resolutions were passed, a committee of twenty was appointed to carry these demands next day to the Hôtel de Ville. Demonstrations occurred on September 21, 22, and 26, in all of which the Committee had a hand, and on each occasion members of

[17] Malon, *Troisième Défaite du Prolétariat Français*, p. 41. See also *Enquête sur le Gouvernement: Annales*, 25:67. Evidence of Corbon.
[18] Malon, *Op. cit.*, p. 41.
[19] *Enquête sur le Gouvernement: Annales*, 21:207. Notes of Chalain. After the 18th of March this committee made something like an official statement of its activities during the siege, signed by the temporary president and twenty-two of its members. "The committee has existed since the 5th of September, 1870. It made the 31st of October, published the 'red poster' (Jan. 5, 1871), and was responsible for the 22nd of January; on each occasion sacrificing some of its members to the prisons. The members of the Central Committee (of the National Guard) and of the Commune of Paris were nearly all of them associated with it." "Le Cri du Peuple," April 4, 1871.
[20] *Les Murailles Politiques Françaises*, I:90.

the government were compelled to harangue the mob which filled the square in front of the Hôtel de Ville. On the last occasion Picard dispelled the crowd at midnight by announcing that Paris had been invaded by the Prussians.[21]

Neither the Central Committee nor its parent the International, however, directed all the opposition to the Government which was born in radical Paris.   Blanqui, Delescluze, Félix Pyat, and Flourens, four of the strongest of the leaders of the revolutionary element, had little or nothing to do with either of these organizations. Flourens, in particular, was a thorn in the side of authority during the siege.[22] His hot patriotism could not brook what he considered to be the blundering incompetence of the Government of the National Defense. On October 5, he attempted to influence the government by a display of force and appeared at the Hôtel de Ville with his battalion commanders, captains, lieutenants and ten armed battalions.[23]

Various members of the government attempted to rea-

[21] *Enquête sur le Gouvernement: Annales,* 21:207.   Chalain.

[22] Flourens was an agitator and rabble-rouser of parts, a representative of what was, in some ways, the best of the French revolutionary tradition. Certainly he was the most attractive figure in the ranks of the Commune. The son of a professor at the Collège de France, Flourens early devoted himself to science and, at the age of twenty, was appointed temporarily to his father's chair. But he possessed a spirit sensitive to injustice and a temper quick to revolt. It must be added that deliberation was not one of his habits.

This quixotic combination of qualities led Flourens in the 'sixties to the Ægean, where he took up arms on behalf of the revolting Greeks. He went from Crete to Italy clad in the native costume, and, in a series of articles on the island campaigns in Italian newspapers, he managed to insert enough criticism of the Italian government to receive a sentence of six months at the hands of the courts. Returning to France in the late 'sixties, when the Republican opposition to the Empire was rapidly gaining force, he threw himself ardently into the cause. Flourens wrote for Rochefort in the newly established "Marseillaise," a series of articles dealing with the relation of the army to the people. This series was so little to the taste of the government that Flourens found himself in jail for another three months. At the funeral of Victor Noir, he counselled the assembled radical forces to march on Paris, but wiser heads vetoed this rash undertaking. By the time of the declaration of the Republic, he was a well-known and popular leader in the proletarian sections.

[23] *Enquête sur le Gouvernement: Annales* 21:260. Report of Lieut.-Col. Chaper.

son with him. Finally Jules Ferry in an affecting scene recalled the relations between his brother and Flourens' father so touchingly that his lieutenants were won over if he himself was not. The meeting broke up with the words of Kératry, member of the government and Prefect of Police, "If the republic perishes it is you who are responsible." [24]

The visit of Flourens preceded an even more extensive demonstration on October 8th, engineered by the Central Committee.[25] Owing partly to the misunderstanding of directions by subsidiary leaders, however, this movement completely failed.[26] The outcome of the demonstration was a popular counter-demonstration of such magnitude that nothing further was attempted during the month of October. For the moment the opposition to the government was eclipsed. When one of the more persistent of the revolutionary leaders, Sapia, a battalion commander, invited the troops to march on the Hôtel de Ville, he was seized by his own men and conducted to the headquarters of the general staff.[27] In view of the state of public opinion the Central Committee deemed it advisable to curtail somewhat its activities and little more is heard of it until the 31st of October.

The opposition to the policies of the government and the demand for immediate municipal elections, which had been put forward in the demonstrations of both October 5th and October 8th, indicate that the International, the Committee, and the associated radical groups had pinned their faith on the Commune. With these groups were beginning to act officers of the National Guard, an alignment to be cemented in the communal revolution of March

[24] Enquête sur le Gouvernement: Annales, 23:473. Evidence of Arago.
[25] Ibid., 21:207. Notes of Chalain. Also see Dubreuihl, La Commune, p. 258, in Jaurès, Histoire Socialiste.
[26] Ibid., 21:207: Dubreuihl lays the blame on Flourens, who spoiled it with his demonstration a few days earlier; p. 259.
[27] "Journal Officiel," October 10, 1870.

18th.[28] From the 8th to the 31st of October, there is a cessation of armed demonstration, but the cause of the Commune is kept alive by the radical press and in the clubs.

Blanqui had established his paper "La Patrie en Danger" September 7, and in the subsequent numbers devoted long articles to laying bare the weaknesses of the military policy of the government and exposing his own schemes. His disciples with literary gifts supplemented these dissertations on strategy with praise of the Communards of 1792 and '93 who, in their history, simultaneously crushed the reaction within and destroyed the enemy without. This laudation of the Commune of '93 was seconded by Delescluze in "Le Réveil" and by Pyat in "Le Combat." In the clubs too, talk of the first Commune of Paris and praise of the "Heroes of '93" ran freely. An orator at the Club de la Porte Saint Martin ventured on a political justification of a revolutionary seizure of power by the party of the Commune.[29]

The government occupied itself frequently in its daily sessions with the state of radical opinion and the agitation in the clubs,[30] but nothing was done about it. Kératry, Prefect of Police, announced in the session of October 10 that twelve heads of battalions led by Blanqui and Flourens had signed a resolution demanding the overthrow of the government and the proclamation of the Commune.[31] He requested the closing of the clubs but the request was refused. The arrest of Blanqui and Flourens was voted unanimously by the government, excepting Rochefort and Arago, but Blanqui from long experience was elusive. The police agents refused to go to Belleville, a proletarian faubourg and a center of revolutionary agitation, where

[28] G. Bourgin, La Commune de Paris et le Comité Central, op. cit., p. 6.
[29] October 25. The speech is preserved at the Archives de la Seine.
[30] Unofficial notes of these sessions, expurgated and edited, were furnished to the Committee of Enquiry, by M. Dréo, one of the secretaries of the government of September 4th. See Annales, 20:131, 132, 134, 135.
[31] Dréo, Notes on the Sessions of the Government: Annales, 20:134.

Flourens, protected by his armed followers, held court. The situation was explosive and required but a small spark to set it off.

AN ATTEMPT AT REVOLUTION; THE 31ST OF OCTOBER, 1870

Paris woke on the 30th of October to find posted on its walls an announcement of the surrender of Metz by Marshal Bazaine with his entire army. On the same day it was learned that Le Bourget, gallantly taken by the French two days before, had been retaken by the Germans. To cap the climax, the government chose this unpropitious occasion to inform the citizenry that M. Thiers had returned to France from his peregrinations in foreign capitals with certain plans for an armistice in his pocket.[32] Like a prairie fire the news spread over the city. To make matters worse, the government stood convicted, in the minds of the populace, of falsehood. When, on the 28th of October, one of the best known of the radical journalists, Félix Pyat, had announced the fall of Metz, claiming to have received his information indirectly from Rochefort, the government indignantly denied it. Far from surrendering, Marshal Bazaine had not for one moment ceased "to harass the enemy by brilliant sorties."[33] Aroused by Pyat's apparently treasonable action, patriotic Parisians had sacked his publishing shop and burned the copies of his paper, "Le Combat." And now the government was forced to recant, and the "traitor" basked righteously in his martyrdom.[34]

The city was shaken as it had not been since the begin-

[32] Announced in "Journal Officiel," issue of October 31.
[33] "Journal Officiel," October 28. Partie non officielle.
[34] There is no evidence that the government was officially aware of the surrender of Metz until the arrival of M. Thiers, who had come through the Prussian lines on October 30th. The rumors had been circulated earlier by the Prussians themselves but, as Trochu announced in a poster of November 1st (see *Murailles Politiques Françaises*, I:311), rumors from this source were hardly to be relied on.

ning of the siege. Bazaine was charged with treason by the newspapers. The mayor of the 18th arrondissement, Clémenceau, then a young man in his late twenties, issued a bitter protest against an armistice. "The municipality of the 18th arrondissement indignantly protests against an armistice which the government cannot accept without treason." [35] The resignation of the government and, particularly of Trochu, military governor of Paris, was demanded.[36] In the clubs the agitation was feverish, and the evening of the 30th witnessed impassioned appeals for the Commune in the radical districts of the capital. It came to the ears of Arago, mayor of Paris, that a demonstration was planned for the next day and he consequently notified the Prefect of Police, but no extraordinary precautions were taken.

The insurrection of the following day came as a surprise to the government. So accustomed was it "to demonstrations, to visits by deputations, armed or unarmed,—by officers of the National Guard, 'avengers' etc., that it lived in the midst of perpetual alarms without believing that one day these demonstrations might prove more dangerous than hitherto." [37] By half-past nine in the morning people had begun to gather in the square in front of the Hôtel de Ville. The crowd was swelled from time to time by the adhesion of onlookers and the arrival of deputations of one sort or another to interview the government. By noon groups of National Guards began to assemble with cries of "no armistice" and "the levée en masse."

The mayors of Paris themselves were dissatisfied with the conduct of affairs by the government. Assembling at the Hôtel de Ville in the morning of October 31, they discussed the state of public opinion in Paris and came to the

[35] *Enquête sur le Gouvernement: Annales,* 21:67.
[36] *Ibid.*
[37] *Ibid.,* 21-68.

conclusion that immediate municipal elections were necessary. They had formulated this opinion in writing and dispatched M. Arago to carry it to the government, sitting
in another room in the same building, when the door of
the assembly room was forced and in came the mob. Led
by Pyat and Delescluze a number of leaders addressed
the tumultuous gathering, proclaiming the necessity of
abdication of the government and the election of the
Commune.

In the assembly room Arago was laying the request
of the mayors before the government. Meanwhile,
outside, Rochefort was haranguing the mob with small success. The Commune was demanded and a list of members
taken from the revolutionary groups of Paris was drawn
up.[38] When Arago appeared with the consent of the government to a municipal election he was roughly handled by
the crowd. Advocates of the revolutionary Commune threw
from the windows written lists of the proposed officials to
the people below. Towards four o'clock in the afternoon
the mob inside the Hôtel de Ville broke into the hall occupied by the deliberating government, led by several members of the International and of the Comité Central des
Vingt Arrondissements.[39] It was at about this time that
Flourens with five hundred of his Belleville infantry
appeared upon the scene, shortly followed by Blanqui.

Revoutionary Paris was gathered at the Hôtel de Ville
and the Government of the National Defense was held
prisoner in its own assembly room. The leaders of the
revolution demanded the resignation of the members of the
government, without success. After some difficulty in collecting his associates, Flourens proclaimed the new government and towards six o'clock messengers were sent out

[38] One list included the following names: Dorian, Blanqui, Delescluze,
Louis Blanc, Félix Pyat, Bonvalet, Ledru-Rollin, Verdure, Schoelcher, Jacque-
mart, Greppo, Martin-Bernard. But there are a number of variations in the
lists drawn up at this time. *Enquête sur le Gouvernement*, 21:73.
[39] Among them Lefrançais, Lévrault, Vermorel, Chassin, Cyrille. *Ibid.*, 74.

to various sympathizers to announce the new dispensation.[40] Under the leadership of Blanqui, who at this point more or less took charge of affairs, the revolutionary committee entered upon its functions with a series of decisions, ordering subordinates to lead military forces to the Hôtel de Ville, occupy the Prefecture of Police and to guard the gates of Paris.[41] The new government thus created included the following names: Flourens, Dorian, Félix Pyat, Mottu, Avrial, Ranvier, Millière, Blanqui, Delescluze, Raspail, Ledru-Rollin, Rochefort, Louis Blanc and Victor Hugo. A committee of public safety composed of the most revolutionary—Delescluze, Blanqui, Millière, Ranvier and Flourens—was also established.[42]

Louis Blanc and Victor Hugo had taken no part in the demonstration. Dorian and Rochefort were members of the Government of the National Defense. Raspail and Ledru-Rollin were old republicans who played a small part in the events of this period. The eight remaining names were to come to a greater prominence in the Commune of March 18th. In addition, the leaders of the revolution named a "Provisional Municipal Commission" of one hundred twenty. At least fifty of these one hundred twenty names were of men who were later to occupy positions of importance in the Commune. The list represented the "flower" of revolutionary Paris.[43]

The new government at the Hôtel de Ville had communicated with its lieutenants in the faubourgs, and some of its orders were executed. The offices of the mayor of the 19th arrondissement (Belleville) were invaded by the novelist Jules Vallès, later a Communard, and his follow-

[40] See Flourens' account reprinted in *Le Journal du Siège de Paris*, published by "Le Gaulois," Paris 1871, p. 187; Blanqui, "La Patrie en Danger," November 4; Millière's account reprinted in *Enquête sur le Gouvernement*, 25:537-47.
[41] *Enquête sur le Gouvernement*, 21:79. The decrees are printed here. See also Blanqui, "La Patrie en Danger," November 4.
[42] *Enquête sur le Gouvernement*, 21:79.
[43] The list is given, *Enquête sur le Gouvernement*, 21:79.

ers; the mayor seized and held as a prisoner until the next morning.[44] At nine o'clock twenty representatives of the Commune presented themselves at the Prefecture of Police to take possession but were unable to make headway against the polite refusal of M. Adam, the prefect.[45] In the 6th arrondissement (Luxembourg) the provisional mayor, Robinet, a radical republican, summoned the National Guard without notifying the battalion commanders. In conjunction with the Republican committee of the district, which included a number of the future leaders of the Commune, he prepared to support the revolutionary government. The Republican Committee of the 6th arrondissement, sitting in the same place, declared its adhesion to the new government and nominated its candidates for the Commune.[46] The revolution in the arrondissements, however, made insufficient headway to afford material assistance to its leaders assembled at the Hôtel de Ville, and the following day the local chiefs were busily occupied in manufacturing excuses for their precipitant activities.

During this time the members of the Government of the National Defense, uncomfortably detained in the Assembly Hall, were jostled here and there by the rampant Parisian proletariat. Flourens strode back and forth on the table knocking over inkwells and scuffing up the green covering with his spurs. Blanqui, Millière and Delescluze were busily engaged in writing dispatches in behalf of the new Committee of Public Safety. At seven o'clock the march of revolution was rudely interrupted by the intrusion of a commandant of the National Guard and four hundred of his

[44] Proclamation posted by the mayor of the 19th arrondissement, Richard. Reprinted in *Le Journal du Siège,* p. 184.

[45] "Le Gaulois," November 1, 1870, *Le Journal du Siège,* p. 188.

[46] These events in the 6th arrondissement are established by a series of telegrams, copies of which are to be found in the Bibliothèque de la Ville de Paris. The candidates proposed for election to the Commune were Robinet, Rousselle, Goupil and Varlin. These names will be met with again during the reign of the Commune. See also the proclamation posted by Robinet in *Murailles Politiques Françaises,* I:308.

troops.[47] "Down with Flourens, long live the Government
of the National Defense," shouted his followers. "Down
with these 'calotins,' down with these reactionaries,"
answered the representatives of Belleville. In the confusion
that followed no shots were fired and the intruders finally
retired from the hall, but safely in their midst walked General Trochu, Émanuel Arago and Jules Ferry, of the National Defense. The doors were closed and the remaining
members of the government were herded into a corner, but
the damage was done. Dangerous enemies of the revolution were at large.

The issue did not remain long in doubt. The vast majority of the city's population stood behind the government.
By ten o'clock twenty-five or thirty battalions of the National
Guard were assembled at the Place Vendôme and led to the
Hôtel de Ville under the direction of Jules Ferry. At midnight it was surrounded by from 50,000 to 100,000 men and
the revolutionaries, peering from the windows, became
alarmed. The end of the fiasco came with the entrance of
two battalions of light troops from Brittany. In order to
prevent a mêlée in which the lives of the imprisoned members
of the government might have been lost, General Le Flo, one
of these members, took command of the situation. The revolutionary leaders protected by the members of the government quietly retired, accompanied by their followers. At
3:25 A.M., Charles Ferry could telegraph to the mayors
of the arrondissements and to government officials, "The
Hôtel de Ville has been evacuated without the shedding of
a drop of blood."

The revolution of October 31st had not been planned.
There is no evidence of concerted action on the part of
leaders of the Paris proletariat or of the radical groups in
the capital.[48] Yet practically the whole of radical Paris took

[47] *Enquête sur le Gouvernement*, 21:78.
[48] Dubreuihl, *La Commune*, p. 259, has it that the 31st failed because the
action initiated by "La Corderie" "was drowned in an unregulated and confused agitation, led by no firm will and following no particular design."

part in it. The demonstration was the clear outcome of military reverses and of the announcement of the possibility of an armistice. Although the revolution was unforeseen and unplanned, it furnishes ample proof, however, of the extent of the organization of the radical element in Paris. Republican committees and vigilance committees in the arrondissements, central committees and the International, the followers of Flourens, Blanqui, Millière and others, were all in close touch by means of interlocking memberships, attendance at the revolutionary clubs and through personal affiliations.

The delegates of the Committee of the Twenty Arrondissements held a convocation on the morning of the 31st at the familiar No. 6, Place de la Corderie. But that they had concerted no plan of revolution is shown by the fact that they marched to the Hôtel de Ville with only three or four hundred men.[49] The action of Flourens also was the impetuous product of the announcements of the previous day. After a meeting with four or five of his friends on the morning of the 31st, notice of an assembly was sent to twenty-three commandants of the National Guard known for their opposition to the government, to which meeting Flourens repaired with his five hundred "sharpshooters."[50] Nor had the Blanquists, who numbered at that time about 3,000, concocted a plan of insurrection. Blanqui came to the Hôtel de Ville alone and, according to his own story, only after he had learned that his name was on the list of the new government.[51] The insurrection represented the spontaneous protest of the radical opposition to the Government of the National Defense.

What was to be the attitude of the government towards this opposition? This was the question which occupied its sessions during the first few days of November and which

[49] *Enquête sur le Gouvernement,* 21:207. Papers seized at the house of Chalain, second secretary of the committee.
[50] Flourens' account reprinted in *Le Journal du Siège,* p. 186.
[51] "La Patrie en Danger," November 4.

led to the resignation of two of its members. The names of the revolutionary leaders were known, the evidence of their guilt complete, but it was equally obvious that a considerable section of Paris was with the opposition. The police force was thoroughly disorganized. In all probability one third of the National Guard sympathized with the insurrection.[52] Furthermore, at least one member of the government, Dorian, had committed himself to a complete amnesty of the leaders of the insurrection. In his attempts to rid the Hôtel de Ville of the mob he had given promises to Delescluze and others, the breaking of which must be followed by his resignation. Yet Dorian was by far the most popular member of the government of September 4th and, through his direction of the munitions industry, the hope of the defense. His resignation was unthinkable.[53]

The opposition itself provided the government with its solution. Certain arrondissements were still occupied by revolutionary forces on the morning of November 4th.[54] In addition there was some talk in the clubs and elsewhere of a further attempt at revolution.[55] This evidence of continued activity on the part of the revolutionaries was enough to smooth over Dorian's rather easily satisfied scruples and

[52] Jules Simon, *Souvenirs du 4 Septembre* (Paris, 1874), 2:180.

[53] The question of the agreement entered into by members of the government and the leaders of the insurrection is somewhat baffling. According to Dorian and to Didier, le Procureur de la République, the convention of amnesty was signed by the imprisoned member of the government. See *Enquête*, 25:540 and Flourens, *Le Journal du Siège*, p. 187. However, it is flatly denied by J. Favre, J. Simon and Tamisier, who assert they never signed nor agreed to such a proposal. See *Enquête*, 21:86. M. Favre reiterates his denial in his book, *Le Gouvernement de la Défense Nationale* (Paris, 1872), II:9. Likewise M. Simon, although not so forcibly, in his *Souvenirs du 4 Septembre* (Paris, 1874), II:181. After the defeat of the Commune a copy of this amnesty was discovered in the search of the papers of Delescluze (reprinted, *Enquête*, 21:84). While stating the agreement concerning the election of the mayors and the vote on the Government of the National Defense, it does not specifically deal with the question of amnesty.

[54] Notably the 6th, 11th and 19th.

[55] M. Cresson, the new Prefect of Police, presented evidence to the government on November 3rd, of further plots by Blanqui and Flourens. *Enquête*, 21:94 and Dréo, *Procès-Verbaux*.

the government decided on a prosecution. But Adam, Prefect of Police, convinced that the government was acting dishonorably, tendered his resignation. He was followed in a few days by Rochefort, a radical who had always been somewhat uncomfortable in the councils of the government. Arago, mayor of Paris, was replaced by Jules Ferry; and Tamisier, commandant of the National Guard, by General Clément Thomas.

The government of September 4th, by reason of its origin, found itself in an unenviable position in this matter of prosecution. At the very moment of the invasion of the Hôtel de Ville, the invaders took care to remind their prisoners that this was another September 4th, initiated for the same patriotic reasons. Blanqui described it as merely a 4th of September which failed.[56] The government, in spite of continued debates on the subject had not, up till this time, submitted its position to a popular vote. However much it may or may not have represented the "general will" it was, as a matter of fact, merely the creation of the Paris mob of September 4th. The legal representatives of the government were somewhat sensible of this position, particularly M. Hémar, avocat-général, to whom was given the task of preparing the case against those accused after October 31st. This possibility of comparing October 31st with September 4th would not fail, he thought, "to create considerable embarrassment in the assize court and might very well lead to an extremely distasteful debate."[57] This vulnerable spot was thoroughly probed by the radical opposition in the months which followed.

THE CLUBS

November was a period of consolidation of the government's position and of repression of the radical opposition. The plebiscite of November 3rd put the question, "Will

[56] "La Patrie en Danger," November 4.
[57] *Enquête sur le Gouvernement,* 23:827.

the population of Paris support the authority of the Government of the National Defense, yes or no." [58] The answer was unmistakably conservative; 557,996 in favor, 62,638 against. The municipal elections of November 4th were of the same tenor. Except in the 19th and 20th arrondissements where Delescluze and Ranvier were elected mayors and the 18th, 19th and 20th where nine of the leaders of October 31st were elected adjutants, the appointees of the government were in general retained. [59] It was decided to prosecute twenty-four leaders of the opposition and on November 4th Cresson, the new Prefect of Police, announced that fourteen had been safely arrested.

However, a number of flies were busily buzzing about the ointment and some few slipped in. As usual, Blanqui, gliding shadow-like around the nooks and corners of Belleville, escaped the clutches of the police entirely. Others, barricaded in their favorite strongholds, were slow in being apprehended. A large section of the Paris press condoned the actions of the accused as being merely political offenses and showed a tendency to confuse October 31st with September 4th. No conclusive evidence was forthcoming against Félix Pyat, who on this as on other occasions had demonstrated an ability amounting almost to genius in avoiding implication. Pyat, who had appeared at the Hôtel de Ville just when the revolution appeared to promise success and had disappeared at the first evidence of its failure, had to be released. [60] Delescluze had formerly been attached to the procureur-général by business links of such intimacy that his prosecution became an impossibility. [61] The difficulty

[58] *Murailles,* I:329.
[59] The 18th arrondissement was Montmartre, the 19th Belleville, the 20th La Villette, three of the proletarian and radical districts of Paris important in the Commune of 1871.
[60] Cresson seems to think that Pyat was released because of the personal friendship of members of the Government, particularly Arago. See his *Cent Jours du Siège à la Préfecture de Police,* p. 53, and his evidence before the "Enquête." However, there actually seems to have been a lack of evidence against Pyat. Evidence of Hémar, 23:826.
[61] *Enquête,* 23:826. Evidence of Hémar.

of securing evidence against others accused led to the release of a few and caused the enquiry to drag on until the end of January, 1871. And, although the 31st had apparently broken up the Comité Central des Vingt Arrondissements, the membership drifted into other radical groups and swelled the numbers and enthusiasm of the clubs.[62]

The position of the political clubs of Paris during the siege and the Commune merits some attention. Their function and importance can in no sense be compared with that of the Jacobin clubs during the French Revolution when the Commune dominated the National Assembly. At the same time they served as centers for the dissemination of radical opinion and added a certain amount of cohesiveness to the radical opposition. When, after the law of June 6, 1868, public meetings were again permitted in France, the clubs established themselves with some difficulty. The question of politics was forbidden but the veterans of 1848 joined together with the younger members of the International and other societies to discuss "la question sociale." After September 4th no subject was barred. The attendance at the clubs augmented rapidly with the coming of the cold weather and the dwindling of the family fuel supply. Then too, the decree of Kératry closing the theatres at the same time made the clubs the chief centers of entertainment and supplied them with comfortable halls of assembly.

The thin line of Prussian troops which ringed Paris from the end of September till the end of January provided the orators of the clubs with one of their chief subjects. During October in particular the rostrums were occupied by inventors and amateur strategists who expounded their pet schemes for the defense of the capital and the extermination of the enemy. Germain Mérigot, the "rediscoverer" of Greek fire, was especially applauded by the club orators who calculated elaborately amid general enthusiasm the number

[62] *Enquête,* 21:208. Papers of Chalain.

of Prussians who might be exterminated per hour.[63] Unfortunate inventors whose military innovations were rendered valueless by the unfathomable ignorance and endless red tape of the Government were listened to nightly.[64] There was a scheme for destroying the invaders by poisoning the Seine from which they drew their drinking water. Another suggested the liberation on the Prussian lines of the wild animals of the Jardin des Plantes. Jules Allix, later of the Commune, and still later of the madhouse, exposed the advantages of his "prussic finger" which was to protect the virtue of French women and, incidentally, exterminate a few Prussians, should the latter succeed in entering Paris.[65] The "levée en masse" and the "sortie torrentielle" were popular down to the end of the siege and were later resurrected during the Commune.

The public, however, soon tired of the inventors and turned its attention to political and social questions. The two issues which dominated all others were the war and the preservation of the Republic. If the government were attacked it was on the ground of its incompetence to conduct war or its unwillingness to defend the Republic. If the Commune were proclaimed it was because the Commune presented the sole means of bringing France victory and of saving the Republic. The International showed itself to be as thoroughly patriotic in its intentions as any other radical group. At the Club of the Rue de l'École-de-Médecine, one of the centers frequented by the International, the problem of the defense of Paris altogether

[63] See Germain Mérigot, *Le Feu Grégeois* (Paris, 1870). Administration Centrale et Comité du Feu Grégeois, 3me d'Isly. Maxime Vuillaume in his *Cahiers Rouges, Cahiers de la Quinzaine,* 11th series, 9th Cahier, p. 82, has an interesting account of Mérigot.

[64] Molinari, *Les Clubs Rouges pendant le Siège de Paris* (Paris, 1871), p. 16.

[65] Henri d'Almeras, *La Vie Parisienne pendant le Siège et sous la Commune* (Paris, 1927), p. 111. Allix was the famous discoverer, in 1850, of the "sympathetic snails." "Snails could," according to Allix, "communicate with one another over great distances, which made possible a sort of living telegraph system" (d'Almeras, p. 109).

overshadowed the question of socialism. If the advantages of socialism were expounded, as frequently happened, these advantages were demonstrated to be intimately connected with the winning of the war.

The incapacity of the members of the Government of the National Defense was patent to all the orators at the Clubs. It became in their mouths the "Gouvernement de la Démence Nationale," or the Government of the National Inertia. Trochu, in particular, was incompetent. He was accused of scheming to kill off the friends of the Republic by putting them in the most dangerous sectors. At the Salle Favier, one of the most important and most revolutionary clubs of Belleville, Trochu was denounced as a traitor to the Republic and was threatened with assassination.[66] When a well-meaning but misguided defender of Trochu protested, he was hustled out as being a secret agent of the ministry. Trochu's catholicism was a red rag to the anticlerical revolutionaries of the clubs. To them he was "Saint Trochu," or "the holy Trochu," engaged in telling his beads when he ought to be supervising the defense of Paris, opposing the organization of Republican battalions in order to turn the country over to the reaction. Jules Favre and Thiers had similarly malignant intentions. "Trochu, Jules Ferry and Jules Favre want to restore a monarchy. Glais-Bezoin is too fond of sleeping; Crémieux is too old; Gambetta is too idle." In consequence, says an orator of the Salle du Pré-aux-clercs, it is necessary "to seize the government by the slack of the trousers and deposit it in a safe place." [67]

In the face of this organized stupidity and reactionary hostility to things republican on the part of the Government, the clubs resort to the Commune. An orator at the Club des Montagnards, November 3rd, is depressed at the

[66] *Enquête sur le Gouvernement*, 25:571. Reports on the Clubs submitted by Cresson, Prefect of Police, November 28, 1879.
[67] December 22, 1870. *Enquête*, 25:580.

vote of confidence in the government but asserts that "that will not prevent us from having the Commune. If they won't give it to us, we shall take it." [68] All the radical clubs ended their meeting with a "Vive la Commune" and at the Salle de l'Élysée-Montmartre the whole evening of December 25th was devoted to the Commune. The Commune alone can render the Republic durable, says one orator. Without the Commune the people will again fall under the dominance of a government of thieves, as during the Empire. The Commune is demanded in order that the laborer may live by his work, "without privation and without exploitation." [69] The Commune became a fetish in the minds of the habitués; not only would it win the war, preserve the Republic and regenerate society but it would, according to one orator, "instantly bring back our beans and our lentils." [70]

The question of social revolution, although overshadowed by the problems of the defense of Paris and the maintenance of the Republic, was occasionally aired in the clubs. The membership of the Club de la Révolution (Élysée-Montmartre) was limited to those who were willing to sign the profession of faith which proclaimed as its political aim the creation of a universal republic and, as the economic, the establishment of collectivism. The means avocated were revolution and the establishment of the Commune. [71] "La République démocratique et sociale," a favorite phrase of the socialists, resounded from many platforms. At the Club of the Rue de l'École-de-Médecine, Armand Lévy and other members of the International explained nightly the principles of a socialist organization of society and associated these principles with the Commune, so popular in radical Paris. At the Salle Favier and the Club of the Rue d'Arras the orators talked often of the approaching day when the

[68] Molinari, Les Clubs Rouges.
[69] Enquête, 25:577.
[70] Molinari, Les Clubs Rouges, p. 195. Club Favier. December 29th.
[71] Ibid., p. 147.

people "would share the unjustly acquired property of the bourgeoisie." [72] Inequalities and injustices in the rationing of foodstuffs and fuel during the siege quite naturally fostered socialist convictions and inflamed the populace of the proletarian quarters.[73] But, on the whole, the opposition to the government did not revolve to any very important extent around socialist principles.

After the 31st of October the clubs remained the chief centers of radical agitation and organization in Paris. But during the months of November and December the revolutionary movement was in partial eclipse. The arrest of important leaders had given it a decided check. Flourens, after remaining at large, protected by his sharpshooters, until December 7th, was finally apprehended. Blanqui's paper "La Patrie en Danger," which had flourished for a while on the violence of its opposition, found it impossible to prevent this violence from becoming monotonous. It died from lack of nourishment early in December. Blanqui himself, although still at large, was deprived of influence. Unable now to preside at his clubs,[74] he must see them pass into other and less capable hands. His disciples still attempted to keep his name alive in the mind of the public, but without too much success. At the Salle du Grand Pavillon, a meeting was held on behalf of Blanqui as candidate for mayor in the 20th arrondissement.[75] According to one of the speakers, "we have only one more chance of safety and that is to elect Blanqui, the enemy of jesuits and traitors; Blanqui, who has conspired for the democratic and socialist Republic for more than fifty years." The public, however, seemed apathetic in the face of the merits of this great conspirator.

[72] *Enquête*, 25:571. November 27th at the Rue d'Arras.
[73] One recalls the medal struck by the fourteen diners at the restaurant Brébant during the siege to commemorate and celebrate the fact that the fare was as good as it had ever been before the war.
[74] In the Rue d'Arras and the Rue St. Denis.
[75] See Molinari, *Les Clubs Rouges*, p. 105.

Even Cresson, the nervous Prefect of Police, who, as Jules Favre remarked, "always feared the worst," was cheered up by the situation of the revolutionary party in December. On the 19th of that month, the leaders are "contenting themselves with talking in the clubs"; on the 21st, "things are very tranquil"; on the 26th "the leaders of revolution are without followers"; and on the 5th of January, the opposition of these leaders to one another is so great that they are all held inactive.[76] But the next day there appeared a revolutionary poster which excited a great deal of comment in the clubs and which indicated a certain degree of cohesion among the revolutionary chiefs. And the 22nd of January witnessed a demonstration which ended in a bloody carnival on the square in front of the Hôtel de Ville.

THE NATIONAL GUARD IN PARIS

The Commune of Paris of March 18th, 1871, was to a very considerable extent the work of the National Guard. The early infiltration of radic ' nd revolutionary elements, the utilization of the organization for counter-governmental propaganda, the eventual establishment of a central committee which accepted the responsibility of the administration of Paris after the government forces had been driven out, all bear witness to the relation of the National Guard to the Communal revolution. So significant was this relation in the opinion of contemporaries that immediate steps were taken for the dissolution of the National Guard, after the re-establishment of lawful authority in May, 1871. It may be said without exaggeration that the dissolution of the National Guard was the most important single effect of the Paris Commune on the history of France. In the light of these facts it becomes necessary to examine the position of the National Guard during the siege and its relation to the parties of the left.

The military situation of Paris on the advent of the new

[76] *Enquête*, 25:562-567.

government, September 4th, was not favorable. The imperial war minister, de Palikao, had pursued the avowed policy of denuding Paris of its defenders in order to strengthen the armies of France.[77] Early in August, after a series of reverses had shown the possibility, if not the probability, of the siege of Paris, steps were taken to put the capital in a state of defense. The minimum strength necessary to garrison the forts surrounding Paris was estimated at 40,000 men, to which must be added at least 80,000 regular troops for action between the forts and for relief purposes.[78] To meet these demands there were available on September 4th, 9,000 marines, 10,000 to 12,000 police, who had to be used for service in the city, 6,000 special troops (artillery and engineers), 4,000 in the process of organization, and 13,500 mobile troops of a rather undisciplined character.[79] In addition there were 60 battalions of National Guard, about 90,000 men, in process of reorganization.

The defeat of Sedan had removed the last serious obstacle to the march of the Germans on Paris. By the 18th of September the capital was besieged. But between these events its military resources had been augmented by the remnants of the 13th and 14th army corps and by 100,-000 of the Mobile Guard summoned to the colors before the 4th of September. Unfortunately these troops were badly organized and the policy pursued by the Government of the National Defense did not improve this organization. Various members of this government had committed themselves, during their long years of political opposition, to a democratic organization of the army. This taken in conjunction with their lack of military experience led to the decree of September 16th which discharged the existing officers of the guard, appointed under the Empire, and pro-

[77] *Enquête sur le Gouvernement,* 23:149.　Evidence of Gen. de Palikao.
[78] *Ibid.,* 21:220.　Note 1. Lieut.-Col. Chaper.
[79] *Ibid.,* 21:220.

vided for election by the troops. As might have been expected large numbers of severe but capable and experienced leaders were supplanted by "beaux parleurs." Furthermore the example had a deplorable effect upon the troops of the line and the National Guard of Paris, which was in process of formation.

The National Guard of Paris was in existence in Paris during the Empire, but its character and the quality of its personnel were supervised with extreme care. Quite naturally the imperial government pinned its faith on the standing army and viewed the more democratic guards with some suspicion. Quite naturally also the republican opposition picked out the army as an obvious point of attack and advocated the adoption of the principle of a citizen militia. On August 12, 1870, the Empire in full retreat, unable to withstand the increasing public pressure, authorized the reorganization of the National Guard. But, even in Paris the reorganization proceded slowly and circumspectly until the Revolution of September 4th.

One of the first acts of the new government was the decree of September 6th authorizing the organization of 60 new battalions of National Guard.[80] Patriotic Paris responded as one man. Within a few days not 60 but 194 new battalions were formed and the total of the National Guard increased to something over 300,000. Old and young, capable and incapable, radical and conservative, flocked to the colors and the new units were created in the midst of incredible but natural confusion.

The elections were held shortly afterwards and resulted in a not very reassuring set of commanders. The soap-box performers, the rabble-rousers, the notorieties of revolutionary Paris, were selected in large numbers, particularly in the proletarian quarters. Blanqui, Flourens, Millière, Sapia, Tibaldi and many other militant, but hardly military, popular heroes found themselves battalion commanders.

[80] *Enquête sur le Gouvernement,* 21:239.   Report of Lieut.-Col. Chaper.

The government viewed this situation with some alarm but for one reason or another abstained from taking action. The 31st of October discovered these commanders marshalling their troops but not in the defense of Paris. One of the results of this uprising was the cashiering of 16 chiefs of battalion, all of whom were subsequently members of the Commune.[81] And in spite of the indulgence of the government, or rather its fear of the radical opposition, it was found necessary to discharge a very large number of the elected officers of the National Guard during the course of the siege.[82]

But the elective system had other and perhaps more deplorable results. The discipline without which a body of men can scarcely be called an army was sadly lacking. The officers of the National Guard were too often the servitors rather than the commanders of their men.[83] On one occasion, when the General Staff singled out for praise a chief of battalion on account of the firmness of the control of his troops, the battalion became so incensed at this reflection on its liberty that the commander's position was no longer tenable.[84] The radical press and the clubs popularized the notion that discipline is non-essential in a republican army. The dissolution of a battalion of sharpshooters of Belleville greatly excited the Club Favier. An orator with whom the audience was in close sympathy declared, "They accuse us of lack of discipline; but of what use is discipline? How has it served us up to the present time? It has resulted in our being beaten by the Prussians. It was the disciplined troops which lost at Reichshofen, at Forbach, at Sedan; it

---

[81] *Enquête sur le Gouvernement,* 24:26. Evidence of Lieut.-Col. Chaper.

[82] Thirty-six battalion commanders, 171 captains of companies, 14 adjutant-majors, 147 lieutenants, 119 second lieutenants, 8 second lieutenant-standard-bearers; and the government deprived of their rank a considerable number in addition. *Enquête,* 21:44. Report of Daru. These figures are for the period between September 27, 1870 and March 18, 1871.

[83] *Enquête sur le Gouvernement* 24:6. Evidence of Lieut.-Col. Chaper.

[84] *Enquête sur le 18 Mars,* p. 724. Evidence of Col. Montagut, Chief of the General Staff of the National Guard.

was the disciplined troops which capitulated at Metz," etc.[85]

The hasty creation of the Paris militia, together with certain faults of the system of direction, equipment, and remuneration, accentuated its tendency towards anarchism. So rapid had been the flow of enlistments that little if any attention had been given to the quality of the personnel. It has been alleged that twenty or thirty thousand ex-convicts were distributed among the new units formed, though there is little evidence to support this estimate.[86] Certainly, the number of untrustworthy recruits was large;[87] so large that the General Staff was in the habit of distinguishing between "good" battalions and "bad" battalions, the good ones being those which could be relied upon to obey commands.[88] If the control of the National Guard had been under the direction of the Ministry of War these unreliable elements might have been whipped into shape. But in spite of the protest of General Trochu, the democratic and republican sentiment of the majority of the government confided the direction to the Minister of the Interior, Jules Favre.[89]

The pay of the National Guard, which constituted an important part of the system of government relief, did not tend to improve the calibre of its man power. The closing of Parisian industries and other economic activities, the consequences of the siege, threw out of work a considerable part of the laboring population. Large numbers of this

[85] Meeting of December 7, 1870. Molinari, *op. cit.*
[86] *Enquête sur le Gouvernement*, 21:238. Report of Lieut.-Col. Chaper. But more reliable observers put this number considerably lower. For example, M. Adam, Prefect of Police for three weeks in October, puts the number of ex-convicts in the National Guard during the siege at around 4,000, with an additional 8,000 coming in after the end of January. *Enquête sur le 18 Mars,* p. 492. This agrees with the estimate given by M. Claude, head of the department of safety. (Service de la Sûreté.) *Ibid.,* p. 533.
[87] General Trochu mentions the figure of 23,000, and Col. Montagut, 35,000. *Enquête sur le 18 Mars,* p. 725.
[88] *Enquête sur le Gouvernement*, 21:243. Report of Lieut.-Col. Chaper.
[89] *Ibid.,* p. 253.

population were necessitous and a government decree of September 12th attempted to provide relief by establishing a daily pay of one franc, fifty centimes for members of the National Guard. Since this was a form of poor relief as well as a military measure, those who qualified for relief were at least as forward in enlisting as those who were qualified for military service.

The distribution of arms and equipment by all accounts seems to have favored the radical battalions. Fear of the reaction within often exceeded the fear of the Prussian without, on the part of those responsible for the distribution. There is no evidence that the central authorities associated with the mayors of Paris favored in this respect the revolutionary units.[90] But certain of the arrondissement officials appointed on the 5th of September either intentionally or through negligence delegated this authority to equipment committees not entirely impartial in their activities. Of the great variety of guns parcelled out to the National Guard of Paris, the most modern of the rapid-fire arms appear to have been secured by the battalions of Flourens, Tibaldi and other revolutionary leaders.[91] It is not necessary to suppose, however, that this mal-distribution was the effect of an intentional policy on the part of municipal officials. The military units of the proletarian quarters, represented by vociferous chiefs, were more militant in their demands. Here as elsewhere the groups which made the most noise received the best equipment.

It was not until the middle of October that the government attempted to transform the National Guard into fighting troops by selecting the most capable man power. On

[90] The Committee on the Commune of March 18th in examining Floquet, who assisted the mayor of Paris, Étienne Arago, in organizing the distribution of military equipment, tries to make him admit that the authorities favored republican battalions. But Floquet, while agreeing that this service was often delegated to officials whose radical opinions alarmed the majority of the government, refused to admit that a policy of favoritism had been adopted. See *Enquête sur le 18 Mars,* pp. 601-619. Evidence of Floquet.

[91] *Enquête sur le Gouvernement,* 21:242. Report of Lieut.-Col. Chaper.

October 16th a call for volunteers was made. But out of the approximately 344,000 troops only a few over 6,000 responded.[92] In consequence of the failure of this volunteer system, a decree of November 8th ordered the formation in every battalion of four fighting companies, designed to produce an effective force of one hundred thousand men. Thus it was only after nearly two months of siege that adequate measures were taken to make of the National Guard a fighting force. The Ministry of War had been against this policy of arming the population from the start. Only the widespread popular fear, shared by the government itself, that the Prussians were about to make an attack upon Paris in September had overcome this resistance.[93] Now, after arms had been given to the populace, very little was done to create effective troops. A few of the National Guard regiments saw action outside the walls of Paris, and undoubtedly the presence of this vast number of armed men within the city added something to its defense. But the arming of a large unruly element of the population occasioned considerable trouble for the Government of the National Defense and the problem of disarmament became one of major importance at the end of the siege.

Large groups of comparatively idle men, loosely organized in the cadres of the National Guard, provided an ideal situation for revolutionary propaganda. The ground was rendered more fertile by the natural dissatisfaction with the Government of the National Defense. Encouraged by the radical press, and even by certain elements in the government, to believe itself a capable fighting force, the National Guard demanded action against the enemy. The "sortie torrentielle" which would engulf the thin Prussian line was much discussed. But as the siege wore on and no attempt was made to utilize these forces disaffection became widespread. The "plan Trochu," universally condemned in

[92] *Enquête sur le Gouvernement,* 21:248.
[93] *Ibid.,* 21:241.

the clubs and radical press, apparently assigned to the National Guard a position of complete inactivity. When, at the end of the siege, the Guard was led into action at Montretout, it was distinctly felt that the object was a little blood-letting, not the defense of France. In the words of a colonel of infantry, before this engagement, "we are going to scramble the National Guard up a bit since that is what they seem to want." [94]

A considerable number of the officers of the Guard belonged to the International, to the committee of the Twenty Arrondissements and to other radical groups. Quite naturally the revolutionary groups in Paris attempted to put to their uses the National Guard. Invitations were continually sent out by Blanqui, Flourens and others to the battalion commanders to meetings at which plans were discussed for "overseeing the reaction." [95] The National Guard, armed or unarmed, took part in all the radical demonstrations at the Hôtel de Ville from the 22nd of September till the 22nd of January. Newspapers and placards announced in advance the place of assembly of the various military units.[96] Leaders of the radical battalions were in the forefront of the opposition to the government during the whole of the siege.

Yet it is distinctly the consensus of informed opinion that the vast majority of the National Guard were on the side of order up to the time of the capitulation of Paris. The influence of the extra-legal revolutionary committees organized in various battalions, family councils, vigilance committees, etc., was by no means general. In the words of a member of the general staff of the National Guard, "We were always able to overcome the influence of these committees until the capitulation; during the siege the spirit of the National Guard was good; it was sustained by patriotic

[94] *Enquête sur le Gouvernement,* 24:15. Evidence of Lieut.-Col. Chaper.
[95] *Ibid.,* 24:34.
[96] *Ibid.,* 21:259.

sentiment and by the desire of avoiding disagreements in Paris. . . ." [97] But, after the attempted revolution of January 22nd and the declaration of the armistice, the situation changed.

JANUARY 22, 1871

Distrust of the executive capacity of the Government of the National Defense and of the military direction of its leader, Trochu, waxed mightily during December and January. First given voice in the clubs and radical associations it spread through the newspapers, attaining even the most conservative, and finally made its appearance in the councils of the government itself. In the clubs vile rumors of the "sale of Paris" to the enemy circulated. In "Le Réveil," "Le Combat" and other radical journals suspicions of insidious reactionary attempts to destroy the Republic were hatched. Conservative journals preached the downright incapacity of Trochu and his staff. As early as the twenty-fourth of December Jules Favre demanded in a meeting of the government the revocation of the military governor of Paris.[98] One must recognize the great spirit of General Trochu, said the Minister of the Interior, but one must doubt his military ability. The populace demanded action, the sole desire of the National Guard was to fight and the Government of the National Defense remained quiescent.

Meanwhile the supply of foodstuffs was running low and the suffering of certain sections of the population was intense. The good citizens of Paris were eating up the city's stock of horses at the rate of seven hundred a day. They had long before proceeded to dogs and cats and now prime rats were going in the market at 3 francs a head.[99] Long lines of housewives stood hours before the distributing centers for the daily ration of bread and vegetables, and com-

[97] *Enquête sur le 18 Mars*, p. 752. Evidence of Baudouin de Mortemart.
[98] Procès-Verbaux (Dréo), *Enquête*, 20:159.
[99] See d'Almeras, *op. cit.*, p. 24.

plained bitterly of the quantity and quality of the foodstuffs received. An extraordinarily cold winter intensified the suffering. Mobs broke into churches and made off with the benches for firewood. The old cry of the proletariat of 1848, "Give us bread or lead," was heard again in Paris and the spectre of famine began to take on flesh and blood. Yet the spirit of the populace continued high; "no capitulation" and "resistance to the last" was the only policy contemplated. But the misery of the people had its effects on the growth of the radical opposition. The Government of the National Defense became the sign of all calamity, the origin of all evil.

The two or three serious attempts at military action outside the walls of Paris ended in rather miserable failure. The battles of the Marne (Châtillon) which lasted from November 28th to December 2nd were followed by the retreat of the troops to Paris on the 3rd. In the words of Trochu, "The battle of Châtillon, audaciously directed by an audacious general, proved only that the army did not exist." [100] It was on this occasion that the sharpshooters of Belleville who had shouted loudest for action shouted even more loudly for inaction. After fleeing precipitantly before the enemy, two companies of this battalion refused to obey the command to return and were ignominiously ordered back to Paris.[101] The attack on Le Bourget begun December 21st ended in much the same way. The emotion in Paris was extreme. The newspapers and the clubs again demanded the resignation of Trochu and the Government of the National Defense. The mayors of Paris were joined by the government in their search for a military successor. The final attempt of the Parisians was the battle of Buzenval, the 19th of January. On this occasion the National Guard took that active part for which it had yearned, without too

[100] Procès-Verbaux (Dréo), *Enquête,* 20:160.
[101] Mentioned in the Order of the Day of General Clément Thomas, December 6th, *Enquête,* 21:460.

great success. Green battalions got out of hand and fired on their comrades.[102] This and the other events of a disastrous day resulted in the usual charges of treason and intensified the general belief in the military worthlessness of the leaders.

During January, following closely on the beginning of the bombardment of Paris, the revolutionary opposition massed and organized its forces. On the 6th Paris rose to discover the "red poster" of the delegates of the Twenty Arrondissements affixed to its walls.

> "Has that government which on the 4th of September was charged with the national defense fulfilled its mission? No!

> "We have 500,000 soldiers and 200,000 Prussians hem us in! To whom belongs the responsibility if not to those who govern us? They have spent their time in negotiating instead of founding cannon and manufacturing arms.

> "They have refused the levée en masse.

> "They have left in office the Bonapartists and put in prison the republicans.

> "The policy, the strategy, the administration of the Government of the 4th of September, a perpetuation of the Empire, are judged. Give place to the people! Give place to the Commune!"[103]

The signers of this document were 140 of the leaders of revolutionary Paris; Blanquists, members of the International, of the Committee of the Twenty Arrondissements, of the Republican League, and of every other opposition group in the capital. The majority later took an active part in the Commune and undertook that direction of the defense of Paris against the besieging French which they were denied at this time against the Prussians. The government was thrown into a flurry, the Prefect of Police attempted

[102] *Enquête,* 24:282. Evidence of General Vinoy.
[103] This poster published in *Murailles Politiques Françaises,* I:490-491.

a number of arrests of which some were accomplished, and discussion at the clubs became explosive and vindictive. Trochu attempted to counteract the agitation by a placard charging the revolutionary element with exploiting the misery of the population to its own interest and against that of the defense. His proclamation ended with the famous phrase, "The Governor of Paris will never capitulate." [104] The delegates of the Twenty Arrondissements reasserted their position in a poster of the 8th but the efforts of the Prefect of Police assisted by General Vinoy succeeded in silencing the "Delegates" until after the armistice.[105]

The defeat of Buzenval brought to a climax the scarcely repressed revolutionary opposition in Paris and ignited the insurrection of January 22nd. All the revolutionary movements of this period followed closely upon military catastrophes. In the words of General Vinoy, "The disaster of Sedan was followed by the 4th of September; the fall of Metz by the insurrection of the 31st of October; the defeat of Buzenval led to the 22nd of January, and the capitulation of Paris gave us later the Commune." But on this occasion the government was forewarned. When the news of the defeat of Buzenval was brought to the awaiting government, Jules Simon foresaw the approaching outbreak and urged preparation.[106] A series of telegrams from the Prefect of Police to Colonel Vabre, commandant at the Hôtel de Ville, warned him of revolutionary preparations in the radical clubs.[107] In consequence Vinoy brought troops into Paris, battalions of regulars were stationed at the Hôtel de Ville, and the gates closed.

During the day of the 21st the crowd surged to and fro

[104] See *Murailles*, I:710.

[105] On the events of these days see G. Bourgin, *La Commune et le Comité Central*, pp. 9-14.

[106] Procès-Verbaux (Dréo), *Enquête*, 20:171. See also Molinari, *op. cit.*, p. 263.

[107] *Ibid.*, 23:807. Evidence of Colonel Vabre.

on the square. Feeling the need of an energetic leader an attempt was made in the night to release Flourens, incarcerated in the Mazas prison. Owing to the weakness of the prison director not only Flourens but a number of other radical leaders, imprisoned for attempts against the government, were rescued. The government, in session on the 22nd, was informed by the Prefect, in tears, that Flourens, gathering together the National Guard of Belleville, was moving on the Hôtel de Ville, that the Prefecture of Police was surrounded, and that the police were no longer masters of the situation.[108]

But M. Flourens was not to take an active part in the events of that day. Sapia, Sérizier, Allix, Malon, and others, later notorious in the Commune, marshalled various battalions of the radical National Guard in front of the Hôtel de Ville, while Blanqui, of but not in the movement, kept in close touch at a nearby café. Various delegates were dispatched to present demands to the government in session. These demands were received by Chaudey, assistant to Jules Ferry, the mayor, who promised to present them to the government. The crowd, little satisfied with this reception and strengthened by the appearance of the 101st battalion of the National Guard, later the crack military unit of the Commune, opened fire on the regular officers stationed at the gate.[109] The government troops replied and the crowd fled in all directions, leaving some fifty dead and wounded in the square. It required little time to clear the surrounding houses and shops of insurgents and by 5:30 Ferry was able to dispatch a reassuring telegram to the mayors of Paris, concluding, "Thus it is, through the crime of a few, that this sorrowful extremity has not been spared

[108] Procès-Verbaux (Dréo), Enquête, 24:282. Evidence of Vinoy.
[109] Enquête, 23:807. Evidence of Vabre. Although it is alleged by Louise Michel, La Commune, Arthur Arnould and other supporters of the Commune that the government troops fired first, the evidence of all the witnesses interrogated by the Committee of Enquiry is to the contrary.

to our glorious and unhappy Paris. An aggression as cowardly as it was foolhardy has soiled so pure a page," etc.[110]

A great deal of the force of the insurrection had been
destroyed by the announcement, on the morning of the 22nd,
of the resignation of Trochu. His successor, General Vinoy,
aided by the sentiment of genuine disgust at the insurrection
felt by the majority of the population, carried out a policy
of severe repression. The government, partially at his
instigation, decided to close the clubs; the radical papers
"Le Combat" and "Le Réveil" were suppressed, and a
number of leaders of the revolt arrested. The siege was now
practically at an end and the Government of the National
Defense, so harassed by the radical opposition in Paris, soon
surrendered its powers, in general obloquy, to the National
Assembly elected on the 8th of February.

Paris and the National Assembly

On the 28th of January, the 135th day of the siege, after
five days of negotiation between Favre and Bismarck, the
armistice was declared. It was time. Provisions for eight
days only existed in Paris and the three armies which at
that time held the field for France gave no promise of relief
to the capital. The external defenses of the city remained
intact and were guarded by 250,000 troops not including
the National Guard. The magnificent spirit of the population continued high and refused still to admit defeat. Lack
of food alone led to the capitulation.

The humiliation of Paris was keen and the rankling bitterness which possessed all classes of the populace fed the
already strong opposition to that authority which had governed France in defeat. The armistice, which was of 21
days' duration, provided for the election of a national assembly to decide the question of the continuation of the war.
Paris was required to surrender its forts, pay an indemnity
of 200 million francs within fifteen days and submit to the

[110] Copy of this telegram in the Archives de la Seine.

disarming of its 250,000 troops, with the exception of 12,000 for service inside the city.[111] The National Guard, which retained possession of its arms, was responsible for the maintenance of order in Paris. This retention of arms by the National Guard was later seen to be a fact of primary importance among the causes of the communal revolution. Jules Favre, speaking in the National Assembly after the outbreak of the revolution, demanded pardon of God and man for not having insisted upon disarmament.[112] But it is difficult to see how it could have been accomplished at the time without Prussian assistance, since possession of a gun represented the 30 sous per day upon which a large mass of the population relied for support.[113]

The fighting troops, disarmed, disgusted, and weary, swelled in Paris the ranks of the discontented and revolutionary element. The well-to-do middle classes which had sent their families to the provinces before the commencement of the siege left as soon as possible to join them. This depleted the ranks of the conservative battalions of the National Guard and, more significant still, deprived a considerable number of military units of commanding officers.[114] The gates of Paris having been thrown open, large numbers of the disbanded French troops in the provinces flocked to Paris accompanied by groups of military adventurers, mainly Poles and Italians, who had fought for France during the war. Vinoy, at that time military governor,

[111] The limitation on the garrison of Paris was later raised to 40,000 on the plea of Thiers.

[112] Session of March 23rd.

[113] The evidence of military experts on the possibility of disarmament presented to both commissions of enquiry is divided, but it leans toward the view that such disarmament was impossible at the time.

[114] According to the evidence of M. Louis de Saint-Pierre (*Enquête sur le 18 Mars*, p. 168) about 100,000 people left Paris after the armistice and remained in the provinces until after the Commune. To prevent resignation of officers of the National Guard, General Clément Thomas asked that permission to leave the capital be granted by himself, but the government delegated this power to the Prefect of Police. When de Paladines became Commandant, these resignations were pouring in at the rate of 60 or 70 a day. *Ibid.*, p. 750. Evidence of de Mortemart.

attempted to improve the situation by organizing and staffing a number of units to be led to the provinces, but this had the disadvantage of further depleting the corps of officers in the capital.[115] General Thomas and Colonel Montagut, commanding officers of the National Guard, in the face of the disorganization and disaffection of their troops, resigned.[116] Thomas was replaced March 3rd by General d'Aurelle de Paladines, a conservative, cordially hated by the radical element in Paris.

Meanwhile the Government of the National Defense was having great difficulty in relieving itself of the responsibility of governing France. Gambetta, chief of the government delegation at Tours, now at Bordeaux, refused to admit that the capitulation of Paris was anything other than an incident in the war against Germany Fiery, buoyant, persuasive, and an able organizer, Gambetta was determined on "la guerre à l'outrance." The elections which the government at Paris envisaged as the culmination of its power and the transfer of responsibility to other shoulders, he considered merely as a means of strengthening and legalizing existing authority. To this end Gambetta desired the exclusion from voting privileges of certain non-republican elements, particularly the office-holders under the Napoleonic empire. The government at Paris succeeded in supporting its views by the dispatch of three representatives to Bordeaux, and, amid great difficulties, elections were held in Paris, February 5th, and in the provinces, February 8th.

The result of the Paris election was an overwhelming repudiation of the Government of the National Defense and a strong approval of the radical opposition. Among the 43 newly elected representatives of the Seine were 10 future

[115] *Enquête sur le 18 Mars,* p. 29.
[116] The committee charged Colonel Montagut and General Thomas with having caused the disorganization of the National Guard by their resignations, but according to Montagut (*Enquête,* p. 722) the resignations were the result of the disorganization.

members of the Commune, including Félix Pyat and Delescluze, whose journals had been suppressed January 23rd, Malon and Millière,[117] both of whom had taken part in the insurrections of October 31st and January 22nd. In addition were Henri Rochefort, one of the ablest and most bitter of the radical opposition, whose paper, "Le Mot d'Ordre," was suppressed by Vinoy on March 11th, and several of the radical mayors who had distinguished themselves by their attacks on the government during the siege. Thiers was 20th on the list and Jules Favre, the only member of the government resident in Paris to be elected, very near the bottom.[118]

The outcome in the provinces was completely different. Here the opposition to the Government of the National Defense was not less but the representatives elected were conservative and monarchical rather than radical and republican. Very few Bonapartists were returned to the National Assembly, but its complexion was none the less monarchical. The majority, for the most part, was composed of politically unknown industrialists, soldiers, and agriculturists. It early evinced its distrust of the republic and by a series of measures quickly earned the disdain of the more or less radical metropolitan centers. Gaston Crémieux, a young journalist from Marseilles, sneered from the balcony during one of the first sessions, "You are only a rural majority," and the title stuck. Incompetent, this assembly certainly was, but it nevertheless elected as "head of the executive power" (*chef du pouvoir exécutif*) the ablest statesman in France, the conservative Adolphe Thiers.

[117] Millière was not a member of the Communal Assembly but took a very active part in the affairs of the Commune.
[118] It was during the electorial campaign that the already insupportable difficulties of M. Favre were increased by the cowardly revelations regarding the illegitimacy of his children and his falsification of birth certificates in this connection. The information, supplied by one Laluyé, a former friend, was published at the Club of "La Reine Blanche" by Millière and in "Le Vengeur" by Félix Pyat.

The new government of France had no sooner met at Bordeaux than it became evident the war was over. The irreconcilable Gambetta and his belligerent confrères from Paris received little satisfaction from the National Assembly or its executive committee.[119] In consequence the radical opposition in the capital transferred its point of attack from the Government of the National Defense to the National Assembly with no diminution of its bitterness. The new government at Bordeaux was a government of capitulards prepared to exceed in its infamy that of the National Defense. Thiers had no sooner been suggested for office than Pyat described him as the "ex-minister of father Philippe, the future minister of Philippe the son, the president of the chamber while awaiting the king's cabinet, the inventor of peace at any price, the author of the principle of each one for himself . . . the forts for the Prussians and [the prison of] Mont St. Michel for the republicans," etc.[120] The traditional hatred of Paris in the provinces and the disdain of the provinces in Paris was obvious in the attitude of the metropolitan newspapers. "The more I think about it," writes Henri Maret, "the more I become convinced that we are attaching too much importance to the decisions of the 600 cow fanciers who ornament our National Assembly."[121]

The more radical of the Parisian representatives, finding the atmosphere of Bordeaux most unsympathetic, marked their disapproval by a series of resignations continuing through February and March. Delescluze, Pyat, Millière, Rochefort, Victor Hugo found the determination of the Assembly to make peace incompatible with the dignity and the traditions of France. Pyat maintained that the Assembly, elected for the whole of France, automatically dissolved

[119] The new government as constituted included Jules Grévy, president of the Assembly; Thiers, chief of the executive power; Jules Favre, Foreign Affairs; Dufaure, Justice; Ernest Picard, Interior; Jules Simon, Public Instruction; de Larcy, Public Works; Lambrecht, Commerce; Le Flo, War; and Pothuau, Navy.
[120] "Le Vengeur," February 15.
[121] "Le Mot d'Ordre," March 11.

itself with its ratification of the cession of Alsace and Lorraine.[122] Meanwhile the Assembly, exhibiting a disregard for the interests and the state of feelings of Paris which amounted almost to a challenge to revolution, proceeded to liquidate the military situation of France.

The first of a series of measures which provoked the proletariat and the petite-bourgeoisie of Paris and threw large numbers of normally law-abiding citizens into the forces of the Commune, was the so-called "law of maturities" passed by the Assembly on March 11th.[123] The siege had very naturally seriously altered the normal commercial transactions of the capital. In so doing it had, in a number of circumstances, made it impossible for merchants to meet their engagements. A law of August 13th had taken account of this situation by postponing the maturity of financial obligations. These obligations had very largely passed into the hands of the banks and discount houses during the siege. The law of March 11th made them payable within a short interval of time.[124] Considerable numbers of small dealers in Paris were faced with bankruptcy. Even the conservative journals protested and commentators hostile to the Commune have admitted the unwisdom of the government policy on this matter.[125] The Committee of Enquiry on the 18th of March, so anxious to justify the acts of the National Assembly on all possible points, confesses that on this occasion "the Assembly . . . erred in adopting a measure which it recognized later as entirely insufficient. The maturities fixed on March 13th placed a considerable section of the business men of Paris in a position of inevitable failure, that is to say, of ruin and dishonor." [126]

[122] See "Journal de Paris," March 8.
[123] For a good discussion of this law see Lepelletier, *Histoire de la Commune de 1871* (Paris, 1911), Vol. I, pp. 281-286.
[124] Obligations contracted before or after the law of August 13 and falling due after April 12, 1871, could not be postponed. Those contracted between August 13 and November 12, 1870 were payable, with interest, seven months after the maturity fixed.
[125] For example, see Maxime Du Camp, *Les Convulsions de Paris*, I:40-41.
[126] *Enquête*, p. 29.

At about the same time it was intimated that the Assembly intended to enact in the near future a measure providing for the collection of building and land rents which had been prorogued during the siege. The laboring class, which had subsisted during this period upon very irregular wages or the allowance to members of the National Guard, was thrown into consternation.[127] Also, during March, proprietors, some of whom had fled to the extremities of France during the siege, began to collect current rents which had lapsed for several months and to evict tenants still unable to find work. A bourgeois witness of this procedure estimated that the Commune recruited its adherents largely from the class threatened with dispossession. "As one of them said to me," he reports, "a soldier of Italy and a good patriot: 'Rather than see the authorities sell my furniture, I'll risk the shots of their soldiers.' "[128] Both of these situations turned to the service of the Commune classes of society normally stable and conservative.

On the 10th of March, M. Thiers, tired of attempting to transact business with part of his government at Paris and the rest at Bordeaux, persuaded the Assembly to establish itself at Versailles. Conservative and provincial elements in the legislative body, distrustful of Paris and all things Parisian, would have preferred Bourges, but yielded to the head of the government. In the light of the whole situation it is difficult to maintain that the decision of Thiers to avoid Paris was a mistake.[129] The turbulent element in the capital had seriously threatened to overthrow the Government of the National Defense on October 31st and January 22nd. This same element was not only still in existence but had considerably augmented its forces. The National Guard, 300,000 strong, was still armed and had been depleted only by the exodus of propertied and conservative citizens. The

[127] See Lepelletier, I:286-288.
[128] From L. Thomas, *Documents,* p. 247.
[129] Lepelletier, favorable to the Commune, states (I:269), "The Assembly, having nothing in particular to fear from Paris, decided to sit at Versailles."

radical opposition had already transferred its animus to the National Assembly. The government possessed very few reliable troops for its defense, and the history of France bore eloquent testimony to the influence of Parisian mobs on its legislative assemblies. Yet, at the same time, this abandonment of the traditional capital of France for the historic seat of the monarchy was a severe blow to Paris and intensified its opposition. A new "Père Duchêne," reminiscent of revolutionary days, had come to birth in March, and devoted a whole number to "The infamous treason of the royalist blackguards who wish to steal from Paris its title of capital in order to kill the republic." [130] Even the mildly liberal "L'Avenir National" is alarmed at this abandonment of the rightful capital of France.[131] It has been maintained with some justice that the failure of the government to assume its responsibilities in Paris and to deal with the opposition on its own ground, contributed greatly to the success of the revolution of March 18th.

The revolution was in the making; the unrest in the metropolis was viewed with foreboding by those in touch with the situation, which included almost every one except the members of the National Assembly. February 24th and 26th were given over to celebrating the February revolution of 1848. On the 26th a former gendarme, an innocent spectator of the demonstration, fell victim to the hatred of the mob for the former imperial police, and was drowned with cruelty in the canal near the Place de la Bastille.[132] The appointment of de Paladines as commander of the National Guard, together with the initiation of what appeared to be a policy of repression, excited the radical opposition. According to "Père Duchêne" it was the purpose of the new commander to break up the National Guard by a slow process of disorganization, and it predicted that the Guard

[130] "Père Duchêne," 19 Ventôse.
[131] "L'Avenir National." March 10.
[132] See *Enquête sur le 18 Mars*, p. 19.

would never obey him.[133] On the 11th of March "Père Duchêne" and five other revolutionary journals were suppressed.[134] An attempt was made at the same time to close the clubs again, but with the coming of spring the streets provided as good a place of congregation as the prohibited halls.

At about the same time the military court announced its decision on those inculpated in the affair of the 31st of October. Blanqui, Flourens, Lévrault and Cyrille, all at liberty, were condemned to death. Goupil and Jules Vallès were given prison sentences, but the remainder, including Jaclard, Eudes and Régère of Commune fame, were set at liberty. The agitation in Paris had not been lessened by the triumphal entry of the Prussians on March 1st. Favre and Thiers had worked hard to save Paris this indignity, but since Bismarck demanded either a triumphal entry or the surrender of Belfort, the former evil was accepted. The haste of the Assembly to ratify the terms of peace had permitted of a stay of only two days, but during this period the excitement was extreme. Some of the more pugnacious leaders of the National Guard had advocated an attack on the invaders, though cooler counsel prevailed. After the exodus of the German army certain restaurants on the Champs-Élysées which had served the enemy were sacked by the indignant mob.

The entrance of the invaders had been used as a pretense by various battalions of the National Guard for the removal of cannon and other military equipment from certain artillery parks and their installation on Montmartre and other "safe" places. This possession of armament by suspected units of the Guard was a serious embarrassment to the government and led to a number of dangerous situations. It caused the Comte de Barthélemy to announce by

---

[133] "Père Duchêne," 16 Ventôse (March 6).
[134] "Le Cri du Peuple," of Jules Vallès, "Le Vengeur," of Félix Pyat, "Le Mot d'Ordre," of Henri Rochefort, "La Bouche de Fer," of Paschal Grousset, and "La Caricature."

poster at Rennes that a "criminal insurrection is being organized in Paris." [135]   A collision between troops of the line
and battalions of the National Guard protecting the cannon
on Montmartre was narrowly avoided.[136]

The "Journal Officiel" published an appeal for order in
Paris, to which most of the reputable newspapers of the
capital added their support.   It was pointed out that the
June days had killed the Republic in 1848 and that a repeti-
tion of these disturbances might well prove fatal to the
Republic in 1871.[137]   But these appeals passed unheeded.
Even M. Clémenceau, the mayor of the stormy arrondissement of Montmartre, although accustomed to the excitations
of the capital, found the situation dangerous.   A band of
sharpshooters had seized a house in his district and apparently no force at the disposal of the authorities could evict
them.[138]   Prophetic after the fact, the Committee of Enquiry
asserts that "Everyone saw the struggle coming; society was
faced with a great battle, the situation was worse, more
terrible than in the June days of 1848." [139]

The Central Committee

No revolution has been made without organization and
leadership, nor was that of the 18th of March.   Suffering,
misery, dissatisfaction with existing authority, humiliation,
and defeat, are influences which must be shaped and guided
to attain results.   The situation in Paris in the month of
March was ripe of revolution, but it required the Central Committee of the National Guard to harvest the
crop.

The origins and purposes of this organization are obscure.
Military witnesses before the Committee of Enquiry were
of the opinion that the initiative came from various sub-

---

[135] See "Journal de Paris," March 9.
[136] Ibid.
[137] "Le Petit Moniteur Universel," March 10.
[138] Enquête sur le 18 Mars, p. 666.   Evidence of M. Dubail (Mayor).
[139] Ibid., p. 12.

sidiary organizations of the National Guard, though they were unable to agree upon which.[140] Others professed to see the hand of the International, which was certainly not correct. It is fairly obvious that the idea of an organization of the National Guard received general circulation during the agitation which accompanied the elections to the National Assembly of February 5th to 8th. At a meeting of representatives of the National Guard units called together at the Cirque National, February 6th, by seven relatively unknown officers, a list of candidates was recommended.[141] The invitation to the Assembly was sent out "in no exclusively partisan spirit"; what was desired by the organizers were "results valuable for our country and for the Republic"; but the sense of the meeting was overwhelmingly radical. The candidates endorsed by the National Guard were those already proposed by four committees; the Central Committee of the Twenty Arrondissements, the Montagnard Club, the International, and the workers' delegations of the Republican Union, the Republican Alliance, the Republican Socialists and the Defenders of the Republic.

There is no particular reason why this Federation of the National Guard should not have disappeared with the election excitement, or why it should have had a more tenacious existence than the hundreds of republican committees and associations which were forming and dissolving at this time in Paris. But once assembled the representatives of the units of the Guard were impressed with the possibility of concerted action by the two hundred-odd armed battalions in defense of the Republic. Another meeting was called for February 15th at Tivoli-Vauxhall, one of the Parisian dance centers, with the ostensible object of replacing representatives to the Assembly who might see fit to resign. The 3,000 delegates who attended paid no attention to the question of

---

[140] See *Enquête sur le 18 Mars*. Evidence of the Colonels Mortemart and Lavigne. Also G. Bourgin, *Le Comité, op. cit.,* p. 23.
[141] The poster convoking this meeting is given *Murailles,* I:846.

the candidates but occupied themselves with the organization of the National Guard.   Commissioners were appointed from all the arrondissements represented, and in the course of the next few days the unification of battalions in each section of Paris proceeded, accompanied by the amalgamation of the Federation with a "Federal Republican Committee," which was occupied with the same task.   By February 24th the organization was completed and at another reunion at the Vauxhall, the constitution of the Federation was laid down.[142]

This constitution has it that the duty of the Federation is to oppose the Monarchy and to support the Republic. The National Guard is the natural military arm of the Republic and must replace the standing army, which is only an instrument of despotism.   "In the end of making more precise and of presenting the duties of expressing and defending the rights of citizens, and also for the establishing and the strengthening of that unity and solidarity which must make of the citizen militia the sole national force, to the exclusion of all other, there is established a central committee of the National Guard, whose composition, attributes and functions are set forth in the statutes." [143]   The meeting of February 24th broke up to permit the delegates to conduct a demonstration on the Place de la Bastille in honor of the Martyrs of 1830 and 1848.

There was nothing particularly revolutionary or socialistic about either the Federation or its official representative body, the Central Committee.   The International had had no hand in its formation, though it was soon approached. The Central Committee requested that four delegates be appointed from the association and Varlin, one of the most influential members both of the Comité and of the International, attempted to utilize the latter in the organiza-

[142] Lepelletier, op. cit., I:230-237 is particularly good on the formation of the Central Committee.
[143] The complete constitution is published in the Enquête.   See also Bourgin, op. cit., pp. 28-30.

tion of the National Guard.[144] Varlin also maintained that
the Committee was socialist in its membership and sympathies.[145] However, there is no indication of any intention
to use the National Guard organization for the furtherance
of socialist programs and, in fact, it was explicitly recognized
by members of the International who sat in the Committee
that this was outside its scope. It was the hope of Varlin
that association with the Committee might advertise and
popularize the International.[146]

To tell the truth, this organization was in a bad way,
its strength having diminished rather than augmented during
the siege. The impoverishment of the Parisian working
class had seriously decreased the payment of dues and the
association found it extremely difficult to keep alive the
small newspaper enterprises on which it had embarked.

The entrance of a Blanquist communistic and revolutionary element, during the siege, had changed the character of
the International somewhat, but does not seem to have
strengthened it.[147] Marx, at the London office, noting the
tendency of the Parisian sections to play a part in politics,
publicly laments the departure from the true strategy of
social revolution.[148] In spite of its alteration and disorganization, the Federal Council of the Paris sections, however,
was setting itself to rebuild the International, with some
success during February and March.

The association of the Central Committee with the International was not accompanied by a domination of the former
by the purposes and methods of the latter. The acts and
declarations of the Central Committee before the 18th of
March were completely free of socialist or revolutionary
tendencies. Its influence, on the whole, was one of restraint
rather than provocation. The Committee regarded with dis-

[144] *Les Séances Officielles de l'Internationale à Paris* (Paris, 1872), p. 78.
[145] *Ibid.*, p. 84.
[146] *Ibid.*
[147] *Enquête.* Evidence of Héligon, member of the International.
[148] See his poster, *Murailles,* I, p. 975.

favor any attempt on the part of the National Guard to oppose with arms the entrance of the Prussians and set forth its attitude clearly in a publication of February 28th.[149] On that occasion the National Guard limited itself to transporting the cannon from Ranelagh and the Place Wagram to Montmartre and the Place des Vosges, and to the seizure of rifles and ammunition from the war depots.[150]

The consolidation of the National Guard and its control by the Central Committee meant, however, the creation in Paris of a possibly dangerous and certainly irresponsible power, observing allegiance to the government only when it appeared advantageous to do so. By the third of March the Committee was claiming the right to discharge any battalion commander who refused to obey it and, at the same time, asserting that in case the National Assembly deprived Paris of its title of capital it would declare the Department of the Seine an independent republic.[151] It claimed at this time the support of 200 battalions in the National Guard, something over 200,000 men.[152] At the same time the disorganization of the regular troops was at its worst and, between February 26th and March 12th, the National Guard took over arms and equipment on a great scale.[153]

The conservative press in Paris was decidedly alarmed, as was the government and the large body of public opinion which it represented. A note in the "Journal Officiel" which condemned the action of the National Guard, under its Central Committee, in taking possession of arms and ammunition was applauded by these papers.[154] There was a great deal of talk of "occult" influences in the National Guard and the Central Committee was treated as a secret and sinister

[149] This poster is in *Murailles*, I:971.
[150] See Bourgin, *op. cit.*, p. 32.
[151] *Enquête sur le 18 Mars: Pièces Justificatives*, p. 45.
[152] See poster, March 4, *Murailles*, I:988.
[153] Bourgin, *op. cit.*, p. 34.
[154] "Journal Officiel," March 4.

body. Édouard Moreau, one of the members, moved by these attacks, published a letter of denial. "A certain number of republicans, informed by a common study of the past, have united to prevent the Republic from once more being the plaything of the reaction; knowing well that this reaction will attempt to disorganize the National Guard, in order to form it into two camps, which it will then proceed to excite to bloodshed." [155]

There was certainly no attempt at anonymity on the part of the Central Committee. It published its acts and its posters were signed.[156] The members of the Committee, however, were quite unknown to the mass of the population in Paris. For the most part small chiefs of no more than local notoriety, their names affixed to important decrees awakened no recognition in the average reader. There were three or four members of the International, among them Pindy, Varlin, and Babick. The Blanquist party was represented by Casimir Bouit, who had edited Blanqui's "La Patrie en Danger" in book form, Eudes, and possibly one or two others. Assi, Varlin and Lullier had achieved sufficient fame in Paris to be advanced as candidates for the National Assembly in the February elections. Otherwise the membership of the Committee had been conspicuously inconspicuous, though several, among them Moreau, Billioray, Bergeret and Jourde, achieved a sort of fame during the Commune.[157]

The meeting of delegates at the Tivoli-Vauxhall on March 10th presented the intentions of the Federation to the people

[155] Published in "Le Vengeur," March 11.

[156] In addition, one of its members had had an interview with Picard, of the government, the beginning of March on the nature and purposes of the Committee and had published the results of his interview a few days later. See Lanjalley and Corriez, *La Révolution du 18 Mars* (Paris, 1871), p. 21.

[157] See de Gastyne, *Mémoires Secrets du Comité Central* (Paris, 1871) for a conservative characterization of the various members of the Central Committee. This membership changed considerably before the 18th of March, at which time it consisted of 30 members representing 13 arrondissements. See Bourgin, *op. cit.,* 38, 39.

of Paris. The Federation represented itself to be the custodian of the general will of the citizens of the metropolis.

"What does the population of Paris want?

"It wants to preserve its arms, to elect its commanders and to revoke them when it no longer has confidence in them.

"It wishes the army to be disbanded and sent home, in order to return to the families of France their dear ones, and to French industry its laboring population." [158]

Although there is no talk of a social revolution or any suggestion of important political or economic reforms, it is significant that a closer relation was developing between the Federation and its committees and the International. Pindy, a member of the International, presided at the Assembly on March 10th. The "Cri du Peuple" of Jules Vallès besought the committees of the National Guard to associate themselves with the International.[159] The International, however, as an organization had no relation to the Central Committee nor to any other agency of the Federation of the National Guard. After the revolution of March 18th, but before Paris was definitely ranged in arms against Versailles, various members of the General Council congratulated the International on having no responsibility for the insurrection.[160]

The assembly of the delegates of the Federation, on March 15th, the last before the revolution, showed 215 battalions of the National Guard adhering to the Central Committee.[161] General de Paladines and Colonel de Mortemart thought, on the 17th, that the government could count on 40 "good" battalions, devoted to order.[162] But this was

[158] Poster, March 10, *Murailles,* I:992.
[159] March 6th.
[160] *Les Séances Officielles, op. cit.,* p. 126.
[161] *Enquête: Pièces Justificatives,* p. 52.
[162] *Enquête.* Evidence of Colonel de Mortemart, p. 759.

only on the assumption that these battalions would not have to leave their own arrondissements.[163] On the 11th the general commanding the National Guard had sent a list of 28 men, active in the organization of the Federation of the National Guard and its committee, to the Prefect of Police, with directions to arrest these men. Not only was the Prefect impotent, but Colonel Mortemart himself found it impossible with the aid of a "safe" battalion to make the arrests.[164] Control of the National Guard, the only significant armed force in Paris, had passed from the hands of the government and its representatives.

The revolution was really prepared, as Lepelletier asserts, when, on February 28th, the "army of Paris" notified France of its existence; when the separate units of the National Guard had bound themselves together for common action.[165] The real commander of the National Guard in March was not d'Aurelle de Paladines but the Central Committee. As the Committee reported to the Assembly on March 10th, with respect to the appointment of de Paladines, "It remains to be seen whether citizens will confirm this appointment; whether the National Guard will continue to receive commands from others than those elected by it; if not, the plan of d'Aurelle de Paladines will go to join the plan of Trochu; it will not be executed, and this general will be asked to go hide in private the glory which he acquired in beating a retreat from Orleans." [166]

It required but a very small issue to range the forces of the National Guard against the forces of the government. The Federation and the Central Committee had formulated a theory of the position of the National Guard in a republic and had set forth in the existing situation a line of action which could be accepted by no government which pretended to hold authority. The Federation would admit of no

[163] *Enquête.* Evidence of Colonel de Mortemart, p. 759.
[164] *Ibid.*, 754.
[165] *La Commune*, I:249.
[166] *Enquête: Pièces Justificatives*, p. 50.

government other than the Republic; within the Republic
it would admit of no armed force other than the National
Guard; within the National Guard it would admit of
no authority other than that elected by the rank and file.
The will of the National Guard was apparently the ultimate
and the immediate repository of sovereignty. In the preamble to the statutes formulated for the meeting of the
Federation on February 15th, it is stated, "The duty of a
citizen is the defense of his country and the maintenance
of internal order, not of a monarchical order, but of an
order resting upon principles frankly republican.

"His rights are those of being an elector and of having
arms necessary to the accomplishment of his duty; the National Guard must henceforth replace permanent armies
which have never been anything other than the instruments
of despotism." [167] The destruction of the standing army
and the prevention of an attempt on the part of the government to disband the National Guard became the two
chief aims of the Federation. "The standing army takes
men and turns them into slaves. It degrades the character
of citizens, makes them lose the taste for work and furnishes
recruits to the odious police, who foster corruption rather
than protect morals; and it lends its hand to all the crimes
against the liberty of the citizen." [168]

This theory of the position of the National Guard in the
constitution of France was not palatable to the government,
but still more unpalatable was the position of the Federation and its representatives on the custody of the cannon
and other armament at the moment in the possession of the
National Guard. As long as 215 battalions of the National
Guard, obeying an authority other than that responsible to
the government, retained possession of the fighting equipment of Paris installed strategically at Montmartre and
other places, the government could hardly be sure of its
position.

[167] *Enquête: Pièces Justificatives,* p. 34.
[168] From a National Guard poster in the 6th Arrondissement, *ibid.,* p. 46.

CONCLUSION: THE COMMUNE BEFORE THE 18TH OF MARCH

The Commune of Paris was a unique event, the product of a multiplicity of causes. Many attempts have been made, particularly among socialist writers, observing the revolutions which have rapidly succeeded each other in 19th century Europe, to construct a theory of revolution. The phenomenon, they maintain, may be treated scientifically; certain uniformities are distinguishable; and we have seen recently the formulation of several "natural laws" of revolution. The Commune, however, does not easily lend itself to such treatment. It arose out of a situation, complex in the extreme, in which a large number of elements, each necessary to the outcome, were interwoven inextricably. It is quite impossible to assign mathematically to each element its importance. All that can be done, all that we have tried to do, is to focus attention upon causes of such significance that the absence of any one of them would have appreciably altered the event.

Of primary importance among the antecedents of the Commune was the defeat of France by Germany. It destroyed the Empire, it destroyed the Government of the National Defense, and the revolution of March 18th was an attempt to destroy the government of M. Thiers. No government can be popular in defeat and few governments forced to sign the treaty of peace which France had to accept in 1871 could avoid attack. The radical opposition in Paris and the Commune into which it developed was patriotic, thoroughly so. The insurrections of October 31st and January 22nd were demonstrations for war to the last ditch. The Commune was a revolution against the "capitulards" of Bordeaux and Versailles. All the radical groups of Paris, the Blanquists, the Proudhonists, the Jacobins, and the members of the International, were nearly chauvinist in their attitude. Their opposition was directed against the supposed military weakness and the executive incapacity of the war leaders of France. Without the defeat, there would have been no Commune.

The radical opposition in Paris was effective because of the internal political weakness of the government. Itself the product of revolution, the Government of the National Defense had never secured its position by an appeal to the electorate of France. After the insurrection of October 31st, it is true, its position was strengthened by the vote in Paris, but this position still lacked the support of a national plebiscite. The revolutionary origin of the Government of the National Defense together with its unconsolidated legal position was a severe handicap in its dealings with those revolutionary groups in Paris which were in part responsible for its power. This weakness was accentuated, under the circumstances, by its republican and democratic principles, or prejudices, against political repression. Revolutionary clubs, journals, committees, and societies, were allowed to breed and multiply in the capital without interference. The police system inherited from the old régime and thoroughly discredited in a republic proved of little service. It is impossible to say whether a government strong internally would have been able to hold in check the radical opposition fed by military reverses, but certainly the Government of the National Defense left to its successor a situation in Paris made doubly difficult by the strength and multiplicity of revolutionary organizations.

This situation became untenable because the radical opposition gradually secured control of an army, the largest armed force in France, the National Guard of Paris. The population of the capital, hastily and carelessly organized, proved a source of embarrassment during the siege and a source of danger after it. The method of electing officers led only too often to the selection of demagogues and intensified the lack of discipline which is frequently a failure of such military organizations. For the most part congregated inactively in Paris, the National Guard, dissatisfied with its position in the defense, easily fell a prey to the arguments which circulated nightly in the clubs. After the armistice it was the only considerable body of men to retain its arms and its complexion became decidedly more revolutionary with the departure of the conservative middle-class elements from Paris. Without the support of the armed body of the National Guard it is more than doubtful whether the Commune could have been made.

The natural tendency after the Commune was to find the cause of the revolution in the activities of socialist and communist revolutionary societies in Paris, particularly the International. The Marxian interpretation, which has been followed by most of the socialist commentators, has it that the Commune was the product of a proletarian and socialist revolution. Although this is emphatically and notoriously untrue, the part played by revolutionary organizations in Paris was important. Unfortunately it is extremely difficult to evaluate. The International in Paris, disorganized by the prosecutions of 1870, had partially reconstituted its sections by the outbreak of the war. Although seriously handicapped during and after the siege by the poverty of its members it did act as a cohesive influence in amalgamating the opposition. The Committee of the Twenty Arrondissements was in large part the direct creation of the International. The central office at 6 Place de la Corderie was the "local" of a large number of socialist republican political associations and labor organizations and, at the same time, a favorite meeting place for representatives of all the opposition groups in Paris. Members of the International took an active part in the insurrections of October 31st and January 22nd. Other revolutionary groups, the Blanquists, a small though well-knit society, the Jacobins, particularly Delescluze, Pyat and their respective followings, and individual leaders such as Flourens, Sapia, and Tibaldi, were also actively responsible, together with the radical clubs

and newspapers, for a considerable cohesiveness in the ranks
of the opposition. The Communal revolution, though certainly not socialist, and not distinctively proletarian,
depended upon this organization of the socialist and revolutionary proletarian element.

Finally, the creation of the Federation of the National
Guard and its organ the Central Committee was indispensable. Organized on the occasion of the February election,
the Federation soon advanced beyond its original purposes
and became a powerful force working for the maintenance
of the Republic, the dissolution of the standing army and
the perpetuation of the National Guard. Controlling the
armed forces of the capital the Central Committee set itself
up against the government on a number of points and
finally came into collision with it on the question of the
surrender of military equipment. The National Guard unorganized, or obeying its legal commanders, was not dangerous. In the hands of the Federation and its Committee,
it was bound to provoke a revolution.

There is little or no evidence that the form the revolution took was actively present in the minds of those
responsible for it. The word "Commune" was bandied
about in the clubs, radical newspapers and revolutionary
societies before the 18th of March; it acted as the rallying
cry in the insurrections of October and January; but no one
appeared to have a definite conception of its meaning. An
orator at the Club Favier put the matter very well when
he said, "I'll wager that even here, at the Club Favier, three
quarters of the audience does not know what the Commune
means. [Protests, denials, tumult, shouting. 'He's a police
spy!' Others: 'Well, go ahead and tell us what it is.']
The Commune is the right of the people, it is equal treatment for all, it is the levée en masse and the punishment
of traitors; the Commune, finally, is the Commune." [169]

[169] Molinari, *Les Clubs Rouges,* p. 213. Meeting of January 6, 1871.

CHAPTER III

PARIS IN REVOLUTION

PARIS, through a series of social and political insurrections which occurred with nearly as much regularity as business crises, achieved during the course of the 19th century the reputation of being the city of revolutions. In 1830, 1848, and 1871, its streets were covered with barricades and blood and its population split into opposing armies. In the intervals, attempts at revolution, such as those of 1839 and 1858, disturbed the peace much as occasional flurries in the stock market interrupt, but do not seriously alter, the ebb and flow of the business cycle. To the conservatives of France and of Europe the turbulence of Paris was evidence of the moral degeneracy and criminality of a proletariat which included the scum of the continent. To the revolutionaries, and for the same reason, Paris appeared as the "city of light," disseminating its gospel of revolt against the evils of a corrupt society, to the uneducated and oppressed of Europe.

The uprising of the Commune in 1871 was the bloodiest and most bitter revolution in the history of 19th-century Europe. The revolutionaries of Paris were not to be subdued until 15,000 had been killed in the city streets and as many again imprisoned or deported. Yet the overthrow of the government in the capital was accomplished with scarcely a shot fired and with the death of a very few men.

The immediate occasion of the conflict between the forces of the government and the forces of the Commune was the affair of the cannon. As we have already mentioned, very considerable quantities of military equipment were

sequestered and guarded by the Paris militia at Montmartre, the Buttes Chaumont, the Place de la Bastille and
elsewhere.[1] The military authorities had made a number of
half-hearted attempts to seize this artillery, notably on the
8th and 16th of March, but inadequate numbers of troops
of the line when faced with the possibility of conflict with
the National Guard had retired without accomplishing their
aim. The sole result had been to awaken resistance in the
faubourgs and to strengthen the determination of the
National Guard to hold the cannon.

When Thiers came to Paris on the 15th of March the
government was in an embarrassing position. The first
meeting of the Assembly at Versailles had been set for the
twentieth. The National Guard of Paris was organized and
armed and had laid down a program, involving the maintenance of the Republic, the preservation of its arms, and
the dissolution of the standing army, which might put serious strictures upon the policy likely to be adopted by the
Assembly. It was notorious that the organized militia was
decidedly antipathetic to the political tendencies of the
government. The possession of artillery might not augment
the military strength of the National Guard or increase its
willingness to act. Nevertheless, a government too weak to
seize it was demonstrably a government not to be feared.

The taking of the cannon, however, was a matter beset
with difficulties. If de Paladines, commander-in-chief of the
National Guard, had issued an order to the battalions
guarding the artillery requesting its surrender, such an
order would undoubtedly have been disobeyed. On the 15th
of March, it is true, the Vigilance Committee of Montmartre was seriously considering the surrender of the
cannon, but a delegation sent by the Federation of the

[1] The transfer of the cannon to Montmartre was the work of a vigilance
committee of the National Guard of the 18th Arrondissement; its object seems
to have been "to intimidate the partisans of monarchy, if they attempted to
impose on Paris a political system opposed to its aspirations." See Lanjalley
and Corriez, *Histoire de la Révolution du 18 Mars* (Paris, 1871), p. 22.

National Guard assembled at the Vauxhall strengthened the determination of the local committee to resist.[2] The government might have entered into negotiations with the Central Committee or some other agency representing the recalcitrant guard, but this policy was open to a number of objections. First, to do so would have been to recognize the authority of the extra-legal Committee and virtually to destroy the power of de Paladines or any other commander of the Paris militia. Second, it would have been an admission of the impotence of the government which would have greatly increased the strength of the opposition. Third, such a program would have been long drawn out; and, meanwhile, the Assembly had been summoned for the 20th of March.

An alternative to negotiation was direct action by the regular troops under the command of Vinoy, and this alternative was much more sympathetic to the nature and temperament of Thiers. The executive of France was, at this time, an energetic, irascible old man of 73. The author of many considered pages on the wars and revolutions of France, he fancied himself something of a military strategist. At the same time he was a stiff-necked conservative, resolutely antipathetic to popular movements, absolutely opposed to any political action on the part of the proletariat and particularly detesting socialism or anything which smacked of this heresy. In his conversations with Nassau Senior, Thiers had succinctly expressed his political faith: "By birth I belong to the people; my family were humble merchants in Marseilles; they had a small trade in the Levant in cloth, which was ruined by the Revolution. By education I am a Bonapartist; I was born when Napoleon was at the summit of his glory. By tastes and habits and associations I am an aristocrat. I have no sympathy with the bourgeoisie or with any system under which they are to

[2] "Petit Moniteur Universel." March 16, 1871.

rule." [3] Shocked by the Revolution of 1848 and the socialist schemes advanced at the time he wrote a polemic against "all those odious, puerile, ridiculous but disastrous systems; sprung like a swarm of insects, from the decomposition of all governments, and filling the atmosphere in which we live." [4] Since he detected socialistic tendencies in the organized opposition in Paris, his course was clear.

Thiers favored the plan of taking the cannon by force. After consultation with the generals Le Flo, de Paladines, and Vinoy it was decided to dispatch a force of 15,000 troops of the line and 3,000 police on the night of March 17th to 18th. "I was of the opinion," said Thiers later, "that it was a fearful resolution we were taking and that success was doubtful. However, it was impossible not to have a try at it." [5] The events of the next few days demonstrated that success was more than doubtful.

The plan of Thiers was based upon two very serious misconceptions, in which he was no doubt influenced by his military advisers, but for which he must take the responsibility. As a result of the experience of the siege he had a very low opinion of the military strength of the National Guard. At the same time he seems to have had confidence in the reliability of the troops of the line. The events of the Commune showed the fallacy of the first opinion; the error of the second should have been obvious from the start. The regulars, stationed in Paris after the armistice, had quickly caught the fever of the mob. Vinoy had found it necessary to make disorder and lack of discipline the subject of a communication addressed to the officers of the army in Paris on March 16th, two days before the attempt on Montmartre. [6]

[3] Nassau Senior, *Conversations. . . . Second Empire,* I:39.
[4] Thiers, *The Rights of Property; a Refutation of Communism and Socialism.* English translation (London, 1848), p. 5.
[5] *Enquête sur le 18 Mars,* p. 362. Evidence of Thiers.
[6] Reprinted in Vinoy, *L'Armistice et la Commune* (Paris, 1872), p. 389.

At best, Thiers' plan was one of great difficulty. The government troops had to be split up into ten or twelve sections for a simultaneous march upon objectives scattered all over Paris.[7] The numbers of cannon deposited at various centers (at Montmartre there were 171), made it impossible that the operation of moving them to the École Militaire could be accomplished without considerable time and disturbance. If the troops under the direction of Vinoy had been of the best, and perfectly disciplined, the transfer of the cannon would have been difficult; but with those actually at his disposal, it was impossible.

At three o'clock on the morning of March 18th, the troops left for their various objectives. The division under General Susbielle, composed of brigades led by the Generals Lecomte and Paturel, moved on Montmartre. The summit of the hill was attained without disturbance, but the cannon could not be moved without horses and equipment and by the time this had arrived it was eight o'clock in the morning. The proletarian quarter of Montmartre had risen early, disturbed by the sound of marching men. The soldiers were subjected to the insults of the women and children gathered on the street corners and the National Guard of the quarter quickly responded to the alarm. The 88th battalion under General Lecomte refused to fire on the approaching National Guard and the police themselves fired only a few shots. Soon the regulars fraternized with the guards, the women of the quarter added their blandishments and, discipline destroyed, General Lecomte was seized by the crowd and conducted to the headquarters of the National Guard of Montmartre.

The government's attempt met with the same failure in all directions. General Paturel had succeeded in moving a few cannon halfway down the hill when his men were surrounded by the populace, the traces cut and the artillery

---

[7] Vinoy, *L'Armistice et la Commune*. The orders for the movements of the troops on March 18th are reprinted, pp. 411-417.

taken back to Montmartre. At the Luxembourg, too, the
soldiers fraternized with the mob. With the troops checked
at the Buttes Chaumont, the Place de la Bastille and Belleville, victory was secured for the opposition by eleven o'clock
in the morning.[8] Under the leadership of local chiefs, barricades sprang up all over town. De Paladines attempted
to summon the battalions devoted to order, but scarcely six
hundred men responded to the appeal and they rapidly
dispersed when faced with the situation.[9] Along towards
noon the Minister of the Interior, Picard, got out a placard
calling upon the National Guard to defend "your homes,
your families, your property," against these men "obeying
unknown leaders, who are directing the cannon destined for
the Prussians, against Paris itself," but he succeeded in
raising little enthusiasm.[10]

General Lecomte, imprisoned since early morning, was
finally transferred in the middle of the afternoon to the
headquarters of the Vigilance Committee of the 18th Arrondissement for purposes of examination. He was soon joined
by another captive, General Clément Thomas. Thomas was
particularly detested by the revolutionary element because
of his part in the repression of June, 1848, and because of
his action during the siege against certain favorite battalions
of Belleville.[11] Commander of the National Guard of Paris
during the siege, he had resigned shortly after the armistice.
The Vigilance Committee put in no appearance and various
officers of the National Guard who, until this time, had
succeeded in restraining the mob were finally forced to give
way. Between four and five o'clock the two Generals were
seized by the frenzied crowd and shot in the little garden
behind the house.

Meanwhile Thiers, a witness of the failure of his scheme

[8] For a good and recent account of the events of this day see Georges
Bourgin, *Premières Journées de la Commune* (Paris, 1928), pp. 51-72.
[9] *Enquête*, p. 362. Evidence of Thiers.
[10] Reprinted in *Murailles*, II:4.
[11] See p. 88.

in all directions, was forced to change his plans. It was under these circumstances that the scholar and statesman bethought himself of an historical precedent. On the 24th of February, 1848, he tells us, "the King asked me, after affairs had taken a bad turn, what it was necessary to do. I replied to him that it was necessary to get out of Paris in order to return with Marshal Bugeaud and fifty thousand men.

"This occasion remained in my memory; and also, I recalled the example of Marshal Windischgraetz, who after having evacuated Vienna returned victoriously some time afterwards." [12] With the evidence of history in his mind Thiers ordered Vinoy to conduct a retreat upon Versailles. Between three and four o'clock he left Paris, shortly followed by what remained of the regular army.

Commune apologists and sympathizers, writing later on the events of this period, and still dominated by the hatred of Thiers which existed during the revolution, have exploited the theory that the revolution was the outcome of a Machiavellian plot hatched by Thiers and molded to his selfish purposes.[13] The theory may be simply expressed. The opposition had no interest in an insurrection so long as the Republic was maintained. Thiers, on the other hand, had a very definite interest in provoking an insurrection. The strong repression of such an insurrection would convince the Assembly of his capacity, even indispensability, and permit him to hold in check the reactionary and monarchical majority which had begun already to give trouble. The means necessary to this end were, (1) a provocation of the recalcitrant element in Paris; (2) a refusal of all conciliation; (3) repression accompanied by disarmament of the National Guard.[14] The capture of the cannon was

[12] *Enquête.* Evidence of Thiers, p. 363.
[13] See particularly Arthur Arnould, *La Commune;* Lepelletier, *Histoire de la Commune de 1871* (Paris, 1911), and Gaston Da Costa, *La Commune Vécue.*
[14] Lepelletier, I:273.

merely a prelude to complete disarmament. Master of the situation, the strong man of France would be voted what he wanted by an admiring Assembly. Since the opening of the Assembly was determined for the 20th of March, the "psychological hour" was the 18th.

It may be readily admitted that neither the National Guard nor the radical opposition in Paris had any interest in revolution so long as the three or four leading claims of the Central Committee were granted; i.e., maintenance of the Republic, perpetuation of the National Guard, election of officers by military units, and dissolution of the standing army. It may also be admitted that the government had a very definite interest in destroying the strength of an organization which might hamper it in the determination of policy and that the capture of the cannon was a step in this direction. There is no doubt that this step, if successful, would have been followed by an attempt to disarm the National Guard. Yet there is no evidence that Thiers had a special end of his own, or that his personal interests in this matter were any different from those of the government. Nor is there the slightest evidence that he anticipated and desired that the seizure of the cannon would lead to an insurrection.

It can hardly be seriously maintained that the removal of the artillery in the possession of the National Guard was an unjustifiable procedure. In the radical quarters and opposition journals there was much talk before the 18th of March, and more talk afterwards, to the effect that the cannon belonged to the city of Paris which had paid for them during the siege, and that the National Guard as the military representatives of the city were the rightful custodians. This line of argument was defended by a number of the apologists of the Commune after the event.[15] The

---

[15] This is the usual socialist position. Marx talks about Thiers' "burglarious attempt" to "steal" the cannon, and, as usual, his socialist and communist disciples follow him carefully. See p. 314.

absurdity of such a claim is too patent to necessitate discussion.

Nevertheless it is fairly clear, in the light of all the facts, that the seizure of the cannon in a clandestine manner was an ill-conceived project, poorly carried out and deserving of failure. A surprise movement was at the same time doomed to failure as a surprise and highly provocative to the mob. The conservative papers of Paris had announced for several days that the army was being organized to take the cannon by force if necessary.[16] It was impossible to march 15,000 troops through the streets of Paris unbeknownst to the population. And yet the affair was secret enough to suggest to the nervous and suspicious population a monarchist coup or some other "reactionary plot."

At the same time Thiers' plan was vitiated by the unreliability of his troops, their division into eight or ten separate units acting over a wide area, and, possibly, the faulty leadership of some of these units. The obviousness of the first point was, naturally, more apparent after than before the event. Nevertheless the unreliability of the troops was recognized by General Vinoy and known to Thiers. The advisability of simultaneous and secret action at various points in Paris rested upon two assumptions, (1) that the removal of the cannon was a task requiring only a few hours' time, and (2), that secrecy could really be secured. Neither of these assumptions was in accordance with the facts. Finally, as almost all commentators have insisted, the execution of the plan left something to be desired.[17]

The Committee of Enquiry exculpated Thiers in the question of the cannon, saying, that "in the situation which had come about, the government could no longer temporize; it was necessary either to disarm the insurrection or give up

[16] For example, "Le Journal de Paris," March 16 and "La Liberté," March 18.
[17] Evidence of General Le Flo before the Committee of Enquiry and other sources, Lepelletier, Bourgin, etc. Lepelletier, I:425.

to it the government's position."[18]   But there were various
ways of disarming the insurrection and it seems probable
that M. Thiers' irascibility, implacable hatred of radicalism
in any form, and penchant for strong and energetic measures, led him to select the wrong way.

THE GOVERNMENT OF MONSIEUR ASSI

The advance of the revolution did not stop with the
retreat of Thiers and the army from Paris. Towards the
middle of the afternoon, order in the revolutionary ranks
began to replace the sporadic, unrelated efforts of leaders
in the various sections of the capital. Part of the Central
Committee came together and then separated in order that
the various members might in their own precincts direct the
progress of the movement. Brunel, arrested for leading a
revolt on January 28th, took charge of a group of the
National Guard, captured the Prince Eugène barracks and
marched on the Hôtel de Ville. Early in the evening Pindy,
of the International, and Ranvier, a friend of Flourens,
arrived with the National Guard of Belleville. The Hôtel
de Ville was surrounded and Ferry, the only member of the
government remaining at duty, was forced to relinquish his
post.[19]   Meanwhile Duval had occupied the Prefecture of
Police and lines of barricades were erected all over town
in defense against the possible return of the regulars or the
rising of the conservative units of the National Guard.

When the Central Committee met on the evening of
March 18th the revolution had conquered Paris. But who
was to govern it? The Committee recognized that it had
no legal title. Yet the government had left for Versailles
and the mayors who remained in Paris were without author-

---

[18] *Enquête*, p. 30.
[19] The meeting of the mayors and adjutants of Paris assembled in permanence at the Mairie of the 1st Arrondissement, was informed by Ferry's
secretary on the evening of the 18th, that the Hôtel de Ville was being
evacuated. A delegation was appointed to take possession, but on its arrival
it was informed by the National Guard that the custody of the Hôtel de
Ville did not concern the mayors of Paris.

ity over the National Guard or the mob. It was the single power in Paris capable of maintaining order, carrying on the municipal services and restraining the revolutionary elements which had made the 18th of March. In consequence the Committee decided to assume the responsibility until a municipal assembly representative of Paris could be elected. At the same time it appointed a drunken fool named Lullier, who had achieved a certain notoriety in the cafés as a bad man, to the post of commander of the National Guard.

The Central Committee had not made the revolution; in fact it would be much truer to say that the revolution made the Central Committee. Since the 10th of March it had not held a single meeting. The attack of the government in the early morning of the 18th was totally unexpected and not until the afternoon was the Committee even partially assembled.[20] The forces of Thiers and Vinoy were routed and the principal places of Paris captured by the insurgents before the Committee was really aware of the course of events. Those responsible for the shooting of Generals Lecomte and Thomas had no relation to it nor was the Committee aware of this catastrophe until hours afterwards.

All this was contrary to the opinion of the government and the conservative element at the time and to the attitude of the Committee of Enquiry which has reported on the revolution and the Commune since. Along the boulevards on the 18th and 19th of March they spoke of the revolution consummated by the Government of Monsieur Assi.[21] In the "Journal Officiel" the ministers of the government still remaining in Paris denounced the Committee as the author of the revolution and murderer of Thomas and Lecomte.[22]

[20] Gaston Da Costa, La Commune Vécue, I:108.
[21] Assi's name generally headed the proclamations of the Comité Central during the first few days of its existence. Then, too, except for Varlin and Lullier, he was the single member who enjoyed any notoriety in Paris.
[22] March 19. After this date the "Journal" was published in Versailles.

"Who are the members of this committee?

"No one in Paris knows them; their names are new to everyone.[23] No one can say to what party they belong. Are they communists, Bonapartists or Prussians? Are they agents of a triple coalition? Whatever they are, they are the enemies of Paris which they give over to pillage, of France which they deliver to Prussians and of the Republic which they surrender to despotism."

The Official Enquiry found the Central Committee guilty of the organization and direction of the revolution and of the murders of the Generals Thomas and Lecomte.[24] This committee, according to the Enquiry, was composed of anti-patriotic revolutionaries, "nearly all affiliated with the International." [25] Nothing could be more false. The Committee, composed of fanatically patriotic representatives of the National Guard, including only four or five members of the International, unaware of the murder of the two Generals, found itself the head of a revolutionary power, through no immediate fault of its own, and unsupplied with anything remotely resembling an administrative program. At nearly every point in Paris the revolution represented a spontaneous uprising against the attempt of the government and at first the Central Committee counted for next to nothing.

This mistake of the authorities, however, was rather natural since the Committee rapidly assumed leadership and made itself responsible for the direction of the revolutionary forces and policy. It even claimed the credit for having initiated the revolution. A proclamation of March 19th to the citizens of Paris begins:

[23] As a matter of fact the government was not nearly as unacquainted with the Committee and its purposes as this proclamation would suggest. See Chapter II, p. 77.
[24] *Enquête,* pp. 34 and 43.
[25] *Ibid.,* p. 43.

"You have charged us with organizing the defense of Paris and the preservation of your rights.

"We are conscious of having fulfilled this mission; assisted by your generous courage and admirable sang-froid, we have overthrown the government which betrayed us." [26]

The Committee proceeded to take over the National Press and the Official Journal of the Republic, which it immediately turned to the justification of the revolution. Commissions were delegated to administer the services abandoned by the government; the telegraph, the offices of the interior, the finances, the Prefecture of Police, and service of war. But, at the same time that the Committee assumed the functions of government, it announced by placards and in the Official Journal that it had no pretense to govern.

"If the Central Committee were a government, it could, to support the dignity of its electors, disdain to justify itself. But since its first pronouncement declared, 'that it did not intend to take the place of those whom popular opinion has displaced,' it takes the part of honesty in remaining exactly within the express limits of the mandate confided to it; it remains a body of personalities who have the right to defend themselves.

"Child of the Republic which inscribes on its banner the great word: Fraternity, it pardons its detractors; but it wishes to persuade honest people who, through ignorance, have listened to calumny." [27]

There follows a list of grievances against the government of France. The government has made an attempt at civil war, it has led the provinces against Paris, it has preserved a standing army whose soldiers desired to return to their homes, it wished to impose upon the National Guard

[26] *Murailles,* II:6.
[27] "Journal Officiel," March 20. See also *Murailles,* II:12, 13.

a general-in-chief, it has attempted to take away the cannon, and, finally, it sought to deprive Paris of its right to be the capital of France.

The new governors of Paris proclaimed themselves to be the saviors of the Republic and interpreted the action of Thiers on the 18th of March as an attack on the Republic. Yet it is a little hard to see that this was so. Although the majority of the National Assembly was monarchist, Thiers himself ostensibly at least held it as one of his chief functions to keep the reactionaries in check and to maintain the Republic. As one of the conservative papers of Paris stated, "Since the revolution of September 4th, and the meeting of the National Assembly, no one has tried to attack the Republic; it has not even been contested. It is then quite impossible to explain the deplorable misunderstanding which has led to actual conflict. Many republicans have taken arms to save the Republic, and the government declares that it has never wished anything else than to maintain it." [28]

The fact is, the revolution of March 18th was the product of the spontaneous uprising of an exasperated populace; and the Central Committee, which assumed responsibility, found it a little difficult to determine its position and to know what to do next. It began with an announcement of its own resignation. In its first proclamation to the National Guard, announcing the fulfillment of its mission, i.e., the overthrow of the government, the guards are asked to prepare for the elections. "Give us the single recompense for which we have ever hoped: that of seeing established the true Republic." [29] And the same day, the 19th, the elections were set for the 22nd.[30]

Nevertheless it performed during its few days in power a number of the functions of government. A decree of

[28] "Journal de Paris," March 20. See to this effect also, "La Liberté," March 20.

[29] *Murailles,* II:6.

[30] *Ibid.,* p. 7. Election proclamation.

March 20th guaranteed the regular payment of the National
Guard. This meant, of course, that part of the National
Guard which supported the Committee. As to the battalions
of law and order, "there was no objection to their collecting
from the government at Versailles." [31] The National
Guard stationed in Paris was charged with surveillance
of the large numbers of ex-convicts who had drifted
to Paris, and a few days later the Central Committee came
out with a fearsome placard announcing death to all thieves
taken in the act.[32] The new government of Paris postponed
the maturity of business obligations for a month and at the
same time decreed that proprietors could not evict their
tenants until further order.[33] In view of the disorganization of government services, the Committee declared that
any employee of the public administration who had not
resumed his occupation before the 25th of March should be
discharged.

The performance of these functions, and particularly the
payment of the National Guard, required funds. The Central Committee occupied itself with this matter from the
first moment of its rise to power, since a failure to maintain
the pay of the Paris militia would have rendered its position
untenable. There was some talk in the sessions of the Committee of collecting a forced levy from the railway companies serving Paris; but the financial delegates Varlin and
Jourde made this unnecessary by borrowing 500,000 francs
from Rothschild, who had important interests to safeguard
in the capital, and by securing from the governor of the
Bank of France an advance of a million. By the 21st of

[31] So stated in the sessions of the Central Committee, March 22, as
published by G. Arsac in his *Conciliabules de l'Hôtel de Ville* (Paris, 1871).
This is a reprint of the reports published in a conservative newspaper, "Le
Paris-Journal," during the Commune, and said to have been furnished by
Assi. These reports are by no means thoroughly reliable; there exists no
authoritative record of the deliberations of the Central Committee. See on
this, Lepelletier, *La Commune,* II:67, 68.

[32] "Journal Officiel," March 24.

[33] "Journal Officiel," a series of decrees proclaimed in the issue of
March 24.

March the National Guard was receiving its pay and the popular support of the Central Committee was secure. The financial delegates had called at the Treasury only to find that the keys to the vaults had been taken to Versailles, but the Committee, finding it possible to secure funds peaceably, was not compelled to debate the advisability of a forcible seizure.

Its attitude towards the Paris press also was, on the whole, amicable. The offices of "Le Figaro" and "Le Gaulois," two of the most reactionary papers in Paris, had been stormed by the National Guard, an act which was severely condemned by Republican papers. Except for this incident the newspapers of Paris were not interfered with during the reign of the Committee. The Committee expressed itself immediately as supporting the republican traditions of freedom of speech and of the press and, in spite of severe provocation and of counsel on the part of friends to abandon this piece of "sentimentality," it pursued these traditions. Nevertheless, after thirty-three Paris papers had publicly declared against the Commune elections, an ominous note of warning creeps into the language of the delegates to the official journal. "As it has already declared, the Central Committee of the National Guard, sitting at the Hôtel de Ville, respects the freedom of the press, that is to say the right which every citizen has of commenting on, of discussing, and of criticizing its acts with the aid of all means of publicity; but it intends to make respected the decisions of the sovereignty of the people of Paris, and it will not permit opponents to continue to attack this sovereignty with impunity, by exciting the populace to disobedience of its decisions and its orders.

"A severe repression will be the consequence of such attempts, if they continue to occur." [34]

Although the representatives of the National Guard had disclaimed all pretense of being a government, the attitudes

[34] "Journal Officiel," March 22.

of its official journal and of the radical press were somewhat contradictory. The delegate to the Journal Officiel in
his leading article of March 22nd, poses the question, "Does
the sovereignty of the people lie with Versailles or with
Paris?

"To suggest this question is to answer it.

"The Assembly, sitting first at Bordeaux and now at
Versailles, was elected under particular circumstances, and
charged with a mission determined in advance, a sort of
restricted mandate.[35]

"In view of the fact that this mandate has been fulfilled,
that the representatives of Alsace and Lorraine and a number of liberal members have resigned, and for other reasons, the Assembly is no longer an expression of the will of
the nation. The will of the nation can be expressed only by
an Assembly freely elected, and in the interim it is the manifest right and duty of the Central Committee of the
National Guard to administer affairs."

The Committee fluctuated between revolution and legality, between governing and resigning, between action and
inaction; it was without either a revolutionary program or
ideas of how to force the National Assembly to meet the
demands of the National Guard. Revolutionary writers on
the Commune have criticized it for not going far enough—
conservative authors have condemned it for proceeding too
far. To the latter, the fact that the Committee assumed
responsibility on the 18th of March put it not only outside
the law but outside consideration; to the former this act
should have been but the prelude to revolution. "To a
revolutionary situation," says Dubreuihl, "and for a revolutionary struggle, the Corderie offered a revolutionary procedure. . . . On the other hand, a confluence of divergent
currents, a chaos of jumbled and confused aspirations, the
Central Committee of the National Guard was deprived by
its nature of the power of decision so indispensable in an

[35] "Journal Officiel," March 22.

hour of crisis; of that decision which saves everything because it dares everything." [36]

Both groups of commentators have not, perhaps, realized adequately the position in which the Central Committee found itself. It assumed power because, in a certain sense, it was forced into power; in no sense was it the representative of a socialist or communist revolutionary movement. Without having made the revolution it was yet of the revolution and could do no other than accept the authority which the flight of Thiers had left vacant. There was no question of pursuing a socialist program, for neither the committee nor the rank and file of the National Guard envisaged such an end.

The fact of the matter is that a bewildered group of incompetent individuals found themselves at the head of, and responsible for, a movement which had far outrun its original intentions. Unwilling to go forward and incapable of going back, the Central Committee was forced by circumstance to govern illegally while frantically striving to achieve legality. It attempted at the outset to shift both power and responsibility to an assembly elected by the municipality. The elections set for the 22nd, however, were postponed until the 26th and, in the meantime, the Committee was compelled to govern. It proposed to limit itself to the transaction of purely municipal affairs but continually and irresponsibly neglected this limitation.

Thiers had abandoned the forts to the south and west of Paris, and these were taken over by the National Guard; but the incapable Lullier had neglected to occupy the fortress of Mont Valérien, which commanded the principal routes from Paris to Versailles, and this was retained by the government troops. Nothing was done to make of the

[36] *La Commune*, p. 284. In the same tenor see Lepelletier, *op. cit.*, II:26 and Da Costa, *op. cit.*, I:295. The great mistake of the Central Committee, according to Marx, was its failure to march at once on Versailles. The Russian communists have considered this regard for legality a fundamental weakness of the revolution of 1871. See p. 350.

National Guard a fighting force and meanwhile Thiers was busy carefully reorganizing what remained to him of an army. In consequence the "Government of Monsieur Assi" saw not only its opportunity of revolution, which had never been envisaged, disappear, but also the possibility of extorting from Thiers those demands which the National Guard had proclaimed so loudly even before the 18th of March.

THE RETREAT TO VERSAILLES

The question of whether or no the Central Committee was justified in assuming the functions of government, a problem which transcends legal limitations and encroaches upon the realm of ethics and politics, is paralleled by the question whether or no Thiers was justified in abandoning Paris. His decision to do so quite naturally shaped the whole course of the communal revolution; and was hotly criticized at the time, and has been since, by conservative as well as radical opinion. It was an open recognition of the strength of an insurrection which, safely arrived at Versailles, he characterized as the terrorism of a handful of brigands and assassins. Since the administration and policing of Paris were under the direct control of the central government, the abandonment of the capital apparently left the population at the mercy of this handful of criminals. Jules Ferry, the mayor of Paris, remained at his post at the Hôtel de Ville until the evening of the 18th, but with his departure not a single member of the government stayed to rally or to direct the opposition to revolution.

The Official Enquiry declared that it was "inertia and the abstention from action of honest men which made the revolution." [37] Certainly there was little or no opposition to the Central Committee or its forces either from the conservative units of the National Guard or the bourgeois quar-

[37] *Enquête*, p. 43.

ters of Paris. With the complete disappearance of leaders and those government officials about whom the forces of "law and order" might have gathered, this is not surprising. A number of important journals maintained that the decision of the Assembly to sit at Versailles was the main reason for the success of the mob. A petition presented to the Assembly on April 4th, urging the government to return to Paris, voiced the same opinion.[38] "Monsieur Thiers reproaches Paris for not saving itself," wrote Varigny, a middle-class conservative remaining in Paris, "when the government has valiantly retreated to Versailles."[39] And the effect of Thiers' policy upon Rossel, the ablest military commander in the Commune's army, is significant. "The 19th of March," said Rossel, "a dispatch of M. Thiers, posted officially at Nevers, announced the evacuation of Paris by the government with forty thousand troops in good order. If I had not had a leaning toward the revolution before, this would have determined me. As if the army had not covered itself with enough shame in this war but that forty thousand men must leave Paris without fighting, when confronted with an enemy as insignificant as an insurrectionary force always must be, and after having the advantage of being on the offensive, which is the only possible position favorable to an insurrectionary force!"[40]

This statement of the military strength at the disposal of Thiers was, it is true, exaggerated; but the exaggeration was

[38] See "La Liberté," April 5. This paper asked, "Are not the most culpable those who have tempted the mob by providing it with so simple and easy a problem?"
[39] L. Thomas, *Documents*, p. 108. In this connection the testimony of Desmarest, mayor of the 9th Arrondissement, is also interesting. *Enquête*, p. 715. "It is impossible not to recognize that the retreat of public functionaries, abandoning the Prefecture of Police and all the ministries in order to attain safety in Versailles, led to a general disintegration in all authority remaining in Paris. The municipal authorities invested in part with the government of the city did not have the strength to win back that which the government had lost."
[40] L. Rossel, *Papiers Posthumes*, p. 87.

his own work. It was part of that general policy of propaganda designed to convince the provinces that the insurrection in Paris was the work of a small group of criminals, "the scum of Europe," that the troops at the disposal of the government were numerous and well disciplined and that the re-establishment of authority in Paris could be expected in short order. To this end the telegraph lines from Paris were cut, the official journal was set up in Versailles, and the provinces were daily supplied with news which was reassuring if not exact.

The position of the government during its first few days in Versailles was not enviable. Instead of 40,000 troops Thiers had barely 22,000 at his command and these none too reliable.[41] He described the situation to the Committee: "We spent 15 days at Versailles doing nothing. These were the worst days of my life. The opinion spread in Paris: 'Versailles is done for; we have only to advance and the soldiers will join us.' I was pretty sure this was not so; however, if we had been attacked by 70,000 or 80,000 men, I should not have wanted to answer for the stability of the army."[42] So precipitate had been the retreat from Paris that important papers were left in all the administrative offices, considerable sums of money at the ministry of finance and a number of military units forgotten.[43] The latter did not succeed in reaching Versailles until the 23rd of March. The Committee of Enquiry justified the abandonment of Paris. But, it declared, "History will blame the culpable ignorance with which the plans of M. Thiers were executed."[44] In one essential point, however, the execution was better than the plan. Thiers had ordered the abandonment of Mont Valérien, the key to the defense of Versailles,

[41] *Enquête sur le 18 Mars,* p. 364. Evidence of Thiers.
[42] *Ibid.* Evidence of Thiers.
[43] *Ibid.,* p. 36. Troops stationed at the Luxembourg. See also L. Fiaux, *Histoire de la Guerre Civile de 1871* (Paris, 1879), p. 86.
[44] *Loc. cit.*

and it was only after being hauled out of bed by General Vinoy at three o'clock on the morning of the 19th that he authorized measures for its reoccupation.[45]

While Thiers was advancing in hot haste upon Versailles, the evening of March 18th, Jules Favre and Picard attempted to pour oil on the waters by cashiering de Paladines as commander-in-chief of the National Guard and by the appointment of Colonel Langlois, who enjoyed a certain notoriety as a liberal.[46] As we have seen, the Central Committee refused to recognize the new commander. Nevertheless certain attempts were made to rally the conservative element in Paris during the next few days, which promised more success.

There is not much doubt, even after the heavy exodus of the propertied class following the armistice, that the supporters of Versailles were in the majority in Paris. The Commune forces were never more than a minority, though at this time a very strong one. Over certain bourgeois quarters in the capital the revolution never succeeded in extending its power. As Cattalain, Chef de la Sûreté under the Commune, remarks, "In those quarters hostile to the Commune, it was sufficient that one wore on his helmet a number of one of the Belleville or Montmartre battalions to put his life in danger. And many a morning one collected the corpses of those of whom it was the sole crime." [47]

During the days following the 18th of March the conservatives and friends of law and order grouped themselves about the Bourse to deliberate on means of defense. Certain conservative newspapers, conceiving that the support of the revolution came from the unemployed, opened a free labor

---

[45] *Enquête sur le 18 Mars,* p. 442. Evidence of Vinoy.

[46] De Paladines retaliated by ridding himself of all responsibility for the fiasco of the 18th. "It was the lawyers [i.e., Favre and Picard] who wanted it. However, I told them it would end this way. They thought they could count on the army and the army fraternized with the mob." See Lanjalley and Corriez, *op. cit.,* p. 44.

[47] Cattalain, *Mémoires,* p. 143.

exchange.[48] The influence of the press was thrown over-whelmingly on the side of Versailles. Thirty-three of the most influential papers in Paris signed the protest against the elections sponsored by the Central Committee. From the Bourse was launched, on the 22nd of March, the demonstration against the Committee which ended in the bloody shooting in the Rue de la Paix.

This was the only bloodletting which occurred during the reign of the Committee. Several thousand demonstrators, led by the royalist journalist Henri de Pène, and bearing banners inscribed "Vive l'ordre" and "Vive la République," proceeded down the Rue de la Paix through the conservative sections of the 1st and 2nd Arrondissements. En route a couple of National Guard sentinels were disarmed and the crowd gathering impetus and excitement shouted, "Down with the Committee!" "Down with the assassins!" While it was not an armed manifestation, large numbers of sword-canes and assorted firearms were available for action. At the Place Vendôme the parade encountered several battalions of the National Guard led by Bergeret, who attempted to arrest the march, only to be hissed and insulted for his pains. The testimony of eye-witnesses is so conflicting that it is impossible to say which side began the hostilities. At any rate shots were fired on both sides and the demonstrators fled leaving a dozen dead on the street. Two of the National Guard were killed and several wounded.

The Central Committee ordered an enquiry into the events of the 22nd, which found the demonstrators guilty of the aggression and attributed to the firmness of General Bergeret the avoidance of more serious bloodshed.[49] To the government at Versailles the affair offered further evidence, if more were needed, of the criminality of the Central

[48] "La Petite Presse," "Le Moniteur Universel" and "Le Petit Moniteur." See "La Petite Presse," March 23.
[49] "Journal Officiel," March 25.

Committee and its cohorts. The shooting in the Place Vendôme effectively checked further conservative manifestations. Nevertheless a number of arrondissement centers still remained in the hands of conservative battalions of the National Guard and served as focal points of the opposition to the Central Committee.[50] The appointment by the mayors acting for the government, on the 22nd, of Vice-Admiral Saisset as provisional commander-in-chief of the National Guard of Paris was a step designed to attract the moderate element to the cause of law and order.

The conciliators in the capital, particularly those mayors who were feverishly seeking a plan of mediation between Paris and Versailles, hit upon Saisset as a man who had distinguished himself during the siege and recommended to Thiers, as his adjutants, Langlois and Schoelcher, both popular with the liberals. Unfortunately Saisset had compromised himself by his applause of Favre's oratorical flight before the Assembly on March 21st in which the latter had denounced the Committee and its followers as brigands and assassins. Also his presence in the manifestation of the 22nd and his attempts, though half-hearted, to organize the resistance to the Central Committee in Paris were not likely to recommend him to the revolution. Nevertheless, he appeared to open the way to final agreement between the Committee and the government when he published on the 23rd what purported to be concessions from Versailles: complete recognition of the municipal franchises of Paris, the election of all the officers of the National Guard including the general-in-chief, a modification of the law of maturities, a rent law favorable to tenants.[51] However, as

[50] Notably the 1st and 2nd. Some 25,000 of the "law and order" guards gathered around these two centers. No doubt the publication by the mayors on March 23rd of a decree announcing themselves as the sole custodians of the public funds destined to the payment of the National Guard had something to do with this.
[51] *Murailles,* II, p. 62.

it turned out, these concessions were unauthorized by Versailles and entirely unacceptable to the Assembly.[52]

Thiers had assured the mayors in a vague and general way of his willingness to compromise and had apparently authorized them to make what concessions were necessary.[53] But no one of these specific concessions could be considered. It is hard to avoid the conclusion that during the first few days following the 18th of March, Thiers was supporting conciliation simply as a means of gaining the time necessary to organize his army. Tirard, mayor of the 2nd Arrondissement, seems to admit as much when he says in his testimony, "I must tell you, gentlemen, that the principal end we followed in this resistance was to prevent the Federals from marching on Versailles.

"I am persuaded that if, on the 19th or 20th of March, the Federal battalions had left by the Châtillon route, Versailles would have run the greatest danger, and I am of the opinion that our few days' resistance permitted the government to organize its defense."[54]

On the other hand, the Central Committee, while of course willing to accept the proposals of Saisset, was not willing to abdicate its authority and to leave the municipal elections in the hands of Thiers. In a special and secret session the Committee decided to accept the proposals but to insist upon immediate elections in Paris. To the appointment of Saisset, Schoelcher and Langlois as chiefs of the National Guard the governors of Paris responded by putting the control of military forces into the hands of the "Generals" Brunel, Eudes and Duval. Brunel quickly destroyed the 1st Arrondissement center as a point of con-

---

[52] If Saisset was not inspired by Thiers he was incredibly stupid in making such promises; Thiers himself had not the authority, without consultation with the Assembly. Lanjalley and Corriez, *op. cit.*, p. 119, explain Saisset's concessions as a mental aberration.

[53] See letter from Thiers to Desmarest, March 23rd. Reprinted in Lepelletier, II:292.

[54] *Enquête.* Evidence of Tirard, p. 658.

gregation for the opponents of the Committee, and the resistance led by Saisset and others quickly melted away. The Admiral, after three days of stupid blundering, authorized the National Guards to return to their homes and left for Versailles.

The opposition to the revolution in Paris had practically vanished. Nevertheless it had done its part, along with the incompetence of the drunken Lullier and the lack of a program in the Committee itself, in securing to Versailles the time so necessary for a reconstitution of the army. It is not necessary to suppose that this farsighted, if vindictive, policy was actively present in the minds of the conciliators in Paris. The opposition to the Commune in the capital was conducted in the main by those genuinely interested in finding a compromise between Paris and Versailles.[55] But the result was to strengthen the latter and weaken the former. Thiers was busy forming the army which was to justify his abandonment of Paris.

The question, however, was not, as the conservatives and monarchists in the assembly envisaged it, whether or no the government, France and civilization were to be destroyed by a mob of cosmopolitan criminals assembled in Paris. The question was not, as Thiers apparently envisaged it, whether the Central Committee and the National Guard of Paris or Thiers and the National Assembly were to rule France. The real problem involved was the handling of a strong and recalcitrant opposition with the least possible bloodshed and disturbance. Possibly compromise was necessary, certainly time and study were. Thiers decided to act after he had been but a few days in Paris and without adequate

[55] The communist historians of the Commune draw a moral lesson from the effects of these attempts at conciliation. According to Lavrov, e.g., *Parizhskaia Kommuna*, p. 225, a commentator much followed by the Bolshevist historians, the Commune was defeated by reconcilers of one sort or another—the mayors, e.g., who sympathized with the Commune, who were listened to by the Committee and who consequently prevented an attack on Versailles when that attack gave the greatest promise of success.

consideration of the strength of his own forces or that of
the opposition. Having acted and failed he encouraged the
opposition by completely withdrawing from Paris and turn-
ing over government to the Committee. Having made civil
war probable before arriving at Versailles, he made it inevitable by his uncompromising position. In this manner
the revolution was conquered, but at the expense of 15,000
lives, the burning of a part of Paris, the destruction of over
a billion francs in property and the intensification of class
hatred not only in France but in Europe. Whether or no
the abandonment of Paris by Thiers was justified in the light
of these facts is doubtful.

The only extenuation of Thiers' policy is to be found in
the nature of the Assembly.[56] At the same time monarchist,
intolerant and stupid, the Assembly and its management presented difficulties of the first order to the chief of a nascent
republic. The Assembly had not shown itself particularly
sapient in the treatment of the problem of Paris while still
in Bordeaux. There was not much evidence that its intelligence was going to increase in the climate of Versailles.
Whether in view of this situation Thiers would have been
able to study the situation in the capital and to proceed with
a policy of conciliation and compromise is somewhat dubious. Taking, as he did, the line of hard-handed repression,
he was often subjected to criticism by the deputies for his
leniency. With a more tolerant and intelligent Assembly,
Thiers might not have been forced to armed action, the
abandonment of Paris and subsequent civil war. On the
other hand, this policy, this attitude towards a democratic
and rebellious movement, was not inconsistent with what
we know of Thiers' character and politics.

[56] Lockroy, liberal deputy from Paris, expresses fairly well the opinion
of this Assembly held by the deputies and mayors who favored conciliation.
"If these men have not seen that the Federal army was very strong, if they
have not understood that its resistance would be fierce and desperate, they
are senseless and blind. If they have foreseen this and, foreseeing it, have
continued their policy, then they may regard themselves as the true authors
of the disaster." *La Commune et l'Assemblée* (Paris, 1871), p. 47.

THE MAYORS OF PARIS AND THE CENTRAL COMMITTEE

The reign of the Central Committee ostensibly ended with the election of a municipal assembly, the Commune, on the 26th of March. The Committee, fearful of undertaking revolutionary action itself, and wishing to be relieved of responsibility at the earliest possible moment, had first set the elections for the 22nd.[57] The Versailles government, anxious to postpone the creation of a municipal assembly until such time as the army could be sufficiently strengthened to support Thiers' program, had wished to put over the elections until some time in April. The liberal mayors of Paris and deputies in the National Assembly, anxious to avoid bloodshed, acted as mediators between the two unyielding parties. In what the conservatives called the "capitulation of the mayors," these mediators finally gave their sanction to the communal elections, and, in so doing, gave a certain air of legality to that municipal body which was for the next two months to direct the revolution against Versailles. The "capitulation" and the events leading up to it were profoundly important in shaping the history of the Commune.

The faith of the Central Committee in the municipal elections was naïve and is a little difficult to understand. Having assumed the direction of a revolution, a revolution which had driven the government from the capital, the Committee assumed that the election of a communal assembly would settle all problems and guarantee to Paris all the rights which it demanded. That the government at Ver-

[57] It appeared that on the 20th, the Committee was willing to relinquish civil authority altogether. Its representatives had entered upon an agreement with the mayors whereby the latter were to occupy immediately the Hôtel de Ville. The Committee was to confine itself to the control of the National Guard. However, when the mayors presented themselves at the Hôtel de Ville they found that the Committee had changed its mind. Its members, having consulted the arrondissement committees, discovered that any delegation of civil authority to the mayors was unacceptable. See Lanjalley and Corriez, *op. cit.*, pp. 60-61 and 72.

sailles would not recognize the municipal assembly was hardly to be thought of. When Jourde suggested this possibility to the Committee, it replied that, if the National Assembly refused to recognize the Commune, it would be necessary for the latter body to lay down the constitution under which Paris must be governed. "But, at the same time, one cannot suppose that the Assembly would dare disapprove of the Paris elections; this would be too serious a step, particularly in view of the attitude of large provincial cities ready to unite themselves with the capital." [58]

This being true one might suppose that the Central Committee could afford to consult the convenience of Versailles by allowing the elections to be postponed. Not at all; the elections must be held immediately and under the supervision of the Committee in order to insure that the new municipal assembly would be representative of the revolution. If the elections were held under the direction of Thiers and time given the reaction to organize itself, the cause of the 18th of March was lost. [59] The Committee felt itself to be master of the existing situation; immediate elections would give Paris a radical communal assembly and the government at Versailles would have no other alternative than to recognize it. If, by any chance, this recognition failed, at least the Committee would have transmitted the direction of a civil war, become necessary, into other hands.

The elections set for the 22nd the Committee found advisable to postpone by reason of difficulties involved in preparing voting lists. Although the government at Versailles was willing to hold elections on April 3rd, the Committee, feeling it was dangerous to wait this long, set them for the 26th. Nevertheless, it appeared on the 24th that a compromise might be reached. General Brunel, ordered by

[58] *Comptes-rendus des Séances du Comité Central et de la Commune.* Meeting of March 25th.
[59] *Ibid.,* meeting of March 24th; secret session.

the revolution to take possession of the 1st Arrondissement, entered into negotiations with the mayor, Adam, and one of the adjutants, Meline. After considerable argument and consultation with the authorities of the 2nd Arrondissement, Brunel and Protot, on one side, and the mayors and adjutants, on the other, managed to agree on the 30th of March. In view of this apparent concord, there was great rejoicing in Paris and considerable fraternization between the National Guard representing the forces of order and that representing the revolution.

The celebration, however, was premature. Both the Committee and the national government were unwilling to accept this date. The opinion of the Committee, expressed by Ranvier, was that to postpone the elections until the 30th would be simply to allow Versailles more time to arm itself against Paris. If the revolution desired and was preparing at this time for war with Versailles there would have been point to this objection. As it was, to reject the offer of the mayors who claimed authority, delegated by the government, was to take a high-handed attitude which only immediate military action could justify. To speak in the vernacular, the committee was "feeling its oats." A report had just come from Lyons that 18 out of the 24 battalions of the National Guard in that city were ready to ally with Paris.[60] Resistance to the revolution had broken down in the capital itself and the Committee was convinced that Thiers' army was so disorganized and unsympathetic with the position of the National government as to be of little support to Versailles.[61] As it turned out, however, this stiff-necked and uncompromising attitude cost the Committee considerable support in the provinces and weakened its position among the moderates in the capital.[62]

[60] "Journal Officiel," March 26. Report from Amouroux made March 24th.
[61] Comptes-rendus, March 24th.
[62] So strong a sympathizer with the Commune position as Lepelletier refuses to justify the Committee in its attitude. See his Histoire de la Commune, II:356-360.

On the other hand, there is small reason for believing that Versailles looked with greater favor upon the compromise. Thiers, it is true, was attempting to persuade the Assembly to permit municipal elections for April 3rd.[63] At the same time, however, the Assembly, in spite of the critical situation in Paris, was in no hurry to declare its position.[64] In discussing the situation with various of the mayors of Paris, Thiers emphasized these necessities: (1) the election in Paris of "republicans devoted to the maintenance of order," (2) the avoidance of bloodshed and (3) the gaining of time in which to reorganize the army. If the elections could be postponed until the 3rd, the first objective might be won, but since, under present conditions, this postponement appeared impossible, it must be sacrificed to the other two. The substance of Thiers' advice to Tirard, mayor of the 2nd Arrondissement, was then that the mayors must take what steps were necessary in order to avoid bloodshed during the few days required for organizing the army. If this meant a capitulation to the Central Committee on the question of early elections, well and good.[65] It did not follow that the government of Versailles felt itself bound to recognize the results of this election.

However much Versailles favored the postponement of the elections the Central Committee undertook full responsibility for refusing to compromise with the mayors. Its position, already weak with the Paris electorate, was further injured. The thirty-one influential newspapers in the capital which had declared against elections sponsored by the Committee took their stand on the question of legality.

[63] Enquête, p. 658. Evidence of Tirard.
[64] A bill introduced by Arnaud (de l'Ariège), setting the municipal elections at the earliest possible date, was before the Assembly at this time. Despite the entreaties of the deputies of Paris interested in conciliation, the consideration of this bill proceeded deliberately. At the close of a night session on March 24th, Clémenceau declared, "You are taking upon yourselves, gentlemen, the responsibility for what is going to happen." "Journal Officiel de Versailles," March 25.
[65] Enquête, pp. 658, 659. Evidence of Tirard.

"Considering that the convocation of electors is an act of national sovereignty;

"That the exercise of this sovereignty belongs only to authority derived from universal suffrage;

"That, in consequence, the committee now sitting at the Hôtel de Ville has neither the right nor the position to order such a convocation;

"Therefore the representatives of the journals mentioned above consider the elections fixed for the 22nd null and void, and invite the electors to take no account of them." [66]

This attitude expressed toward the elections of the 22nd was carried over to those of the 26th and was intensified by the intransigent stand assumed by the Committee.

On the other hand, the papers supporting the Commune besought the electorate to register its support of the insurrection at the polls, and various radical political organizations in Paris placarded the walls of the capital with announcements of their intention to vote.[67] The "Cri du Peuple" discovered a sacred duty of voting as a protest against the unsocial exhortation of the reactionary journals.[68] It seemed for the moment that the elections of March 26 were to record the clear-cut opinion of insurrectionary Paris, supporting the Committee while recognizing its illegality.

However, on the 25th, the mayors of Paris and certain deputies of the Seine threw a covering of legality over the vote by an agreement with the Central Committee. The representatives of the Hôtel de Ville, Ranvier and Arnold, sent to the mayors on the evening of the 24th to obtain their cooperation in the elections of the 26th, had failed in their mission. Nevertheless, a series of events was forcing the

[66] *Murailles,* II:14.
[67] Several proclamations of radical organizations published in *Murailles,* II:72 and 73.
[68] "Le Cri du People," March 24.

mayors into cooperation. In the first place there was no unity in their opposition to the Committee. Of the eighty mayors and adjutants in Paris, about ten or twelve whole-heartedly favored the Commune and the rest were for conciliation and compromise.[69] The majority of the actively interested populace of the metropolis believed, rightly or wrongly, that the elections meant peace and the return of order. Indeed, Ranvier was not far wrong when he represented the Committee's determination on early elections as forced upon it by popular opinion. The vote had been postponed once and the Committee was fearful of the consequences of a further postponement.[70]

The situation veered further in the direction of cooperation with the arrival, on the morning of the 25th, of certain mayors and deputies from Versailles, where they had been urging conciliation upon the National Assembly. Clémenceau and Floquet brought back the rumor, which they received from Jules Simon, that the government was contemplating the appointment of the Prince de Joinville as Lieutenant-General of the army.[71] This rumor, which turned out to be groundless, had a tremendous effect upon the municipal officials. To staunch republicans this looked like the beginning of the return to monarchy. Furthermore, the deputies and those of the mayors who had come in contact with the Assembly were deeply depressed by the unwillingness of the majority to take a step in the direction of compromise.[72] As Clémenceau expressed himself to the mayors,

[69] *Enquête*, p. 719. Evidence of Desmarest, mayor of the 9th Arrondissement.

[70] For Ranvier's argument see Lepelletier, *op. cit.*, II :365.

[71] *Enquête*, 721. Evidence of Desmarest, p. 840. Evidence of Héligon, adjutant in the 14th Arrondissement. Apparently the news of Saisset's concessions to the revolution had created a furor in monarchist circles in Versailles. There was considerable talk of deposing Thiers, talk which had come to the ears of Simon, Minister· of Public Instruction.

[72] A delegation of the mayors of Paris visited Versailles, March 23, to lay a communication on the situation in the capital before the Assembly. Their appearance had occasioned such an impassioned exchange of recriminations between the left and the right that the president, unable to preserve order, had been forced to terminate the session.

"They don't want to understand anything or to do anything."

The Central Committee, which had sent its delegates to interview the mayors on the morning of March 25th, was apparently willing to reinstate them in their mayoral offices. In consequence of all these things—the impossibility of dealing with the Assembly, the rumor of the return of the monarchy, the demand of the Parisian populace, and the promise of reestablished mayoral authority—forty-one mayors and adjutants and six representatives to the Assembly joined with the Central Committee in declaring elections for the 26th of March. The mayors had capitulated and the position of the Central Committee before the Paris electorate was enormously strengthened.

"The Central Committee of the National Guard, with which is allied the deputies of Paris, the mayors and adjutants, convinced that the sole means of avoiding civil war, the shedding of blood in Paris, and, at the same time, of securing the affirmation of the Republic, is to proceed immediately to the elections, convokes for to-morrow, Sunday, all of the citizens in their electoral colleges.[73]

"The inhabitants of Paris will understand that, under present circumstances, patriotism obliges them to vote, in order that the elections may have that serious character which alone will assure peace to the city."

The result of this proclamation was rejoicing and celebration in the capital. The majority of those who had made the 18th of March considered their ends attained, and at that without the civil war which, at any moment, had seemed

[73] *Murailles*, II:87. This proclamation represents a distortion at the hands of the Central Committee of the agreement entered into by the mayors. The latter, without making a formal protest, published the exact version, the first lines of which read, "The deputies of Paris, the elected mayors and adjutants, reestablished in the mayoral offices of their arrondissements, and the members of the Federal Central Committee of the National Guard, convinced," etc. (See "Journal Officiel," March 26.) The Committee in its version sought to pretend that the municipal officials had allied themselves to the program of the Commune, which was not true.

imminent. The municipal council, the Commune, was to be established and this conception, this abstraction, no better understood now than on the 31st of October, had lost none of its attraction. The radical journal, "La Commune," flamboyantly voiced the satisfaction of its party: "The peace is made. The blood of Parisians will not be shed in this great capital of civilization. Universal suffrage will speak and the whole world will bow respectfully before its decision." [74]

The conservative papers still grumbled. "Le Bien Public" on the day after the elections, maintained that, "illegally sanctioned, they had not been held under those indispensable conditions of security, equality and liberty." Nevertheless, Paris had voted and the vote, all things considered, was large: 229,167 out of a registration of 485,569. Versailles, stressing the abstentions, found the vote small and evidence of the fact that the revolutionary party in Paris was in the minority. Still, 229,000 votes hardly justified Jules Favre's and Thiers' remarks on the "handful of bandits and assassins." After all, the abstentions could scarcely be considered to measure the forces of law and order in Paris. The registration figures were those of Napoleon's plebiscite of the spring of 1870. Since then the war had taken a heavy toll in Paris and the exodus of the better classes in February and March had run close to a hundred thousand.

It was a surprisingly heavy vote and for it the "capitulation" of the mayors was largely responsible. The Committee of Enquiry on the 18th of March was inclined to judge the mayors harshly.[75] To cover the Commune with the cloak of legality, a legality inadmissable by Versailles, was to strengthen the revolution and prolong the civil war. Nevertheless these deputies and mayors who had believed in conciliation as opposed to the government's policy of

[74] "La Commune," March 26.
[75] *Enquête*, pp. 51-54.

out-and-out repression defended their action before the Committee of Enquiry, and declared that if it had to be repeated they would do the same.[76] Bloodshed and civil war had been avoided for the moment; the responsibility for the future rested with the Commune.

WAS THE REVOLUTION PROLETARIAN AND SOCIALIST?

The rule of the Central Committee appeared to be terminated. In a proclamation posted on the walls of Paris and published in the "Journal Officiel," it pointed with dignified pride to its accomplishments and admonished the citizens to cast their ballots with perspicacity.

"Our mission is ended; we are going to give up our place in your Hôtel de Ville to the newly elected, your regular representatives.

"Assisted by your devotion and your patriotism, we have brought to a favorable termination the difficult enterprise undertaken in your name. Thanks to your continued cooperation, Solidarity is no longer a vain word; the safety of the Republic is assured.

.   .   .   .   .   .

"Do not forget that the men who will serve you best are those you will choose from your own class, living your own life, enduring the same difficulties.

.   .   .   .   .   .

"Finally, look for men of sincere convictions, men of the people, resolute, active, having a sense of justice and a recognized honesty. . . . Show your preference for those who do not ostentatiously solicit your votes; true merit is modest, it is the duty of the voters to know their men."[77]

[76] For example: Evidence of Schoelcher, *Enquête,* p. 642.
[77] "Journal Officiel," March 27; *Murailles,* II:86.

The elections of March 26th, which called the Commune into existence, brought to a close the first phase of the revolution. Governmental authority had been driven from the capital, which had been ruled for eight days by a committee representative of the insurrectionary forces. Now Paris had elected its own municipal assembly, into whose hands the future of the revolution was committed. It is pertinent at this point to enquire to what extent the movement had been that proletarian and socialist revolution which the Marxian mythology of the Commune describes.

That the insurrection of March 18th was largely a proletarian movement can hardly be denied. Generated in the proletarian faubourgs of Montmartre and Belleville, which had been the centers of revolutionary excitation all during the siege, it had drawn its rank and file from the working class element incorporated in the National Guard. Of the thirty-six members of the Central Committee who signed the agreement with the mayors, at least twenty belonged to the working class and six or seven of the remainder, including Lisbonne, Bouit, Lullier, Lacord, Fortuné and Billioray, belonged to that semi-literary and artistic bohemia which, half-proletarian and largely revolutionary, is a well-known aspect of metropolitan areas and particularly of Paris. Quantities of small shopkeepers and petty business men attached themselves to the cause of the Central Committee and voted for the Commune. Journalists in large numbers espoused the claims of Paris as against Versailles and played a very prominent part in the events of April and May. Nevertheless the uprising of March 18th and the personnel of the National Guard which assumed control was, in the main, proletarian. The movement sprang as much from the working class as any other revolutionary uprising in the 19th century.

Nevertheless, in spite of Marx and the Marxians this does not mean, necessarily, that the revolution was socialist. There is no cosmic necessity leading the working class toward socialism, such that the proletariat and socialism are inseparable entities, nor is any connection of this sort visible in the revolution of the 18th of March. There were socialists in the Central Committee and socialists in the rank and file supporting the Committee, socialist ideas were disseminated in the journals allied with the Commune and the importance of their ideas and of their disseminators grew steadily during the revolution. But it was not as socialists that the Committee and its allies took part in the events of the 18th of March. There was no preparation in revolutionary circles for the overthrow of Thiers and his government on that day. The uprising was spontaneous and unexpected and the spirit of unrest in the populace, from which it sprang, was the product of patriotism outraged by the experience of Paris during the siege. Socialist ideas were in the air and socialist ambitions had a profound effect upon the course of the Commune, but to understand the 18th of March, not much more is necessary than a knowledge of the events in Paris which intervened between that date and the 4th of September.

This, it is needless to say, was not the opinion of the Committee of Enquiry which filled a thousand pages with its report on the causes of the 18th of March. Nor was it the opinion of the majority of the Communards themselves, who later wrote on the revolution. Contemporaries, both conservative and radical, were inclined to see in the insurrection an attempt to overthrow existing society. As the editor of "Le Bien Public" put it, "This is no political revolution but a social revolution. The leaders do not see this—they are looking at it politically. But they do not know the nature of the forces they are leading." [78]

The magniloquent address of that old revolutionary-republican, Félix Pyat, to the citizens of Paris expresses the same idea. "You have made a revolution without example in history. Your revolution of the 18th of March has a par-

[78] "Le Bien Public," March 28.

ticular quality which distinguished it from all others. Its especial grandeur lies in its being completely popular, entirely collective, communal—a revolution en commandite, anonymous and unanimous, and, for the first time, without directors (*gérants*)." [79]

Pyat was typical of the ineffectual, idealistic, and bombastic revolutionaries, responsible for so many of the stupidities of the Commune.

Although it is fairly obvious that the 18th of March was, in its motivation, anything but socialist, the reign of the Central Committee was marked by the adhesion of a number of socialist organizations and the spread of socialist opinion. The stone hewers of Paris seized the occasion presented by the revolution to meet in order to discuss whether or no "we can continue to allow those who produce nothing to live in luxury; whether the social system we have lived under for so long is destined to last forever, even though it is completely opposed to our interests." [80] The Paris sections of the International in declaring their adhesion to the cause of the Central Committee, asserted that the independence of the Commune will "put an end to class antagonism and will assure social equality.

"We have demanded the emancipation of the working class and this communal assembly is its guarantee, for it gives to every citizen the means of defending his rights, or controlling in a satisfactory manner the representatives charged with the care of his interests, and of determining the progressive application of social reforms." [81]

The International in Paris, which had hesitated at first to ally itself with the Committee, for fear of linking its existence and future prospects with the fate of the revolution, finally came out with a proclamation, posted in all the Arrondissements and printed in the "Journal Officiel,"

[79] "La Commune," March 27.
[80] *Murailles*, II:25.
[81] *Ibid.*, 52-53. And in the "Journal Officiel" of March 26.

whole-heartedly espousing the cause of the Committee.[82] The adherence of the International was accompanied by the formation of lists of candidates, and statements of principle, on the parts of the socialist clubs of the various arrondissements.[83] They were rewarded on March 26th by the election of a large number of socialists to the Commune.

Socialist propaganda creeps into the pages of even the "Journal Officiel." The ablest and most intelligent of the editors, the man who drafted a large number of the proclamations of the Central Committee, was Charles Longuet, a convinced socialist and disciple of Proudhon. He was later to marry one of the daughters of Karl Marx and to serve as one of the important popularizers of Marxism in France. In a number of the well-written articles with which he graced the pages of the journal, the 18th of March is envisaged as a class struggle by which the proletariat hopes to emancipate itself from its bourgeois masters. "The proletariat, confronted with a permanent menace to its rights, with an absolute negation of all its legitimate aspirations, with the ruin of the country and all its hopes, has conceived as its imperious duty and its absolute right the taking in hand of its own destinies and the assurance of its own triumph by the assumption of power.

"That is why it has answered by means of a revolution the criminal and insensate provocation of a blind and culpable government, which has not hesitated to let loose a civil war in the presence of a foreign invasion and occupation." [84]

The Central Committee, in contrast, kept entirely off this subject. In spite of a number of socialists in its ranks, in none of its pronunciamentos is there the slightest hint of socialist desires or pretentions. Whatever the attitude of

[82] *Séances Officielles de l'Internationale à Paris.* Meetings of March 23rd and 24th.
[83] A large number of the socialist election posters are reprinted in Vol. II of *Murailles.*
[84] "Journal Officiel," March 21.

160 THE PARIS COMMUNE

its members may have been, the proximity of the elections and the fear of frightening the moderate vote by too revolutionary an attitude was enough to keep the suggestion of socialism from its declarations.

The Committee, as a matter of fact, proceeded no great distance in formulating the aims of the revolution. The conservative journals were quite justified in protesting that no one could discover exactly what the trouble was all about. In the clearest presentation which the Committee vouchsafed, there is no appreciable change from the demands of the National Guard before the 18th. "What do we demand?" it exclaims on March 24th:

"The maintenance of the Republic as the sole possible and indisputable government.

"The common rights of Paris, that is to say an elected communal assembly.

"The abolition of the Prefecture of Police, as the Prefect Kératry himself demanded.

"The abolition of the permanent army and the right for you, the National Guard of Paris, to be the sole authority responsible for order in Paris.

"The right to elect all our officers.

"Finally, the reorganization of the National Guard on principles which will give guarantees to the people." [85]

These are far-reaching changes but there is nothing of socialism in them. The last four, though in a somewhat modified form, had been the continuous demand of the republican opposition all during the reign of Napoleon III. They grew quite naturally out of French political experience in the 19th century. With the standing army Napoleon had made the 2nd of December, the coup d'état which made him Emperor of France. The highly developed Prefecture of Police, with its elaborate political department, he had used to hunt down and eliminate the more dangerous of the republican opposition. A National Guard with officers

[85] "Journal Officiel," March 25.

elected by and responsible to the rank and file, that is, the citizenry of France, was designated to guard against the recurrence of such practices.

The first principle, the maintenance of the Republic, was hardly at issue. Whatever the political complexion of the National Assembly might have been, the legal representatives of Paris, the mayors, their adjutants and the delegates to the National Assembly were almost unanimously and whole-heartedly republican. It has been the claim of most apologists for the Commune, that the revolution of the 18th of March saved the Republic. How much truth there is in this contention we shall discuss later.

It was the second demand of the Committee, the Commune, which excited the hopes and fears of Paris. It could mean everything or nothing. To the communists it meant communism, to the socialists, socialism, to the Proudhonists, federalism, to the moderates, very little. In the eyes of the Central Committee and of the insurrection, the Commune could define its own powers and limit its own duties. "That constituent power which is accorded so largely, so indefinitely and so confusedly for France to the Assembly, it must exercise for itself, that is to say, for the city, of which it is only an expression." This statement of the delegate of the Central Committee to the "Journal Officiel" apparently means that the Commune was to have in Paris all the legislative power which the Assembly possessed for France. The Municipal Assembly might not exercise its powers to their full capacity, but if so the restraint would be of its own volition and not imposed by the National Assembly. "A free Paris, in a free France," was the cry of the revolution; but, so far as one can see, there was no inclination on the part of its leaders to give a thought to the difficult problems of the relation between the Commune of Paris and the Assembly, on the one hand, or between the Commune of Paris and the other communes of France, on the other. All this was to be left to the Municipal Assembly elected by the democracy of Paris on the 26th of March. In the meantime, every one was free to paint the Commune any lovely color his heart desired.

Paris and Versailles at War

The inhabitants of Paris, casting their ballots for the Commune, hoped for peace, but they got war. In the vote of the 26th the revolution won all along the line. Except in the 1st and 2nd Arrondissements, where the existing mayors and their adjutants were reelected, the men who had led the opposition on the 31st of October and the 22nd of January, the orators of the revolutionary clubs and the editors of the radical journals were established in power.

The installation of the Commune on the 28th of March was a magnificent affair. The huge balustrated and decorated platform erected in front of the Hôtel de Ville was surrounded by the Federals, as they were called now, singing the "Marseillaise" and rejoicing in their municipal independence. The spirit of 1793 when, under the first Commune, Paris was not only master of itself but of France, had returned. Amid general celebration the Commune "declared that the National Guard and the Central Committee have merited well of the country and the Republic." [86] Boursier, of the Central Committee, read out the list of those elected, and Ranvier, a close friend of Flourens, after announcing the transfer of authority from the Committee, proclaimed the Commune in the name of the people. In the high-flown phrases of the Central Committee's proclamation, "Today, we have had the privilege of viewing the most glorious popular spectacle that has ever met our eyes or stirred our souls; Paris greeted and acclaimed its Revolution; Paris opened a white page of the book of History and thereon inscribed its puissant name." [87]

The Commune did not disappoint these ardent anticipa-

---

[86] "Journal Officiel," March 29.
[87] Proclamation of March 28th. *Murailles,* II:124-125.

tions. It quickly assumed a position toward Versailles which would have made concilation impossible for a government much less intolerant than that of M. Thiers and the National Assembly. In its second session the new Municipal Assembly abolished conscription, decreed that no armed force other than the National Guard could ever be created or brought into Paris, and laid it down that all able-bodied citizens were, *ipso facto,* liable for service in the National Guard. None of these matters fell within the purview of a municipal council. Prefacing a law on rents with the statement, "Whereas labor, industry and commerce have met all the expenses of the war and it is therefore just that property bear its part of the country's sacrifices," the Commune granted a generous postponement of obligations to the tenants of Paris. Employees in the public services were warned to take no cognizance of orders emanating from Versailles, under penalty of immediate dismissal.[88] At the same time the Commune appointed its executive commissions, displaying an energy and initiative in these first two or three meetings that were visible only infrequently thereafter.

The first address to the citizens of Paris was couched in a language extremely uncomplimentary to Versailles. "A cowardly and aggressive power has seized you by the throat; you have, in your legitimate defense, excluded from your walls this government which sought to dishonor you by imposing on you a king.

"Today, these criminals, whom you have not even cared to pursue, are abusing your magnanimity by organizing at your very doors a center of monarchical conspiracy. They are invoking civil war; they are employing all sorts of corruption; they beg for any assistance; with lies they encourage the support of the foreigner.

"We summon them from these despicable activities to the judgment of France and the world."

The address proceeded with the enunciation of a pro-

[88] All of these decrees to be found in the "Journal Officiel" for March 30.

gram calculated to exclude the national government completely from the administration of the affairs of Paris. Good
news from the provinces no doubt emboldened the note
struck by the Commune. The communal revolution at Lyons,
which had broken out on the 22nd, appeared at this time to
favor Paris, and Amouroux, one of the newly elected members of the Paris Commune, was quickly dispatched to
cement an alliance. The "Journal Officiel" of March 28th
printed the news of the proclamation of the Commune of
Toulouse.[89] At St. Étienne a revolutionary mob invaded the
Hôtel de Ville and assassinated the Prefect, M. de l'Espée.
The Commune was proclaimed at Narbonne on the 23rd,
and was set in motion in Marseilles on the same date. Revolutionary disturbances occurred in Creusot on the 24th and
in Nanterre on the 3rd and 4th of April.[90] These communal
revolutions in the provinces were short in duration, but they
served to encourage the Commune of Paris, at the outset, to
take up an intransigent attitude toward Versailles.

The first meeting of the new Municipal Assembly was
held on the evening of March 28th in the hall of the Municipal Commission under the Empire. In spite of a considerable amount of confusion and hesitation, the general temper
of the Assembly became fairly clear. It was expressed by
Paschal Grousset, editor of the radical "L'Affranchi," in the
course of a debate on whether or no the deliberations were
to be published. "The Commune is essentially a council of
war. There is no reason why we should inform the Assembly,
our enemy, of our decisions."[91] There was opposition to

[89] The Communal revolution was overthrown by the Prefect of Police
Kératry on the 27th, after two days of existence, but the news penetrated to
Paris only after considerable delay.

[90] On these provincial revolutions and the relation of the Commune of
Paris to them see Bourgin's *Le Mouvement Communaliste dans les Départements en 1871*, "Revue Socialiste," 49:412, May, 1904.

[91] *Procès-Verbaux de la Commune de 1871*, Vol. I. Edited by G. Bourgin
and G. Henriot (Paris, 1924), p. 23. This is the first of three volumes,
utilizing the manuscript of the *Procès-Verbaux* deposited in the Bibliothèque
de l'Institut d'Histoire, de Géographie et d'Économie Urbaines de la Ville
de Paris. The other two have not yet appeared.

this attitude toward publicity. Throughout the duration of the Commune the question of publication of the deliberations was continuously debated. But there was no opposition to the opinion that the Commune was necessarily the enemy of Versailles. The frank recognition of this state of latent war gave Tirard, former mayor of the 2nd Arrondissement and elected member of the Commune, his opportunity to resign. Ignoring the violent hostility of his colleagues he took the position that, since his electors were under the impression that they were voting for him as a member of a municipal council limited in its powers by the constitution of France, and not a council of war or a government set up in opposition to Versailles, he felt it his duty to withdraw.[92]

It is interesting to contrast the impressions which the Hôtel de Ville at the time of this first meeting of the Commune made upon two of its members, Tirard who withdrew to Versailles and Arnould who remained with the Commune. In the words of Tirard: "The National Guard filled the Hôtel de Ville. Soldiers were eating in the corridors and in the Assembly room. The smell of tobacco, wine and food choked and suffocated me. An infernal racket assaulted the eardrums. It was a sickening spectacle." [93] Arnould, on the other hand, found the scene colorful and inspiring; the people in revolution. "One thing which must have attracted the notice of every observer was that all the soldiers had newspapers which they were reading eagerly.

"That alone would have been enough to demonstrate at the first glance that they were not the soldiers of an established power but the volunteers of a revolution. The fighter in repose became the citizen occupying himself with the public interest, instructing himself in the sacred cause for which he had offered his life yesterday and for which he was going to die tomorrow." [94]

[92] *Enquête,* p. 659. Evidence of Tirard.
[93] *Ibid.*
[94] A. Arnould, *Histoire de la Commune de Paris* (Brussels, 1898), II:67.

Despite the truculent attitude of the Commune and its precipitance in exhibiting its power, there were some lofty-minded and idealistic members who believed apparently that the reasonableness of its ideas and the righteousness of its cause would conquer France bloodlessly and without delay. The doyen of the Commune and, consequently, its first president, old Charles Beslay, Proudhonist and sentimental socialist, voiced the beliefs of a number of colleagues in his opening address. "The Republic is today no longer what it was in the great days of our first revolution. The Republic of '93 was a soldier who, to fight against external and internal enemies, found it necessary to centralize under its direction the whole strength of the country; the Republic of 1871 is a worker who has need of liberty to fructify the peace.

"Peace and labor! There is our future! There is the guarantee of our revenge and our social regeneration, and, thus understood, the Republic can still make of France the sustainer of the weak, the protector of labor, the hope of the oppressed throughout the world and the foundation of the universal republic." [95]

Whatever peaceful penetration these ideas might have enjoyed in France, they did not proceed far at Versailles. Thiers might assure the provinces of his benign intentions and willingness to compromise, but the Assembly showed itself as unheeding as the Commune. If to Paris the Assembly was known as the "Prussians of Versailles" the "royalist conspirators," and the "six hundred cretins," the Communards passed in Versailles as blackguards, assassins and brigands, the "scum of proletarian Europe."

The proposal of the deputies of Paris for early municipal elections in the capital was rapidly disposed of in the Assembly on March 22nd. In spite of the fact that M. Thiers in a long speech urged moderation and discretion in debate, feeling ran very high. The "martyred" generals Lecomte

[95] Printed in the "Journal Officiel," April 2.

and Thomas had been voted a monument in the previous session and their families given a pension by the state. The Assembly, on March 23rd, enacted a law providing for the organization in the provinces of battalions of volunteers charged with protecting the national sovereignty and repressing Paris.[96] On the twenty-seventh the assassinated Prefect of St. Étienne, M. de l'Espée, was amid enthusiasm declared to have "merited well of his country." The conservative majority was in a determined mood and the liberal deputies of Paris preserved that discretion which is held not to be inconsistent with valor.

The next day, however, sharp words passed. Clémenceau, unsympathetic with the policy of the government, and incapable of exerting a moderating influence in the face of the huge conservative majority, resigned. "In the profound conviction that I can no longer try to be useful to the country by continuing to sit in the National Assembly, I have the honor of presenting you with my resignation from this assembly." [97] Count de la Rochethulon, in a most provocative speech, aroused a storm of protest from the liberals. "I pray my honorable colleagues of the Left to impart the news to their friends in Paris, that henceforth, towards them, I consider myself in a state of legitimate defense." [Lively approbation on the Right. Fiery replies on the Left.][98]

The resignations of a number of the Paris deputies followed that of Clémenceau. The letter which accompanied Delescluze's was not calculated to pacify the conservatives.

"To the citizen president of the assembly meeting at Versailles.

"Citizen,

"Having discontinued, eight days ago, taking part

[96] To enact such a law was, according to Tolain (the only member to speak against it in the Assembly) "purely and simply to organize civil war in France."

[97] "Journal Officiel de Versailles," March 29.

[98] *Ibid.*

in the deliberations of the Assembly over which you preside, in which Assembly I remained solely for the purpose of following the condemnation of the dictators of September 4th [protests from several benches] and not wishing to associate myself with its insanities and passions [exclamations] [voices—'This is insolence!'] I have the honor of notifying you of my resignation as representative of the people for the Department of the Seine.

"I add, that, honored by the votes of two arrondissements for the Commune of Paris, I accept this responsibility." [99]

Clémenceau and several of the representatives of the Seine, having resigned from the Assembly, proceeded to form the "Republican Union of the Rights of Paris," an association devoted to conciliation, in which end it proved as abortive as all the other attempts to spread the spirit of compromise.

Thiers announced to the country on the 28th that order had again been established at Lyons and Toulouse, the revolution was on the wane in Marseilles, Narbonne and St. Étienne and that, consequently, the attempts of Paris to encourage insurrection in the large cities of France had entirely failed. The elections in Paris, in his opinion, demonstrated that the party of order had deserted the Commune. "The whole of France was united behind this government, freely and legally elected." [100] There remained only the task of conquering by military force the small band of desperados in the capital.

CONCLUSION

Civil war was prepared; irreconcilable aims and an uncompromising behavior on both sides had made it in-

[99] "Journal Officiel de Versailles," April 1.
[100] Telegraphic dispatch reprinted in *Murailles,* II:131.

evitable. It required but a few days' time and the natural course of events to bring the National Guard of Paris and Thiers' renovated army to blows.

The ten days which elapsed from the 18th of March till the 28th, when the Commune was installed, saw a spontaneous and unorganized uprising taken in hand by a planless and incompetent committee. Unwilling and afraid to go ahead to overthrow the government, incapable of checking the movement for which it had assumed responsibility, the Central Committee was borne by the flow of events along a course which lay between revolution and legality. Since the program which it proposed to Versailles was obviously unacceptable, and since the moderation of these demands seemed impossible, even if desirable, in view of the pressure from behind, the Committee was faced with the alternative, either of using force or of shifting the responsibility. Rejecting the first it pinned its faith on the mythical and mystic Commune. Meanwhile sufficient time had elapsed to allow Thiers to rally his disorganized and dispirited troops and begin the formation of an army. The golden moment for revolutionary action had passed.

Thiers, in the face of an admittedly difficult but not impossible situation, had adopted a plan of attack without an adequate examination of his own resources or those of the opposition. The failure of this plan, assisted by incapable direction, was the signal for revolution. Whereupon the government of France, deserting its traditional capital, left Paris in the hands of what was certainly, on the 18th of March, a minority. Safe in Versailles, Thiers pursued the only policy which the intransigent behavior of the Assembly and that of Paris permitted; i.e., preparation for war. Meanwhile he sought to gain time by encouraging the plans of conciliation of the mayors and deputies of Paris.

The revolutionary uprising which had upset the calculations of M. Thiers drew its strength from the proletariat of Paris organized in the battalions of the National Guard.

It was socialist in neither its motivation nor its program. The incentive to insurrection, while undoubtedly influenced by the socialist and communist propaganda plentiful in Paris at the time, sprang chiefly from the events of the siege and the humiliations of the war. The program was primarily political and republican. In the minds of many, it is true, the Commune possessed a socialist significance, but before the 28th of March no content had been given to this symbol. It required the events of the next two months to give a meaning to the conception of the Commune.

CHAPTER IV

THE COMMUNE OF PARIS

THE election of the Commune Assembly, in bringing to an end the tentative period of negotiation, vacillation and uncertainty, gave body and substance to the revolution and determined the direction of its course. It ceased to be an uprising of the National Guard of Paris and became a political movement. Not that the Central Committee and other representatives of the citizen militia faded out of existence; on the contrary, the Committee continued to flourish and its activity in the administration of military resources was an ever-present source of annoyance to the Commune and the occasion of bitter debate and recrimination. But the National Guard henceforth was used as an instrument in the pursuance of a policy not of its own determination. The majority of the Assembly had little or no connection with the Guard at the outset and were brought in constant contact with it only because other interests of the Commune had to be subordinated to the defense of Paris.

All the important figures of the revolution belonged to the Commune or became prominent during the period of its administration. The program and policies with which the revolution is associated were formulated or modified by it or under its direction. No able man, it is true, was produced by the revolution or seriously shaped its course. Its policies and ends were vague and formless, to say the least. Nevertheless, what ideas and personalities the movement did contribute to history were associated with the events of the two months which elapsed between the inauguration of

the Assembly on the 28th of March and the final defeat of
the Communards in the recesses of Belleville on the 28th
of May. Between these dates the Commune governed
Paris, conducted the municipal administration, directed the
armed forces of the revolution and instituted a number of
economic and political reforms.

It is not the purpose of this and the following chapter
to record in detail the course of the military action between
Paris and Versailles, except in so far as the organization and
direction of the Commune's troops sheds light upon the
executive capacity of the new municipal assembly and its
methods of administration. As an episode in the history of
the socialist movement, if it were such, the importance of
the Commune lies in its reforms, its ideas and programs,
its organization, its legislative and executive capacity and
the means and sources from which it drew its following.
This was the first time since the beginning of the socialist
movement that a government in any sense socialist and
proletarian had held power. The character of this administration is then a matter of some importance.

Karl Marx, in writing on the Revolution of 1848, delivered himself of some sound advice on revolutionary tactics,
advice which the leaders of the Commune might have, but
did not follow. "Firstly, never play with insurrection unless
you are fully prepared to face the consequences of your
play. Insurrection is a calculus with very indefinite mag-
nitudes, the value of which may change every day; the forces
opposed to you have all the advantage of organization, discipline and habitual authority; unless you bring strong odds
against them you are defeated and ruined. Secondly, the
insurrectionary career once entered upon, act with the
greatest determination, and on the offensive. The defensive
is the death of every armed rising; it is lost before it measures itself with its enemies. Surprise your antagonists while
their forces are scattering, prepare new successes, however
small, but daily; keep up the moral ascendancy which the

first successful rising has given to you, rally those vacillating elements to your side which always follow the strongest impulse, and which always look out for the safer side; force your enemies to a retreat before they can collect their strength against you; in the words of Danton, the greatest master of revolutionary policy yet known, *de l'audace, de l'audace, encore de l'audace."* [1]

Such, however, was not the revolutionary policy of the Commune. When the enemy forces were scattering to Versailles, the revolution was hesitant in Paris; instead of acting on the offensive the Commune was always on the defensive and proud of the fact. Far from preparing every day a success, however, small, the military leaders of the Commune prepared every day a failure, however large, the succession of misfortunes continually increasing the difficulty of recruiting the revolutionary forces in Paris. Thus, the elements in the population which vacillated between Paris and Versailles at the outset drifted rapidly toward the latter party after the Commune reverses of April 2nd, 3rd and 4th.

The first encounter in the struggle between Paris and Versailles occurred on the morning of April 2nd in Courbevoie, a small village on one of the main roads to Versailles.[2] The insurgents, or Federals, as they were now called, had thrown up a few hastily constructed barricades against which the reorganized government troops directed their attack. The Commune Assembly was busily engaged in debating the question of freedom of conscience and the separation of church and state, unconcerned for the moment with military difficulties. The day was Sunday and the populace of Paris wandered in the suburbs oblivious to the imminence of war. The Commune generals, Bergeret, Eudes and Duval, in council, were considering the advis-

[1] *Revolution and Counter Revolution*, p. 120.
[2] Occasional shots had been exchanged between the sentinels and outposts for several days.

ability of an attack on Versailles, though no adequate
provisions had been made.

The question as to who was the aggressor in this opening
of hostilities, though a matter of inconsiderable importance,
has occupied at length historians of the Commune. The
facts seem to be that the Commune troops in reconnaissance
had thrown up light barricades in Courbevoie, Neuilly and
elsewhere. On the morning of April 2nd, at six o'clock,
Versaillese troops under the leadership of Vinoy set out to
take these defenses.[3] The chief surgeon, riding considerably
in advance of the troops, and mistaken by the insurgents
for a colonel of the gendarmerie, was shot by the National
Guard and the battle was on.[4] The first shot was fired by
the Commune but the first attack was planned and executed
by Versailles. The undisciplined and unorganized troops
under Rossel, later chief of the Commune forces, beat a
somewhat disordered retreat and Courbevoie was occupied
by the Versaillese.[5]

The effect of this news in Paris was profound. The
revolution aroused itself and demanded battle. Units of the
National Guard in all the arrondissements formed and
assembled to march at a moment's notice. At two o'clock

[3] Telegraphic dispatch of Thiers. April 2, 1871. Reprinted. *Murailles,*
II:157.
[4] It is interesting to note the reports of the government and the revolution
on this occasion.
    Thiers.—"The wretches whom France is reduced to fighting have com-
    mitted a new crime; the chief surgeon of the army, M. Pasquier, having
    advanced, alone and without arms, too close to the enemy positions, was
    unworthily assassinated."
Dispatch of April 2nd.
    Henri, Colonel of the General Staff under the Commune.—"Bergeret
    himself is at Neuilly. According to his report the enemy fire has ceased.
    Spirit of the troops excellent. Soldiers of the line arrive and declare
    that, except for the superior officers, no one wants to fight. Colonel of
    the gendarmerie who attacked was killed."
Murailles, II:156.
[5] Rossel thereupon attempted to weed out the incompetent officers in his
battalions and introduce the necessary discipline, but this immediately brought
him into conflict with the Arrondissement Committee of the National Guard
and he was taken to the Prefecture of Police to be locked up. Rossel, *Papiers
Posthumes,* p. 98.

in the afternoon Bergeret ordered a general summons and
by evening tens of thousands of the Commune troops were
assembled.[6] The executive commission of the Commune
published a bombastic and high-flown appeal to the National
Guard of Paris, beginning,

"The royalist conspirators have ATTACKED.

"In spite of the moderation of our attitude, they
have ATTACKED.

"Not being able to count any longer on the French
army, they have ATTACKED with the pontifical
zouaves and the imperial police." [7]

Meanwhile the hubbub, confusion and uproar were
increased by the revolutionary bands of women who performed the functions, says Lepelletier, one of the combatants, of a tragic chorus. "They lamented the victims, cried
for vengeance, stimulated courage, reawakened ardor, demanded the presence of men under arms, and ordered the
resumption of battle." [8]

In the evening General Cluseret, whose military prestige
was high in the radical quarters of Paris, was put in charge
of the Commune's army. This Cluseret, who during April
was general-in-chief of the revolution, is an interesting
example of the old-style, conspiratorial, secret-society socialist, who conspired through love of conspiracy, fought for
the sake of fighting and who embraced the cause of socialism
largely because his merits were, in his own eyes, inadequately
recognized elsewhere. As a henchman of Cavaignac he
attacked the barricades of 1848; he fought in the Crimea,
distinguished himself in Africa, joined the forces of Garibaldi in Sicily, became a general in the Northern forces

[6] A telegram (copy preserved in the Archives de la Seine) dated April 2,
2:15 P.M., makes it clear that the attack on Versailles of April 3rd
and 4th was the work of Bergeret, Eudes and Duval. They acted without
orders from the Commune and against the wishes of an important section
in the Assembly.
[7] *Murailles*, II:154.
[8] *Histoire de la Commune*, III:189.

during the American Civil War and led the Fenians in Ireland in the 1860's. Shortly afterwards he affiliated himself with the International and passed among the socialists of Paris as a misunderstood and unappreciated Napoleon during the Franco-Prussian War. Even the Republican government of September 4th could find no place for this doughty warrior worthy of his capacity, so France was left without the service of his arm. As he himself has said, "What I saw was that the government had no place for the only Republican general in France." [9] In consequence he occupied himself with stirring up revolution in Lyons and Marseilles and, as one of the leaders of the League of the South, helped to establish in the latter city a short-lived revolutionary Commune.

Cluseret had been put in charge of the Commune's troops before the advance on Versailles of April 3rd, but it is doubtful whether he, or any one else, could have checked this unprepared, foolishly directed but impetuous attack. The Revolution demanded blood and its generals, Eudes, Duval and Bergeret, were too ignorant and inexperienced to foresee that, with such an unorganized and undisciplined rabble, this blood would not flow from the Versaillese.

It was a mob rather than an army which marched out of Paris in the early morning of April 3rd, and a mob in a festive mood. The memory of the easy victory of March 18th was still warm in the minds of the National Guard. The regular army had fraternized with the citizens of Paris on that occasion; would they not do the same again? The Versaillese troops contained, it is true, a few hundred imperial police and perhaps a few thousand "Papal zouaves" and "Breton fanatics" but, after these had been scattered, the soldiers from the provinces would not fire on their brothers from Paris. Artillery was left behind, provisions were neglected and the units of the National Guard ad-

[9] Cluseret, *The Paris Commune of 1871,* "Fraser's Magazine," March, 1873, p. 368.

vanced without ambulance or medical services. The merry soldiers of the Commune broke ranks frequently and, far from maintaining the silence expected in an approach on the enemy, filled the air with song and laughter. "One would have said," remarks Lepelletier, "that it was a band of turbulent pic-nickers, setting out gayly and uncertainly for the country, rather than an attacking column directing itself toward a formidable position." [10]

The army, divided into three parts, intended to proceed toward Versailles by three routes. The troops commanded by Bergeret and Flourens, advancing to the west and northwest, took a route which passed beneath the guns of Mont Valérien. Duval commanded the southern division and Eudes the southwestern. Through an oversight, inexplicable and unexcusable, the Commune, the Executive Committee, and the three generals had all neglected to take account of the fortress of Mont Valérien, abandoned by Thiers on the 19th but unoccupied by the revolution owing to the stupidity of Lullier. The fortress had been reoccupied by the Versaillese on March 20th upon the insistence of Vinoy and was now restocked and revictualed for defense. How Bergeret and his colleagues could have imagined Mont Valérien as favorable to the Commune, or at least neutral, exceeds the power of understanding.[11] Nevertheless this appears to

---

[10] *Histoire de la Commune,* III:231.

[11] When summoned to surrender on the 20th, the commander of Mont Valérien had replied that he would take orders only from the ministry of war, but that he would never fire on Paris. See Lanjalley and Corriez. *Op. cit.,* p. 188. Nevertheless, the Federals appear to have contemplated an attack on the fort, doubting its neutrality. A telegram said to have been found on the body of a telegraph officer, a copy of which is preserved at the Archives de la Seine, reads:

Police 5h. 10. (Date without doubt is April 2.)
Urgence.
Police à Guerre et Place.
J'expédie 2 hommes sûrs l'un du pays et une clef de poterne du fort du Mt. Valérien.
Nous préparons expédition nocturne sans bruit en avant quelques hommes résolus et dévoués soutenus par détachements échelonnés. Prévenir Bergeret si possible.

Pour copie

à Mallet.

178   THE PARIS COMMUNE

have been the belief of the Commune's generals and it was certainly the belief of the citizens of Paris.

When the division led by Bergeret and Flourens came abreast of Mont Valérien, the fortress, quite naturally, opened fire. The National Guard, completely taken by surprise, cried treason and fled along the road in both directions. The column was cut in two, one part returning to Paris and the other, more disorganized than before, if possible, pressing on toward Versailles. Bergeret and Flourens managed to effect a junction and attain Bougival, only six kilometers from Versailles, but the resistance they afforded to the regular army was short and the road back to Paris was filled during the night of April 3rd with Commune troops retreating in the utmost confusion.[12] Nor were the divisions under Eudes and Duval more successful. Eudes in the center and Duval on the left wing, although carrying on their skirmishes with the enemy for two days, were decisively defeated. Duval and fifteen hundred of his men fell into the hands of the Versaillese. The revolutionary enthusiasm of the Commune troops was no compensation for their inexperience, nor did it withstand successfully two sleepless nights and the incapacity of their commanders.

Certain of the Communards taken prisoner and recognized, or supposed to have been recognized, as deserters from the army were shot on the spot. In addition Vinoy,

---

[12] Bergeret puts the blame for his failure on the state of his troops. Telegram preserved at Archives de la Seine:

1 h 20 m.
de matin
4 avril.

Place à Commune et guerre.
minuit 10. En ce qui me concerne j'ai fait prudemment replier le peu d'hommes qui me restaient, sur Neuilly qui par mes ordres est formidablement fortifié.

Il était impossible de rester plus longtemps à Asnières avec des hommes indisciplinés, ivres et dépourvus de leurs chefs lesquels les ont abandonnés depuis ce matin.

Sans discipline pas de soldats, avec l'élection actuelle pas de chefs.

Rien n'est compromis, loin de là, mais il faut d'abord relever le moral par de bonnes mesures et recommencer dans de meilleures conditions.

Général Jules Bergeret.

in cold blood, ordered Duval and his chief of staff executed. Although the Versaillese and their apologists have denied this execution, it is clear from the evidence of Colonel Lambert of the government forces, himself an eye-witness, that this is what happened.[13] On this and other occasions the forces of Thiers treated their prisoners in a manner they would never have dared to treat the Prussians. The Official Committee of Enquiry, while viewing with horror the "terrible law of the hostages," under color of which the Commune executed its prisoners, says nothing about the shooting of prisoners by the Versaillese.[14]

Thiers repeatedly denied the execution of prisoners and in reply to a protest of Monsignor Darboy, Archbishop of Paris, pointed to the large number of prisoners held in Versailles as evidence of his assertion. When the International Society condemned this violation of the convention of Geneva, Thiers retorted that, "The Commune not having adhered to the convention of Geneva, the government at Versailles is not compelled to observe it." [15] The only admission of these executions which emanated from Versailles was contained in Thiers' succinct statement, "Some men recognized as belonging to the army and seized with arms in their hands, have been shot according to the rigor of military law which condemns soldiers fighting their own flag." [16] The extreme improbability that any recognition of this sort preceded the shootings of April 4th, led to the protest of Paris papers not generally favorable to the Commune.[17]

It also led directly to the seizure of the hostages who

[13] *Enquête*, p. 572.
[14] *Ibid.*, p. 58.
[15] "Journal Officiel de la Commune," May 13. The Commune thereupon declared its adherence.
[16] "Journal Officiel" (Versailles), April 6. General Gallifet, in a proclamation of April 3rd, refers to the executions ordered by himself as follows: "I declare a war without truce and without pity on these assassins. It was necessary to make an example this morning; let us hope it was salutary; I do not wish again to be reduced to such an extremity."
[17] For example, "Le Siècle," April 7.

were later miserably shot during the last frenzy of the
Commune, in the bloody killings of the rue Haxo. The
Executive Committee aroused the people of Paris with a
proclamation beginning, "The monarchists sitting at Versailles are not making upon you a war of civilized men;
they are making a war of savages.

"The Vendéens of Charette, the agents of Piétri, *shoot
their prisoners, throttle the wounded and fire on
ambulances.*" [18]

This exaggerated tone is continued in another manifesto
of the Commune itself.

> "Every day, the bandits of Versailles throttle or
> shoot our prisoners, and not an hour goes by without
> bringing us news of one of these assassinations. The
> criminals, you know them; they are the gendarmes and
> the imperial police, they are the royalists of Charette
> and Cathelineau, who march against Paris to the cry
> of 'Vive le roi!' white banner at their head.
>
> "The government of Versailles has put itself outside
> the laws of war and of humanity; it will be necessary
> to use reprisals.
>
> "If, continuing to ignore the conditions customary in
> war between civilized peoples, our enemies massacre
> one more of our soldiers, we shall reply with the ex-
> ecution of the same or a double number of our own
> prisoners." [19]

The lack of prisoners taken in battle was easily remedied
by the seizure of prominent civilians in Paris sympathetic
to the cause of Versailles.

The expedition of the 3rd and 4th of April, inadequately
prepared and unskillfully executed by an inexperienced
soldiery led by commanders on the whole incapable, suffered heavy losses in killed, wounded and captured. In
addition it cost the Commune Duval and Flourens, two of

[18] *Murailles,* II:176, April 4.   [19] *Ibid.,* II:179, April 5.

its most energetic leaders and fiery revolutionaries. Duval was a prominent member of the International and Flourens probably the most popular and influential figure in the revolutionary ranks.

Its effect in Paris was even more serious to the cause of the Commune. The lukewarm supporters of the revolution, shifting sides with the tide of battle, began to swerve in the direction of Versailles. The change in tone was evident in a number of the newspapers which had welcomed the 18th of March.[20] Furthermore, although it should have been obvious that the sole chance for success lay in carrying the battle to Versailles while the forces of the government were still comparatively weak, the defeats of April 3rd and 4th strengthened that element in the Commune which wished to confine military operations to the defense of Paris. Lefrançais had already resigned from the Executive Commission because of his opposition to the aggressive tactics of the majority, and the unfortunate issue at Mont Valérien and elsewhere offered a certain justification for his position. Finally, the confidence of the rank and file in its leaders was profoundly shaken. However legitimate this distrust might have been, it did not increase the verve and esprit of the revolutionary forces. "Le Père Duchêne," which had rapidly become the most popular revolutionary paper in Paris, appeared on 17th Germinal (April 7th) with an attack on those members of the Commune responsible for the appointment of incapable commanders, and the demand for the immediate establishment of a Committee of Public Safety.[21]

Bereft of its confidence in the military capacity of popular leaders, the Commune now pinned its faith on a man of the trade, Cluseret, who, although appointed on April 2nd, took command of its forces only after the 4th of April.

[20] See "Le Siècle," April 7. "A number of papers which associated themselves with the Commune rather frankly a couple of weeks ago are now rejoicing at the victories of Versailles."
[21] "Père Duchêne" in common with a number of other Commune publications followed the revolutionary calendar.

One of his first acts was to cashier General Bergeret, who had so strangely overlooked Mont Valérien. Bergeret was promptly imprisoned by order of the Commune Assembly for military incapacity and insubordination. The military leaders of the Commune acquired the habit of capping their periods of command with a period of enforced meditation in the municipal jails. Cluseret followed Bergeret, and Rossel, Cluseret's successor to the supreme command, escaped this fate only by hiding in the suburbs.

Despite the military promise of Cluseret, the destiny of the revolution was determined by the battles of the 3rd and 4th of April. French prisoners released by the Germans at the solicitations of Thiers were swelling the ranks at Versailles. The government troops were inspirited by their successes and the forces of the Commune proportionately depressed by their defeats. It became now a question only of how long the revolution could hold out against an increasingly superior enemy. Nevertheless the leaders of the Commune refused to face the facts. A telegram to the Communal Assembly on the 3rd of April had announced that the forces of Bergeret were already in Versailles, and this is typical of the optimism of the leaders of the revolution during the course of the siege.[22] Victory after victory was announced in the face of accumulating disaster and not until after the actual entrance of the government forces into Paris, apparently, did the Commune admit the possibility of defeat.

THE COMMUNAL ASSEMBLY

The Communal Assembly which met for the first time on the 28th of March and which was to govern Paris for the next two months was, like most elective bodies, a heteroge-

[22] Copy of the telegram to be found at the Archives de la Seine:
  Place à Commune, Guerre et Interieur.
  Plusieurs artilleurs arrivent et affirment que nous sommes à et dans Versailles, et Valérien cerné. Attendez confirmation avant annoncer.
                                                                Henri.

neous affair, embracing a wide diversity of political beliefs, social position, and economic employment. It was neither consistently socialist nor proletarian. It contained one or two artists of significance, one or two authors, a lawyer, a few men of wealth and position, a few members of the petite bourgeoisie, a large group of journalists and a considerable sprinkling of working men. The amorphous and indistinct substance of the Commune, its vague yearnings, violent verbosities and general lack of a coherent and tangible program were well reflected in its Assembly. For the most part, the citizens of Paris elected the candidates recommended by the "Conseils de Légion" of the National Guard and by the republican and socialist arrondissement committees. Since these organizations agreed on very little except their opposition to the government of Thiers, their representatives possessed to a very small degree that community of interest and policy required by the situation.

There were 9 Blanquists, including Blanqui, who was himself elected in two arrondissements despite the fact that he was at the time forcibly detained by the emissaries of Thiers in the South of France.[23] The International counted 17 representatives but failed to form a definite and important unit in the assembly.[24] Its members divided on several significant questions as did, for that matter, the Blanquists. There were 15 moderate republicans, most of them former officials of the municipality, all of whom resigned from the Commune within the first few days of its existence.[25] Six radical republicans with leanings toward Gambetta resigned before the tenth of April.[26] The remainder of the 85 members of the Communal Assembly

[23] Tridon, Duval, Rigault, Eudes, Protot, Chardon, Ferré, Miot and Blanqui.
[24] The representatives of the International were: Pindy, Lefrançais, Clémence, Gérardin, Beslay, Varlin, Vaillant, Champy, Babick, Assi, Avrial, Thiéry, Fränkel, Clément, Langevin, Chalain and Malon.
[25] Adam, Rochart, Méline, Barré, Brelay, Tirard, Chéron, Loiseau-Pinson, Leroy, Ferry, Murat, Mast, Desmarest, Dr. Marmottan and Bouteiller.
[26] Goupil, Robinet, Lefèvre, Ranc, Parent and Fruneau.

were in the main revolutionaries of a wide variety of complexion. Jacobins such as Delescluze and Cournet mingled
with tentative and provisional socialists such as Vermorel
and Arthur Arnould. However, after the withdrawal of
the 21 moderate and radical republicans, the assembly was
pretty consistently socialist and rather strongly revolutionary. Most of the remaining members had ideas, however
indefinite, on the inadequacy of the "bourgeois" order, and
conceptions, however little in agreement, of a desirable and
radically altered society of the future.

The wealthy, bourgeois sections of Paris returned the
moderate republicans who resigned almost immediately. On
the first day after the elections the 1st and 2nd Arrondissements (Louvre and Bourse), were deprived of all their
representatives. The 9th Arrondissement (l'Opéra) lost
its membership almost as rapidly, as did the 16th (Passy).
In addition three of the five members of the 6th (Luxembourg) resigned before the 10th of April. The populous
and proletarian arrondissements of the Panthéon, Popin-
court, Gobelins, Batignolles-Monceau, Buttes-Montmarte,
Buttes-Chaumont, and Ménilmontant, returned revolutionary socialists. These were the representatives who remained
in the Assembly to rule the Commune.

The "démissionnaires" were in the main well-known
political figures most of whom had been prominent in republican circles during the Empire. The 64 who remained to
constitute the Commune, on the other hand, were for the
most part new to government and unpracticed in politics.
A small number, among them Delescluze, Pyat and Tridon,
had been elected to the National Assembly, and 7 or 8 more,
among them Ranvier, Lefrançais, Miot and Malon, had
been connected with the municipal administration after the
4th of September and during the siege of Paris; nevertheless, it remains true that the Communal Assembly was
untried in the business of government. Its members had
been elected to represent the people on the basis of their

activities in the clubs, in the International and, in particular, in connection with the radical journals antagonistic to the Empire. Thirteen had already achieved a certain prominence as members of the Central Committee.[27] Twenty-one enjoyed a local notoriety as familiar and habitual orators in the political clubs, established since 1868, and particularly active during the siege.[28]

The majority of the permanent members of the Commune were from the professions, journalism in particular, but there was a large sprinkling of working men; large enough to give this assembly an economic composition new in the history of European politics.[29] It cannot be said, however, that this representation of the proletariat had any significant effect upon the acts and policies of the Commune. On important questions the working-class members divided in much the same manner as did their colleagues.[30] The majority and minority parties into which the Commune soon split had about equal proportions of working men and "bourgeoisie." The divisions in the Assembly, numerous enough on other grounds, were never determined by differences in class or employment.

An analysis of the membership of the Commune ought not to be concluded without consideration of a fact of some interest and, perhaps of some importance; i.e., the difference in ages between the men of Paris and the men of Versailles. In the government of France, at this time, there was not a man under fifty, and its two most important members,

[27] Bergeret, Ranvier, Billioray, Henri Fortuné, Babick, Geresme, Eudes, Jourde, Blanchet, Brunel, Clovis Dupont, Mortier and Antoine Arnaud.
[28] Amouroux, Jules Allix, Champy, Émile Clément, Demay, Charles Gérardin, Goupil, Ledroit, Lefèvre, Leo Meillet, Martelet, Ostyn, Oudet, Puget, Régère, Rastoul, Urbain, Ulysse Parent, Fruneau, Parisel, and Descamps. From Malon, *Troisième Défaite du Prolétariat F.*, p. 135.
[29] There were 23 members of the Assembly who could be called working men: Avrial, Amouroux, Assi, Bergeret, Varlin, Dereure, Clovis Dupont, Durand, Gérardin, Geresme, Victor Clément, Clémence, Langevin, Malon, Ostyn, Pindy, Régère, Theisz, Fränkel, Chalain, Champy, Chardon, and Eudes.
[30] See Arnould, *La Commune*, II, p. 86.

Thiers and Dufaure, were respectively, 74 and 73.[31] On the other hand the Commune was made up of comparatively young men. Beslay it is true was 75, Delescluze 62 and Blanqui 66, to mention its oldest members. But Beslay was a person of little importance in the municipal assembly and Blanqui was not in attendance. The ages of the first executive committee were as follows: Bergeret 38, Eudes 27, Duval 30, Lefrançais 45; Pyat 61, Tridon 30, and Vaillant 30. This is a pretty fair indication of the age distribution of the Commune as a whole. The composition of the first Committee of Public Safety illustrated the same fact. The ages of its members were: Antoine Arnaud 30, Leo Meillet 29, Ranvier 54, Pyat 61, and Charles Gérardin 26.

The Communal Assembly was then, speaking generally, a body of young men, inexperienced in politics, pretty strongly revolutionary and socialist, composed largely of laboring men and radical journalists who had made their way into the public eye by their oratorical activities in the political clubs and their journalistic efforts against the Empire and the government of September 4th. It was a body without a program, without unity of purpose, and without both the capacity and the opportunity to produce either the one or the other. Although composed of men of more ability than those of the Central Committee, it exhibited almost as much indecision as the Committee. The revolution drifted on following pretty much its own course, carrying the Commune along and molding rather than being molded by it. The Assembly was distinguished by many and vigorous talkers but produced few men of action.

The first three or four days of its existence were passed in verifying election returns, appointing commissions to take over the services abandoned by Versailles and in discussing the scope and limitations of the Commune's authority. The military preparations of Versailles were ignored and, within

[31] The ages of the members of Thier's government were as follows: Thiers 74, Dufaure 72, Barthelémy-Saint-Hilaire 71, de Larcy 66, Jules Favre 65, V. le Franc 62, General de Cissey 59, Admiral Pothuau 57, Jules Simon, 56, Poyer-Quertier 54, Lambrecht 53.

the Assembly itself, nothing was said regarding the advisability of an attack on the government. It appeared to be the consensus of opinion that a policy of watchful waiting and legitimate defense was the only one conceivable in the situation. The Commune waited for Versailles to put itself in the wrong by an armed attack on the city justly defending its rightful franchises.

The skirmish of April 2nd and the battles of April 3rd and 4th answered a number of questions which the Assembly had been unable to decide for itself. The Commune at once assumed an aggressive attitude, issued manifestos right and left, published decrees and, forced by events, made some little progress in defining its own functions. With a grave formality, scarcely less stupid than silly and impotent, it declared the leading members of the national government criminals and sequestrated their property in Paris pending their appearance before "the justice of the People." This decree began—

> "Considering that the men of the government of Versailles have ordered and commenced civil war, attacked Paris, killed and wounded National Guardsmen, soldiers of the line, women and children;
>
> "Considering that this crime has been committed after premeditation and wilfully, contrary to all justice and without provocation,
>
> "It is decreed,
>
> "Act 1. MM. Thiers, Favre, Picard, Dufaure, Simon and Pothuau are legally accused," [32] etc.

Attempts at conciliation by intermediaries in Paris were indignantly prohibited by the Executive Commission.

> "Reaction assumes all guises: to-day it is that of conciliation.
>
> "Conciliation with the 'chouans' and 'mouchards'

[32] Decree of the Executive Committee, April 6th, forbidding a public assembly held to discuss the question of arbitration. Reprinted in *Murailles,* II:197.

who throttle our generals and kill our disarmed prisoners!

"Conciliation under such circumstances is treason."

Pointing to the Communal uprising in Limoges, Guéret, la Nièvre and Vierzon, the Executive Commission assured Paris that Thiers' appeal to the provinces for help would meet not only with refusal but with general rebellion against the "gendarmes of Versailles."

"If Paris continues to do its duty, if it is as constant as it has been brave, then an end will be put to this civil war and its culpable authors." [33]

Driven to battle the Commune accepted the challenge and turned its attention to the defense of Paris. External events defined its immediate interests and limited the scope of its activity.

Nevertheless a beginning was made at civil legislation in an attempt to right the wrongs inflicted on Paris by the government of Bordeaux and Versailles. A proclamation of March 30th announced to the citizens of Paris,

"You are masters of your destiny. Strong in your support, the representation which you have just established is going to repair the disasters brought about by the authority now fallen; industry hampered, work suspended, the paralyzed municipal affairs are now going to be vigorously taken in hand.

"To-day, the expected decision affecting rents.

"To-morrow that regarding the maturities;

"All public services reestablished and simplified;

"The National Guard, henceforth the sole armed force of the city, reorganized without delay.

"Such will be our first acts." [34]

[33] Manifesto of the Executive Committee, April 7th. See *Murailles,* II:216.
[34] "Journal Officiel de la Commune," March 30.

In conformity with this proclamation the Commune published at the same time a decree remitting to tenants all rents for the terms of October, 1870, and January and April, 1871. Any sums paid as rent for these nine months were applicable against future charges and no tenant could be evicted against his will for a period of three months."[35] Another decree, enacted at the same time, forbade the further sale of deposited articles by the pawnshops of Paris.[36] The employees of the public services were ordered to ignore any communication or direction emanating from Versailles under penalty of discharge.[37] The Commune took into its own hands the administration of affairs and proceeded to satisfy the particular grievances of Paris against the legislation enacted at Bordeaux.

The Commune proceeded, as a matter of fact, much further than an exclusive concern with the business of the municipality could justify. A decree of March 29th abolished conscription and enacted that no armed force other than the National Guard could ever be created in or brought into Paris.[38] Furthermore, on April 2nd, amid the applause of the radical papers of Paris, the Commune announced the separation of church and state.[39] In the words of Félix Pyat, member of the Executive Commission of the Commune and editor of "Le Vengeur," "Yesterday we witnessed two great acts of justice and self-preservation!

"The Commune accuses the culprits of Versailles.

"The Commune separates church and state.

"If these are national rather than local questions, that

---

[35] "Journal Officiel de la Commune," March 30.
[36] Ibid.   [38] Ibid.
[37] Ibid.   [39] Ibid., April 3.
   "Whereas the first of the principles of the French Republic is liberty;
   "Whereas liberty of conscience is the most important of liberties;
   "Whereas the religious budget is contrary to this principle, since it taxes citizens against their own faith;
   "Whereas, in fact, the clergy has been an accomplice in the crime of the monarchy against liberty,
   "Therefore, it is decreed," etc.

is the fault of Versailles. Versailles wants an enslaved Paris
in an enslaved France. The Commune wants "a free Paris
in a free France." [40]

It has often been maintained by partisans of the Commune that its interference in national affairs was necessitated
by the policy of the government of Versailles. The demand
of Thiers, for example, that all government employees in
Paris leave their posts under penalty of permanent discharge, made it necessary for the Commune to perform the
functions of government. As Lefrançais put it, "This decision of Versailles forced us to step out of the limitations we
had first drawn and obliged us to put our noses into affairs
of state." [41] Of course, this is to a certain extent true. The
withdrawal of government officials to Versailles obliged the
Commune to take over the administration of the national
museums, libraries, schools, telegraph and postal service,
and the like, but it hardly explains the decrees on the questions of church and state and of conscription.

The delegate to the official journal, discussing this matter, declared that "to consider the sole end of the revolution
of March 18th to be the establishment in Paris of an elected
municipal body under the despotic tutelage of a highly centralized administration, is a strange and puerile illusion. . . .
It is, as we have said from the first day, to conquer and to
assure in the future, independence to all the communes of
France, and also to all the higher groups, cantons, departments or provinces, linked with one another by a truly
national agreement; it is, at the same time, to guarantee
and to perpetuate a republic finally established on its basic
foundation, that the men of the 18th of March have fought
and conquered." [42]

This was the opinion of Longuet who thus expressed his
ideas on decentralization inherited from Proudhon.

[40] "Le Vengeur," April 4.
[41] *Souvenirs d'un Révolutionnaire,* p. 489.
[42] "Journal Officiel," April 1. Longuet.

Whether or not they would have met with general assent from the Commune, it is obvious from the decrees of the Assembly and its discussion that its ideas of the proper sphere of municipal autonomy were widely divergent from those of the National Assembly. The scope of municipal autonomy would have to be wide indeed to include the legislation on the army and on church and state which came from the Commune in the first few days of March.

The so-called decree of the hostages, which eventually led to the massacres of May 25th and 26th, was enacted at about this time under stress of the news of the defeats of April 3rd and 4th. The Commune in its evening session of April 4th was informed by a member, Chardon, who had taken part in the fighting, of the shooting of Duval. "Cries of anger and vengeance break out. Everyone is standing. It is necessary to avenge them. . . . It is necessary to take reprisals, to do some shooting ourselves. Propositions of the most violent sort were pressed. Rigault wants to shoot the archbishop, arrested the evening before and now imprisoned at Mazas, and to shoot with him the curés and Jesuits arrested at the same time. 'We must open the prisons to the people, who will make their own justice,' cried some one." [43]

The next day the Commune decreed that anyone suspected of complicity with Versailles should be imprisoned as a hostage and that "Any execution of a prisoner of war or of a partisan of the regular government of Paris will be immediately followed by the execution of three times as many of the hostages." . . . [44]

During the next two months several hundred priests, former gendarmes and members of the regular army living in Paris were incarcerated on the charge of complicity, in the prisons of the metropolis.

[43] Account of Maxime Vuillaume, reported to him by Protot, a member of the Commune. Vuillaume, *Mes Cahiers Rouges,* VIII. *Cahiers de la Quinzaine.* 11th Cahier. 13th Series, p. 164.
[44] "Journal Officiel," April 6.

The Administration of the Commune

The Communal Assembly was faced at the outset with administrative problems of considerable magnitude. The division of Paris into arrondissements necessitated the appointment of twenty sets of local officials who were to be chiefly occupied during the next two months with administering relief, helping with the recruiting and equipment of troops, and disbursing pensions promised by the Commune, in addition to their responsibility of popularizing the revolution with the citizenry of the metropolis. Immediately upon the convocation of the Commune the administration of the arrondissements was entrusted to the newly elected representatives, each group being responsible for the section which had returned it to the Assembly.[45] This imposed upon the members of the Commune the double task of legislator and mayor. The numerous executive commissions into which the Commune divided itself provided another occupation for most of the members of the Assembly. They were legislators, ministers of state, and municipal officials rolled into one. In consequence, all responsibilities tended to be neglected. We find the Commune complaining on occasion of the absence of representatives from the debate, these representatives being engaged at the time on a problem of city government or occupied in a session of one of the committees. At other times we discover a member of the Assembly complaining that the Executive or War Committee is making decisions which belong properly to the province of the Commune, and that none of the members of the committee is present to answer the charge.

At the same time it was a familiar criticism that the various administrative committees were composed of men unfamiliar with the technical problems which faced these committees. Moreover, the time necessary to acquaint themselves with the problems was lacking because of the

[45] March 30th.

demands of the Commune, which met daily and often twice a day. Similarly, in many of the arrondissements, claims for pensions and redress piled up unheeded, the administrative organization was disordered and disrupted and the whereabouts of those in charge were often undiscoverable because of the conflict of other duties.

It is impossible, however, to consider adequately the question of the administration of the Commune. The evidence we possess is scanty in the extreme. The commissions appointed by the Commune left no, or very meager, records, the reports of observers are ludicrously contradictory, and circumstances over which the Commune had no control oftentimes created a situation such that it is impossible to tell good administration from bad. What we can say, nevertheless, is, in the first place, that the administrative organization of the Commune was defective and ill conceived; in the second place, that the Commune as a legislative body light-heartedly undertook responsibilities which the Commune as an executive could not fulfill; in the third place, that certain feasible administrative tasks were badly performed; and, in the fourth place, in one or two arrondissements, authority was placed in the hands of egregiously incompetent officials. It is equally certain that the admittedly difficult circumstances in which the Commune was placed do not satisfactorily explain its weaknesses. The fault lay in the men and the machinery rather than in the circumstances.

The Assembly appointed its executive committees on the 26th of March and designated sixty-one of the representatives, practically the whole of its personnel, as members.[46] The committees formed were the Executive, Finances, Military, Justice, General Safety, Supplies, Labor-Industry-Trade, External Relations, Public Services and Instruction. Except for the Ministry of Cults which was suppressed, these commissions resembled too closely the organization of

[46] Five or six were members of two committees.

ministries under the government of France not to suggest that the Commune was stepping outside the limitations of purely municipal functions. Certain of these committees appear to have remained for the most part inactive.[47] Another, the committee on External Relations, limited itself to issuing high-flown, but ineffective, appeals to the provinces. The others were active in greater or lesser degree and ofttimes came into conflict with each other and the Commune. The Commune never defined accurately the authority of any of these auxiliary bodies and consequently it depended in large part on the aggressiveness and obstinacy of their respective members.

The chief of the Committee of General Safety, (Sûreté Générale) Raoul Rigault, was a particularly headstrong and stubborn executive and consequently came frequently into conflict not only with the directors of other committees but with the Commune itself. As his old master Blanqui described him, Rigault was a natural-born police detective. He gathered about him at the Prefecture of Police a large number of the young Blanquists of Paris and terrorized not only the foes of the Commune but ofttimes its friends. From the first of April on he was in frequent conflicts of jurisdiction and authority with Protot, the head of the Committee of Justice.

The police was constituted in many respects as an independent power, ignoring at will the orders of the courts.[48] Rigault and his assistants, twenty-year-old scoundrels, as Cluseret called them, made arrests right and left, locked up

[47] The Commission of Supplies, the Commission of Public Services and the Commission of Education. Lissagaray, *History of the Commune of 1871*, English translation by Eleanor Marx Aveling (London, 1886), p. 217, says of the first two that they required merely good will. The regular personnel remained at work and there was little for the delegates to do. Paris was supplied through the neutral zone, which could not be prevented by Thiers.

[48] Laronze, *La Commune* (Paris, 1928), pp. 249-250, cites examples of Rigault's refusal to validate the orders of the Commission of Justice and concludes, "Once again the principle that in revolution the last word is to the most violent is confirmed."

prisoners in solitary confinement, and often refused to examine them until long after their arrest. In the session of the Commune on April 5th, Delescluze demanded that measures be taken against the encroachments of power of the Committee of Public Safety and Lefrançais asked for an official disavowal by the Commune of the acts of this Committee and the replacement of its chief.[49] Again, the Prefecture of Police came into conflict with the Executive Committee over the appointment of a new member, Viard, to the Committee of General Safety. Tridon, a member of the Executive Committee, in defending this appointment, said, "We have received so many complaints of the complete disorganization which reigns in the ex-Prefecture of Police, that it is impossible not to take some action to remedy this state of affairs." [50]

The abolition of the Prefecture of Police had been one of the most pressing demands of the revolutionaries during the siege. Rigault met this demand by calling it the ex-Prefecture. However, the ex-Prefecture strikingly resembled the Prefecture except in its personnel. Rigault left unaltered the organization of the imperial police, though it was quite impossible for the Commune to staff such an organization.[51]

Surprisingly good order, however, was maintained in Paris during April and May; on this matter all but the more reactionary observers agree.[52] But it was in spite of and not because of the police. The number of arrests was far above the normal. From the 29th of March to the 23rd of May, 3,201 were incarcerated although two-thirds were

[49] *Procès-Verbaux de la Commune,* p. 124. Cf. Ch. IV, p. 72, Note 1, supra.

[50] *Procès-Verbaux de la Commune,* p. 268, April 18.

[51] Gaston Da Costa, *op. cit.,* II :220.

[52] Edmond de Pressensé, *Les Leçons du 18 Mars,* p. 127, who is decidedly unsympathetic with the Commune, has this to say about it: "Let us recognize, to the honor of the population of Paris, that, during this time of social anarchy, the streets have been as safe by night as by day, theft has been rare and that the unruly element which mingled with the population has been more or less restrained."

released after a short imprisonment.[53] The Executive Committee asserted on April 6, that the streets of Paris had never been so tranquil. "For three weeks not a theft has been committed, nor an attempt at assassination." Socialist and communist authors are accustomed to assert that the situation during the Commune was one of idyllic peace and security. This is not true. Arrests for infraction of the common law increased.[54] Nevertheless, under the circumstances the population of Paris remained surprisingly law-abiding.

The major part of the arrests were for political reasons and many of those arrested were imprisoned upon no definite charge. The law of the hostages gave Rigault, who as we have seen was intensely anticlerical, an opportunity of imprisoning priests on a large scale, which duties he performed with great relish. When it was observed on the floor of the Commune that priests, uninterested in politics, could not be considered serious hostages, Rigault replied that he considered them to be agents of a very dangerous propaganda.[55] One of the preoccupations of Rigault in his wholesale seizure of the clergy was undoubtedly his hope of exchanging these hostages for Blanqui, a hope which was never realized.

The police were assisted in their attempts to preserve order by the National Guard, whose members acted frequently but not always well. On April 21st, a battalion visited the offices of the municipal gas company and made off with 183,000 francs which were returned only upon the insistence of the Commune.[56] A little before another group had occasioned considerable embarrassment by raiding the

[53] Maxime Du Camp obtained these figures from an examination of the police registers. They are attested by Laronze, *op. cit.*, pp. 334-335, who has made a special study of the departments of Justice and the Police under the Commune.
[54] Laronze, *op. cit.*, p. 335.
[55] *Procès-Verbaux*, p. 148, April 8.
[56] A description of the incident appears in the "Journal Officiel," April 24.

Belgian consulate.[57] In spite of various attempts of the Commune to regularize the situation, the police service in Paris during April and May was in a state bordering upon anarchy.

The continued opposition of the Commune led to the resignation of Rigault, April 24th. The Assembly, scandalized by the methods of the Prefect of Police, had voted the previous day that any member might visit prisoners and examine the reasons for their incarceration.[58] Rigault's resignation, however, did not mean his disappearance from the scene. He became Prosecutor (Procureur), a post held under the first Commune by his hero Chaumette. And Cournet, the new Prefect, lasted only until the 13th of May when Rigault secured the appointment of his henchman, Ferré.

Rigault and his friend Ferré, both Blanquists and both delegates at the Prefecture of Police, were probably the most detested figures of the Revolution. In Versailles these were names with which to frighten little children. Rigault was shot by the Versaillese on May 24th, on the Boulevard Saint-Michel, in the midst of his old haunts of the Latin Quarter, and with the universal applause of the adherents of "law and order" ringing in his ears. Ferré was captured, tried and executed a few months later. "Fortune is capricious; I confide to the future the care of my memory and of my vengeance," wrote Ferré and died with a "Vive la Commune" on his lips. As Maxime Du Camp, the conservative historian of the Commune, has it, "they represented the sottishness, the crudity, the vanity, the cruelty, the ignorance and the debauchery of the Revolution; these two

[57] "Journal Officiel," April 17.

[58] When Arnould protested in the Commune against secret imprisonment, against which the revolutionaries had always protested under the Empire, and described it as immoral, Rigault replied, "War also is immoral and yet we are fighting." After tendering his resignation he is reported to have said to Arnould, "My dear fellow, the happiest day of my life will be that on which I arrest you." See Fiaux, *op. cit.,* p. 300.

imitators of the Terror did an incalculable amount of harm by continually exciting the mass of dreamers to excesses." [59] They died like true revolutionaries without recantation and without regret.

Rigault, Ferré and their following were hated almost as much by the moderate party in the Commune as by their enemies at Versailles. Arnould, who represents this point of view, called the military and police administration the weakest points in the Commune. Rigault and Ferré were not the right men. "From the political point of view . . . they were the most conspicuous among those who completely misunderstood the particular and original character of the Commune of 1871, who saw in it only a continuation, more or less intelligent, of the first revolutionary Commune." [60]

Da Costa, who himself was the "chef de cabinet" of the Committee of General Safety under the Commune, attempts to defend the police service in Paris during the second siege. But he is forced to admit that Rigault was nothing as an administrator and that the Prefecture was in a more or less continual conflict with the other administrative divisions of the Commune. Rigault "put off everything till the arrival of Blanqui: to see Blanqui was his constant dream. Without Blanqui nothing could be done; with him everything. Thus he let himself drift along, hitting out wrongly and at cross purposes, not for the sake of showing his position, as has been said, but for fear of passing as one lacking energy." [61]

The Prefecture of Police was not the only source of friction within the administration. The military command was frequently in difficulties with the Executive Committee and the Commune, as was the Executive Committee with the Commune. The absence of a clear-cut limitation of function of the various administrative organs was one of the principal reasons for the formation of the supposedly all-powerful

[59] *Convulsions de Paris*, I:79.
[60] Arthur Arnould, *La Commune*, II:220.
[61] Da Costa, *La Commune Vécue*, II:220.

Committee of Public Safety, reminiscent of the great Revolution, on April 30th. The Commune found itself in opposition to the Committee of Public Safety quite as often as it
had previously to the committees which the Public Safety
supplanted.

General Cluseret and his successor, Rossel, found this lack
of clarity in the division of function embarrassing on a number of occasions. On others it was nearly disastrous.[62] As
Andrieu viewed the matter in the session of the Commune
on April 20th, "There is only one committee which, considering the circumstances, has functioned regularly up to the
time; that is, the Executive Committee . . . I demand that
a Committee of Organization be appointed to delimit the
functions of all committees and to create, what does not
exist at the present time, a certain harmony between the
acts of the different committees." [63]

The distribution of the time and energy of members of
the Commune among committees, the Assembly, and municipal administration, was certainly the simplest way of securing the neglect of all responsibilities. As early as the 9th of
April we find a member of the Commune complaining that
the committees are often not represented in a meeting of
the Assembly by a single delegate, and suggesting that
these committees at least send a secretary.[64] The absence of
members from the meetings of the Assembly became so
numerous and so frequent that it was decreed by the Commune that the absentees were to be deprived of pay.[65] This
measure at least made it probable that the committees and
the arrondissements were more likely to be neglected than
the Commune. Oddly enough, the members of the municipal
assembly exhibited no inclination to delegate their authority,
in fact, they were continually on the lookout for more.

[62] The difficulties of the military administration are discussed in the
next section.
[63] *Procès-Verbaux*, p. 311, April 20.
[64] *Ibid.*, p. 151, April 9.
[65] *Ibid.*, p. 155, April 9.

There is a mania in the Commune, said Billioray, one of its members, for seizing positions. "In fact, all the ministries and all the administrations are in our hands; it is impossible to cope with so many problems, and the Commune, when it finds intelligent people, ought to delegate authority." [66]

The Commune itself did nothing to ease the situation through its legislation. On the contrary, it created new functions and responsibilities with the greatest sangfroid. Not only did the various administrative committees show the greatest unwillingness to delegate authority, but new services were continually created and administered by members of the Commune. The ambulance service was directed by a member of the Commune, Miot; Gambon and V. Clément formed a committee to inspect the prisons; the Assembly appointed from its own members a committee of five to discover shelter for the inhabitants of the bombarded town of Neuilly. These instances are typical; the Commune showed no capacity to concentrate on matters of importance and to delegate detail to subordinates.

With an impressive gesture the Commune adopted, on the 2nd of April, the families of those killed in battle and proceeded, on the 10th, to allot pensions to widows and orphans in a large-handed way.

"Act 1.—A pension of 600 francs will be granted to the wife of a National Guard killed in defense of the rights of the people, after an inquest to discover her rights and needs.

"Act 2.—Each one of the children, whether legitimate or not, will receive until the age of 18, an annual pension of 365 francs, payable monthly." [67]

This, certainly, was generous provision, but there is grave doubt whether the widows and orphans ever saw much of this money. The administrative machinery which the Commune set up was a committee of six in every arrondissement, presided over by a member, for that arrondissement, of the

[66] *Procès-Verbaux*, p. 268, April 18.
[67] "Journal Officiel," April 11.

municipal assembly. A committee of three members was to perform the functions of centralization. The reception and investigation of pension claims was an occupation which the Commune took upon itself lightly. It was discovered only later that the occupation involved a certain amount of attention. We find, in consequence, a member of the Assembly asking, eight days later, for the appointment of a committee of investigation into the pension situation, since the Minister of Finance is being besieged with claims, the validity of which he knows nothing.[68]

A member of a municipal assembly, which sat twice a day, who was also a member of one of the ministries, and, in addition, in charge of the administration of his arrondissement, head of the pensions committee and occupied with several other government services, could hardly be expected to execute all functions properly.

We shall not attempt to consider in order the administration of the various government services under the Commune. Something has been said already of the Prefecture of Police. The organization of the military administration will occupy us in the next section: we shall reserve for future consideration the Commissions of Education and Labor,

[68] *Procès-Verbaux*, p. 272, April 18. (Varlin.) Among the widows demanding compensation was the wife of the lamented Colonel Bourgoin, one of the trusted military officers of the Commune, killed on April 6th. His funeral had been the occasion of a great demonstration; ten thousand people took part in the ceremonies. Yet we find the widow Bourgoin writing the following letter to Urbain, member of the Commune and delegate from the 7th Arrondissement, on May 19th, two days before the Versaillese entered Paris:

"I have the honor of recalling to you that you have promised to citizens Mallet and Ranvier to attend immediately to my pension and the assistance to which I am entitled as widow of Colonel Bourgoin, since April 6th.

"You already know that I am responsible for three small children of which the eldest is only 8 and that my situation merits all your attention.

"P. S. My dead husband had not yet received his last month's salary in the battalion. I have gone to see you many times without ever having been able to find you in."

From a letter preserved at the Archives de la Seine. Documents relating to the 7th Arrondissement during the Commune.

Industry and Trade. Since the Commissions on Supplies and on Public Services have already been dismissed as unimportant, there remain the administration of the finances and of justice.[69]

The revolution was faced, of course, from the beginning with serious financial difficulties. The pay of the National Guard together with the pension promises made by the Commune necessitated a large and constant flow of funds. The Central Committee through its delegates, Jourde and Varlin, had solved the problem for a few days by borrowing 500,-000 francs from Rothschild and a million from the Governor of the Bank of France. But the municipal assembly came into power with an empty exchequer and heavy and immediate commitments.

The Committee of Finance appointed by the Commune on the 29th of March was composed of Beslay, Varlin, Jourde, Victor Clément and Régère. Beslay was named as delegate at the Bank of France. The bank reserves consisted of 77,000,000 francs in coin and 166,000,000 francs in bank notes, all of which was, of course, at the disposal of the Commune, if it had cared to seize it.[70] That the Commune did not seize these reserves is due very largely to the influence of Beslay. As the Marquis de Plœuc, Assistant Governor of the Bank, put it, "Without the help that he [Beslay] gave us, the Bank would no longer exist." [71]

The relation of the Commune to the Bank of France has been a chief point of attack by socialists with revolutionary leanings. It is argued that if the revolution had seized the reserves of the Bank at the outset and had used this treasure

[69] The important task of popularizing the Commune in the provinces and abroad was miserably performed by the delegate to the Commission of the Exterior, Paschal Grousset. His activities were limited to the expedition of a couple of addresses to the provinces and the dispatch of a few men to encourage the communal revolt in other cities. See on this, Bourgin, *Le Mouvement Communaliste dans les Départements*, "Revue Socialiste," 49:412. The Russian communists, learned in the technique of propaganda, have rightly considered this to have been one of the weakest services in the Commune administration.

[70] *Enquête sur le 18 Mars*, p. 788. Evidence of Marquis de Plœuc.

[71] *Ibid.*, p. 790.

in the struggle against Versailles the issue would have been quickly and favorably decided. The Blanquist element in the Commune was all for this action and it is doubtful whether, if the Communal delegate had been some one other than Beslay, the bank could have escaped attack during the sixty-seven days of the siege. After the bloody week in May, when surviving Communards were scattered in all corners of Europe, Beslay was subject to several attacks by his former colleagues for his "treasonable" defense of the bank. Certainly to the Russian communists this bank policy was one of the weakest points in the Commune's tactics.

Beslay's defense of his own policy is, from a revolutionary point of view, pretty weak. "Is it not established," he said, "that the bank as the depository of wealth and the center of credit, represents a national patrimony, whose vitality is a matter of interest not only to France but to the whole civilized world; for today there are no longer any frontiers for capital, credit or business, and the disappearance of the bank would have given a shock to the world." [72]

This would seem to indicate that the delegate to the bank was a Proudhonian visionary, full of vague and beneficent yearnings, rather than a realist interested immediately and solely in the success of the revolution. This was the opinion of M. de Plœuc. "M. Beslay was one of those men whose imagination is without balance and who delight in Utopias; he dreams of reconciling all antagonisms existing in society, between employers and employees, between masters and servants." [73]

As a matter of fact Beslay's policy is thoroughly defensible from a revolutionary point of view, though for other reasons. The Bank of France gave little direct assistance to Versailles, outside of a few hundred thousand francs advanced to Admiral Saisset before the forces of order had left Paris. The Commune, on the other hand, would have

[72] *La Vérité sur la Commune*, p. 80.
[73] *Enquête*, p. 790. Beslay was an old friend and disciple of Proudhon and a mutualist member of the International.

gained little by seizing the bank reserve and would have lost much from the resulting depreciation of bank notes, in the esteem of the citizens of Paris. As it was, the revolution found sufficient revenue to pay all the soldiers who would take service under its flag. The effect on the provinces of an attack on the Bank would have been deplorable. True enough, the Commune received little cooperation from the provinces and hence was doomed to failure, but the failure was not less certain had the treasure of the Bank of France been taken over.

Under the circumstances the Bank of France was the chief source of revenue during the siege. Its total advances to the Hôtel de Ville amounted to 15,040,000 francs, almost half of the Commune's total estimated disbursements.[74] As it happened the city of Paris possessed, on the 18th of March, a credit of 9,400,000 francs, which M. de Plœuc paid out as slowly as possible.[75] After this credit was exhausted he had no other alternative than to meet grudgingly the further demands of the Minister of Finance.

The revenues with which the Commune financed its struggle against Versailles were secured as follows:[76]

Bank of France	15,040,000. francs
Octroi	13,217,526.88
Direct taxes	373,813.
Indirect taxes (tobacco)	2,629,123.15
Stamp and registration tax	800,000.
Municipal markets	814,323.82
Reimbursements from the National Guard	1,000,000.
Special levy on the railroads	2,000,000.
Customs	55,000.
Sums seized at the Hôtel de Ville on occupation	6,008,608.91
	41,988,395.76

[74] From Charest, *Le Bilan de la Commune* (Paris, 1896), p. 44.
[75] *Enquête*, p. 793.
[76] From Charest, p. 44. Charest gets his figures from the account books of Jourde, Minister of Finance under the Commune, now deposited at the Archives de la Seine. Except in the case of the Bank, the revenues from May 1st to 24th are estimated, the estimates representing an extrapolation on the receipts from March 20th to April 30th. Before the Third War Council, Jourde stated the receipts and disbursements of the Commune to be in the neighborhood of 47,000,000 francs.

The collection of "direct" taxes was small despite the warm appeal to the taxpayers of delegates Combault and Faillet.

"The government of Versailles, after having betrayed the Republic, has disorganized all the administrative services.

"It did not count upon our determination to appeal to all for the concern of all.

"To-day the administrations are being reorganized; fifteen hundred active and experienced republicans are replacing ten thousand, a veritable army of parasites.

"Citizens, you are the judges. To fulfill our mission we are appealing to your sense of justice and to your patriotism," etc.[77]

On the other hand, the Commune did not ask the railroads for contributions in such dulcet tones. In place of the former taxes paid by the railroad administrations to the state, the Commune levied a tax of a tenth of the gross passenger and express receipts of the Paris terminals.[78] On the 27th of April the Minister of Finance, Jourde, ordered the payment of 2,000,000 francs within forty-eight hours, which payments he collected only, according to Da Costa, with the help of Rigault's police.[79]

Whatever may have been the faults of the financial administration of the Commune, it fulfilled its chief purpose of providing the funds needed by the Hôtel de Ville. Lissa-

[77] *Murailles,* II:155.
[78] "Journal Officiel," April 28th.
The tax was levied as follows:

La compagnie du Nord	303,000 frs.
La compagnie de l'Ouest	275,000 "
La compagnie de l'Est	354,000 "
La compagnie de Lyon	692,000 "
La compagnie d'Orléans	376,000 "
	2,000,000 frs.

[79] *La Commune Vécue,* II:222.

garay has described Jourde as a person of inexhaustible
garrulity, but he held the confidence of the majority of his
colleagues, and with the occasional assistance of Varlin,
maintained an order in his department which was not to be
found elsewhere. Aided by his wife's habit of doing the
family washing he passed for an upright and honest man.

The head of the Commission of Justice also was a fairly
able man. The rest of the delegation was incompetent and
without the special knowledge required by the task.[80] The
Commission of Justice, therefore, was Protot, and he gathered about him a group of capable assistants, mostly young
Blanquists. However, he was impossibly handicapped in his
functions by the antagonism of the Prefecture and the dispersion of the police power among numerous and often
irresponsible agencies of the National Guard. Charged by
the Commune with "taking the steps necessary to guarantee
individual liberty," he was not provided with the machinery
for accomplishing this task, nor was he strong enough to
force through the municipal assembly the measures necessary
to give to the courts and to his department their proper ascendancy over the police.[81]

[80] See Laronze, *op. cit.*, p. 180.
[81] Certain subsidiary services under the Commune, particularly the
administration of the Post, the Mint, and Public Assistance seem, considering the circumstances, to have been well managed. Theisz, a laborer and
member of the International, had been appointed to the Postal Service by the
Central Committee, and his appointment was confirmed by the Commune.
He found the situation in the greatest disorder, for the existing director,
Rampont, had retired to Versailles with the cash box and the most important
materials. In addition all the chiefs of bureaus resigned and most of the
head clerks. With the assistance of a few socialists in the service he
restored some semblance of order after two days of effort, during which
the population of Paris was without mail. Within the city, mail delivery
was carried on as usual; letters for the provinces had to be smuggled out of
Paris and letters from the provinces were brought by privately organized
companies. The best account of this service appears in Theisz' report to
Lissagaray, *op. cit.*, pp. 471-74.
The telegraph service was even more disorganized and here order
appears never to have been reestablished. The Commune attempted to train
new telegraphers without much success. A long letter from an employee,
now preserved at the Archives de la Seine, to Urbain, delegate to the 7th
Arrondissement, complains that Pauvert, the man put in charge by the
Commune, is utterly incompetent and that cabals and intrigues of all sort

Available data on the administration of the arrondissements are even more scanty than on the various executive
delegations. The members of the Commune responsible for
this administration were assisted usually by a commission,
called a municipal commission, which undertook the greater
part of the work.[82] These commissions were composed of
local notorieties who had obtained their training in the clubs
and who were usually more versed in oratory than in municipal management. In the 1st Arrondissement, where the
early resignation of the moderate members left the district
without Commune representation, the extempore municipal
commission published an optimistic proclamation of its program.

> "We intend, to the extent of our powers, to insure
> that our device, Liberty, Equality, Solidarity, shall at
> last represent the truth and that, consequently, frater-
> nity shall not be a vain word.
> "We want to free the proletariat, we want a situa-
> tion in which every one can live by his own work.
> "No more idleness! No more parasites! No more
> exploiters! No more exploited!"

In addition to the municipal commission, every arrondissement had its Legion Council and Legion General Staff, under
the general supervision of the Central Committee. These
organizations had a finger in the administration and the
inexact division of function was a cause of considerable

---

continually disrupt the service. Inexperienced men were put at the head
of various departments, etc.

At the Mint Camelinat, a bronze worker and member of the International,
was in charge. He appears to have done well. He printed emergency
stamps for the Post Office and, before the end of the Commune, had coined a
certain amount of money bearing the stamp of a coin of 1848. See on this,
M. Vuillaume, *Cahiers de la Quinzaine*, 10th Series, No. 8, p. 213.

The Public Assistance was in the hands of Treillard, an upright and
honorable man shot by the Versaillese on May 25th.

[82] A. Arnould, *op. cit.*, III:53.

friction.[83] The mass of complaints which appear in the records of certain mayoral offices seized after the defeat of the revolution, compels the conclusion that this part of the Commune's task was badly performed. On the 26th of April a project was presented to the municipal assembly proposing a limitation of the duties of members of the Commune in their arrondissements, but nothing was done about the matter.[84]

The 8th Arrondissement was so badly administered that it became a matter of notoriety in the Assembly. The only member of the Commune who fulfilled this function, Jules Allix, was later incarcerated in an insane asylum and, from all accounts, should have been before. On May 2nd the Commune received the complaint of an executive commission of the 8th, declaring that the arrondissement was in a state of complete disorganization, that nothing was being done and that if elections were held there now the Commune would receive a very small minority.[85] But despite the demands of Malon, who declared that Allix was insane, the Assembly did nothing to reorganize the arrondissement administration. The probability is that the government of a number of the others was not much better.

All in all, it appears obvious, from the evidence we possess, that the administrative capacities of the Commune were such as might have been expected in a nondescript group of laborers unfamiliar with affairs, and third-rate orators and journalists unacquainted with public office.

THE MILITARY DIRECTION OF THE COMMUNE

We have seen that the military resources of the Commune, on its inauguration, March 28th, were considerable. The 215 battalions of the National Guard supporting the Central Committee yielded fighting troops to the number of

[83] A. Arnould, *op. cit.*, III: 56.
[84] *Procès-Verbaux*, p. 501.
[85] *Procès-Verbaux, MSS. II*, May 2.

from 75,000 to 90,000, and somewhat over 100,000 sedentary troops. It is estimated that probably 60,000 soldiers of the Commune took part in the march on Versailles of April 3rd and 4th.[86] Munitions and other equipment left over from the siege permitted the revolution to arm its forces adequately.

The 1st of April saw the high point of the military strength of the Commune. From that time on the numbers fell rapidly. The battles of April 3rd and 4th caused an immense cooling in the enthusiasm of the National Guard, and its effective fighting force was cut in half. Saint-Pierre, who reported on the military strength of the Commune to the Committee of Enquiry, estimated the number of its troops in May as 70,000, but this seems highly exaggerated.[87] The partisans of Versailles had a natural interest in exaggerating the forces of the Commune, since this not only glorified Thiers' army but helped to explain how it required two months to subdue the revolution. Lepelletier has given us reason to believe that the troops defending Paris during April did not number more than 25,000 to 30,000 and that the effectives had fallen by the 20th of May to somewhere about 12,000.[88] Cluseret's report to the Commune on April 23rd indicates that he had less than 40,000 troops at that time.[89]

On the other hand, Versailles was represented, after the

[86] *Enquête*, p. 171. Evidence of Saint-Pierre on the National Guard.

[87] General Appert, *Rapport d'ensemble de M. le général Appert sur les opérations de la justice militaire rélatives à l'insurrection de 1871* (Paris, 1875), gives his calculations of the average active troops commanded by the Commune at 96,089 men and 4,500 officers, but this is obviously absurd. He bases his figures upon the statistics of the National Guard as it existed before the 18th of March. The revolution could count on the services of less than half of this number.

[88] *La Commune*, III:365.

[89] *Procès-Verbaux*, p. 399. The Commune was paying wages to far more soldiers than actually bore arms. An order of the War delegate on May 12th remarked on the discrepancy between the numbers of artillerymen receiving pay and the numbers in service. A note of the delegate of Finances on May 19th asserts that, "the pay of the National Guard is subject to scandalous abuses. See the "Journal Officiel," of May 13th and 19th.

middle of April, by 130,000 well-armed, well-disciplined troops, led by the ablest commanders in France. Thiers' decree of April 6th laid down the organization of the besieging army, and by April 11th it had been formed and was ready to commence operations.[90] MacMahon, the commander-in-chief, says of this force and its operations, "The army, assembled at Versailles, conquered, in a month and a half, the most formidable insurrection that France has ever seen. We completed works of considerable magnitude, dug nearly 40 kilometers of trenches, and captured 80 batteries mounting 350 cannon. We took possession of five forts, formidably armed and stubbornly defended, as well as numerous temporary defenses."[91]

The disproportion between the military forces of Paris and Versailles was accentuated by the inexperience of the defenders of the Commune and their rank indiscipline. Accustomed during the first siege of Paris to wearing the uniform and carrying the weapons of a soldier, the National Guard was completely unaccustomed to firm discipline and hardship. This was apparent in the action of the 1st of April against Courbevoie. Rossel marched out at the head of 2,000 troops. "There were," he has said, "at least two battalions completely drunk; others complained of being hungry. The head of the column, which I conducted, followed in good order, but the other battalions, whose officers were without authority, did not wait long before they sprawled out along the sides of the road, quarrelling and complaining; there were two or three panics and finally the most complete disorder."[92]

The commanders-in-chief of the Communal army from the 1st of April till the middle of May, Cluseret and Rossel, both agree on the nearly complete absence of discipline

---

[90] *Rapport sur les opérations de l'armée de Versailles, depuis le 11 avril, époque de sa formation, jusqu'au moment de la pacification de Paris, le 28 mai.* (MacMahon.) "Journal Officiel de la République Française," August 3, 1871.
[91] *Ibid.,* p. 2402.
[92] Rossel, *Papiers Posthumes,* p. 96.

in their forces. "I have seen many organizations," said Cluseret, "and many insurrections in my life. But never have I seen anything comparable to the anarchy of the National Guard in 1871. It was perfect of its kind, and Proudhon would have been satisfied with the fruits which the tree planted by him in 1848 bore in 1871." [93]

Rossel, as chief of the general staff under Cluseret during April, in receiving the complaints of the disaffected, had ample opportunity to observe the disorganization. "Most of my time," he tells us, "was taken up by the importunate and the incapable; delegates of all kinds, men with inventions, searchers after information, and, especially, officers and soldiers who left their posts to come and make complaints of their superiors or of their equipment. There were also, nearly everywhere, particular officers who did not accept or execute orders." [94]

Desertion and disobedience to command was a frequent occurrence which the revolution attempted to check by a Court Martial set up April 18th. The presiding officer was Rossel and one of his first cases was that of Girot, a battalion commander who refused to march against the enemy on the pretext that his men had not eaten for twenty-four hours. Rossel imposed the death penalty. This excited the Commune greatly, since Girot was a revolutionary of good standing, highly esteemed for his political opinions. Consequently the Executive Commission, "considering the democratic antecedents of citizen Girot," changed the sentence to one of civil and military degradation. [95] Despite the protest of Cluseret to the Commune that he was "surrounded by the cowardice of officers," despite his demands that he be given full powers to punish such acts, citizen Girot remained unexecuted. [96]

[93] Cluseret, *Mémoires*, I:114.
[94] Rossel, *Papiers Posthumes*, p. 101.
[95] "Journal Officiel," April 20.
[96] *Procès-Verbaux*, p. 295. Rossel said of the Court Martial (*Papiers Posthumes*, p. 112), "The action of the Court Martial made the Commune uneasy; it feared this new power which punished offenders without regard

The army of the Commune was democratic. Each unit of the National Guard elected its own officers.[97] On April 6th the Executive Committee abolished the rank of general on the ground that, "such ranks are incompatible with the democratic organization of the National Guard." The principle of a hierarchy of superiors commanding through rigid discipline the rank and file, appealed not at all to the Commune. Its survivors, in their reminiscences of the events following the 18th of March, are almost unanimously inclined to criticise Cluseret and Rossel for their lack of understanding of a "republican and revolutionary force." As Lefrançais put it, comparing Rossel with Cluseret:

"He, also, seemed to believe that it was necessary to create an instrument which did not reason and which was content to act without understanding.

"But it is just this necessity of understanding which alone can give to a revolutionary army the chance of victory." [98]

The army of the Commune, like every democratic community, was distinguished by an almost uncontrollable mania for rank, decoration and display. Corporals assumed the uniform of captains, captains the rank of colonels, and colonels the rank of generals. Gaudy uniforms, bizarre attendants and impressive insignia made the Commune's army one of the most colorful, if astonishing, of military assemblages of modern times. Cluseret made this penchant for sartorial distinction the subject of a disciplinary note to the National Guard.

"I have observed with disapproval that, forgetting our modest origin, the ridiculous mania for stripes,

---

to their more or less demagogic antecedents. It discovered, in truth, that the most obvious offenders were firm supporters of the good cause."

[97] Nevertheless, in practice the war delegate nominated the officers of the general staff, and the officers of the general staff of the legions. And in order to prevent a rapid turnover in officers it was decided that no elected officer could be deprived of his position except by a special decree of the delegate of war. See Appert, *op. cit.*, p. 100.

[98] Lefrançais, *Souvenirs d'un Révolutionnaire*, p. 520.

decorations and shoulder knots is beginning to spread among us. Workers, you have for the first time accomplished the revolution of labor and for labor.

"Let us not deny our origin, and, in particular, let us not blush for it. Workers we were, workers we are, and workers we shall remain." [99]

This Spartan advice, however, was not acclaimed in revolutionary circles.[100]

The decline in revolutionary and military enthusiasm after the defeats of April 3rd and 4th, with the consequent decrease in the number of willing soldiers, necessitated measures for encouraging the unwilling. In its decree abolishing conscription the Commune had decided that every citizen would *ipso facto* be a member of the National Guard. The outbreak of hostilities led to a supplementary decree, which made unmarried citizens from 17 to 35 liable for active service.[101] On April 7th Cluseret threw the anti-Commune circles of Paris into consternation by the following order:

"In consideration of the patriotic appeals of a large number of the National Guard who, although married, cherish the honor of defending their municipal independence, even at the price of their lives, the decree of April 4th is modified; from 17 to 19 years, service in active units will be voluntary, and from 19 to 40 years obligatory for the National Guard, married or not married. I advise good patriots to perform the police

[99] "Journal Officiel," April 8.
[100] Lepelletier (*La Commune,* III:203) says of this, "With his austere republicanism, Cluseret acted like a Calvinist, and could not appeal to the emotions of voluntary soldiers. The puritanism which he affected as a pose annoyed his best officers. Many of them had, without doubt, an excessive taste for lace, but this has been a traditional mania in all our armies, and finery and shoulder knots have not prevented them from fighting well; quite the contrary."
[101] "Journal Officiel," April 5. This decree was followed by a proclamation of the Prefect of Police, April 7th, denying passports to those between the ages of 17 and 35.

functions of their arrondissements themselves and to force refractory citizens to serve." [102]

This order does not seem to have increased greatly the fighting strength of the revolutionary troops, but it helped to make life in Paris untenable for Versailles sympathizers. It accelerated the secret exodus from the capital continually going on. Spying and informing became rampant in the arrondissements and those unwilling to serve were forced into hiding.[103] During the last days of the Commune the pursuit of "refractory" citizens assumed the character of a man hunt.

A considerable number of the soldiers of the Commune fought because it was necessary to live. With employers fled to Versailles, factories and shops closed down, and employment impossible to find, laborers with no strong sympathies for the revolution were forced into the ranks to earn the famous thirty sous.[104] The large pension promised in case of incapacity or death was an added inducement.[105]

[102] "Journal Officiel," April 8.
[103] The following letter preserved in the Archives de la Seine is illuminating on this point:

Citizen Deberle to the adjutant of the XIVth Arrondissement.

"I want to defend my country and to remain French; but I do not want to see a young 'garde-mobile' who, having known how to hide himself, comes to laugh in my face when I take my gun.

"Such a one is citizen Opoix, Eugène, born at Pommeuse, canton and arrondissement of Volommers, of the class of 1869.

"E. F. Henry,

"Baker, 24 rue Daguerre, married and having two children while citizen Opoix is single."

[104] Charles de Varigny (L. Thomas, *Documents,* p. 145) tells the story of a young worker with a wife and three children to support. Thrown out of work he saw his savings diminish. When he went to a former employer to ask for menial service, he found the latter had left Paris. In consequence, he was reduced, on May 10, to accept the 30 sous of a *fédéré.*

[105] The pay of the officers of the National Guard was as follows:

Général en chef ....`.....................	500 francs per month
Général en second	450 " " "
Colonel ....‚....	360 " " "
Commandant	300 " " "
Capitaine, chirurgien major, adjutant-major .	225 " " "
Lieutenant, aide-major	165 " " "
Sous-lieutenant	150 " " "

The rank and file of the National Guard can certainly not be called first-class fighting material, despite the presence of a few staunch and well-disciplined battalions. On the other hand, the leaders were, for an insurrectionary force, distinctly capable. Surviving Communards and historians, too sympathetic with the cause, have criticized bitterly Cluseret and Rossel, and have attempted to saddle them with the failure of the revolution. It has been said that both were men of the military trade, unsympathetic with the aims of the revolution and incapable of handing republican and revolutionary troops. This is perhaps true, but men capable of handling such troops have never as yet graced the pages of history. Certainly the armies of Soviet Russia, the most successful revolutionary force yet organized, were officered by commanders who demanded, and were accorded, discipline.

Cluseret had many and notorious faults; he distrusted his men, he considered himself superior to his position and lacked that energy and enthusiasm necessary to the leader of a successful insurrection. Like Trochu, who conducted the defense of Paris against the Prussians, he was pretty well convinced of eventual failure from the outset. Yet he brought some semblance of order out of the chaos into which the troops of the Commune had been thrown after the defeats of early April. And he appointed a set of capable under-officers. Rossel was his choice as chief of the general staff; he appointed a distinguished civil engineer, Roselli-Mollet, as director of fortifications and was responsible for the advancement of Dombrowski, one of the ablest military leaders of the Commune, to the position of commandant of Paris. In his articles on the revolution, published after the defeat, and in his book of recollections, Cluseret showed himself a boastful and self-satisfied ignoramus, but compared with the generals of the Central Committee, he was nearly of Napoleonic stature.

The tactics of this general-in-chief of the Commune were

purely defensive, and possibly rightly so. The time had already passed when the revolution could have carried the attack to Versailles with any possibility of success. He occupied and equipped the formidable fortifications to the south and west of Paris and then began that tenacious defense of the capital, which nearly exhausted the patience of the supporters of Thiers, and ended only after two months of almost continuous bombardment.

Cluseret was not, however, destined to lead the troops of Paris to defeat. On April 28th, he was dispossessed in favor of a younger and abler man, Colonel Rossel, and spent the month of May in the prison of Mazas. No great administrator under favorable circumstances, he found it impossible to satisfy the often opposing demands of all the authorities who occupied themselves under the Commune with the affairs of war. Members of the Assembly, visiting the fortifications, received the complaints of the soldiers and used them against the general-in-chief. On April 23rd the Commune voted an immediate inquiry into the causes of the military disorganization.[106] It was charged that Cluseret was working with the Central Committee and the legion committees against the policy of the Commune, and that consequently he was committing treason.[107] On another occasion, after the lapse of five days, during which Cluseret had made no report to the Commune on the military situation, he was accused of wishing to set up a dictatorship. Finally the Assembly, in secret committee, deposed its war delegate, and ordered him imprisoned on the pretext that he was responsible for the temporary abandonment of the fort of Issy.[108]

[106] *Procès-Verbaux*, p. 406.
[107] *Ibid.*, p. 473. April 25.
[108] "Carelessness and negligence on the part of the war delegate having endangered the possession of the fort of Issy, the executive committee has believed it to be its duty to propose to the Commune the arrest of citizen Cluseret; it was so decreed." "Journal Officiel," May 2.
That the affair of Issy was not Cluseret's fault is indicated by the evi-

The Commune appointed in his place Cluseret's former chief of staff, Rossel. Saint-Pierre, who reported to the official Committee of Enquiry on the subject of the National Guard, said of Rossel, "We can say that the Commune lasted an extra month, thanks to his active direction and his talent for organization, united with his great energy." [109]

The new war delegate was uninterested in politics and indifferent, if not antipathetic, to the ideals of the Commune. He had allied himself with the revolution because it was an uprising against the government which had made peace with Prussia. "The 19th of March," he said later, "I learned that a city had taken up arms and I clung desperately to this fragment of France. I did not know who the insurgents were, but I knew against whom they were rebelling and that was sufficient." [110] He continued to fight for the Commune after he understood its aims and learned to know its leaders, because he saw no honorable way of withdrawing. [111]

Rossel considered the aims of the Commune visionary and its leaders impotent, and he was not always careful to keep these opinions to himself. After the defeat of the revolution, while he was awaiting his trial and execution, he described his ex-colleagues as follows: "The Commune had no statemen, no soldiers, and it did not wish to have them; it spread ruin around itself without having the capacity nor even the desire to build and create. Frightened of publicity because it was aware of its stupidities, frightened of liberty because it was in an unstable equilibrium from which it could

dence presented by Rossel to the Assembly, May 2nd. *Procès-Verbaux*, MSS.

Gambon—"Why was the fort of Issy abandoned?"

Rossel—"Because of the collective cowardice of the National Guard, lacking organization."

[109] *Enquête*, p. 173.

[110] Charles Prolès, *Le Colonel Rossel* (Paris), p. 37.

[111] The following appears in a letter of Rossel to his parents, written April 17th: "I am going to the outposts to make a tour of inspection; if I am wounded, I can honorably retire from this business."—Prolès, p. 46.

easily be dislodged, this oligarchy was the most idious despotism one could imagine." [112] It must be remembered that imprisonment and the prospect of death were not likely to temper Rossel's scorn of his late associates. Nevertheless, he gave his best in that struggle against the "government of the capitulards," which he hated as much as any revolutionary.

Until the time of Rossel's appointment as military delegate, the Central Committee, which had never ceased to exert its influence on the National Guard, was an ever-present source of trouble. Ostensibly the conduct of the revolution was in the hands of the war delegation of the Commune, but the Central Committee existed as a self-appointed auxiliary agent, irresponsible because unofficial, and dangerous because influential. Rossel was more seriously handicapped even than his predecessor. However, with the help of the recently appointed Committee of Public Safety, he drew up a new plan of military administration which made the war delegate responsible for the initiation and direction of military operations, and the Central Committee, under the control of the military commission of the Commune, responsible for the various services of war administration.[113] This decree did no more than to recognize and to bring into the open the true position of the Central Committee in the organization of the revolution. It was taken, however, by various members of the Assembly, as proof of the collapse of the Commune's authority. What was more serious, it did not put an end to the conflict of authorities which disorganized the military administration. On May 4th the formidable redoubt of Moulin-Saquet was captured by the Versaillese. There was the usual cry of treason and the suspicion engendered led to the incarceration of the Dominican monks of Arcueil. A considerable element in this defeat was demonstrated in the Assembly to have been the con-

[112] Rossel, *Papiers Posthumes*, p. 152.
[113] This decree is published in the "Journal Officiel," May 6.

tradictory orders of authorities. The commander, Wroblewski, unknown to Rossel, had been ordered elsewhere by
Félix Pyat of the Committee of Public Safety, and the
redoubt was captured during his absence.[114]

The Commune opened its session of May 9th with the
receipt of the news of the fall of Issy. The members learned
of this catastrophe from the pages of the "Journal Officiel,"
in which Rossel had inserted the following dispatch. "The
tricolor floats over the fort of Issy, abandoned yesterday
evening by the garrison." The war delegate had not only
failed to notify the Commune, but he had had 10,000
copies of this dispatch printed and circulated without con-
sulting either the Commune or the Committee of Public
Safety.

Delescluze, returning to the Assembly after an absence of
several days, castigated his colleagues for their verbosity,
incapacity, and preoccupation with personal affairs.

"I make an appeal to all of you.

"It is this deplorable debate which has taken place
during the last week, which I am happy not to have
attended, that is producing the present disorder among
the population of Paris.

"It is in such a situation as this that you waste your
time in questions of amour-propre. [excitement.] . . .

"To-day the National Guard is refusing any longer
to fight [excitement], and you continue to debate on
the questions of the procès-verbal." [115]

Rossel in a flamboyant and rather theatrical manner announced his resignation to the Commune, in a letter which
he sent immediately to the evening journals.

---

[114] Pyat denied having signed such an order and consequently was thrown
into considerable confusion when confronted with it before the whole
Assembly. Arnould took the affair as evidence of the "disastrous conflict of
powers" which existed and demanded a delimitation of the functions of the
Committee of Public Safety. *Procès-Verbaux, MSS.*, May 5.
[115] *Procès-Verbaux, M.S.S.*, May 9.

"I feel incapable of longer maintaining the responsibility of a command in a situation in which every one deliberates and no one obeys. . . . The central artillery committee deliberates and has prescribed nothing. . . . The Commune has deliberated and has resolved on nothing. . . . Later the Central Committee of the Federation of the National Guard has come to offer almost imperiously its assistance in the war administration. The Committee deliberates and has not known how to act. . . .

"My predecessor Cluseret was wrong in trying to meet this absurd situation in debate. Enlightened by his example, I have two lines to choose from; either to break the obstacles or to retire.

"I will not break the obstacle, for the obstacle is yourself and your weakness. I do not desire an attack upon your sovereignty.

"I resign and I have the honor of demanding from you a cell at Mazas." [116]

Instead of accepting a cell at Mazas, however, Rossel preferred to hide for the balance of the siege.

The Commune met this situation promptly and drastically, if not wisely. It completely replaced the personnel of the Committee of Public Safety; it court-martialed Rossel and appointed Delescluze as civil delegate of war; it resolved to meet only three times a week as a deliberative assembly. The Committee of Public Safety was to sit in permanence at the Hôtel de Ville.

The military situation was grave, to say the least. With Mont Valérien and Issy, the army of Versailles commanded the defenses of the southwest of Paris. With all of Delescluze's courage and revolutionary determination, he knew nothing of the position he was called upon to fill. As his biographer has observed, "He lost himself in the midst of

[116] "Le Moniteur Universel," May 12.

his difficulties;—the technical side of military affairs escaped him completely, and he found himself confronted by problems of which he knew not the first word." [117]

The Commune, prompted by Delescluze, attempted to bridge the gap which separated a deliberative assembly from the actual direction of the war by the appointment of three of its members as civil delegates. The great Revolution had indicated the road. "Our fathers understood perfectly that this measure alone could save the country from a military dictatorship, which sooner or later ends in a dynasty." [118] But the formula of 1792 could not answer the difficulties.

That the Commune fought on for another nine days and then conducted a stubborn defense within the walls of Paris is to be very largely attributed to the capacity of the military leaders, whom Delescluze had inherited from Cluseret and Rossel: Dombrowski, Wroblewski and La Cécilia. The former two were Poles and the last, although of French extraction, had fought under Garibaldi. In recommending Dombrowski as "commandant de place" the Central Committee had described him as "incontestably a man of war and a soldier of the universal republic." La Cécilia and Wroblewski were no less. The former had been a member of the International, and both Dombrowski and Wroblewski had been associated with the republican and revolutionary element in Paris during the siege.

On the whole, it is true to say that the Commune was considerably more fortunate in its military than its political leaders.

INTERNAL DIFFICULTIES OF THE COMMUNE

The administrative and military difficulties of the Commune were intensified and exaggerated by personal animosities, group rivalries, and irreconcilable conflicts of

[117] Prolès, *Charles Delescluze* (Paris), p. 110.
[118] "Journal Officiel," May 17.

authority. Journalists, of which there were not a few, used the superior news-gathering facilities bestowed by their official position as members of the municipal assembly to their private advantage. Personal hatreds between radical leaders, established in political rivalries before the 18th of March, flared up again in the Commune. The work of the Assembly was disrupted by a series of resignations tendered through pique or wounded vanity. Finally, and much more serious, were the uncompromising conflicts between the minority and majority in the Commune, and between the Commune and the Central Committee.

Underlying and determining these internal conflicts and disturbances was the complete lack of a governmental and administrative tradition. Discussion in the assembly continually degenerated into mere bickering and personal vilification for want of a parliamentary tradition. The hastily conceived division of function and authority left rough edges which use and experience had no time to smooth. The necessarily slow process of adaptation and adjustment was repeatedly disrupted by a radical reconstruction of new administrative machinery. In this situation supposedly interdependent groups strive for independence, limited authorities seek to lose their limitations, criticism is repressed and opposition is trodden under foot; the reign of law becomes a reign of particular prowess, in which the powers of each particular are limited only by the powers of every other. Such was the situation toward which the Commune tended.

Newspaper criticism was resented almost from the outset. Although a great outcry had gone up among the radical journals when Vinoy suppressed six of their number in March, and although many fine words had been written on that occasion regarding the necessity of free discussion in a free state, toleration was not the policy of the Commune or its supporters. As early as April 4th the revolutionary journal, "L'Action," demanded the suspension "sans phrase" of all the papers hostile to the Commune.[119] On April 18th, the Assembly followed this counsel with the suppression of four important dailies, "Le Bien Public," "Le Soir," "La Cloche" and "L'Opinion National," on the ground that "the principle of freedom of the press does not justify the existence in Paris of papers favorable to the interests of the armed enemy."

The government of Thiers was prohibiting in all parts of France the publication of papers favorable to the cause of Paris, and in its next wholesale suppression the Commune used this fact as justification of its own policy. On May 5th, seven more journals were condemned.[120] Most of the eleven papers so far suppressed were definitely favorable to Versailles, though certain of them, at the outbreak of the revolution, had not been hostile to the Commune. On May 19th, however, papers which had been favorable to the revolution met the fate of their predecessors.[121]

"La Commune," for example, published by the principal editors of "Le Combat" and "Le Vengeur," two of the revolution's fieriest sheets, came to grief because of an article on the explosion of a munitions plant, on May 17th. The article, entitled "Responsibility," began as follows: "Treason at Moulin-Saquet, treason at the fort of Issy, treason at the munitions factory of the Avenue Rapp, treason everywhere. But who is doing the betraying?—The agents of Versailles?—That is their business, and we should be happy to treat them in the same way.

"In these cases, however, there is no other treason than the incapacity and imbecility of the blackguards and fools

[119] The editor of this paper was Lissagaray, the author of an important work on the Commune, highly favorable to the revolution.
[120] "Le Petit Moniteur," "Le Petit National," "Le Bon Sens," "La Petite Presse," "Le Petit Journal," "La France" and "Le Temps."
[121] The papers suppressed the 19th were "La Commune," "L'Écho de Paris," "Le Républicain," "La Revue des Deux Mondes," "L'Écho d'Ultramar," and "La Justice."

who have laid hands on public business of which they knew not the slightest detail. In their hands the general safety has been wilfully threatened and the service of police has neglected or abandoned the most elementary guarantees." [122]

This medicine was a little too strong for the Commune to stomach.

Henri Rochefort in his "Mot d'Ordre" was a constant and caustic critic of the Commune, but his popularity with the citizens of Paris and his skill in polemic made him a difficult man to handle. He condemned bitterly the suppression of the freedom of the press, and found it "extremely singular" that Félix Pyat, a member of the Commune, should continue to edit a newspaper, "especially when this elected of the people, to whom he owes his whole time, presides daily over the suppression of other papers which he does not edit." [123]

Pyat, as a member of the Commune, made himself generally unpopular among his fellow journalists, not only because of this policy of suppression, but because he used his official position to the advantage of his paper. "We recall the time," one of these critics asserted, "and it does not lie far in the past, when M. Pyat, journalist, cried,—and with what energy—against the communications made by the Minister of the Interior to certain papers to the detriment of others.

"We could even cite the furious articles of the editor-in-chief of 'Le Combat.'

"Forty mutations ab illo!

"Today Pyat (Félix), member of the Commune, communicates to Pyat (not less Félix), but journalist, the decrees signed during the sessions, and that at an hour when no other paper has received the official documents." [124]

[122] "La Commune," May 19.
[123] "Le Mot d'Ordre," April 9.
[124] "Le Moniteur de Peuple," April 10.

But Pyat (not less Félix) was not the only journalist member of the Commune to reap the reward of political success.[125]

The animosities within the municipal assembly itself often seriously hampered the conduct of affairs, by reason of the considerable amount of time devoted to the airing of private grievances. Pyat and Vermorel, for example, both journalists and both representatives, carried on a running fight in their respective papers and on the floor of the Assembly. Pyat's paper, "Le Vengeur," accused Vermorel on April 24th of being a police spy; Vermorel replied in "L'Avenir du Peuple," April 28th, with a violent attack on Pyat. They brought their grievances to the Commune, where the Committee of Enquiry on Members of the Commune took charge of the affair.

On May 1st, when the important question of the Committee of Public Safety was before the Assembly, Jourde and Pyat wrangled for twenty pages of MSS. over an article by the latter, to which the former had taken offense. "The light of day is the best minister," said Pyat, in discussing the administration of the finances, and Jourde with some justice took this as a reflection upon his probity. It required a vote of the Commune to straighten the matter out.[126] Half the session of May 4th was given over to a four-cornered debate between Pyat, Vermorel, Tridon and Johannard. Pyat pathetically maintained that his work on the Committee of Public Safety was hampered by enemies he had had the misfortune to make in his profession. Vermorel wanted to know whether he could be accused with impunity of being a police spy. Tridon and Johannard explained that, although not in sympathy with Pyat, they had never insulted him. The bickering proceeded interminably and was only concluded by the entrance of Rossel, who shocked the

---

[125] Vésinier, delegate at the Journal Officiel, was attacked in the Commune for doing the same thing. *Procès-Verbaux, MSS.*, May 1.
[126] *Procès-Verbaux, MSS.*, May 1.

Assembly into life by announcing the fall of Moulin-Saquet.[127]

During the early part of May, when the military situation of the Commune was going from bad to worse, discussion in the Assembly became more and more chaotic. The Commune was irreconcilably divided over the Committee of Public Safety and finally, after three days of futile discussion on this matter, the meeting of May 6th broke up in complete disorder. On the 7th, the Assembly failed to meet for lack of a quorum. It took the shock of the fall of the fort of Issy and the subsequent lecture by Delescluze to bring the Commune back to business. "A great revolution is not being made by means of the Assembly," said Delescluze, "but in spite of it and the insufficiency of its members." [128]

The most serious internal difficulties arose over the Committee of Public Safety and the relation of the Commune to the Central Committee. The split in the Assembly over the Committee of Public Safety and the consequent emergence of a majority and minority, completed a cleavage which had existed in embryo from the start. The Jacobin, communist element favoring a dictatorship, repression and a certain degree of terrorism, dominated as it was by the tradition of the great Revolution, voted for the Committee of Public Safety. The moderate, democratic and socialist element voted against it. It is not true, as many writers have suggested, that the latter was exclusively the party of the International. It included a number of others and, on the other hand, certain members of the International, for example, Vaillant, voted with the majority. Nevertheless, the backbone of the minority was the party of the International, and the focus of its opposition was a belief in democratic government.

The ground was prepared for this division into parties from the start. The Blanquist and Jacobin groups envisaged

[127] *Procès-Verbaux*, May 4.
[128] *Ibid.*, May 9.

the aim of the revolution as the overthrow of the government of Thiers and the means as the organization of a powerful and largely irresponsible dictatorship. The reorganization of society on socialist or communist lines, if it entered into the thoughts of certain of them, was a matter which could and should be postponed until the settlement of the business in hand. The minority, on the other hand, while just as much interested in the overthrow of the government of Thiers, tended to consider this the means to the end of social reform. Furthermore, the minority opposed any attempt to take control out of the hands of the Commune, the elected of the people, and to put it in the hands of the more or less irresponsible group which the Committee of Public Safety promised to be.

That the cleavage was deep and exclusive is seen clearly enough in the various histories of the Commune left by surviving Communards. They fall pretty sharply into two classes; the one, which is Jacobin or communist, attributing the failure of the Commune, in large part, to the vacillating, anemic policy of the sentimental socialists, i.e., the International; the other, finding a considerable cause of the failure of the revolution in the despotic, terroristic and undemocratic behavior of the majority, with which the rank and file was out of sympathy.[129] The socialist movement, particularly in France, has always tended to split into these two groups, and in this situation is to be found one of its most considerable weaknesses.

The Committee of Public Safety was first suggested by Miot, one of the Blanquists, on April 28th, "in view of the

---

[129] One of the best examples of the first class is Gaston Da Costa's *La Commune Vécue,* a very readable and often penetrating account of the Commune, in three volumes. Da Costa describes the International as Napoleonic in its origin, which is untrue. "Its theories were affirmed only by timid decrees with no sanction, on the maturities, night work for bakers, and the reorganization of the pawnshops. Time childishly lost to the profit of Thiers and at the expense of organization for battle." III:70.

Arthur Arnould, *La Commune,* in 3 vols., is a good example of the second class of histories.

gravity of the situation and the necessity of taking promptly the most radical and energetic measures." [130] He proposed that it be given complete authority over all other committees and that it be responsible only to the Commune. This proposition was supported by many members of the majority, frankly on the grounds that it meant a dictatorship and that a dictatorship was necessary in the situation. The minority opposed it on the same grounds, i.e., that a dictatorship meant the abdication of the Commune, which was the only body elected by and responsible to the people.

After a discussion which split the Commune into its two parties the Committee was voted by a small majority on May 1st. [131] Its first members were Arnaud, Meillet, Ranvier, Pyat and Charles Gérardin. This new power was to centralize all authority. As a matter of fact, created without defined functions, it came into continual conflict with the Commune and added one more unassimilated element to the general disorder. The five delegates went everywhere and mingled in everything, their orders frequently conflicted and they succeeded in pleasing no one. Criticism of the committee occupied nearly half the time of the Commune during the first few days of May. Finally, in the desperation created by the news of the fall of Issy, three of the members of the Committee were dismissed and Gambon, Eudes and Delescluze elected to take their places. From the 9th of May until the fall of the Commune the 2nd Committee of Public Safety administered Paris, responsible only to the Commune. [132]

The 2nd committee was a majority creation without representation of the minority. The moderates in the Com-

[130] *Procès-Verbaux*, p. 556.

[131] The dispute over the Committee was so bitter that it was resolved not to print it in the "Journal Officiel." As Grousset put it, "I do not attempt to hide from you the fact that if the abstention from the vote which we have seen is known to-morrow, it means the death of the Commune." *Procès-Verbaux, MSS.*, May 1.

[132] When Delescluze became delegate of war on May 12th, Billioray was elected to take his place.

mune were further disgruntled by the dismissal of their delegates on the war committee and the appointment of Jacobins and Blanquists.[133] Convinced that their presence in the Assembly was henceforth useless, 23 of them published a manifesto on the 16th, stating their position, and prepared to withdraw.[134]

"By a particular and precise vote, the Commune of Paris has abdicated its power in favor of a dictatorship, which it has given the name of Committee of Public Safety.

"The majority of the Commune has, by its vote, declared itself irresponsible, and has abandoned to this committee all the responsibilities of our situation.

"The minority, to which we belong, affirms, on the contrary, this idea: that the Commune owes it to this revolutionary, political and social movement to accept all responsibility, declining none, however capable may be the hands to which it wishes to entrust this responsibility.

"Convinced, in addition, that the war outweighs at this time all other matters, we shall devote the leisure permitted by our municipal functions to the cause of our brothers in the National Guard, and will take our part in this decisive struggle maintained in the name of the rights of the people."

The manifesto of the minority was really secession in the ranks of the revolution itself and was so recognized in the Commune. Public opinion in Paris among the revolutionaries was, on the whole, in favor of the majority, although

[133] The Committee of Public Safety maintained that the dismissal of the members of the war committee was necessary because of disobedience to orders, in permitting the escape of Rossel. See *Procès-Verbaux, MSS.,* May 17.
[134] Ch. Beslay, Jourde, Theisz, Lefrançais, Eug. Gérardin, Andrieu, Vermorel, Clémence, Serrailler, Longuet, Arthur Arnould, V. Clément, Avrial, Ostyn, Fränkel, Pindy, Arnold, Vallès, Tridon, Varlin, Gustave Courbet, Malon. Most of them were members of the International.

the secession had its supporters.[135] As it happened, however, the majority called a special session for the next day, May 17th, and the minority responded meekly by returning to the fold.[136] Nevertheless, the discussion of May 17th in the Assembly showed clearly in what a hopeless situation the Commune had fallen. The session closed shortly after the following words of Billioray, member of the Committee of Public Safety:

"The schism is made, now you can do with me what you will.

"I wish to make a confession; this word is not too strong and is perhaps true. I am 48 years old and have never before been a member of a popular assembly. I come from the working class and am not familiar with the ways of politics; and I see here things which astonish me. I had thought I should find in this assembly something greater and more worthy." [137]

The struggle between the Commune and the Central Committee of the National Guard was even more disorganizing than the dissension within the municipal assembly over the Committee of Public Safety. Upon the election of the Commune the Committee had retired from the leadership of affairs with fine words of resignation. "Citizens, we have just put in your hands what you have charged us with establishing, and, now, at this last moment of our ephemeral

[135] E.g., the following account in "La Justice," May 17: "A fraction of the Commune, as one will see by the text of this manifesto, has just broken with the sterile parliamentarianism in which it was engulfed. It has withdrawn from the government to return to the problem of municipal administration and to that business in which it will render greater service than in the deliberations of the Hôtel de Ville.

"After the regrettable abdication of the Commune in favor of the Committee of Public Safety, this was the sole attitude which it could and should take."

[136] The Federal Council of the Paris sections of the International took strong exception to the action of its representatives in the Assembly and impressed upon them the necessity of maintaining the unity of the Commune. See Laronze, *Histoire de la Commune*, p. 156.

[137] *Procès-Verbaux, MSS.*, May 17.

power," etc. Yet at the end, we find the Committee issuing decrees on questions within the province of the Commune, taking charge of the internal defense of Paris, and slaughtering hostages in the Rue Haxo. The Committee, in truth, never completely relinquished its hold upon the direction of the revolution.

Ostensibly it had resumed its position as a mere internal institution of the National Guard, an agency for the redress of grievances and the discussion of matters of interest to the citizen militia. Yet we find, as early as April 3rd, rumors of a clash of authority between the Committee and the Commune. In the words of Rochefort, "The Central Committee, having officially transferred its power to the municipality, is constituting itself a 'Conseil de famille' and continues to impress upon the National Guard a political direction." [188]

Since the National Guard was the only armed force in Paris and consequently the army of the revolution, to control the Guard meant to control the revolution. Both the "Journal Officiel" and the Central Committee vehemently denied any such control and asserted that the Committee, "Considered by the Commune and recognizing itself as the great 'Conseil de famille' of the National Guard, has been allowed by the war delegate of the Commune to assist in the reorganization of the National Guard." [139] From "assistance in the reorganization," however, the Committee passed to something more important and more serious.

The conflict of authorities during April, while serious enough to hamper the administration of the war, as Cluseret later insisted, was not serious enough to disturb the Commune greatly. Certain early difficulties were cleared up sufficiently to permit· Pyat, on behalf of the Executive Committee, to inform the Commune, April 2nd, that all friction

[188] "Le Mot d'Ordre," April 3.
[139] "Journal Officiel," April 6. A similar statement by the Committee, April 7.

was at an end.[140] The Committee sent delegates to the Commune disclaiming any pretensions to political power and asking that its functions be defined as including merely the reorganization of the National Guard and the control of supplies (l'Intendance).[141] These powers were granted by the Executive Committee.

Nevertheless, certain members of the Commune were uneasy. Citizens Lefrançais and Ledroit observed that "the Central Committee has not lost its desire to be a power." [142] We find citizen Meillet, on April 16th, protesting against a "new encroachment of the Committee." [143] And on April 25th, citizen Chalain demanded, with a certain amount of approval from his colleagues, the dissolution of this dangerous body.[144]

That there was some justification for this attitude is obvious from a consideration of the Committee's program of war administration.[145] It proposed a complete control of all policies and measures initiated by the war delegate. Although this official was appointed, and could be dismissed, by the Commune, it was absolutely necessary, for the smooth functioning of the service, that he remain on good terms with the Committee. This both Cluseret and Rossel discovered to their sorrow.

After the dismissal of Cluseret the Central Committee came out frankly asking for the suppression of the war delegation and the placing in its hands of the administration and control of the National Guard and the defense of Paris.[146] From May 1st, the friction between the Commune and the Committee became more and more serious.

[140] *Procès-Verbaux*, p. 102.
[141] *Ibid.*, p. 115.
[142] *Ibid.*, p. 117 (April 4).
[143] *Ibid.*, p. 250.
[144] *Ibid.*, p. 473.
[145] *Enquête: Pièces Justificatives: Annexes*, p. 60. This program was formulated in the meeting of March 27th, the purpose of which was to discuss the Committee's rôle in the Commune.
[146] Session of May 3rd. *Enquête: Pièces Justificatives: Annexes*, p. 115.

The first Committee of Public Safety showed itself amenable to the claims of the Central Committee and decreed a division of powers between the war delegate and the Committee which very greatly increased the scope of the latter's recognized activity. The delegate of war, now Rossel, was charged with the "initiation and direction of military operations," and the Central Committee, "with the various services of war administration, under the control of the military commission of the Commune." [147]

The Committee soon came in conflict with the Military Commission, the membership of which was strongly of the minority group in the Commune.[148] The question of the encroachments of the Central Committee on the authority of the Commune became part and parcel of the controversy over the Committee of Public Safety. The majority party in the Commune sided with the Central Committee and when the Military Commission had been made more acceptable to the latter by the dismissal of its minority members, the split in the municipal assembly was complete. As the minority viewed the situation, the Commune had sold out to the Committee of Public Safety and the Committee of Public Safety had sold out to the Central Committee of the National Guard.

Before and immediately after the 18th of March the leaders of the communal revolution had demanded as one of their aims, the control of the National Guard by itself; i.e., by its own elected officials. This was now precisely the thing to which the Commune, or at least its minority, was objecting. It had discovered that a government which has lost control of its army has ceased to rule.

DECLINE OF THE COMMUNE

The incapacity of the Commune's administration, the

---

[147] Decree of 15 Floréal (May 6th). *Murailles,* II :423.
[148] As is evident in the sharp decree of the Military Commission limiting the functions of the Central Committee, May 8th. See *Murailles,* II:450.

succession of military reverses and the internal dissension and dispute which, in the course of time, became obvious to even the least astute, led to a rapid decline in the popularity of the revolution. This is obvious from the newspapers, from the results of the complementary elections of April 16th, from the response to the Commune's appeals for military recruits and in many other ways. As the municipal assembly lost its hold on the substantial citizenry of the capital, it fell more under the influence of the violent and irresponsible riff-raff. Its progress during May was marked by a quantity of "revolutionary" acts as impotent as they were silly; the destruction of the Vendôme column, the house of M. Thiers, the Brea Chapel, the burning of the guillotine, and others of the same order. It became obvious to the intelligent by the middle of April that the revolution was going to fail, and the cloud of impending disaster hung ever lower over the Commune during May.

The revolutionary newspapers are illuminating on this point. The Commune could and did suppress the most bitter of its critics, but objection, discontent and prophecy of disaster were rife in journals ostensibly favorable to the revolution. The most popular and one of the most revolutionary of the contemporary papers, "Père Duchêne," charged the Commune with being no longer at the head of the revolution. "We must say to you—you lack energy, you have not that ancient vigor which made so admirable in their time the men of '93, because they had arms strong enough to execute the decrees which their brains conceived." [149]

The futile discussion of the Assembly was often a subject of attack. "There is in France no time worse spent," said "La Commune," "than that in the sessions of the Hôtel de Ville; at least one must so judge from the verbal report in the official journal." [150]

"La Justice" was even more critical. "We have seen be-

---

[149] "Père Duchêne," 30 Germinal (April 19).
[150] "La Commune," April 27.

fore now strong governments which rested upon a weak, that is to say, a false principle.

"The Commune presents us at the present time, the rare spectacle of a weak government which rests on a strong principle . . .

"The Commune, such as we see it, weak, inconsistent, unconsequential, divided, lacking intelligence and with a political ignorance which exceeds anything we can imagine, resists and holds good in spite of everything.[151]

And again, "not only has the Commune not known how to organize the governmental administration of Paris, but it has not even known how to organize the defense.

"All the faults committed during the Prussian siege by the government of the 4th of September, the Commune has revived and aggravated.

"It is Trochu's plan without Trochu." [152]

The Committee of Public Safety in its order of May 18th suppressing ten papers, among them "La Commune" and "La Justice," decreed that no new paper could be established in Paris until the end of the siege, that all leading articles must be signed by their authors, and that any attack on the Commune was to be referred to the Court Martial. In spite of this, the secret police had the following report to make two days later on one of the few surviving papers.

" 'La Vérité' attacks bitterly the decree which suppressed ten of its confrères and calls this new measure monstrous. The Committee of Public Safety is accused of being merely a plagiarist of the Marquis de Tinguy and of Vinoy, and of instituting reaction to an extent the Empire never would have dared. In common with the evening papers which protested against this measure, 'La Vérité' persists in confusing a normal and regular state of society with a state of war. In consequence of this bad faith and its evident desire to misrepresent the facts and to falsify principles, it would be

[151] "La Justice," May 12.
[152] Ibid., May 13.

prudent to apply to this journal the new law of the Committee of Public Safety." [153]

The supplementary elections of April 16th showed clearly the shift of public opinion and in so doing covered the Commune with gloom. As a result of the numerous resignations and certain deaths there were 21 vacancies to be filled and the various revolutionary arrondissement and municipal committees, along with the International, selected their candidates with care.[154] Precautions were taken to get out the largest possible vote. Rochefort's paper, "Le Mot d'Ordre," printed on election day an appeal which was duplicated by most of the other journals supporting the Commune.

"It is in this situation that we appeal to the people to go to the polls. Vote for whomever you wish; for Chaudey who is in prison, or for Gaillard père, who is in charge of the barricades—but vote.

"The essential thing is that to the divagations of the papers of Versailles, we can oppose a substantial number of votes. The insecurely established Thiers who governs the anti-national assembly has declared that the Parisian 'insurrection' is made by twenty thousand ex-convicts. The sole response to make to him is to prove that it is being made by two hundred thousand citizens." [155]

The votes actually cast, however, numbered only 53,680. It was only in the 18th, 19th and 20th Arrondissements, the revolutionary and proletarian sections of Buttes-Montmartre, Buttes-Chaumont and Ménilmontant, that the electors turned out in numbers. The official journal of Versailles rejoiced over these figures, and rightly, for it was a

[153] Archives de la Seine, *Délégation de l'Intérieur et de la Sûreté Générale,* May 20. A daily report on the situation in Paris by Moreau of the Central Committee.
[154] See "Paris Libre," April 17.
[155] "Le Mot d'Ordre," April 17.

serious defeat for the Commune. As Rochefort put it; "Le Mot d'Ordre preached the vote 'à l'outrance.' It is abstention which has won out. The result of the communal elections on Sunday proves, in the first place, that we have no influence, which disturbs us, and, in the second, that the Commune is losing ground, which disturbs us much more." [156]

The vote was so scanty that the provision regarding the eighth of the inscribed voters could not be observed, as it had been, ostensibly at least, in the elections of March 26th. A number of the candidates had not received an eighth, so the Commune shifted its criterion to a bare majority of those voting. Two of the elected, Rogeard and Briosne, refused to sit under these conditions, and that sly dog, Félix Pyat, sensing the ultimate fall of the Commune, made this situation the occasion of his first resignation. [157]

Nor did the newly elected delegates add much to the strength of the Commune. Nine were members of the International, including Cluseret, elected in two arrondissements, and Longuet, who edited the "Journal Officiel." [158] Courbet, the distinguished painter, was elected from the 6th Arrondissement and busied himself chiefly during his term of office with the custody of the arts. The others were, in the main, little known, and not too competent, journalists and club orators. Of the eight elected in the conservative 1st and 2nd Arrondissements, seven were members of the International who stood without opposition.

The elections of April 16th indicated that the citizens of Paris had finally taken sides on the question of the Commune. By that date the issues had been fairly stated, every

[156] "Le Mot d'Ordre," April 20.

[157] The criticism of his resignation, both inside and outside the Commune, was so severe, however, that he was led to reconsider. He resigned again on the occasion of his difficulties in the committee of Public Safety, but again was persuaded to reconsider. However, he managed to extricate himself from the Commune in time to escape safely to England.

[158] The others who were, or had been members of the International, were Vésinier, Andrieu, Pottier, Serrailler, Durand, Johannard, and Dupont.

one realized in a sort of a way what the revolution
proposed and that to take part in the vote meant the statement of allegiance to the Commune. The majority of the
population was conspicuous by its absence. Rid for the most
part of the restraining influence of the conservative middle
class, the Commune entered upon that series of pompous
and often senseless revolutionary acts which marred the last
month of its rule.

The demolition of the Vendôme column, demanded by
"Le Cri du Peuple" of Jules Vallès on April 4th, was voted
by the municipal assembly on April 12th, in the following
terms, "In view of the fact that the imperial column of the
Place Vendôme is a monument of barbarism, a symbol of
brute force and false glory, an affirmation of militarism, a
negation of international law, a permanent insult to the
conquered by the conquerors, a perpetual attack on one of
the three great principles of the French Republic, fraternity, it is decreed that the column shall be destroyed." [159]

Having decreed its destruction the Commune put the
matter off until, goaded by the revolutionary papers, it set
the date of May 16th.

The occasion was festive. The square was decorated with
flags and flowers, the speakers moved by the fall of this
symbol of tyranny were eloquent, the column toppled grace-
fully, breaking in three parts before it landed on its pre-
arranged bed with carefully engineered precision. The
reporter for the official journal in contemplating this event
reflected upon its significance in revolutionary history.

"The 26 Floréal will be glorious in history, for it
consecrates our break with militarism, that bloody
negation of all the rights of man. . . .

"The Commune of Paris accepted the duty of destroying this symbol of despotism; it has fulfilled it.
It proves thus that it placed right above might and that

[159] "Journal Officiel," April 13.

it prefers justice to murder even when the latter is victorious." [160]

The Commune made obeisance to the 1st Revolution and to the Revolution of 1848 in two "great acts of revolutionary justice." On May 6th, the Committee of Public Safety decreed the destruction of the chapel of Louis XVI.

> "Whereas the building called the expiatory chapel of Louis XVI is a permanent insult to the 1st Revolution and a perpetual protest of the reaction against the justice of the people"; etc. [161]

The decree ordering the demolition of the chapel erected to the memory of General Brea, instrumental in repressing the June revolution of 1848, was couched by the Commune in almost identical terms.

> "Whereas the Brea chapel situated in Paris, 76, Avenue d'Italie, is a permanent insult to the conquered people of June and to the men who have fallen for the cause of the people,
> "It is decreed:
> "Article 1. The Brea chapel shall be destroyed.
> "Article 2. The square of the chapel shall be called the 'Place de Juin.' " [162]

The destruction of the Vendôme column caused much gnashing of teeth at Versailles and strengthened the desire for revenge already overdeveloped. Worse than that, it completed the estrangement between the Commune and the provinces. To the provinces the Column was a sacred symbol of the glorious history of France, the value of which the recent disasters of the war with Germany had not lessened. [163] In none of its acts was the ineptness of the

[160] "Journal Officiel," May 17.
[161] *Ibid.*, May 6.
[162] *Ibid.*, May 17.
[163] MacMahon made it the subject of an address to the army: "Soldiers!
"The Vendôme column has just fallen.

Commune more evident than in the destruction of these three monuments.

The razing of the house of Thiers in the Place St. Georges, was, however, if possible, still more futile. On May 10th, the Committee of Safety found time, in spite of its manifold duties and functions, to indite the following order:

"Considering the poster of 'sieur' Thiers, calling himself the chief in power of the French Republic;

"That this poster, printed at Versailles, has been affixed to the walls of Paris by order of the aforementioned Thiers;

"That, in this document, he declares that the army has not bombarded Paris, although every day women and children are victims of the fratricidal projectiles of Versailles;

"That he has appealed to treason in order to gain access to the city, knowing the absolute impossibility of conquering by force the heroic population of Paris,

"It is decreed,

"Article 1. The personal property of Thiers be seized by the domain administration.

"Article 2. The house of Thiers, Place Georges, be destroyed." [164]

Monsieur Fontain, to whom the Commune entrusted the execution of this decree, entered upon his work with zest. After cogitation he issued this remarkable proclamation:

"The foreigner respected it. The Commune of Paris tore it down. Those men who call themselves French have dared to destroy, under the eyes of the Germans who are watching us, this witness of the victories of our fathers against the coalition of Europe," etc.

[164] "Journal Officiel," May 11. It is interesting to observe the anti-clericalism of the committee which appears in its refusal to call the square *Saint* Georges.

"In reply to the tears and menaces of Thiers the
bombarder, and to the laws enacted by the rural assembly, his accomplice,
      "It is decreed," etc.[165]

One of the articles of the decree was, "on the site of
the house of this parricide will be established a public
square."

During these last days of the Commune the tradition of
'93 spread its influence everywhere. The Committee of
Public Safety and the majority in the Assembly were Jacobins or Blanquists, dominated by the memories of the great
Revolution. The "Père Duchêne" of Hébert had been revived in the "Père Duchêne" of 1871, which was by far the
most popular paper among the supporters of the revolution.
The revolutionary calendar was coming into frequent use
by the middle of May, Delescluze and the Committee of
Public Safety adopted it after the 20th, and the last reported
session of the Commune was dated, "1 er prairial, an 79."
The minority had protested against "this false tradition of
1793," but in the last days the majority ruled undisturbed;
the true revolutionaries governed Paris.

[165] "Journal Officiel," May 16.

CHAPTER V

THE COMMUNE OF PARIS (*Continued*)

THE SOCIALISM OF THE COMMUNE

THE chief significance of the Commune lies, as has already been suggested, in its relation to the socialist movement. In chapters six and seven the socialist and communist interpretations of the Revolution of March 18th will be considered. Before undertaking this consideration, however, it will be necessary to examine directly what there is of socialism to be found in the acts and program of the Commune, in the deliberations of its Assembly, and in its clubs and papers. The aims and intentions of the individuals and groups making up the Commune were notoriously diverse and conspicuously vague. Nevertheless, there is a considerable amount of evidence which is pertinent to the question in hand.

The causes of the revolution, we have seen, were only indirectly and very tenuously related to conscious and expressed desires for a socialist society. The outbreak of March 18th was the direct and immediate consequence of the seizure of Paris and its attendant circumstances. The current interpretation of the Commune disposes of it as an incident in the Franco-Prussian War. This view, moreover, has been strengthened by the accounts and reminiscences of surviving Communards. These fall into two fairly well marked groups. Those belonging to or sympathetic with the majority party in the Commune very often profess to see nothing of socialism in the revolution. On the other hand, the exponents of the minority point of view are convinced that the meaning of the revolution lay in its socialism.

242

Gaston Da Costa, a sturdy Blanquist, Rigault's assistant at the Prefecture of Police, concludes in the third volume of his sincere and passionate account of the Commune that "the revolution was above all republican and patriotic, in spite of the socialist philosophy of its leaders, the patriotic and republican will of the people being then its supreme law." [1] Lepelletier, a soldier of the Commune and sympathetic with the majority party, asserts after discussing various socialistic elements in the Commune, "Socialism was the result and not the cause of the revolution of the 18th of March. It profited from a communal régime which it had not created." [2]

On the other hand, those of the minority who survived to write histories of the Commune interpret the movement as being essentially socialist. Arnould, Beslay, Malon and Lefrançais, to mention no others, view the matter in this light and are inclined to maintain that the failure of the majority to understand its true significance, their preoccupation with the obsolete and misleading catchwords of the 1st Revolution, was one of the serious causes of the failure of the Commune.

The acts and decrees of the municipal assembly do not throw a great deal of light upon the motives or the ultimate program of the revolution. In the situation in which the Commune found itself it was not to be expected that serious attention could or would be paid to the various problems involved in a reorganization of society. This was particularly true because of the continual insistence of the majority that the Commune's sole immediate end and excuse for being was the struggle against Versailles. There was plenty of time for building anew after the enemy at the gates of Paris had been destroyed.

[1] Da Costa, *La Commune Vécue,* III:76. M. Georges Bourgin, an authority on all phases of the Commune, believes that many of the prominent leaders of the Commune were revolutionists for the sake of revolution. See his review of Da Costa's book, *Revue d'Histoire Moderne.*
[2] Lepelletier, *op. cit.,* III:30.

Nevertheless, in spite of the concentration upon war, a considerable number of the Commune's decrees exhibit a distinctly socialist leaning. They show a tendency to conceive the 18th of March as a revolution on behalf of the proletariat directed against the possessing class. No doubt a shallow opportunism, a desire to propitiate by legislation the class upon which it depended for support, explains a large part of the Commune's policy. But it does not explain the whole of it. Furthermore, two things in particular must be borne in mind in judging the socialism of the Commune by its works. In the first place, the acts of a radical government in power are never so radical as its program when out of power. Any body of men when brought face to face with the duties and responsibilities of government becomes to a certain extent opportunist; its policy tends to be determined by the situation and not the situation by its policy. The various European socialist and labor governments which have held power since the war furnish us with numerous illustrations of this truism. In the second place, to the France of 1871, many things were socialist which to us are not. In an economic organization permeated with the ideas and policies of an extreme laissez-faire individualism, labor legislation or other tampering with freedom of contract or with the "natural" price of commodities was considered to be socialism. A great deal of light can be thrown on the bearing of particular acts of the Commune by a consideration of contemporary opinion. If the admitted socialists of the time applauded a decree as "a step toward socialism" and admitted conservatives condemned it for the same reason, these opinions should be taken into account.

The revolution of 1871 took the central symbol of the republican device, "Liberté-Égalité-Fraternité," with some seriousness. One of the first decrees of the Commune stated that,

"Whereas in a really democratic republic there can be neither sinecure nor favored treatment;

"It is decreed:

"The maximum salary of employes in all the communal services is fixed at 6,000 francs a year." [3]

This was shortly followed by the decree abolishing the rank of general in the National Guard.

The Commune, however, went no further than this in equalizing remuneration in the public service and indeed maintained in the National Guard a scale of pay which ranged from 1 fr. 50c per day to 16 fr. 50c. In other words it merely proceeded further than most governments in the policy of inadequate compensation for higher public positions.

The Commune did, however, seriously concern itself with the condition of the laboring class. Its chief agency was the Commission of Labor, Industry and Trade, which was specifically charged with the propagation of socialist doctrines.[4] Its most active members, Malon, Fränkel and Theisz, were all of the International. Beginning with the 18th of March, the steady exodus of employers from Paris had led to the closing of large numbers of workshops and a consequent intensification of unemployment. The Commission attempted to meet this situation by a scheme providing for the utilization of abandoned plant and equipment by workers' associations. The Commune accepted the idea in principle and in a decree of April 16th authorized the associated labor unions of Paris (Chambres syndicales ouvrières) to appoint a committee to investigate the matter.

"Whereas a number of workshops have been abandoned by those who directed them, in order to escape their civic obligations, and without consideration of the interests of the laborers;

[3] "Journal Officiel," April 2.
[4] The Commune outlined its functions as follows: "The Commission is charged with the propagation of socialist doctrines. It must look for means of equalizing work and wages. It must also concern itself with the furtherance of French and Parisian industries. This Commission must, at the same time, concern itself with means of developing international trade and of attracting to Paris foreign industries, in order to make of Paris a great center of production."

"Whereas this cowardly abandonment has interrupted a number of works essential to the communal life, injuring thereby the working class;

"It is decreed," etc.[5]

This plan, however, came to nothing at all. Ten days elapsed before the Public Service Commission put an assembly room at the disposal of the projected committee.[6] It was not until May 15th that the delegates of the various labor organizations of Paris were called together to deliberate on means of taking over the workshops. This summons particularly requested the attendance of women delegates. "We ask particularly that 'les citoyennes,' whose devotion to the social revolution has been of such great assistance, shall not remain aloof from so important a matter as the organization of labor."[7]

A second meeting on May 18th was necessary to complete the organization. Four days later the Versaillese were in Paris. If the Commune had lasted longer, this measure might have led to the expropriation of absentee owners; it was certainly a tentative step in the direction of socialism.[8] As a matter of fact, it came to nothing.

A measure which occasioned a great deal more discussion in Paris was the order of the Executive Committee forbidding night work in bakeries.[9] The Committee acted upon the request of the organized labor in the trade, but the employers and a certain number of the workers protested. And, of course, conservative opinion expressed in the papers saw in this order a grave attack upon individual liberty. In the discussion of this matter which occupied the major part of the session of April 28th, certain members doubted the

[5] "Journal Officiel," April 17.
[6] Ibid., April 25.
[7] Ibid., May 10.
[8] The opposition papers treated it as an act of spoliation. See "Le Républicain," May 17.
[9] April 20.

wisdom of a policy of government interference in the labor question and others felt that the application of the decree ought to be postponed for a sufficient time to permit bakeries to reorganize their operations to meet the new conditions. However the majority opinion was expressed by the socialist Fränkel, who headed the commission on "Labor, Industry and Trade":

"I support this decree because I consider it to be the only truly socialist decree which the Commune has so far enacted; . . . we are here not only to legislate on questions concerning the municipality, but also to secure social reforms. [Très bien!] And to secure social reforms, must we first consult the employers? No. Were the employers consulted in '92?"[10]

This order went into effect May 3rd and was actually enforced. On one occasion agents of the Commune descended upon 27 bakeries of Montmartre, seized the baked bread and in other ways demonstrated their vigor in the enforcement of the law.[11] We should certainly not call a legislative prohibition of night work for bakers socialism nowadays, but in a France which had seen almost nothing of labor legislation it was so regarded both by the socialists themselves and by contemporary conservatives.

Another piece of labor regulation secured at about the same time was the order of the Executive Commission on April 28th abolishing fines.

"Whereas certain enterprises have instituted a system of fines or deductions from established wage scales;

"Whereas these fines are often imposed upon the slightest pretext and constitute a real loss to the worker;

"And whereas, in justice, nothing authorizes this vexatious and arbitrary imposition"; etc.[12]

[10] *Procès-Verbaux*, April 28, p. 543.
[11] See "Le Moniteur Universel," May 12.
[12] "Journal Officiel," April 29.

The practice was forbidden in both private and public establishments and orders given that all fines imposed since March 18th be refunded.

While this appears to our eyes a piece of labor legislation of elementary necessity, it was hailed by not too reactionary contemporaries as "A Bounty to Idleness and Incapacity." [13] Certainly what there was of organized labor and organized socialism in Paris felt that in its decrees on working conditions the Commune was showing itself to be the defender of the proletariat and of socialism. The stone cutters' section of the International prefaced an appeal for laical instruction with the following:

"Whereas the Commune of Paris has freely entered upon a policy of political and social reforms such as we favor in our declaration of principles,

"The stone cutters' section of the International Association expresses the hope,

"That the Commune of Paris persevering in this way of the progress of the human spirit," etc.[14]

The laborers in bakeries assembled 1200 to 1500 strong to thank the Commune for its efforts on their behalf.[15]

The Commission of "Labor, Industry and Trade," conceived it as part of its function to assist, wherever possible, the organization and unionization of labor in Paris. For example, we have this notice sent by the secretary of the Commission to all the arrondissement administrations:

"To encourage the development of existing associations is to stimulate the formation of new ones, and, in the same way, to shelter labor from the exploitation of capital is to shelter the individual laborer from the influence of capitalist-monarchists.

"I recommend to your attention the workers' asso-

[13] The headline of an article on this subject, "Le Petit Journal," May 4.
[14] "Journal Officiel," May 11.
[15] Ibid., May 17.

ciations and societies which follow. . . . We believe we are furthering the principle of association in indicating the names and addresses of the various associations actually existing in Paris, and in calling them to the attention of everyone." [16]

The attitude of the Commune on the labor problem is to be seen very clearly in the situation which developed in connection with the production of uniforms for the National Guard. Under the Government of the National Defense, workers on such uniforms were paid at the rate of 6 francs per jacket and 3 fr. 75c per pair of trousers. This scale of rates was taken over by the Commune. But the Assembly discovered to its consternation that, after April 25th, a contract system had been adopted with the disposal of work to the lowest bidder. A report made by Messrs. Lévy and Évette of the International presented the situation clearly. Jackets were being made for 4 fr. and trousers for 2 fr. 50c. "It follows that a price already low is being diminished by almost half, and that those who are doing the work are receiving less than living wages; . . . one can say, then, that the Social Republic has done that which those who are besieging us refused to do; i.e., it has lowered salaries." [17]

The session of May 12th was devoted to a discussion of this situation. Fränkel, after presenting a demand for action from the Commission on Labor, Industry and Trade, added a few words: "We must not forget that the revolution of March 18th was made exclusively by the working class. If we do nothing for this class, we who have as our principle social equality, I see no reason for the existence of the Commune." [18]

The Commune responded by authorizing the revision of

[16] Notice of May 14th, Archives de la Seine. There follows the names of 40 Associations of Production, 7 "Sociétés d'Alimentation," 4 consumers' cooperatives and 34 trade unions.
[17] The report of Messrs. Lévy and Évette is published in *Enquête: Pièces Justificatives: Annexes,* p. 162, and in the "Journal Officiel," May 13.
[18] "Journal Officiel," May 13.

contracts and enacted a decree providing that future ar-
rangements be made directly with workers' associations
where possible. The delegate of labor and the financial delegate were given authority to enter into agreements with
the representatives of these associations.

It was not, however, by legislation on wages and conditions of labor alone that the Commune attempted to improve the position of the proletariat. One of the contributing causes of the revolution had been the laws of the
National Assembly at Bordeaux on rents and the maturities
of financial obligations. The Commune, on the first day of
its existence, proclaimed a general remittance to tenants
of rent obligations and forbade evictions of domiciled inhabitants for a period of six months. On April 1st it asked
various labor organizations and associations of employers
for opinons on the question of the maturities. Until such
time as the Commune should issue a decree on this matter,
all existing financial obligations were suspended.

The credit situation in Paris was undoubtedly bad. The
long first siege and now the second, by seriously hampering
business enterprise, had made it impossible for a large number of debtors to meet their obligations. Other debtors, able
to pay, quite naturally took advantage of the temporary
suspension of their legal liability and refused to satisfy their
creditors. The National Assembly had met this situation
by an admittedly harsh and summary enactment ordering
the payment of obligations within a brief delay under threat
of recourse to the usual legal procedure.

The Commune's handling of this problem throws a great
deal of light upon its economic ideas and its class sympathies. Almost to a man its members were on the side of
the debtors and particularly concerned with the laborers and
small shopkeepers. The only exceptions were Beslay and
his adherents who, in true Proudhonian fashion, thought
that all interests could be harmonized with prejudice to
none. The three most discussed solutions to the problem

of the maturities were those of Tridon, Jourde, and Beslay.

Tridon's scheme, in brief, proposed a suspension of payment for three years during which time the debt was to bear interest at 2 per cent. After hearing Beslay's project he added a clause providing for the establishment of an accounting bank "to serve as intermediary between the opposed interests." [19] Just how these interests were to be reconciled is not stated. When this project appeared for discussion in the Commune, it was supported by a number of the more radical and revolutionary members on the grounds, chiefly, that it was the most socialistic of the schemes,[20] and that it was clear-cut and absolute.[21] The latter quality can certainly not be denied.

Jourde was the Commune's Minister of Finance and while he can hardly be described as a financial wizard, his proposed solution of the credit situation was more intelligent than Tridon's. He was in favor of extending maturities by two years instead of three and proposed a gradual reduction of debts by the payment of an eighth every three months, beginning July 15th, 1871. Any debtor who refused to pay was subject to prosecution for the eighth of the debt due. The scheme was designed to keep alive a certain amount, at least, of the debtor's interest in his obligations.[22]

The project of Beslay was by far the most interesting. Its author was the Commune's delegate at the Bank of France and prided himself on his familiarity with the intricacies of currency and credit. The scheme not only was to secure the eventual repayment of existing debts, but it proposed an immediate liquidation of "frozen" assets through the creation of a bank of account issuing circulating notes on the security of the commercial paper as yet unpaid.

[19] The scheme is published in the "Journal Officiel," April 17.
[20] The opinion of Parisel. See *Procès-Verbaux*, April 14, p. 206.
[21] The opinion of Fortuné, *ibid.*, p. 241. April 16.
[22] Jourde's scheme, published "Journal Officiel," April 16.

A truly Proudhonian solution! Charles Longuet, member of the Commune after the elections of April 16th and delegate to the official journal, greeted this scheme with enthusiasm. It provided not only an answer to the immediate problem but it contained the germ of a solution to more general future problems.

"The legists of Versailles are as foreign to the reality as to the philosophy of things; these men of pretended good sense and moderation are at bottom vulgar empiricists, who, to maintain an apparent order, have for sixty years found nothing better than executions and the contraction of billions of debt; the legists of Versailles face to face with this problem, have had only one preoccupation, to conciliate and to satisfy as much as possible two classes which they believe distinct, debtors and creditors.

"Never having studied the mechanism of credit and the circulation of wealth, they have not seen that these two terms, debtor and creditor, are reducible to one." [23]

Beslay's project, which avoided these vulgar errors, was in substance this; the debtors were to distribute the payment of their obligations over a period of three years in eighteen two-monthly payments, but during this time the creditors were not to suffer for the lack of liquid assets. A "Commercial Bank of Liquidation" was to be formed issuing notes of 20, 50, 100, 500, and 1,000 francs secured by the deposit of the paper drawn between July 1st, 1870, and July 15th, 1871, unpaid at maturity. In addition, the Commune was to assist the bank by opening a credit in its favor to the extent of one-fiftieth of these unpaid obligations. In Beslay's opinion all that was necessary to secure the circulation of the notes at par with the notes of the Bank of France was to declare them redeemable on August 1, 1874. By that time the currency necessary for redemption purposes would have been collected from the debtors. [24]

[23] "Journal Officiel," April 11.
[24] Beslay's project was published in the "Journal Officiel," April 11.

Unfortunately the Commune did not take kindly to Beslay's Bank of Liquidation, and the law on the maturities, enacted April 17th, was a compromise between the schemes of Tridon and Jourde. The act provided for the gradual liquidation of suspended obligations by the payment of one-twelfth every three months beginning July 15th.[25] Certainly the debtors of Paris had no occasion to complain of the harshness of this enactment.

The Commune in its decree on the pawnshops aimed at extending assistance to the poor of Paris who had been forced during the sieges to pawn, often, the necessities of a decent existence. Avrial, member of the Commission on Labor, Industry and Commerce, presented a project to the Commune on April 25th, asserting that "it is necessary to show that we are concerning ourselves with the people who made the revolution of the 18th of March. The people, living on black bread, have the right to ask that we take account of their suffering; and in satisfying their legitimate demands we must not quibble over a few millions. The institution of the pawnshop must disappear; but while waiting for this, the brave men who are fighting must be given some preliminary satisfaction." [26]

The rumor that the Commune was about to permit by decree the gratuitous withdrawal of articles placed in pawn had been circulating in Paris for some time. Quite naturally individuals wishing to benefit from this decree began to pawn their personal property. When this fact was called to the attention of the Assembly by a member it was objected that this was "merely a matter of detail." [27] The majority of the Commune felt that limitation of 50 francs per person on the value of articles withdrawn would prevent abuse of this privilege.

The Commission of Labor, Industry and Commerce pre-

[25] This decree published in the "Journal Officiel," April 18.
[26] *Procès-Verbaux*, April 25, p. 474.
[27] *Ibid.*, p. 475.

sented a report to the Commune on the pawnshops.[28] After
a lengthy review of usury through the ages, it was concluded
that "the liquidation of the pawnshops is indispensable both
because of the immorality of their principle, and the absolute nullity of their economic practice." However the loans
of the Paris pawnshops outstanding totaled 38 million
francs, a sum the Commune did not have at hand. Therefore the Commission suggested a syndicate of liquidation
which should carry on its operations over a period of five
years. "The Commune by means of institutions sincerely
social, by the support it will give to labor, to credit and to
commerce, must tend to render useless the institution of the
pawnshops, which is a resource offered to economic disorder
and debauchery."

However the Commune postponed the eradication of this
evil to a future time and satisfied itself for the present
with a decree permitting the gratuitous withdrawal of
clothing, furniture, linen, books, bedding, and tools pledged
before April 25th.[29] Such withdrawals were not to exceed
a pawned value of 20 francs. In spite of its caution in limiting individual withdrawals to 20 francs the Commune
found itself under heavy financial obligations in indemnify-
ing the pawnbrokers.

None of this economic and social legislation of the
Commune, the laws on rents, maturities, pawnshops, night
work, fines, utilization of abandoned workshops, and so
forth, was socialistic in the narrow sense of the term. None
of it involved the expropriation, strictly speaking, of property owners or the communalization of economic activities.
Yet it was the sort of legislation that a socialist government
in charge of a municipality might be expected to enact under
the circumstances. The belief in a socialist society and the
intention to establish one underlies practically all the discussion of these subjects in the Commune. Under the

[28] Published in "Journal Officiel," May 1.
[29] *Ibid.,* May 7. Enacted May 6.

circumstances, however, it was felt that the more thorough-going social reforms must be postponed in favor of immediate palliatives. As Lefrançais put it in the Municipal Assembly, when discussing the question of the pawnshops, "If the Commune triumphs, as we must hope, everything which is now called public assistance, hospitals, workhouses, pawnshops, etc., will certainly disappear. But this will come about by means of a set of new institutions which you cannot formulate in the articles of a decree . . . before suppressing them it is necessary to make them useless." [30]

The manifestos and proclamations by which the revolution presented its program to the people also throw a certain amount of light on the socialism of the Commune. One would search in vain, however, for an official manifesto of the Commune exposing a socialist program. As Dubreuihl, the author of the volume on the Commune in Jaurès' *Socialist History of France* puts it, "The Commune said little or nothing about this, because it had little or nothing to say. It was, it is necessary to repeat, an extremely composite assembly in which the authoritarian Jacobin element elbowed the international federalist and Proudhonian party; an assembly in which few men had an exact feeling for the immediate situation and still less the sense of the subsequent events which the revolution of March 18th prepared and announced." [31]

An equally important reason for the failure of the revolution to adopt an explicitly socialist program, particularly in its early stages, was the fear of antagonizing the liberal and moderate element which had helped make the 18th of March. The moderates wanted the Republic and were willing to support a movement for the extension of communal autonomy in France, but further than this they were not to be pushed.

Towards the end of the revolution, when the Commune

[30] *Procès-Verbaux,* April 25, p. 477.
[31] L. Dubreuihl, *La Commune,* p. 422.

felt power slipping from its grasp, the Delegate of Exterior Relations, Paschal Grousset, whom Rochefort rightly described as having more exterior than relations, still continued to describe the enemies of the revolution as being monarchism and centralization, though within Paris the partisans of the Commune were talking of the struggle between capital and labor, the bourgeoisie and the proletariat.[32]

The difficulty of agreement within the Municipal Assembly itself, plus the necessity of enlisting the support of "weak-kneed" liberals, prevented the early formulation and statement of a program. It was only the criticism of its friends in Paris which finally goaded the Commune to the publication of the Manifesto of April 19th. In this manifesto there was nothing of socialism; in fact, one gets the impression that the Commune was leaning over backward in its attempt at moderation. This document was to present the claims of the revolution to Paris and to the provinces, and the Assembly realized the danger of frightening those whose assistance and support was sorely needed.

The "Declaration to the French People" proposed, it is true, some significant changes; the 18th of March was described as a revolution on behalf of the proletariat; but nowhere was there a hint of an attack on property or property incomes, nor was the word socialism mentioned.

> "The Communal revolution, begun by the popular initiative of the 18th of March, inaugurates a new era of experimental, positive and scientific politics.
>
> "It means the end of the old governmental and clerical world, the world of militarism, of functionarism, of exploitation, speculation, monopoly, and privilege, to which the proletariat owes its slavery and the fatherland its misery and disaster.

[32] Address of the Commune to the "Great Cities." *Murailles,* II:503, May 15.

"Let this great and dear fatherland, deceived by lies and calumny, reassure itself!

"The struggle joined between Paris and Versailles is not of the order which can be terminated by illusory compromises; the issue is clear-cut and decisive. Victory, pursued with an indomitable energy by the National Guard, will rest with the ideal and the right." [33]

The demands of Paris as stated in the "Declaration" were precise and, except perhaps for the provision regarding the National Guard, not extreme. What the Commune appeared to demand was a highly decentralized republic.

"The recognition and consolidation of the republic, the only form of government compatible with the rights of the people and the regular and free development of society;

"The absolute autonomy of the Commune extended to all the localities of France, assuring to each its integral rights, and to every Frenchman the full exercise of his faculties and aptitudes, as a man, a citizen, and a laborer.

"The autonomy of the Commune will have for its limits only the equal autonomy of all the other communes adhering to the contract; those associations must assure the unity of France.

"The inherent rights of the Commune are:

"The responsibility for the municipal budget, receipts and expenditures; the administration of local services; the organization of the magistrature, of the local police and of instruction; the administration of property belonging to the Commune.

"The choice by election or competition, with the responsibility and the permanent right of control and recall, of all grades of municipal magistrates and functionaries.

[33] *Murailles,* II:314-315.

"The absolute guarantee of individual liberty, liberty of conscience and the freedom to work.

"The continuous cooperation of citizens in communal affairs through the free expression of their ideas, the free defense of their interests; the guarantee of these rights to be given by the Commune, the sole authority charged with the surveillance and assurance of the free and just exercise of the right of assembly and publicity.

"The organization of urban defense and of the National Guard, which elects its own leaders and is responsible alone for the maintenance of order in this city."

This program, however, can hardly be taken at its face value; it represents considerably more than, and at the same time considerably less than, the Commune's probable demands. The opposition papers in Paris rightly pointed out that the Declaration ran exactly counter to the revolutionary tradition in France, to which decentralization was anathema. The program of April 19th, in its politics, was straight Proudhon; but of Proudhon's ideas on economic organization there was nothing. Yet the element in the Commune sympathetic with Proudhonian decentralization was socialist, very largely the party of the International. Its socialism was left out of the program. The party which was indifferent to the question of economic and social reorganization, on the ground that the immediate task was destructive rather than constructive, was steeped in the Jacobin and revolutionary tradition of centralization. To this element, the majority in the municipal assembly, the rights of the Commune meant very little other than the right of Paris to rule France. In the light of this situation the Declaration can hardly be regarded as more than a statement of partial and possible claims, framed with an eye to its reception in the provinces.

Other proclamations, of the Central Committee, the Executive Commission, the various arrondissement associations, and other organizations more or less intimately connected with the revolution, shed more light on this question of the socialism of the Commune. It is necessary to remember throughout that these pronunciamentos are never more than the expression of opinion of small sections of those who were making the revolution. The Commune of 1871, in all its organizations and manifestations, was wordy but essentially inarticulate. It is extremely difficult to draw out of this babble of words anything precise on socialism or any other subject.

The Central Committee, as might be expected, was more direct and less diplomatic than the Commune. While the Executive Commission headed by those arch-Jacobins, Delescluze and Cournet, was assuring France, in an address to the Departments,[34] that "Paris aspires only to establish the Republic and to conquer its communal franchises," the Central Committee in a proclamation to the citizens of the capital adopted a different tone.

> "Workers, do not deceive yourselves: it is the great struggle; it is parasitism and labor, exploitation and production, which are opposed. If you are tired of vegetating in a state of ignorance and stagnating in misery; if you want your children to be men receiving what they produce, and not a sort of animal groomed for the factory or for war, feeding with their sweat the fortune of a speculator or shedding their blood for a despot; . . . Then, workers, be intelligent, arise! and with your strong arms throw this filthy reaction under your feet." [35]

The various arrondissement administrations composed of members of the Commune, who felt relatively free in dis-

[34] See *Murailles*, II:182-83.
[35] *Ibid.*, II:180-81, April 5.

cussing the significance of the revolution with their own revolutionary constituents, almost invariably speak of the aims
of the Commune as being something more than decentralization and the consolidation of the Republic. They all insist in
more or less violent terms that the struggle is one between
labor and capital, between the proletariat and the bourgeoisie, though they do not always use this now commonly
accepted jargon of socialism.

The members of the Commune for the 17th Arrondissement, in contrasting the programs of Paris and Versailles,
assert that the former means "the revindication of the rights
of man; it is the people, master of its destinies; it is justice
and the right to live by working; it is the scepter of the
tyrant broken by the hammer of the worker." [36]

The 17th was represented by members of the minority
party in the Assembly, delegates mainly of the International.
The 11th Arrondissement, on the other hand, had elected
Jacobins, members of the majority. Yet their explanation of
the significance of the revolution is much the same. "Who
can sustain henceforth that the struggle is not between
the Republic and the monarchy, between the proletariat and
capital, between progress and fanaticism, between light and
darkness?" [37]

As the revolution developed and liberal and moderate
support was withdrawn, the necessity for camouflage and
diplomacy disappeared. The tone of the Commune and its
various representative organizations in May is at once more
revolutionary and more socialist than in April. At a meeting
of the electors of the 4th Arrondissement, called for the
purpose of questioning their delegates on the split between
the minority and majority factions, the representatives of
both groups describe the meaning of the Commune as lying
in its socialism. As Lefrançais put it, "The end pursued by

[36] *Murailles*, II:382-83. The members for this arrondissement were
Gérardin, E. Clément, Chalain, A. Dupont and Malon.
[37] Address to the battalions of the 11th Legion. *Murailles*, II:436-37.
Mortier, Delescluze, Verdure and Avrial.

the majority and the minority is essentially the same. They both wish the definitive affirmation of the Republic, an economic transformation which will put the laborer in command and the deposition of those who oppose these reforms."[38] Amouroux, the principal representative of the majority, agreed with Lefrançais that the end of the revolution was the establishment of a socialist order.

The "Journal Officiel," while performing its chief function in publishing the decrees of the Commune, was also in part an expresser of revolutionary opinion. The tone of its leading articles was mildly socialist. However, it must be understood that these articles were not officially inspired and represented, strictly speaking, merely the opinion of their different authors. It published the various manifestos of the International issued during March, April, and May, thus lending its official approbation to the International's interpretation of the significance of the revolution.

The manifesto published in the number of March 27th stated that "the independence of the Commune is the guarantee of a contract whose clauses, freely arrived at, will put an end to class antagonism and will secure social equality."

The address of the International assembly at Geneva to the workers of Paris appeared in the issue of May 7th.[39]

"In the Communal revolution of March 18th, we have welcomed the political uprising of the working class, and we have considered it as the beginning of an era of social reorganization. Your names, *unknown* to the ignorant royalists of the Vendée, are dear to us because of your known and proven devotion to our common cause, and the principles you have enunciated in the proclamations of the Republic of the proletariat, which are those also professed in the great assemblies

[38] *MSS. Procès-Verbaux de la Réunion des Électeurs du IVᵉ arrondissement à la salle du Théâtre Lyrique,* May 20. Preserved at the Bibliothèque de la Ville de Paris.
[39] The address was dated April 15th.

of the International Association, are for us a definite
guarantee that Paris presides at this moment over the
foundation of a new social structure—of the true edi-
fice of liberty, equality and fraternity for all, not for an
infinitesimal privileged minority."

The editors printed the felicitations of the German socialists to the Commune on remaining "faithful in your duty to
yourselves and toward all the proletariat." [40] They quote
with approval a "remarkable article from "La Liberté" of
Brussels on "The End of the Bourgeoisie," extinguished by
the rising proletariat.[41]

After the 22nd of May, when the enemy troops had
entered Paris, the Committee of Public Safety, in a last
desperate appeal to the Versaillese soldiers, described the
revolution in its essence as a class struggle.

"Like us, you are of the proletariat; your interest,
like ours, lies in refusing longer to permit sworn monarchists to drink your blood as they drink our sweat." [42]

The meaning of the revolution in the minds of the
leaders, expressed in the decrees of the Commune and in its
proclamations, we have seen to be highly vague and somewhat unintelligible. While ostensibly fighting for a decentralized republic, there is abundant evidence that in the
minds of most this struggle was one between labor and capital, the proletariat and the bourgeoisie. But what the cause
of the proletariat signified, it would be hard to say. The
majority of the leaders could certainly be called socialist, but
their socialism hardly included a definite picture of the economic and social reforms necessary to reorganize the bourgeois state. It was, however, the socialism of the Commune,
such as it was, which drove the republicans to Thiers and
Versailles. As Mazzini put it in refusing his approval to the

[40] "Journal Officiel," May 2.
[41] Ibid., April 22.
[42] 3 Prairial. Murailles, II:561.

revolution of March 18th, "This insurrection which has suddenly broken out without a preconceived plan, complicated by a socialist element which is entirely negative, abandoned by all the republicans of any standing . . . must surely fail." [43]

There is a feeling among many of the socialist historians of the Commune that its socialism was to be found in the rank and file and not at the Hôtel de Ville. There is no way of recapturing the opinion of the rank and file other than by an examination of the papers, the proclamations of the various groups which sprang up spontaneously in April and May, and the reports of the meetings of the political clubs. This opinion, such as it is, seems to differ in no important respect from that of the members of the Assembly or other leaders of the revolution. There were the same political alignments, the same motive of injured patriotism in opposing the "capitulards" of Versailles, the same slogans of republicanism and decentralization and the same underlying belief in the revolution as a class struggle. The rank and file were neither more nor less socialist than the leaders, though often more violent because of an absence of responsibility.

"Le Père Duchêne," the most popular newspaper of the revolution, was also the most violent. It was frankly Blanquist and wrapped its whole conception of the revolution around Blanqui. In its election proclamation, 17 Germinal, we read,

> "Blanqui, citizens, is the social revolution in person!
> "Blanqui is the honor, the probity, the patriotism, the heroism, the living incarnation of socialism, of the rights of the people and of the demands for universal equality.
> "Name at the head of your lists the good Blanqui."

"Le Père Duchêne" preached the class struggle and envisaged the 18th of March as an expression of the class

[43] "Le Républicain," May 17. From the "Roma del Popolo."

struggle. In its invocation to the dead, buried amid great pomp and circumstance by the Commune on April 6th, it defined the issues.

> "The struggle is between work and parasitism!
> "It is a coalition of workers against capitalists!
> "You have died for that,
> "O citizens!
> "You have died because you wanted to put an end to this theft,
> "Because you wished to live your own lives,
> "And not support nobles, priests, and the wealthy."

Nor was "Le Père Duchêne" the only popular Commune newspaper which interpreted the revolution in terms of socialism and the class struggle. "Le Cri du Peuple" of Jules Vallès, "L'Action" of Lissagaray, and others took this same view.

The political clubs functioned during the Commune as they did during the first siege. The churches in many cases were used as club rooms. The absence of police repression made them more violent and the lack of opposition made them less popular, but otherwise there was little difference. The program adopted at the Club de la Révolution sitting in the church of Saint-Bernard in the 18th Arrondissement, 21 Floréal, gives an idea of the opinion of the more obscure revolutionaries. The following recommendations were voted:

> 1. The suppression of the magistrature and the abolition of the existing code, replacing it by one more in accord with the new institutions and legitimate aspirations of the people.
> 2. Suppression of cults, arrest of the priests as accomplices of Versailles; the immediate sale of their wealth.
> 3. Replacement of the pawnshops decree, by one

THE COMMUNE OF PARIS (Continued) 265

returning free all objects pawned by the defenders of the city and by such women as have justified this favor by their service to the revolution.

4. Any bearer of a purchased passport to be fined or imprisoned and have his passport confiscated.

5. Suppression of houses of prostitution.

6. Work undertaken for the Commune hereafter to be given to the various workers' associations.

7. The execution of an important hostage every twenty-four hours until the liberation and arrival in Paris of citizen Blanqui, member of the Commune."

There is no more of socialism in this series of recommendations than in the programs of the Commune. Underlying these is certainly some conception of the revolution as a class struggle. The address of the "Workers of Paris" to the "Workers of the Country," quoted below, is more explicit in its statement of the right of labor to its full product and may be taken, in recapitulation, as a socialist pronunciamento typical of a very large element in the Communal revolution.

"Brother, they are deceiving you. Our interests are the same. What I demand, you wish also; the freedom that I claim, ought to be yours. What does it matter whether it is in the city or the country that bread, clothing, shelter is lacking to those who produce all the wealth of the world? What does it matter whether the oppressor be called large landowner or industrialist? With you as with us the days are long and the work rough, and they do not yield even that which satisfies the mere needs of the body. To you as to me, liberty, leisure, the life of the spirit and the heart are lacking. We are now and always have been, you and I, vassals in misery. . . .

" Published in "Paris Libre" (Vésinier's paper), May 14.

"The land to the peasant, the tool to the worker, and work for all." [45]

THE ANTI-CLERICALISM OF THE COMMUNE

There was one thing, in the midst of continual disagreement and dissonance, upon which the various parties in the Commune saw eye to eye, and that was their opposition to the church and to religion. Atheism was a cardinal tenet of Blanqui's faith, and his disciple Rigault was an adept at priest-baiting. Proudhon's great antithesis had been the Revolution versus the Church. The Jacobins inherited their anti-clericalism from '92 and '93; and the International opposed religion in the spirit which has dominated all French socialism. There were degrees, it is true, in the intensity of this antagonism. It ranged from a mild declaration of the principle of religious toleration, the wish to see all sects treated alike, to the violent passions released in the last days of the Commune, which resulted in wholesale shootings of the clergy. But whatever its shades and differences, anti-clericalism was a rallying ground of the revolution.

The municipal assembly exhibited its secular sympathies at the outset in a decree separating church and state, suppressing the religious budget and declaring the wealth held by religious bodies in mortmain national property. From the 1st of April the Communal police began to imprison the clergy on the ground that they were natural accomplices of Versailles, and before the middle of May the prisons bulged with them. Darboy, Archbishop of Paris, was one of the first arrested. When the news of the shooting of Duval by the Versaillese came to the Commune, Rigault and others demanded a general massacre of priests in retaliation and were only restrained by the enactment of the decree of the hostages. From this time on, the majority of the hostages

[45] This address, the work of the socialists Malon and Mme. André Léo, was distributed in the provinces by means of balloons equipped with a releasing device.

detained by the Commune came from the clergy. The Commune hoped by the decree of the hostages to deter Thiers from shooting prisoners taken in battle. Whether it was the decree or for some other reason, the Versaillese pursued for a period more civilized tactics, and the hostages accumulated unmolested. Then it occurred to the Blanquists in Paris that the more important of the hostages might be exchanged with Thiers for Blanqui, imprisoned March 17th. Negotiations were undertaken by Flotte, an old friend of Blanqui, who obtained from the archbishop a letter to Thiers proposing the exchange of himself, Deguerry, curé of the Madeleine, Bonjean, ex-president of the Senate, and Lagarde, General Vicar of Paris, for the old revolutionary. But the head of the government refused. Then Rigault authorized the exchange of all the hostages held by the Commune, and Flotte sent this offer to Versailles, but Thiers still refused.[46]

The papal nuncio, and through him, the American ambassador, Washburne, lent themselves to this negotiation, but without success. As Washburne stated the matter to Thiers, the government could lose nothing in placing Blanqui at liberty and it would probably save the life of the archbishop and his colleagues.[47] But Versailles refused to consider the hostages in danger, in spite of the serious warnings of the mediators. Apparently, Thiers feared the presence of Blanqui in the Commune. But the real reason for refusing this exchange was that it would simply encourage the imprisonment in Paris of additional hostages to be used in wringing further concessions from the government.

After the Versaillese had entered Paris, the revolution assassinated Darboy and his associates, as had been predicted. The Communards have persisted in laying the responsibility for this assassination at the door of Thiers. In

[46] See Da Costa, *La Commune Vécue*, I:424.
[47] E. B. Washburne, *Recollections of a Minister to France* (New York, 1887), II:175.

the words of Rochefort, "The premeditated obstinacy of Thiers, who persisted in refusing all negotiation, even for the release of the archbishop, indicated the depth of his plan. He foresaw the execution of Darboy and the curé of the Madeleine so clearly that it would seem as if he himself had given the order. If the Commune, showing magnanimity, had sent him the two priests without conditions, he would certainly have been placed in a serious embarrassment." [48] In other words, Thiers wanted an atrocity to blacken the Commune and to justify the measures of repression which he contemplated. It is more than probable, however, that the release of the archbishop would not have deprived Thiers of his atrocity. The revolution's hatred of the church and the clergy would have assured him that.

The anti-clericalism of 1871, imitating that of 1793, found it ironically appropriate that the churches be used as meeting places for the revolutionary clubs. Religion was denounced from the pulpits, and gothic vaults frequently rang with the condemnation of the clergy. The first church taken over as a club was Saint-Nicolas-des-Champs, and others followed rapidly; Sainte-Geneviève, Saint-Séverin, Saint-Eustache, Sainte-Élizabeth and many others. The "Bulletin Communal," which called itself the organ of the clubs, described the occupation by the people of the 3rd Arrondissement of a church to be used for this purpose. It was a "great revolutionary act," the taking possession of a public monument which, until the present, had been used by the "born enemies of all progress."

"Follow our example, open communal clubs in all the churches; the priests will be able to officiate by day and you can carry on the education of the people in the evening." [49]

A contemporary has described a club meeting in Saint-Nicolas-des-Champs, on April 28th.

[48] *Aventures,* III-32.
[49] "Bulletin Communal," May 6.

"One would have believed himself in the time of the first revolutionary Commune; it was like a vignette of 1793. The church was lighted as if for a great fête; an enormous crowd inundated the central nave and overflowed into the aisles, a noisy, shouting crowd, which saluted with wild applause every wild suggestion. Women were there in large numbers, many of them with children in their arms. The officers sat at the altar, and the president used the bell reserved for mass. The orators mounted into the pulpit."[50]

The Commune was interested in the elimination of religious instruction and the organization of laical schools. A commission of education was appointed, headed by the novelist Jules Vallès; but apparently it was not very active.[51] Nevertheless, a certain number of secular schools were established. The Communal school for boys in the 10th Arrondissement was reorganized to offer "all the guarantees of instruction and morality desirable.

"The instruction, exclusively rational, will include reading, writing, grammar, arithmetic, the metric system, first elements of geometry, geography, the history of France, rational ethics, vocal music, and artistic and industrial design."[52]

In the 3rd Arrondissement three schools were taken out of the hands of religious and entrusted to lay instructors. Almost every arrondissement had its local committee composed of revolutionaries interested in eliminating the church and religion from education. The Communal delegation in the 2nd Arrondissement expresses in its report the typical view on this matter:

"Absolutely convinced of the urgent necessity of preparing a healthy and strong generation, able to utilize

[50] Edmond de Pressensé, *Les Leçons du 18 Mars*, pp. 65-66.

[51] The fact that this Commission had been assigned only 1,000 francs by the Commune for the period March 30th to April 30th gives a measure of its activity.

[52] See *Murailles*, II:325.

in the future the results of the Revolution, we desire to
institute a true system of education; an instruction
which in the field of science will limit itself to known
and proven facts, springing pure and without alloy
from the crucible of the human reason; and in the field
of ethics, to those eternal principles of justice and liberty which should mold the man and the citizen. . . .

"It is necessary that humanity arrive at a precise
realization of that precept, old as society, and the basis
of all true equality: 'He who does not work must not
eat.' " [53]

Rationalism, materialism and progress were the terms
which the Commune opposed to religion, obscurantism, and
reaction. As the Committee on Secular Instruction in the
20th Arrondissement put it:

"The so-called religious dogmas are an obstacle to
progress.

"As opposed to natural and positive science they
tend to deceive the intelligence.

"Their entirely arbitrary morality is hostile to the
sovereign principles of justice and solidarity.

"They have consecrated all privilege and sanctioned
all servitude." [54]

The assistance rendered by the priests and the nuns in
the hospitals and ambulance service was another source of
irritation to the revolutionaries. The representatives of the
church were everywhere regarded with suspicion and, where
their services were not absolutely necessary, with open hostility. It was frequently charged, in the clubs and elsewhere,
that nuns working as nurses in the hospitals neglected the
soldiers of the Commune and aggravated their suffering.

[53] Signed Pottier, Serrailler, Jacques Durand, J. Johannard—of the Commune. This document in the Archives de la Seine.
[54] Archives de la Seine. Signed by the members of the Commune,
Ranvier, Viard and Trinquet.

A poster, published by Doctor Rousselle, under the heading "Administration of Ambulances of the Universal Republic," described the evil effect of religion on the wounded:

> "I have taken particular care to free the wounded of the fatiguing visits of those people who, under the pretext of religion, come to demoralize them by adding to their physical suffering moral tortures, utilizing the weakness of all their faculties to convict them of sin, holding it to have been a crime to fight in the name of the right and of the Universal Republic, to the point almost of making them blush for their wounds." [55]

The period of the Commune was made lurid with the tales of the crimes and secret sins of ecclesiastics. The popular mind, with its natural taste for the melodramatic and its naïve belief in the sexual perversion of the clergy, wallowed in the "revelations" supplied by the revolutionary newspapers and brochures. "The Confessions of a Breton Seminarist," "The Revelations of an Ex-Curé," "The Corpses of the Church of Notre-Dame-des-Victoires" were displayed in the newsstands to an avid public. The mysteries of clericalism, cloistered nuns, the lubricity of the priesthood, were entertaining, not to say exciting, subjects of conversation.

The Commune was relentless in its pursuit of the hidden crimes of the church. At the convent of Picpus, a much used "cradle" was discovered which, after a wave of popular excitement, turned out to be nothing more than an instrument for the treatment of orthopedic cases in the institution. Likewise, the three maidens sequestered in a remote and inaccessible outbuilding appeared, after investigation, to be three middle-aged nuns who had been separated from the main body because of insanity.

But the main crime of the clergy, unveiled during the Commune, was revealed in the discovery of sixteen or eighteen corpses, all but three those of women, in the vaults

[55] Archives de la Seine.

of the Saint-Laurent Church. The passions of the mob were at fever heat. "Credulous mothers," said the "Cri du Peuple," "You who confide your honor and the life of your children to the priests, you for whom any attack on the clergy is calumny or blasphemy, come and see for yourselves what the hideous caverns of the old church of Saint-Laurent disclose. You who complain that the acts and words of your saints are misunderstood or travestied by the revolutionaries;

"Here nothing of that sort is possible. The priest has worked alone in the shadows.

"Here Catholicism is in operation; come and contemplate it." [56]

The Commune ordered an investigation which came to nothing, but Leroudier, of the 10th Arrondissement, made a report which was published in the "Journal Officiel," May 21st, and which reveals admirably the mentality and the superstitions of a large element in the revolution. After drawing a lurid spectacle of the history of Saint-Laurent, in the days when the "tonsured sadists" brought their feminine prey to the caverns by way of secret tunnels, the report turns to the present. Let the pitiful victims of ecclesiastical sensualism speak for themselves:

"The priests, our pitiless persecutors, after having attracted us here by force or ruse, after having made us the object of their brutal lubricity, soon left us; it was necessary to give way to younger and more beautiful girls; after the outrages of the last orgy, we were drugged by a powerful narcotic and delivered, powerless to defend ourselves, to those monsters, who despoiled us of our clothes and bound us so tightly that one can still see the contraction of the bones against one another. At the end of a certain time, the effect of the narcotic being weakened, the consciousness of existence returned to us; terror and inexpressible anguish seized us; we sought instinctively to disengage ourselves

[56] Issue of May 7.

from the earth which oppressed us." [57] But in vain, the poor girls had been buried alive.

Unfortunately for M. Leroudier and for those who wished to believe in the criminality of the clergy, an expert examined what remained of the corpses and reported his findings. They were: (1) that the majority of the women had died at an advanced age, after having lost many of their teeth; (2) that two of the remaining women had been seriously affected by rickets; (3) that while it was impossible to determine exactly the date of burial, it was clear that it had taken place a very long time ago, when the practice of burial in church vaults, on occasion, was still observed. [58]

The revolutionary hatred of the clergy appeared at its height in the executions which blackened the last days of the Commune. It was these executions which captured the minds of contemporaries and furnished an excuse for the brutality of the repression. They have also played, unfortunately, by far too large a part in establishing the Commune's place in history. The revolution of March 18th was neither a particular bloody nor a particularly violent affair. The number of executions before the entrance of the Versaillese was negligible. And outside of the suppression of newspapers, the Commune had not resorted to violent measures. Life in Paris, by all reports, was practically as peaceful and well ordered as in normal times. The execution of the hostages was the chief crime of the Commune and by this crime its reputation was established.

The shooting of priests and gendarmes, however, was not a premeditated act of the Communal Assembly, but the work of vindictive individuals. The municipal assembly disintegrated after the entrance of the Versaillese, and the various members of the Commune made their way to different sections of Paris, either to take part in the fighting or to

[57] *Deuxième Rapport sur la recherche des crimes commis à l'Église Saint-Laurent.* No trace exists of the first.

[58] The report of Piorry, professor in the Faculty of Medicine.

attempt to escape. Any order or central direction in the Commune or in the disposition of its forces disappeared with the appeal of Delescluze calling for a battle of the barricades.

"Enough of militarism, enough of decorated general staffs with gold braid at every seam! Give way to the people, to the fighters with bare arms! The hour of the revolutionary war has struck.

"The people knows nothing of wise manœuvres: but when it has a gun in its hand and the pavement under its feet, it isn't afraid of all the strategists in the whole monarchist school." [59]

Under these circumstances, with barricades springing up all over Paris, with the revolution split up and disorganized into a hundred little groups intrenched at every street corner, what restraint the Commune might have exercised on the passions of the mob or of individuals was non-existent. The hatred of the clergy and the desire to take revenge upon Versailles by the execution of the hostages was not to be controlled. The men of the Central Committee, contemptuous of the feeble shilly-shallying of the Commune, came into their own, and applied the strong measures they had for so long advocated.

Even in the Communal Assembly, before that body disintegrated, there was grumbling that the decree of the hostages, enacted April 6th, had remained a dead letter. On May 17th, Urbain, in the presence of a report that a nurse connected with the ambulance service had been violated and massacred by the Versaillese, demanded that ten of the hostages be shot within twenty-four hours. [60] Amouroux insisted that half of them be of the clergy. "Every time that the Versaillese, who, as you know, have certain religious ideas, kill one of ours, we must immediately shoot not only

[59] 3 Prairial. *Murailles*, II:558.
[60] "Journal Officiel," May 18.

a gendarme or a 'sergent de ville' but also a priest." [General assent.] [61] However, the Assembly took no steps in this matter, and completed its rôle in the revolution without having, as a body, given the order for the execution of a single hostage. Nevertheless, it could hardly wash its hands of the responsibility.

When the last meeting of the Commune broke up on May 22nd, after the enemy had entered Paris and the battle of the barricades had been accepted as the last resort, the more violent of the members, associated with the Committee of Public Safety and with the police, took the matter of the hostages into their own hands. An order of the Committee of Public Safety directed the transfer of the more important hostages from the prison of Mazas, in the line of the enemy attack, to the prison of La Grande Roquette, near the cemetery of Père Lachaise and in the midst of the proletarian and revolutionary quarter close to Belleville. The Committee was aware that this transfer of hostages meant execution. A second decree ordered the Procureur of the Commune, Rigault, to assist Régère in the application of the decree of the hostages in his arrondissement.[62]

Da Costa, who was in charge of the transfer of the hostages to La Grande Roquette, gives us a clear picture in his reminiscences of the temper of these days.

"What was my state of mind during this mission? Did the thought that this transfer was for the prisoners a step towards death torment me? No.

"With all the insouciance of extreme youth, under the very living influence of revolutionary fanaticism, I acted, convinced that I was executing a necessary order. I will avow it, I even experienced some pride. There was an instant, however, when I lost all my calmness; it was the 22nd, in the evening, at a corner in the Faubourg Saint-Antoine; the shrieks of the delirious mob unnerved me. For an

[61] *Procès-Verbaux, MSS.,* May 17.
[62] Cited by Da Costa, *La Commune Vécue,* I:464.

anguishing moment I imagined the conscienceless mass, blind, unchained, and ferocious, overcoming us and massacring on the spot our prisoners." [63]

On the 24th the executions began. The troops of Versailles advancing in a semi-circle had captured the Montparnasse station, were attacking Montmartre and had reached the Luxembourg. Ferré, the assistant to Rigault, called with a squad at the prison of the Prefecture, already in flames, demanded one Veysset, accused of complicity with Versailles, and had him shot on the bridge near the statue of Henri IV. Across the river, on the left bank, the government troops were already assembling for their attack on the *Cité*. The same day Rigault executed Gustave Chaudey, friend of Proudhon, editor of "Le Siècle," whom many revolutionaries had supposed responsible for the massacre of January 22nd at the Hôtel de Ville.

Later in the day, in the center of the revolutionary 11th Arrondissement, Ferré, besieged with the demands of furious Communards who wanted blood, signed the order for the execution of six of the principal hostages of La Grande Roquette. His adjutants, Fortin and Genton, carried out this order. On the evening of the 24th, Darboy, Archbishop of Paris, Deguerry, curé of the Madeleine, Bonjean, ex-president of the Senate, and three associates, all priests, were shot in the yard of the prison.

Next day the scene shifted to the 13th Arrondissement, where the Communards were still holding out in the neighborhood of the Place d'Italie. The victims were the Dominicans of Arcueil, imprisoned since the 19th of May at the fort of Bicêtre. The monks, who inhabited the monastery of Arcueil, had been accused of giving information to the enemy, a charge never substantiated, and were imprisoned on the order of Wroblewski after the capture of the Moulin-à-Moutarde redoubt. Just before Bicêtre fell into the hands of Versailles the Federals, evacuating the fort hastily, took

[63] Cited by Da Costa, *La Commune Vécue*, I:473.

with them their prisoners. They were locked up in the jail of the 9th Sector, but not for long. The thirst for blood was keen in the arrondissement and the revolutionaries found a commander who could satisfy their appetites. Moreau, Wroblewski's chief of staff, gave the order to bring the prisoners into the street where a crowd, made up largely of women, participated in a shooting which turned into a veritable chase, as the victims attempted to escape.[64] Twelve were killed on this occasion.

On the 26th the revolution still commanded the heights of Belleville and the adjacent territory, but the enemy surrounded what remained of the Commune on all sides. The tricolor floated over Montmartre and the Buttes Chaumont. The prison of La Grande Roquette disgorged the hostages who had been transferred there on the 22nd and, to the number of 52, they were marched past Père Lachaise cemetery and up the long hill surmounted by the Rue Haxo. Here the last commander of the revolutionary forces, Hippolyte Parent, had established his quarters. The prisoners were accompanied by a surging, jesting, drunk, and unruly mob clamoring for death. The twenty-eight guards of Paris, ten gendarmes, four civilians and ten priests were huddled together in a small courtyard while Varlin of the Commune pled with the mob for their lives. But the Commune was no longer in power. During the last few days the Central Committee had supplied what there was of leadership in the defense of Paris. And the more criminal and violent of the local leaders of the revolution were no longer held in check. The fifty-two hostages were assassinated in the Rue Haxo by an ungovernable revolutionary mob.

Among the four "civilians" was the banker Jecker, who had been active in the unhappy venture in Mexican finance

---

[64] The usual account credits Sérizier, commander of the 13th Legion, with the responsibility for the killing, and he was executed on this charge by the military court. I have preferred to follow the account of Maxime Vuillaume, *Mes Cahiers Rouges, Cahiers de la Quinzaine 11ᵉ série, 9ᵉ Cahier.* Vuillaume has examined the question with great care.

which marked the reign of Napoleon III. There was something of revolutionary justice in the execution of a precursor of the era of economic imperialism by a revolution which professed something of socialism.

Thus were some seventy innocent men, whose death benefited the cause of the Commune not one whit, sacrificed to the thirst for vengeance which dominated the wild and ungovernable revolutionary mob during the last days of the Commune.

THE FALL OF THE COMMUNE

The troops of Versailles entered Paris through an unguarded breach in the walls, on the night of May 21-22, sixty-four days after the 18th of March. But it was not until a week later, the 28th of May, that the last of the Communal guns ceased its fire in the proletarian 11th Arrondissement. The intervening seven days witnessed the most bloody street battles known in modern times before the Russian Revolution. The June days of 1848 were pale compared to these. Whatever might have been the weakness of the Commune's army outside the walls of Paris, the revolutionaries, with the pavement under their feet, and behind their five hundred-odd barricades, fought like men insane. The women were equally inspired, or bedeviled, and boys from seven to sixteen took their places beside the men. The Commune forces, by the defection of the unwilling or the prudent, had been pared down to the true revolutionaries, but these behaved as such.

The Commune Assembly faded out of the setting on the 22nd of May. Some of its members joined the military units in the arrondissements and fought on until the end. Others, and they were numerous, went into hiding or sought to escape over the frontier. The number of revolutionary leaders who turned up later, unharmed, in Belgium, Switzerland, and England was astonishing.

"What constitutes in our eyes," says Da Costa, "the political crime of the Communal Assembly, in the hours of revolutionary agony, was not the execution of the hostages, although this has been generally said and believed; it unhappily did nothing in this matter. Its crime, on the contrary, was its lamentable self-effacement, its dispersion, its desertion. Its crime, again and above all, was the cowardly attitude of most of its members before the third council of war, when the responsibility of the violent and inevitable acts of the last days was put up to them." [65]

Delescluze died on the barricades, Vermorel perished in the street fighting, Varlin was shot by an execution squad after being conducted through hissing crowds in that 18th Arrondissement from which the revolution sprang. Rigault was captured and executed on the spot, appropriately enough, in the midst of his own Latin Quarter, surrounded by cafés and brasseries from which he had rarely been absent. His assistant, Ferré, captured, tried, and executed, died like a man with a "Vive la Commune!" on his lips.

On the other hand, the ever-prudent Pyat escaped early and safely to England; Arnould, Jourde and a host of others made their way to Belgium and Switzerland; and the fire-eating Blanquists had a large enough contingent in London, some of them former members of the Commune, to give Karl Marx serious trouble in maintaining the control of the first International. The aged Beslay was expedited to Switzerland, with the cognizance of Thiers, under the conduct of the Marquis de Plœuc, assistant governor of the Bank of France. His protection of the Bank against the attack of certain elements in the Commune earned him his life.

The last few days of the revolution, therefore, saw a more or less unorganized mob, retreating from barricade to barricade before the overwhelming superior forces of the

[65] Da Costa, *La Commune Vécue*, I:447.

government troops. A decree of the Committee of Public Safety ordered that every shutter and blind in Paris be kept open, to prevent firing on the revolutionary troops. The defenders of Paris did not hesitate to call the aid of fire to their defense and from the 23rd to the 28th the city was in flames. A dispatch signed by Gambon and Arnaud of the Committee of Public Safety ordered the burning of suspected houses. "Ransack those houses which appear suspect and have them burned if the inhabitants act against the revolution or fire on the national guard."

When Charles de Varigny protested to a Commune officer against the burning of his house, he was shown the following order, which must have been typical of a large number.

> "The chief of the barricade will occupy the house forming the angle and on which the barricade is supported. He will establish there a part of his men and their collection of ammunition. In the event that, after as long a resistance as possible, he is obliged to withdraw before superior forces, he will burn the house and leave behind him nothing but ashes and ruins.
>
> (Signed)   "Varlin." [66]

The number of houses burned in the defense of Paris ran into the hundreds. To what extent this burning was necessary to the plan of defense and to what extent it represented pure vindictiveness it is very difficult to say. Naturally the anti-Communards have found the latter explanation of more importance, and the Communards and their sympathizers, the former. The socialist Guesde, who, of course, was sympathetic with the Commune, says that of all the fires in Paris only two can be attributed to the Commune: the Tuileries and the Hôtel de Ville, and these "were a matter of principle for the republican and socialist revolution of March 18th." The other fires were (1) strategically necessary to the defense, (2) those lighted by the incendiary fuses

[66] L. Thomas, *Documents*, p. 137.

and bullets of MacMahon, or (3) those of undiscoverable origin.[67] This contention will not stand examination.[68]

A belief which had wide currency at the time among the Versaillese and which has been handed down as evidence of the depravity of the Communards is the legend of the "pétroleuses." It was alleged that women circulated in the residential areas of Paris armed with petrol and other inflammable substances to burn the houses indiscriminately. "The rôle played by women in the insurrection," said the "Paris Journal" of May 28th, "exceeds the limits of horror.

"Not only do these Megaeras, organized into bands of 'pétroleuses,' attempt to burn the monuments; but, in the quarters occupied by the army, they burrow, looking for a favorable opportunity to burn the houses which the mitrailleuse has spared."

"Le Gaulois" of May 29th discovered that these women were paid 10 francs a day for their efforts, and described in detail their activities. "The incendiaries, armed with tin cans about the size of a sardine can and containing a composition of petrol, tallow and sulphur, slip into the houses and, lighting a fire, escape."

The Assembly at Versailles debated the case of the pétroleuses, and a law regulating the sale of petrol was proposed. In the same session it was alleged that a number of lower-class women had attempted to help the cause of the insurgents by poisoning the soldiers with liquor offered for the pretended purpose of giving relief.[69]

There is, it is needless to say, no evidence to support these beliefs. It is possible that in isolated cases, houses may have been burned by women, but if so, it does not follow that they were acting under orders of any revolutionary organization or that they were paid for their activities. There

[67] *Çà et là*, p. 55.
[68] See on this Laronze, *op. cit.*, p. 600, note. He has gone into the matter of the responsibility of the Commune for the burning of Paris very thoroughly.
[69] "Journal Officiel" (Versailles), May 28.

were, in all conscience, sufficient explanations of the fires
without resorting to this fantastic legend of the pétroleuses.

For five days the flaming houses and public buildings
illuminated the sky of Paris. It was this horrible sight of
ruin and destruction greeting the eyes of the returning
Versaillese which, as much as anything, explains their implacable spirit of revenge.

The events of the bloody week of May have nothing to
do with the socialism of the Commune, yet any socialist
history of the revolution of March 18th is largely devoted
to this subject. It was in the wild and despairing battles of
the barricades that the true heroes of the revolution
emerged. Almost any socialist knows more about the Mur
des Fédérés than the whole economic, social, and political
policy of the Commune combined. The thousands upon
thousands of the proletariat shot in the streets of Paris have
given the Commune its chief socialist significance. In the
light of this slaughter the feeble, faltering and often incredibly stupid leadership of the Commune is forgotten. In
its death the revolution was far more robust than it had ever
appeared in life. The words of Henry Maret, the collabo-
rator of Rochefort, are very true and very just, "The massacre was not only a crime, it was for the reaction itself a
grievous fault. The Commune which would have faded out
in ridicule assumed a tragic grandeur."

The insurgents were far from understanding their true
situation at the time of the entrance of the government
troops. Just how far can be seen from the terms of conciliation, proposed as from one sovereign power to another,
by the Central Committee on the 4th Prairial, the 24th of
May:

> "We propose to the armed and heroic people who
> have elected us, we propose to the misguided men who
> attack us, the single solution capable of stopping this

bloodshed, while safeguarding the legitimate rights that Paris has conquered:

"1. The National Assembly, whose rôle is finished, must be dissolved.

"2. The Commune will dissolve itself at the same time.

"3. The army called *regular* will leave Paris, and must withdraw to a distance of at least twenty-five kilometers.

"4. A provisional power will be named, composed of delegates of the cities of over 50,000 inhabitants. This body will choose from among its members a provisional government, which will have as its mission the preparation of the election of a constituent assembly and the Commune of Paris.

"5. No reprisals will be taken against the members of the Assembly or the members of the Commune, for events after the 26th of March.

"These are the sole acceptable conditions.

"Let the blood shed in a fratricidal war be upon the heads of those who repulse these conditions.

"As to us, we have, as in the past, fulfilled our duties up to the end." [70]

No document could better illuminate the qualities of mind of the Central Committee, a body thoroughly representative of the revolution, than this. That a collection of men, after two and one-half months in a position of leadership and responsibility, could have been so abysmally ignorant of the realities of the situation as to put forward a proposal of this sort, tells us all about the direction of the revolution that it is necessary to know. The Communal Assembly, it is true, was a shade more capable than this, but hardly more than a shade.

If this plan for conciliation represented the leaders' esti-

[70] *Murailles,* II:571.

mation of the situation on May 24th, they were quickly
disillusioned. The temper of the returning Versaillese and
the soldiers of the regular army soon became evident. On
the first day or two of the fighting numerous prisoners were
taken—after that they became considerably fewer. The
Germans closed what gates of Paris were not in possession
of Thiers. Then the slaughter began. The wanton firing
of the public buildings of Paris exacerbated the fury of the
Versaillese. From shooting merely the leaders of captured
groups of Communards, they proceeded to the shooting of
a large portion of National Guards caught with guns in
their possession. The revolutionaries, finding their retreat
cut off from the rear and realizing that capture meant death,
fought with the desperation of despair.

The National Guards of the party of order who had
either fled to Versailles or remained in hiding during the
Commune distinguished themselves by their violence and
cruelty. Arrayed in their uniforms once more, with their
allegiance to the cause of Versailles indicated by a brassard,
these men who had remained at home the 18th of March
now made their particular function the ferreting out of the
Commune's sympathizers. This function they performed
with an enthusiasm which was nauseating to all the foreign,
and therefore relatively unbiased, observers who happened
to be in Paris at the time.

The spirit of revenge which dominated the Paris of law
and order is evident in the papers which were returning
gradually from Versailles.

"If, in the midst of these frightful and desolating disasters," said the Paris Journal of May 26th, "there is anything which can console us, it is the knowledge that the
guilty cannot escape punishment.

"Tracked down into their last lairs, these wild beasts
have avenged themselves with a horrible vengeance, worthy
of this infamous mob which formed the army of the Commune." At Versailles, during the Commune, the revolution-

aries had been assassins, brigands, beasts in human form, and the like, to the conservative papers, and the battles in the streets did not improve their reputations.

After the 25th, courts-martial established at the Châtelet, the Luxembourg, the Parc Monceau, La Grande Roquette, and at many of the arrondissement centers facilitated greatly the extermination of the Communards. The prisoners who had been seized with weapons, or because they wore the uniform or part of the uniform of the National Guard, or because they had been accused by fellow citizens, were summarily disposed of. After a short interrogation they either went to face the firing squad or were sent to Versailles. Ten, fifteen, and twenty were dispatched at a time, at the Luxembourg and at the Châtelet. The courts-martial operated steadily for a week and finished their work only after the receipt of a special order from Versailles.

In spite of the fact that these courts-martial were set up on the order of the high command, their existence is not even mentioned in any of the official reports on the Commune. It is impossible to determine the total number of executions. Despite the demands, within and without the Assembly, by deputies of the left led by M. Clémenceau, the government maintained its silence on the courts-martial. All we can say is that the executions of men and women, in a number of cases innocent men and women, ran into the thousands.

Maxime Vuillaume, himself arrested and hailed before the courts-martial of the Luxembourg, has given us an unforgettable picture of the slaughter house into which the gardens had been transformed. The executioners shot during the day and it was only after nightfall that the tumbrils carted away one day's harvest to make way for the next. He describes the courtroom itself:

"I found myself again in the little court of the Senate building. It was about one o'clock. The disorder was even more impressive than when I had gone through the first

time, after our arrest. Unkempt soldiers, officers in campaign uniforms, agents with arm bands, groups of unknown
and miserable people scattered here and there whose
emaciated faces one could see behind the gun barrels.

"We turned to the left. An unforgettable spectacle confronted us.

"Crowded between a long wall and the end of a grove of
trees, a mass of men was surrounded by soldiers.

"On our arrival the ranks opened and enclosed me.

"This it was that the provost called the *queue*.

"I had scarcely had time to collect myself when a firing
squad arrived at a leisurely pace, with shouldered guns.
Four soldiers stopped at the head of the group, talked
rapidly with those who stood on guard, and I heard distinctly, two steps from me, this order:

" 'Six, fall out of rank.'

"Six men, the first six, marched forward. They were
quickly surrounded by the soldiers of the firing squad. I
heard a deep volley." [71]

This scene was reënacted all day and every day for a
week by a number of courts-martial in Paris. As might have
been expected many innocent men were executed, how many
no one knows. The papers reported the death of Jules
Vallès three times: three men shot because of a real or
fancied resemblance to the former member of the Commune. Meanwhile the real Jules Vallès escaped safely
across the frontier. Supposititious Billiorays, Courbets, and
Varlins were executed in the same way. A number of Poles
were summarily shot because of the exploits of their fellow
countrymen, Dombrowski and Wroblewski; many more
unknown and innocent men must have been executed though
their deaths were never reported. [72]

This week of May provided a glorious opportunity for

[71] *Mes Cahiers Rouges. A la Cour Martiale du Luxembourg. Cahiers
de la Quinzaine, 9e série, 10e cahier*, p. 62.
[72] On these executions of innocent men see C. Pelletan, *Questions d'Histoire: Le Comité Central et la Commune* (Paris, 1879), pp. 139-42.

the satisfaction of personal revenge. Denunciation of one's enemies to the police, as Commune sympathizers, provided an easy method. In addition, to denounce others was an accepted manner of averting suspicion from oneself. Paris was converted into a city of informers and those informed upon. Since adequate investigation of all the charges was impossible in a short period of time, summary justice, which often took the form of death, was meted out in the suspected arrondissements. More than three hundred and fifty thousand denunciations were received by the authorities. The thoroughness with which the informing spirit gratified itself sickened a little even the police.

The 22nd of May, after the besieging army had entered Paris and when victory became certain, M. Thiers addressed himself to the Assembly. "We are pursuing victory at this moment with the intention of achieving it. But, after the victory, it is necessary to punish. We must punish legally but implacably. Yes, the public conscience must be implacable, but it must be so while acting according to law, with the law and by the law. The military operations once finished, justice will take its course."

If the executions of Bloody Week were according to the law, which presumably means after adequate legal investigation, full reports of the numbers executed must have been preserved by the proper authorities. If these executions occurred in the pursuit of justice, there seems little reason for withholding the figures from the public. But perhaps M. Thiers meant that justice would step forward only after the courts-martial had ceased their work. No doubt this was part of the "military operations" of which he spoke to the Assembly. If so it seems a waste of time and effort to have bothered with courts, which are oftentimes associated with the processes of justice but which play a small part in war.

The number of arrests which followed the Commune was staggering. After the June days of 1848 something over

11,000 had been brought before the courts. But in 1871 the prisoners taken after the Commune were in excess of 38,000, according to the figures of General Appert.[73] Gabriel Hanotaux, including all arrests from the beginning of hostilities to 1875, accepts the figure of 43,521.[74] If we add to this the several thousand who were taken in custody only to be immediately released the number probably exceeded 50,000.[75] At least 35,000 were taken to Versailles and, during the May days, long columns of worn-out, feverish and despairing prisoners marched through Paris between lines of soldiers and crowds of jeering and vindictive spectators howling for their death. At Versailles they were herded into improvised prison yards before being distributed between the penitentiaries along the coast.

The cruelty and ferocity of the repression is now a fact admitted by all historians whether conservative or radical. The contemporary evidence of foreign newspapers certainly not noted for their radical sympathies and whose correspondents were comparatively unbiased, is sufficient. The London "Times," "Standard," and "Telegram" are at one on this point. The "Times," which regarded with horror the activities of the Communards and which filled its editorial columns during April, May and June with praise of the British constitution and repeated assurances that nothing similar could happen in a society so wisely ordered as "our own," could not be accused of antagonism to Versailles. Yet the "Times" was sickened by the cruelty of the repression. An editorial of May 27th reads, "A time will come when the conduct of the French executive will be judged by the world. At this moment of desolation we do not wish to criticize a Government at the crisis of such a struggle. But from the day that Paris was abandoned so hastily to the Democracy, with all its population, riches, monuments and

---

[73] *Rapport sur les Opérations de la Justice Militaire*, p. 178.
[74] *Histoire de la France Contemporaine*, I:211.
[75] See Laronze, *Histoire de la Commune* (Paris, 1928), p. 650.

treasures of art, to the present victory of what may be called the allied operations, there has been much requiring explanation and apology in the policy of Versailles. Paris has been won back at last, but it is a Paris in ruins, both materially and morally—Paris with a fierce reaction triumphant, and a mad revolutionary hatred stifled for the time in blood."

On the same day, the 27th, M. Thiers was castigating the Communards for their failure to observe the laws of war. "Our troops have suffered painful losses. General Leroy de Daïs is dead. Commandant Legoyer was made prisoner by the insurgents in the place de la Bastille, and his captors, without respect for the laws of war, shot him at once. The fact is what we might have expected from men who set fire to our cities, and who even collected a quantity of venomous liquid wherewith to poison soldiers and cause almost instantaneous death."

In the light of the conduct of the soldiers of Versailles this lamentation over the failure of the revolutionaries to observe the laws of war seems somewhat misplaced and the "Times" cannot forbear from remarking, "The laws of war! They are mild and Christian compared with the inhuman laws of revenge under which the Versailles troops have been shooting, bayonetting, ripping up prisoners, women and children, during the last six days. So far as we can recollect there has been nothing like it in history." [76]

As the slaughter continued the "Times" became even more depressed. "The French are filling up the darkest page in the book of their own or the world's history. The charge of ruthless cruelty is no longer limited to one party or to one class of persons. The Versailles troops seem inclined to outdo the communists (*sic*) in their lavishness of human blood." [77]

Again, "the burning of Paris was diabolical; the shooting of the hostages 'a deed without a name.' But it seems as if

[76] "Times," May 29.
[77] *Ibid.,* May 31.

we were destined to forget the work of these maddened savages in the spectacle of vengeance wreaked upon them. The wholesale executions inflicted by the Versaillese soldiery, the triumph, the glee, the ribaldry of the 'Party of Order,' sickens the soul." [78]

The soldiers of Versailles were no doubt fighting under great provocation in this battle of the streets and barricades. Shots fired from behind shutters or from an adjoining roof took a heavy toll in dead and wounded. But their commanders exerted to too small an extent that restraining influence which would have made itself felt had the enemy been other than the Communards. When Marshal Gallifet, directing a march of prisoners to Versailles, ordered eighty out of line for the purpose of summary execution, it could not be said that the soldiers lacked an example.

It is the general consensus of opinion that the soldiers were moderate in their brutality compared to the populace of Paris. The civilians followed with high satisfaction the work of the courts-martial, and crowds assembled at the passage of every Communard prisoner, demanding death. As the conservative historian, Maxime Du Camp, put it, "They have accused our soldiers of cruelty; but if the insurgents had been turned over to the populace, not one of them, not a single one, would have been spared." [79]

As frequently happens the women were more cruel, more vindictive, and less restrained in the repression than the men. They shouted longer and more fiercely for death, they attempted to get at the prisoners to beat them with their umbrellas, they appeared insane. The London "Times" recalled that statement of Voltaire's, "A Parisian woman is half tiger and half monkey," and it seemed entirely à propos.

It is a strange history, the story of the activities of women in the Commune and particularly during the Bloody Week of May. The great Revolution had seen its feminine battal-

[78] "Times," June 1.
[79] See *Convulsions de Paris*, II:401.

ions of the National Guard, 1848 its legion of "Vésu-viennes" and the siege of Paris of 1870, its "Amazones de la Seine." [80] During the Commune, there was no fighting unit composed of women, but Louise Michel, the "red vir-gin," fought with the 61st battalion and had taken part in the insurrection of January 22nd.[81] Elizabeth Dimitreff, a disciple of Karl Marx and the mistress of Outine, one of the International's organizers in Switzerland, and a num-ber of other women were active in the military defense. Women established a number of political clubs, there existed a "Central Committee of the Union of Women for the Defense of Paris and the Care of the Wounded," [82] and a considerable amount of attention was paid to the organiza-tion of the women workers of Paris.

After the entrance of the Versaillese a number of women fought behind the barricades along with the men and took part in the bitter hand-to-hand struggles of the streets. The "Paris Journal" of May 31st, contains the following: "In the midst of the atrocious scenes which shock Paris, the women are particularly distinguished by their cruelty and rage; most of them are widows of Communards. Madness seems to possess them; one sees them, their hair down like furies, throwing boiling oil, furniture, paving stones, on the soldiers, and when they are taken, they throw them-selves desperately on the bayonets and die still trying to fight."

Eight hundred and fifty women were arrested during or after the street fighting. General Appert says of them, "One had seen them fighting in the ranks of the Federals, lighting the fires, massacring the hostages, killing officers and sol-diers with sangfroid in the streets of Paris, everywhere

---

[80] See M. de Villiers, *Histoire des Clubs des Femmes, 1793-1848-1871* (Paris, 1910).

[81] Irma Boyer, *Louise Michel* (Paris, 1927).

[82] The Central Committee was organized "in the name of the social revolution . . . of the recovery of the rights of labor, of equality and of justice." See "Journal Officiel," May 8.

more exalted, more cynical, more ferocious even than the men." [83]

Along with the women were arrested 651 children under the age of 16, all of whom had taken some part in the defense of the Commune. Thirty-eight were between the ages of 7 and 13. [84]

The government published complete information, of course, on the sentences meted out to prisoners taken during and after the Commune. Out of the more than 50,000 rendered, there were 270 death penalties, 175 in default of appearance (jugements par contumace). However, 72 of the death sentences were commuted and only 23 executed. This number included Rossel, the Commune's military commander. Seven thousand four hundred and fifty-nine sentences of deportation were rendered, of which 2,910 were in default. More than 4,000 Communards were shipped to the islands of New Caledonia in the South Pacific and their suffering during the next ten years is a chief theme in the Communard accounts of the revolution. In addition there were more than 3,000 sentences of imprisonment, bringing the total penalties handed down by the military courts to 13,450, of which something over 3,313 were ineffective because of the death or escape of those sentenced and of which nearly 2,000 were either cancelled or reduced. All in all, it was certainly the most extensive judicial repression of modern times.

Undoubtedly a very large number of those killed and sentenced were of the scum of Paris. The Report on Military Justice mentions 7,460 ex-convicts among the thirty-odd thousand prisoners. [85] Of the 850 women, "nearly all," says General Appert, "were nomads, living a life of disorder and prostitution." The very worst element of the great city was undoubtedly attracted to the ranks of the Commune

[83] *Rapport sur la Justice Militaire*, p. 214.
[84] *Ibid.*, p. 215.
[85] *Ibid.*, p. 214.

and helped to lead the revolution into its excesses. However, it is not necessary to believe with Thiers and his friends that no other or better element had made the 18th of March or directed the Commune.

While we have complete figures on the numbers of Communards imprisoned and sentenced after the defeat of the revolution, it is impossible to determine the number killed in the battle of the barricades or by the courts-martial during the week of May. Dubreuihl thinks that somewhere near 2,500 were killed on the barricades, and takes 20,000 as the probable total of the victims shot by the courts-martial and in the street fighting.[86] Like most of the estimates of Communards and their sympathizers, this is probably an exaggeration. Malon, in his *Troisième Défaite du Prolétariat Français,* puts the losses at 37,000.[87] Vésinier gives the absurd figure of 40,000, ten thousand of which he asserted were women.[88]

On the other hand Maxime Du Camp, anxious to defend Versailles, is much too conservative when he puts the killing at 6,500.[89] He bases his calculations on the burials in the various cemeteries of Paris from the 20th to the 30th of May and adds to this the numbers of those exhumed for reburial from May 24th to September 6th. However, it seems evident that these figures are not complete. Many bodies, thrown into the Seine, had no burial places. Vuillaume has shown that the interments at the Charonne cemetery, which Du Camp fixed at 134, were in reality 800.[90] Others, hastily buried, were never exhumed and never reported.

Any figure for the total executed and shot on the barricades during May is a guess. It is probable that the total

---

[86] *Histoire de la Commune de Paris,* p. 472.
[87] P. 523.
[88] *Histoire de la Commune de Paris,* p. 419.
[89] *Convulsions de Paris,* II:424-26.
[90] *Mes Cahiers Rouges, Cahiers de la Quinzaine, 9ᵉ série, 10ᵉ cahier,* p. 96. Vuillaume puts the total at 20,000.

number of Communards engaged in the street battles was not above 10,000. But we have the statement of Corbon, former mayor and a close witness of the street fighting, that the Versaillese shot more men than there were behind the barricades.[91] The Commune sympathizers have made a great deal of the supposed statement of General Appert that 17,000 revolutionaries were killed in Bloody Week. That the General ever made this statement is very doubtful.[92] MacMahon considered it a greatly exaggerated figure.[93] It seems likely to the writer that the number killed in the streets and by the courts-martial exceeded 10,000 and fell short of 15,000.

Whatever estimate is accepted, even the most conservative, it is evident that the Commune witnessed the bloodiest revolutionary street fighting and repression in modern times. The cruelty and severity of the reaction had never been equalled. In the June days of 1848 only a few hundred men were killed in the streets and less than half as many sentences imposed upon the imprisoned as in 1871. If one takes the historical precedent of which M. Thiers was so fond, in justifying his retreat from Paris, the difference is shocking. After Marshal Windischgraetz had succeeded in conquering the revolutionaries in Vienna in 1848 he proved himself to be lenient in the extreme. The reactionaries in France have succeeded in making the Commune live by the very senselessness of their revenge.

The last resistance of the revolution in the 11th Arrondissement ended on May 22nd. Some 300 of its military leaders took refuge in the fort of Vincennes and refused to surrender unless given an amnesty. But MacMahon's preparations to attack caused them to think better of it and

[91] See E. Zevort, *Histoire de la Troisième République* (Paris, 1896), I:243.
[92] *Enquête*, p. 376. Vacherot, who received this figure from General Appert, was uncertain whether it included the fatalities of the whole siege and whether it was the total figure of dead and wounded.
[93] *Ibid.*

they surrendered on the 29th. However, the battle in Paris was over on Sunday the 28th. On the morning of that day the survivors of the Commune in the cemetery of Père Lachaise, to the traditional number of 147, were lined up before the wall, the now famous Mur des Fédérés, and shot. They fell into a common ditch.

CHAPTER VI

THE COMMUNE IN SOCIALIST MYTHOLOGY

THE Commune left in France a heritage of hatred, but its historical effect could hardly be called profound. An immediate result was the dissolution of the National Guard, so prominent in the revolutions of 1830, 1849 and 1871. It was some time before radicals in France dared speak of the advantages of a popular militia. Another result was the Dufaure law of 1872 which excluded the International from France and hastened its dissolution in Europe. The Commune, however, vanished, leaving hardly a trace on the economic, social, or political life of France.[1] Like the bird of Omar Khayyam it came to the firelight out of the night and into the night returned.

The socialist movement, however, it affected otherwise, and the real significance of the Commune must be sought here. It has made its contribution to the socialist calendar of saints and has embellished socialist mythology with many a dramatic episode. Henri de Man tells us of how, as a youth, awe-struck and with veneration, he gazed on a piece of petrified butter said to have been handed down from the Paris Commune. It was upon the occasion of his introduction into the socialist party in Antwerp, that a veteran

---

[1] Any number of the Communards assert that the Commune saved the Republic for France. This contention will hardly bear serious examination. The argument seems to be that the revolution of March 18th demonstrated how serious was the opposition to the mere possibility of the reestablishment of the monarchy. There is no doubt that the monarchist sentiment in France was strong in 1871, but it was certainly not weakened by the Commune. It would be much truer to say that the Commune all but lost the Republic. Republican papers in Paris, immediately after the revolution, were doing their utmost to divorce the Republic from any relation with the Commune. E.g., see "La Cloche" of June 6. Article by Louis Ulbach.

exhibited this precious morsel to the boy of sixteen. A copy of Picchio's painting, Le Mur des Fédérés, hangs in almost every socialist home in Europe and the United States. The leaders of the Commune, Varlin, Delescluze, Duval, Flourens and others, have given their names to streets and public squares wherever the socialist party has had influence. In Russia the 18th of March is a national holiday, and, as Engels remarks, "the anniversary of the Paris Commune became the first general holiday of the entire proletariat." [2] The annual pilgrimage to "the Wall" in the cemetery of Père Lachaise provides the occasion for a reaffirmation and regeneration of the faith. Many a pilgrim from foreign lands in contemplating this sacred spot has renewed his hatred of capitalist and bourgeois society.

The socialists have taken the Commune as their own and have made of it one of the first and most important battles in that long and incessant war between proletariat and bourgeoisie which is to culminate in the victory of socialism. In the words of Bebel, since become famous, spoken before the Reichstag at the time of the Commune, "Paris may be conquered this time but I warn you that the battle being waged is only a little outpost skirmish; the decisive battle in Europe is still to be fought; before many years the war cry of the Parisian proletariat: war against the palace, peace for the cottage, death to poverty! will be the war cry of the proletariat the world over."

The Commune has had its part in popularizing the idea of the class struggle and of the conception of socialism as one of the combatants in that struggle. The classical interpretation of the Commune, the interpretation which has persisted in socialist and communist circles until this day, is, of course, that of Marx. The "Civil War in France" made of the 18th of March a proletarian and socialist revolution, and so it has remained. Even the non-Marxian socialists, the anarchists, Marx's adversaries, regard the Commune in

[2] Introduction to Marx, *Klassenkämpfe in Frankreich* (London, 1895).

the same way. Thus from a relatively simple episode in the history of France, it has become a relatively important episode in the history of socialism.

THE COMMUNE AND CONTEMPORARY SOCIALISTS

The revolution of March 18th was accepted at the outset by contemporary socialist organizations as proletarian and socialist. Socialist societies in Berlin, Geneva, and elsewhere sent congratulations; the International everywhere declared itself in complete sympathy. In the defeat of the Commune and the events of Bloody Week European socialism saw a grievous, though temporary, set-back in the class war. "The flower of European socialism and revolution were destroyed; once again the past had triumphed over the future. For all revolutionaries in Europe it was the worst day of their lives." [3]

There can be no doubt that the Commune and its defeat not only added cohesion to the International socialist movement but contributed something very real to the consciousness of class among the European laboring population.[4] While the bourgeoisie all over Europe was shocked and horrified at the crimes of the Commune and applauded the victory of Versailles, organized labor, outside as well as inside the socialist movement, sympathized with the revolution and was deeply stirred by the cruelty of the repression. Even in England where Frederick Harrison was almost alone among "respectable" commentators in espousing the

[3] Fritz Brupbacker, *Marx und Bakunin,* p. 101, a socialist study.
[4] Lavrov (*Parizhskaia Kommuna,* 1878) gives the best account in socialist literature of the effect of the Paris Commune on contemporary socialism. Reviewing the period from 1871 to 1878 he remarks, "First of all it is obvious that all workers' parties, irrespective of their divisions and dissensions with each other, and irrespective of their nationality, have recognized and do recognize in the Paris Commune of 1871 their own cause. . . . In the capital of the new German empire as in the various towns of the kingdom of Italy; in Switzerland and in the North American republics, the day of the 18th of March holds solemn memories for all; the realization of the struggle of the proletariat against the governing class." 4th ed. (Moscow, 1925), p. 194.

cause of the Commune, where the upper class viewed the revolution with horror and Earl Russel attributed its "horrid deeds" to atheism, the working class, in so far as it followed events, was on the other side. The feeling was widespread that the revolution was made by workers in the interest of the oppressed. The English working class saw the execution of the hostages as a justifiable retaliation for Versaillese atrocities. "When Paris was taken," wrote a British contemporary, "there was the most passionate indignation among the working classes of this country at the manner in which communist prisoners were butchered by the mercenary soldiery." [5] There was a general tendency to take the news furnished by the reputable journals as the fabrication of class interest.

As we have mentioned, Communard refugees were received as brothers by socialist organizations in England, Belgium, and Switzerland. When these countries refused to sanction the extradition of Communards, much to the indignation of conservative France, on the ground that their crimes were political, communities of escaped Parisians established themselves abroad and worked in cooperation with local socialist groups. The General Council of the International in London was of great assistance to the Commune émigrés and for several months following May, 1871, devoted its chief efforts to raising funds for this purpose. In Switzerland, Committee of Assistance for the refugees were formed in Saint-Imier, La Chaux-de-Fonds, Le Locle and Neuchâtel, all centers of Internationalist activity.[6]

Needless to say, socialist papers the world over espoused the cause of the workers of Paris as their own. "La Liberté" of Brussels, "La Solidarité" and "L'Internationale" in Switzerland, the "Volkstaat" of Leipzig, and the "Proletarier" of Augsburg, with many others, all held the

[5] From an illuminating article in "Fraser's Magazine," July, 1871, p. 64, "The English working class and the Paris Commune." Signed—"The Journeyman Engineer."
[6] J. Guillaume, *L'Internationale*, II:155.

Communal revolution to have been both proletarian and socialist.

In Germany the socialist party, the party of Bebel and Liebknecht, was passionately sympathetic with the Commune. At the Dresden Congress, held on August 12th, 13th, and 14th, the delegates were ordered by the inspector of police to omit all allusion to the Commune. But the report tendered to the Congress by Johann Most, which was violently adulatory, was accepted without debate.[7] "We decided," says Bebel, "to express our gratitude to the Paris Commune without debate by rising from our seats."[8]

Although the struggle and defeat of the Communards strengthened the class consciousness of the proletariat in all lands, and provided a "glorious tradition" of incalculable worth to the socialist party,[9] the immediate effect of the dispersion of refugees all over Europe was disorganizing. The International had already entered upon the period of dissension and internal strife which was to culminate in its virtual dissolution at the Hague Congress of 1872. The General Council under the leadership of Marx was preparing to give battle to the forces of anarchism grouped around Bakunin. The Communards settling in England, Belgium and Switzerland threw themselves energetically into this struggle where the prestige of their revolutionary experience gave them weight and substance. Unfortunately their ideas and principles exhibited the same divergence now as during

---

[7] Most, who was later hailed before the Prussian courts for remarks made in speeches favorable to the Commune, has given an account of the views on the revolution held by German socialists and by Prussian officials in his pamphlet, *Die Pariser Commune vor den Berliner Gerichten* (Braunschweig, 1875). For another presentation of the German socialist point of view see Wilhelm Blos, *Die Geschichte der Kommune* (Braunschweig, 1876).

[8] *Aus meinem Leben. Zweiter Teil*, p. 233 (Stuttgart, 1922). Bebel later set forth in detail his position in the Commune in a speech given March 10, 1876, in Leipzig, which he gives in full in his autobiography, Vol. II, pp. 348-369.

[9] Lavrov, *op. cit.*, p. 211, attributes the "regeneration of Russian socialism" after 1870 very largely to the "fact of the Commune."

the revolution. They added disturbing elements to an already disordered situation. The Blanquists, who had settled in force in London, found it impossible to agree either with their colleagues of the Commune or with Marx and the General Council. After months spent in trying to bring them to heel, Marx wrote bitterly and unpleasantly in a letter to Sorge, "Here is my recompense for having worked nearly five months on behalf of the refugees and for having saved their honor by the publication of the 'Address on the Civil War.' "

In Switzerland the Communards, led by Malon and Lefrançais, sided for the most part with the opponents of Marx.

Despite the imminent schism in the International, both sides, as has already been remarked, embraced the cause of the Commune and held the same view of its historical significance. Bakunin immediately took up his weapons in defense of the revolution of March 18th against the attacks of Mazzini.[10] He explained the meaning of the Commune in a manner which met with the full approval of his followers. Bakunin's interpretation of the Commune is important since it did for socialist opinion of the revolution in the Latin countries what Marx's *Civil War in France* did for socialist opinion in Germany, England and the United States.[11]

Quite naturally Bakunin saw in the Commune a movement in the direction of his own anarchist federalism. "I am a partisan of the Commune which, having been massacred and drowned in blood by the butchers of the monarchical and clerical reaction, only became more living

[10] Mazzini, in a series of articles published in his newly established "Roma del Popolo," attacked the Commune as a revolution without meaning, purpose or direction.

[11] It is a curious and somewhat significant fact that the followers of Bakunin's anarchism were recruited almost entirely from Italy, Switzerland, Spain and France. The *Civil War in France* circulated very little in these countries. See Guillaume, *L'Internationale*, II:191.

and more powerful in the imagination and heart of the
European proletariat; I am a partisan particularly, because
it has been an audacious negation, strongly pronounced, of
the state." [12]

A negation of the state and of all authority, the Commune proclaimed the autonomy of small groups, it represented a federalism in which the individual units were free.
"The future social order," Bakunin remarks, "must, from
top to bottom, be made only by the free association and
federation of workers, in association first, then in communes,
in districts, in nations, and, finally, in a great international
and universal federation." [13] The Commune was a step in
this direction.

These are the ideas of Proudhon but to them Bakunin
added the conception of revolution. To him the significance
of the Commune lay in the fact, as he thought, that it was
a spontaneous revolution of the workers of Paris for a
society patterned on the ideas of Proudhon.

The socialist element in the Commune, as he recognized,
was small. These socialists, led by Varlin, were opposed by
a Jacobin majority, more adept and more experienced in
the ways of politics. But the Jacobins, determined by the
logic of events, could not escape becoming socialists themselves. "These generous Jacobins, at whose head was
placed, naturally, Delescluze, a great soul and a great character, desired before everything else the triumph of the
revolution; and as there is no revolution without the masses,
and as the masses to-day are filled with the socialist instinct
and can make no revolution other than an economic and
social revolution, the Jacobins, permitting themselves in
good faith to be carried along by the logic of the revolu-

[12] Although written in June, 1871, these pages in the Commune were
first published under the editorship of Élisée Reclus in a pamphlet entitled
La Commune de Paris et la Nature de l'État, 1878. Bakunin wrote copiously
on the Commune for socialist journals of the time. These citations are
from his *Œuvres*, IV:253.
[13] *Œuvres*, IV:264.

tionary movement, ended by becoming socialists in spite of themselves." [14]

In consequence, the Communal revolution was, according to Bakunin, proletarian, because it was the product of a spontaneous uprising of the workers of Paris; socialist, because an attack upon property rights and unearned income was inherent in it; and anarchist because it sought as the political unit of society the independent commune, organized and governed by the cooperation of free men.

The associates and followers of Bakunin, Élisée Reclus the great geographer, himself a member of the Commune, Prince Kropotkin, Guillaume—a principal organizer of the opposition to Marx in the International—all held the same view of the Commune. In the opinion of Kropotkin, "The Revolution of 1871 was above all a popular one. It was made by the people themselves, it sprang spontaneously from the mass, and it was among the great masses of the people that it found its defenders, its heroes, its martyrs. . . . And, at the same time, its moving spirit was the idea of a social revolution; vague certainly, perhaps unconscious, but still the effort to obtain at last, after the struggle of many centuries, true freedom, true equality for all men. . . . Communal independence was then but a means for the people of Paris; the social revolution was their end." [15]

That the revolution sprang out of the defeat of France and was in large part the insurrection of exacerbated patriots against a government believed to have betrayed them is not to be considered. "Paris inaugurated a new era"; announces Bakunin, "that of the emancipation, definitive and complete, of the masses and their solidarity henceforth really established, across and in spite of the frontiers of states. Paris killed patriotism and established on its ruins

[14] Bakunin, *Œuvres*, IV:256. Marx and Engels took exactly the same view. The Blanquists and Jacobins were forced by the logic of events to act as good socialists would.
[15] *The Commune of Paris*, pamphlet published in London, 1896.

the religion of humanity; Paris proclaimed itself humanitarian and atheist, replacing divine fictions by the realities of social life, and faith in science." [16]

Interpreting the Communal revolution as essentially anarchist, the anarchists of the "Fédération Jurassienne" profess to have been greatly astonished that their great opponent Marx, an avowed authoritarian collectivist, should also applaud the revolution and hail it as proletarian and socialist. The Commune seemed to them the negation of everything which Marx held dear. Bakunin was inclined to attribute the Marxian attitude to a natural but regrettable desire to benefit from the enthusiasm for the Commune everywhere apparent in the proletariat.

"The effect of the communalist insurrection was so great everywhere that even the Marxians, all of whose ideas were contradicted by this revolution, were obliged to take off their hats before it. They went further: in opposition to the simplest logic and their own true sentiments, they proclaimed that its program and its ends were their own. It was a truly clownish travesty, but necessary. They had to do it, on penalty of seeing themselves rejected and abandoned by everyone, so powerful was the passion which this revolution had evoked all over the world." [17]

THE MARXIAN INTERPRETATION OF THE COMMUNE

Certainly Marx was, or appeared to be, deeply moved by the Communal revolution and its tragic death. Two days after the cannon had ceased firing in the cemetery of Père Lachaise he had completed the first draft of his *Civil War in France,* one of the most powerful pamphlets he ever wrote and, in the words of his biographer, "the classical

---

[16] *Œuvres,* IV:254.
[17] Published by Nettlau in *La Société Nouvelle* (Brussels, 1894). Reprinted by Guillaume, *L'Internationale,* II:192. According to Guillaume, also, "The Commune, which was an affirmation of the federalist idea, had nothing in common with the socialist state or Volkstaat which the Marxian Sozialdemokratie inscribed on its banner."

account of the Commune of Paris."[18] Undoubtedly it is the classical socialist interpretation.

Marx was avidly interested in events in France during March, April and May. He read every word of the "Journal Officiel," carried on correspondence with Varlin, Fränkel, and other members of the International active in the revolution, and thought and talked of little else. Here in the events in France he fancied he saw unfolding the confirmation of his philosophy and theory of history. The bourgeoisie which had used the proletariat as a tool in all its revolutionary progress since the advent of the capitalist epoch was now seeing the former ally differentiate itself and turn against the exploiters. The movement of history, in which the class struggle appeared as the dynamic element, was proceeding on the lines chalked out by Marx.[19] The Commune came to demonstrate that the Marxian view was right, that the long-heralded war of the world proletariat against the world bourgeoisie was reaching the stage of actuality.

It is impossible to understand the socialist interpretation of the Commune without an understanding of the Marxian theory of history. If Marx gave to socialism the classical interpretation of the Commune it is because modern socialism has taken its stand on the Marxian interpretation of history. The *Civil War in France* was the final item in the series of polemical writings in which Marx applied his economic interpretation of history to the march of political events in France.[20]

[18] Franz Mehring, *Karl Marx,* 3rd edition (Leipzig, 1920), p. 458.

[19] Although Marx took the history of England as typical of economic development under capitalism, he saw in France the political structure and situation typical of the capitalistic epoch. It seems a little difficult to fit this conclusion into an interpretation of history which made the nature of economic activity, the mode of production, the determining cause of all else, including the development of political life and institutions. See, on this point, Bober, *Karl Marx's Interpretation of History* (Cambridge, Mass., 1927), p. 279.

[20] Composing this series are *Revolution and Counter-revolution, The Eighteenth Brumaire of Louis Napoleon, Die Klassenkämpfe in Frankreich*

Marxian socialism appealed to the socialists of his generation and appeals to ours largely because of the perfect faith it inculcates in the inevitableness of the ultimate victory of the proletariat over the bourgeoisie. "The stars in their courses are fighting for socialism." It was from the history of France that Marx largely drew his examples and his conviction. The great Revolution had destroyed the bulwarks of feudalism and had given to the bourgeoisie a hand in the control of the state. In the revolutions of 1830 and 1848 the bourgeoisie had consolidated its position, utilizing the proletariat to fight its battles.

"The evolution of the conditions of existence," he says, "for a numerous, strong, concentrated and intelligent proletarian class, goes hand in hand with the development of the conditions of existence for a middle class. The working-class movement itself never is independent, never is of an exclusively proletarian character until all the different factions of the middle class, and particularly its most progressive faction, the large manufacturers, have conquered political power, and remodelled the state according to their wants. It is then that the inevitable conflict between the employer and the employed becomes imminent and cannot be adjourned any longer; that the working class can no longer be put off with delusive hopes and promises never to be realized." [21]

The conditions for a "numerous, wealthy, concentrated and powerful middle class" had been attained in the France of Napoleon III. The reign of Louis-Philippe was government by capitalists; the Republic under Louis Napoleon had seen for a brief space of time the unification of the exploiting classes in a government directly antagonistic to the producing classes; and then this "joint stock enterprise"

and, to some extent, the articles composing the volume entitled *The Eastern Question.* All are in part applications of the theory of history enunciated clearly in the Communist Manifesto.

[21] Marx, *Revolution and Counter-revolution,* p. 8.

had given way to the Empire, "the only form of government possible at a time when the bourgeoisie had already lost, and the working class had not yet acquired, the faculty of ruling the nation." [22] The movement of history with its inexorable material forces had brought to its fruition the epoch of capitalism. But the fruit was already overripe, the old world was pregnant with the new, and the empire of Louis Napoleon stood as evidence of the further incapacity of the bourgeoisie to rule.

"Imperialism is, at the same time, the most prostitute and the ultimate form of the state power which nascent middle-class society had commenced to elaborate as a means of its own emancipation from feudalism, and which full-grown bourgeois society had finally transformed into a means for the enslavement of labor by capital." [23]

The Commune was the answer to this historical situation. The proletariat, no longer fighting the battles of the bourgeoisie, stood upon its own feet and made its own government. It had supplanted the bourgeoisie as the revolutionary class, and the Commune was the first trial of its budding powers. "This was the first revolution," says Marx, "in which the working class was openly acknowledged as the only class capable of social initiative, even by the great bulk of the Paris middle class—shopkeepers, tradesmen, merchants—the wealthy capitalist alone excepted." [24] The Commune was socialist because it was proletarian, and as such it takes its heroic place in the history of the socialist movement. This is its true significance.

"Workingmen's Paris, with its Commune, will be forever celebrated as the glorious harbinger of a new society. Its martyrs are enshrined in the great heart of the working class. Its exterminators, history has already nailed to that eternal pillory from which all the prayers of their priests will not avail to redeem them." [25]

[22] Marx, *Civil War in France*, p. 73. American edition, New York Labor News Company, 1919.
[23] *Ibid.*   [24] *Ibid.*, 81.   [25] *Ibid.*, 105.

The *Civil War in France* claimed the Commune for social-ism, though no one knew better than Marx that the Paris International had practically nothing to do with the revolu-tion of March 18th and had always been the minority party in the municipal assembly. In the years to come various voices arose in the socialist party to condemn Marx for linking the International with the detested Commune and thus drawing on the shoulders of the association the attacks of bourgeois governments all over Europe. But by and large European socialism has accepted Marx's interpreta-tion of the Commune at its face value. It glories in this "socialist" revolution and has enshrined the leaders of the Commune in its calendar of saints.[26]

Although it is very evident that his philosophy of history affected Marx's interpretation of the Commune, it is very difficult to assess the importance of the reverse influence. Did the Commune cause Marx to alter his views on the movement of history, on the manner in which the capitalist epoch disappears to give way to a proletarian and socialist society? Longuet, Marx's son-in-law, who wrote the intro-duction to the French translation of the *Civil War in France,* seemed to think so. "There is no doubt," he says, "that the historical events of 1871 had their effects upon the equivocal formula, in any case 'trop simpliste,' of 1847." [27] (i.e. of the Communist Manifesto.)

Marx and Engels countenance this same view in their introduction to the 1872 edition of the Communist Mani-festo. The Commune has made the program of the Mani-festo, in certain places, out of date. "Especially did the Commune demonstrate that the 'working class' cannot simply seize the available ready machinery of the state and set it going for its own ends."

[26] For example, see Karl Kautsky's *War die Pariser Kommune Deutsch-feindlich?:* "Die Gesellschaft" (1925), p. 227. This leading interpreter of Marx describes the Commune in the words of the master, "the first prole-tarian workers' government."

[27] Reprinted in *Le Mouvement Socialiste,* Vol. 5, p. 76. (1901.)

It is the familiar interpretation of Marx that the socialist and proletarian revolution will be introduced by the seizure of the institutions of the bourgeois state. These institutions and, in particular, the repressive machinery with which the bourgeois state was accustomed to defend the economic interests of the exploiting class against the encroachments of the proletariat, could then be used, in a typical Marxian phrase, "to expropriate the expropriators." After which the state would wither away, having performed its only possible function.

The *Civil War in France,* as Bakunin and the anarchists hastened to point out, seemed to deny this formula. Marx appeared to find the significance of the Commune in its attack upon the state in all its manifestations. The revolution of March 18th proclaimed the birth of the small autonomous group with whose existence the necessity of the centralized state disappeared at the outset. Marx applauded this proclamation.

The Commune not only "shattered" the institutions of the state, but it devised a type of governmental machinery which in the future must take the place of the state.

Those who like Bismarck see in completely new historical creations only the counterpart of older and even defunct forms of social life, find the Commune to be a mere copy of previous protests against governmental centralization. "Thus, this new Commune, which breaks the modern state power, has been mistaken for a reproduction of the medieval communes." [28] But, as a matter of fact, Marx holds, the Commune is a political form altogether new, the form, he suggests, into which a proletarian and socialist society must be cast.

"The multiplicity of interpretations to which the Commune has been subjected, and the multiplicity of interests which construed it in their favor, show that it was a thoroughly expansive political form, while all previous forms of

[28] *Civil War in France,* p. 76.

government had been emphatically repressive. Its true secret was this. It was essentially a working-class government, the product of the struggle of the producing against the appropriating class, the political form at last discovered under which to work out the economic emancipation of labor." [29]

When all due allowance for Marx's momentary enthusiasm for the Commune has been made, this is a significant statement. It is one which throws much light on his conception of the transition to a socialist society. It is not, however, in such flagrant contradiction with his previous views on the subject as his anarchist commentators would have us suppose.

Bakunin, Guillaume, and their friends had it that Marxian "authoritarian" socialism proposed the centralized state, the "Rechtsstaat" of the Germans, controlled by and in the interests of the proletariat. The antithesis between Marxian socialism and anarchism as it stood in their minds was, then, authoritarian and centralized state socialism as against decentralized, libertarian, antistate anarchism.

This was a complete misunderstanding. In the fully developed socialist society of Marx, a society as Utopian as anything of Fourier or Cabet, law and authority had no place. It was only in the transition period between capitalism and socialism that the instrumentality of the "Rechtsstaat" must be preserved and utilized in eradicating all opposition to the better society to come. This transition period was the period of the "dictatorship of the proletariat" of the "withering away of the state," the period in which the familiar repressive institutions of the state disappeared one by one as the occasion for their use vanished. Since the state is the determined product of the economic forces released by the capitalistic mode of production, it must disappear with the disappearance of capitalism. But there is necessarily a transition period.

[29] *Civil War in France*, p. 78.

The history of the Commune then did not alter Marx's views on the nature of socialist society, views which he purposely left vague and undefined, but altered his conception of the transition period between capitalism and socialism. The Commune gave flesh and blood to the Marxian phrases the "dictatorship of the proletariat" and the "withering away of the state."

"Do you want to know how this dictatorship looks?" asks Engels in his introduction to the *Civil War in France*. "Then look at the Paris Commune. That was the dictatorship of the proletariat."

The dictatorship of the proletariat preserves some of the forms of a political state. The Commune indicates which forms. In the words of Engels it was not a state "in the proper sense," because it abolished those instrumentalities of bourgeois despotism, the police, the standing army, and the church as an arm of the state. At the same time it retained the forms of political government now become truly democratic for the first time. For the time being, at least, the Commune becomes for Marx and Engels the source of example and precept on the revolutionary road to be followed by the proletariat from capitalist oppression to socialist liberty.

THE HISTORY OF THE COMMUNE ACCORDING TO MARX

Marx, as we have seen, derived the significance of the Commune from his materialistic interpretation of history. From this vantage ground also he surveyed and assessed the historical causes of and events in the revolution of March 18th. Although the *Civil War in France* is a polemic against the bourgeois Government of the National Defense and bourgeois government in general, it pretends also to be a history of the revolution. Under color of this pretense it has created a legend of the Commune which socialists, on the whole, have shown themselves willing to accept.

For a scientist, coolly concerned with abstract historical

forces determining the march of events, Marx waxes exceedingly warm in places. Although he had demonstrated to his own and his party's satisfaction that bourgeois morality and bourgeois justice are the only morality and justice possible in a society determined by the capitalistic mode of production, he is stirred to fierce anger and horror at the actions of men whose conduct could not be other than completely determined, according to his logic, by forces outside their own control. Marx, the dispassionate philosopher, has been set aside for the moment in favor of Marx the passionate partisan, to the great advantage of the ardor and tempo of his style.

Thiers, Favre, Simon, Trochu, instead of being mere pawns shoved here and there by unseen but irresistible influences, are either knavish monsters or prodigies of incapacity personally responsible for their horrid misdeeds. Thiers, in particular, is a fiend in not very human form. He is a "monstrous gnome," the "historical shoeblack of the first Napoleon," a "master in a small state roguery, a virtuoso in perjury and treason." "With the elevated vanity of a parliamentary Tom Thumb, permitted to play the part of Tamerlane, he denied the rebels against his littleness every right of civilized warfare, up to the right of neutrality for ambulances." Marx took all the epithets hurled at Thiers by the revolutionaries in Paris during the Commune and out of them created his historical estimate.

The Government of the National Defense which took office on September 4th assumed as its chief task, according to this Marxian legend of the Commune, not the organizing of France for war, but the holding in check of the revolution in Paris. This bourgeois government with full appreciation of its class interest saw as the true enemy the working class of the industrialized capital. "In this conflict between national duty and class interest, the Government of the National Defense did not hesitate one moment to turn into a Government of National Defection." [30]

In his evaluation of the government of September 4th during the siege of Paris by the Prussians, Marx accepts at face value all the wild charges made by revolutionary orators in the radical clubs. Trochu's "plan" for the defense of the capital becomes a plan of capitulation. While the "Bonapartist cutthroats" in charge of the defense of Paris exchanged ribald jokes concerning this mockery of a defense, Jules Favre admitted that the policy of the government was the suppression of the proletariat. What they were defending Paris against was not the Prussian soldiers but the working men of Paris. Thiers was sent on his mission to the courts of Europe to ask for mediation upon the promise that the Republic would be betrayed in the interests of monarchy in France.

The capitulation of Paris set the stage for that civil war in which Thiers and his class now had the assistance of Prussia. Their aim was the destruction of the Republic, for "it was only by the violent overthrow of the Republic that the appropriators of wealth could hope to shift on to the shoulders of its producers the cost of a war which they, the appropriators, had themselves originated." [31] The only obstacle was Paris, for the working men of Paris were armed and alive to their interests.

Thus the causes of the revolution of March 18th, in the Marxian analysis, are seen to be the class antagonism of proletariat and bourgeoisie, centering around the attack upon and the defense of the Republic.

By an ingenious bit of reasoning, borrowed largely from Pyat, Delescluze and other journalists of the Commune, and as superfluous to his general argument as it is fallacious,

[30] *Civil War in France,* p. 48. This is a phrase borrowed from the revolutionary clubs during the first siege.
[31] *Ibid.,* p. 58.

he seeks to prove that the Bordeaux assembly, elected February 8th, had no mandate from the people of France to govern. The real custodian of sovereignty was the working class of Paris.[32] The Empire having been overthrown on September 4th by the working men of Paris, the Government of the National Defense had no source of authority except this same Paris proletariat. Since the elections of February 8th had been sanctioned by the Government of the National Defense for the purpose, and the sole purpose, of making peace with Germany, the mandate of the Bordeaux assembly expired with this act.

This assembly in seeking to govern was exceeding its powers. Now this same Paris whose workingmen's revolution of September 4th provided the only legal title of the National Assembly was asked to lay down its arms "at the insulting behest of the rebellious slaveholders of Bordeaux." Paris refused to do this and in so doing was only within her rights.

The only course open to Thiers, consequently, was that of goading Paris into rebellion for the purpose of disarming the proletariat. Marx sees the acts of the government of France during February and March as all a part of a deliberate plan to provoke Paris into civil war. Vinoy, "the *Décembriseur*," was appointed as military governor; Valentin, "the Bonapartist gendarme" as Prefect of Police; d'Aurelle de Paladines, "the Jesuit General," as commander-in-chief of the National Guard. The seat of government was transferred to Versailles instead of to the historical capital. Finally, Thiers, resorting to the "most barefaced of lies" asserted that the artillery of the Paris National Guard belonged to the state and asked for its surrender. When this failed, the revolution of March 18th was invited

[32] Although Marx laboriously and frequently demonstrates in his writings that bourgeois law, justice and morality, are merely class creations for the preservation of economic interests and that the law, justice and morality of the proletariat are something quite different, he is always at pains to justify the actions of the proletariat even by bourgeois standards.

by the "burglarious" attack on Montmartre, Thiers' criminal attempt to steal property which the Guard had bought and paid for.

This recital of the events leading up to the 18th of March is a recapitulation of the revolutionary oratory and argument rife in Paris during the rule of the Government of the National Defense. It exhibits Marx as an assiduous, but hardly critical, reader of the radical Paris journals. The *Civil War in France* attempts to fit these events, as seen through the eyes of the Communards, into the Marxian mold of the class struggle. Consequently the revolutionaries of Paris are all, either members of the working class, or representatives of the working class. In the second place, their ultimate aim is the defense of the interests of the proletariat, although this is obscured by lesser but more immediate purposes. His conclusion is that civil war was forced upon the proletariat of Paris by the machinations of a bourgeois government, economically interested in the suppression of the working class and shrewdly, though knavishly, led by Thiers. "The glorious workingmen's revolution of March 18th," therefore becomes an heroic episode in the history of the class struggle.

Marx has singularly little to offer in criticism of the acts of either the Central Committee or the Communal Assembly. Later, both socialists and communists were to dissect the conduct of the Paris revolutionaries in search of lessons on revolutionary policy, in an adversely critical manner. Marx confined himself to a condemnation of the Committee for its failure to march immediately upon Versailles, when Thiers and his army were at the mercy of Paris. This is attributed to the Committee's understandable reluctance to continue the civil war commenced by Thiers. Its members in true democratic fashion preferred to resort to the ballot box, and to transfer their authority to the duly elected representatives of Paris. It was none the less a mistake.

He says nothing of the failure of the Commune to loot

the Bank of France which the communists were later to consider a revolutionary mistake of the first order. Indeed he speaks with admiration of the financial measures of the Commune, "remarkable for their sagacity and moderation." Shortly afterwards, however, Engels attributed the failure of the Commune in part to this same moderation toward the Bank of France, a mistaken policy for which Proudhon's disciple Beslay was responsible.[33]

All other measures, both of the Committee and the Commune were admirable. The execution of Lecomte and Thomas was not the work of the Paris proletariat but of the soldiers of these same generals. In the shooting of the Place Vendôme the National Guard of Paris was defending itself against an attack by the "notorious familiars of the Empire." The lives of the hostages shot in May had been forfeited many times over by the persistent execution of Commune soldiers. The burning of Paris was a necessary measure of defense. "If the acts of the Paris workingmen were vandalism, it was the vandalism of defense in despair," and of considerably less importance than "the vandalism of a Haussmann, razing historic Paris to make place for the Paris of the sightseer!"

So, too, the positive acts of the Commune met with the approval of Marx and Engels. In order to justify this approval it was necessary to show that the Communards, although followers of the despicable petit-bourgeois socialist Proudhon and the well-meaning, but misguided, Jacobin Blanqui, were not governed in their policies by the ideas of these masters.

Proudhon's ideas never had much influence in France, according to Engels, despite the large number of his followers. "This became obvious during the Commune. Although the Proudhonists were strongly represented in it, not the slightest attempt was made to liquidate the old society or to organize the economic factors according to

[33] *Zur Wohnungsfrage. Separatabdruck aus dem "Volkstaat"* (1872), p. 55.

the principle of Proudhon. On the contrary, it stands to the highest honor of the Commune that, in all its economic measures, it pursued simple practical needs instead of relying on that 'spontaneous impetus' of [Proudhon's] predilection. Therefore these measures, the outcome of an association of laborers, were not in the spirit of Proudhon, but in that of German scientific socialism. The single social measure which the Proudhonists carried through was the preservation of the Bank of France and in part this was the cause of the fall of the Commune. In the same way the so-called Blanquists, just as soon as they ceased to be merely political revolutionaries and became a group of socialist workers with a definite program—such as that which the Blanquist émigrés have published in their manifesto, 'Internationale et Révolution'—refused to follow the principles of Blanqui's plan of social salvation, and adopted almost letter for letter the views of German scientific socialism on the necessity of the political action of the proletariat and its dictatorship during the transition to a society without classes and without a state, views which have been enunciated in the Communist Manifesto and many times since." [24]

Thus, although the writings of Marx and Engels were practically unknown in France, and although German scientific socialism was a meaningless phrase to the Paris proletariat, this same proletariat, when it came into power, acted in accordance with the principles of scientific socialism laid down by Marx.

Because the revolution was proletarian it had to be socialist, and socialist according to Marx. "The great social measure of the Commune was its own working existence. Its special measures could but betoken the tendency of a government of the people and by the people."

The unenlightened observer would, perhaps, have difficulty in perceiving evidences of Marxian socialism in the acts of the Commune. The abolition of night work for bakers, the decree on the pawnshops, might appear to him

[24] *Zur Wohnungsfrage,* p. 55.

merely innocuous, opportunistic measures calculated to heighten the popularity of Communal representatives among their electors. It was not so to Marx.

The Commune in meeting the immediate needs of the situation was acting in socialistic fashion. The needs of the situation were the maintenance in power of the proletariat and the pursuit of its class interests and this is socialism. Public ownership of the instruments of production, work according to capacity, and distribution according to need are far-off ends having little to do with the immediate needs of the working class. To those who deny the socialism of the Commune, because its acts did not primarily affect either the control of the instruments of production or the distribution of wealth, Marx would reply that this argument is beside the point.

He reviews these beneficent socialist measures of the Commune and sets his stamp of approval on each. In its first decree the Commune rid itself of the standing army and the police, those necessary defenders of bourgeois interests without which these interests could not exist. Having got rid of these "physical force elements of the old government" the revolution set about to break the "spiritual force of repression," the church. Education was divorced from the control and restraint of superstition and "science itself freed from the fetters which class prejudice and governmental force had imposed upon it." Judicial functionaries were to be divested of that "sham independence which had but served to mask their abject subserviency," and in their place "magistrates and all judges were to be elective, responsible and revocable." At the same time the revolution buried another institution of bourgeois society, parliamentary government. "The Commune was to be a working, not a parliamentary body, executive and legislative at the same time." Its members served the public at workmen's wages.

The political changes necessary to the period of the dictatorship of the proletariat were quickly followed by legislation affecting the economic and social position of the working class. "The political rule of the producer cannot coincide with the perpetuation of his social slavery. The Commune was therefore to serve as a lever for uprooting the economic foundations upon which rests the existence of classes, and therefore of class rule."

The actual measures enacted by the Commune seemed to proceed but a very little way toward this desirable end. Marx can only mention the decree abolishing night work for bakers, the abolition of the practice of imposing fines upon laborers and the decision to surrender abandoned factories to associations of workers. But he tells us that "the working class did not expect miracles from the Commune. They have no ready-made Utopias to introduce *par décret du peuple*. They know that in order to work out their own emancipation, and along with it that higher form to which present society is irresistibly tending, by its own economic agencies, they will have to pass through long struggles, through a series of historic processes, transforming circumstances and men. They have no ideals to realize, but to set free the elements of the new society with which the old collapsing bourgeois society itself is pregnant."

Not only was the legislation of the Commune enlightened and beneficent, its administration of affairs left nothing to be desired. This was the first time that "plain workingmen . . . dared to infringe upon the governmental privilege of their 'natural superiors,' " but "under circumstances of unexampled difficulty, [they] performed their work modestly, conscientiously, and efficiently—performed it at salaries the highest of which barely amounted to one-fifth of what, according to a high scientific authority, is the minimum required for a secretary to a certain metropolitan school board."

Marx's uncritical acceptance of the Commune, including its institutions, laws and administration, almost reaches the stage of absurdity in his credulity toward its stories of Versaillese atrocities. He believed everything unfavorable to the counter-revolution which managed to get printed in the revolutionary journals, even the faked-up scandals of convent orgies and of the extraordinary lubricity of the Catholic priesthood. "It is irritating, indeed, to the Rurals," he tells us, "that at the very same time they declared the return to the church to be the only means of salvation for France, the infidel Commune unearthed the peculiar mysteries of the Picpus nunnery and of the Saint-Laurent church."

But then, Marx was without the experience of this generation in the credibility of atrocities. Certainly the conduct of the partisans of Versailles in that bloody week following the entrance of Paris would lend truth to any story, however unplausible, of their capacity for sadistic satisfaction.

Naturally he makes the most of Bloody Week and the counter-revolutionary repression. The chief significance of the Commune, for the rank and file of the socialist party, will always rest in the executions at the Mur des Fédérés and the massacre in the streets of Paris.[35] Marx, along with every other socialist historian of the Commune, found here an historical fact which could be turned to the account of the party just as it stood, without varnish or embellishment.

Apart from this, the Marxian history of the Commune is, from beginning to end, almost pure myth. His vested interest in the economic interpretation of history and the

[35] Lavrov, op. cit., p. 195, speaks rightly when he says, "The Commune effectively represents itself to socialists of all varieties of opinion, not as a special program of organization, not as a particular dogma, but as the very step which established the historical foundation for a united struggle of the modern proletariat against its persecutors. The continued martyrdom of the representatives of labor under oppression, sucking the vital source of their strength by capital, is here concentrated in the tragedy of the great martyrdom of Bloody Week. Unwisely, in the name of equality for all citizens, in the name of the democratic Republic with popular elections, in the name of the device 'liberty, equality, fraternity' flaunted from walls bespattered with the blood of the killed, the Versaillese republicans shot ten thousand of the proletariat who had risen in this cause."

theory of the class struggle made him see in the revolution of March 18th an internationalist, a proletarian, and a socialist movement in what was in reality an essentially patriotic, not to say chauvinist revolt, only partially proletarian and only secondarily socialist. Nevertheless this myth is the generally accepted socialist history of the Commune.

The "Lesson" of the Commune

A philosophy of history implies that historical events have meaning, a meaning which is to be found by relating the event to the general principle or principles of historical change which constitute the philosophy. The historian equipped with a philosophy does not limit himself to a plain description of the event; indeed, such a description is impossible; he must also search out its significance. The danger to our historian, particularly if his philosophy be as precisely formulated as the materialistic interpretation of Marx, is that his account of the event will be very full of significance but very short on history. This seems to be true of the *Civil War in France*.

A philosophy of history, and, in particular, the Marxian interpretation, implies at the same time that lessons may be learned from the observance of historical phenomena. We know from the Marxian interpretation of history that capitalist society will disappear and make room for socialism and that the change will be effected through the class struggle. The developing and expanding proletariat will eventually overcome the declining and degenerating bourgeoisie. But what are the steps in this process? In the unfolding of history they become evident to the careful observer, and the representative of the proletariat may draw from succeeding events lessons by which the advance of his class may be accelerated.

Just so, the Commune of Paris holds a lesson, and all socialists agree it is a very important one. The problem is to find it. Or, to put the matter in the form in which it usually presents itself to socialists, the problem is to find what Marx thought about it, and on this matter there is much dispute.

As the question has been formulated in recent socialist controversy, will the transition to a socialist society be made by means of a forceful revolution or a peaceful evolution? Lenin maintained that revolution was the method of Marx and he supports his case very largely by reference to the Marxian treatment of the Commune.[36] The interpretation of the German Social Democrats runs counter to this. According to them Marx drew quite another lesson from the Commune.

The truth of the matter seems to be that Lenin is correct in his interpretation of the *Civil War in France* but that the Social Democrats were closer to the views of Marx and Engels as expressed in their later years. The Social Democrats, from the vantage point of their parliamentary successes, came to look upon the Commune and its methods as relics of an earlier day. Revolution by force was, in general, to be considered a vestige of the immaturity of socialism. Although an heroic and never-to-be-forgotten landmark in the history of the movement, the Commune had no lessons to give it at this stage in its development. Until the time when the Russian communists appeared upon the scene to claim the Commune as the first step towards the dictatorship of the proletariat and government by soviet, the revolution of March 18th was dismissed in socialist circles as an unfortunate, because a mistaken and untimely, attempt to seize power.[37]

Marx and Engels appear, finally, to have come round to this view. In their letters on the Gotha program in 1875 they still clung, it is true, to the views of the Communist Manifesto, that the institutions of bourgeois society in the

36 *State and Revolution.*
37 See Karl Kautsky, *The Social Revolution* (Chicago, 1902), p. 98.

main can be dissolved only by force.[38] As Marx had put it in the first volume of *Capital*, "Force is the midwife of every old society pregnant with a new one." [39]

But when Engels, a few years before his death, and in the midst of dramatic parliamentary successes on the part of the German Social Democracy, wrote the introduction to Marx's *Klassenkämpfe in Frankreich*, the tone seems definitely to have changed. Reviewing the history of revolutions in France and the lessons which he and Marx had learned from them, Engels was inclined to confess that the views of the Communist Manifesto were wrong, or at least too sharply put. The old-style revolution with its barricades, its heroic sacrifices, its sudden and often unprepared onslaughts was a thing of the past.[40]

The new weapon in proletarian warfare is the vote, and the socialists of Germany have shown their comrades in all countries how to use it. "The irony of history," says Engels, "turns everything upside down. We the 'revolutionists,' the 'revolters,' prosper far better by lawful measures than by unlawful measures and violence. The law and order parties, as they call themselves, go to ruin under the legal conditions which they themselves have established. They cry out in despair with Odilon Barrot: 'la légalité nous tue,' 'lawfulness is killing us.' While we, under this lawfulness, are getting firm muscles and rosy cheeks and are the picture of eternal life." [41]

The lesson of the Paris Commune must, therefore, be reread. Engel's remarks on the revolution of March 18th are in decided contrast with the tone of the *Civil War in France*. "It was again demonstrated that in Paris no other

[38] Engels' letter to Bebel, published in Bebel's *Aus Meinem Leben*, II:322. Marx's letter to Bracke, republished in the *International Socialist Review*, Vol. VIII, p. 642.
[39] I:824.
[40] See Bober, *Karl Marx's Interpretation of History* (Cambridge, 1927), Ch. XIII, for a discussion of the views of Marx and Engels on the question of revolution.
[41] *International Socialist Revolution*, 3:12.

revolution is possible any more, except a proletarian one. After the victory the leadership fell uncontested into the lap of the working class, just as a matter of course, and again it was shown how impossible it was even then, twenty years after the former effort, for the leadership of the working class to be successful. On one hand, France left Paris in the lurch and stood by looking on while it was bleeding under the bullets of MacMahon; on the other hand, the Commune wasted its strength in a barren quarrel of the two disagreeing factions, the Blanquists, who formed the majority, and the Proudhonists, who formed the minority, neither of which knew what to do. The victory of 1871, which came as a gift, proved just as barren as the forcible overthrow of 1848." [42]

The working class must organize itself, discipline itself in the maintenance of an established political party. A revolutionary minority acting in advance of the existence of an organized proletariat has no chance of success, even though it succeed in seizing power. Furthermore, once the proletariat is organized and disciplined the occasion for the use of force has in all probability disappeared. This is the lesson of the Commune.

Thus it is that socialists read the lesson and continue to read the lesson. The communists, as we shall see, are inclined to see the Commune in quite another light. And their views are probably closer to the *Civil War in France* than those of the socialists. The dispute furnishes an interesting and illuminating example of the uses to which history may be put.

[42] *International Socialist Revolution,* 3:5.

CHAPTER VII

THE COMMUNIST INTERPRETATION OF THE COMMUNE

THE Russian Revolution and the expansion of the Communist party has given new birth to the study of the Commune. The events of 1871 have acquired a new significance and are now seen, at least through the eyes of their Russian interpreters, to be of decisive importance, as first steps on the road followed by bolshevism. The "opportunist" and "philistine" dismissal of the Commune as insignificant for the present stage of the proletarian movement, a view current in socialist circles, became an issue of first-rate importance in the division between the 2nd and 3rd International. The revolution of March 18th, thanks to communism, has become what Marx predicted, "the glorious harbinger of a new society."

A glance at the voluminous literature on the Commune which has poured out of Russia since the revolution of 1917 is sufficient to fathom the importance which this "first government of the proletariat" has assumed in the eyes of communism. The introduction to a popular book of readings on the Commune designed to provide entertainment for workers' clubs on the anniversary day of the 18th of March assesses its significance as follows: "In the history of the proletarian revolutionary movement, there is no stage which possessed such universal historical significance as the Paris Commune of 1871. It was the first serious attempt on the part of the proletariat to proclaim a laborers' government. Furthermore, the Commune in this way outlined the political form of the deliverance of the workers, which received its broad, clear and full realization some forty-six years later in the October revolution of 1917." [1]

This statement is typical. The writings of the leaders of communism, Lenin, Trotsky, Zinoviev; the dozens of small propagandist pamphlets designed for circulation in the workers' clubs; the considerable number of serious Marxian histories of the Commune which have appeared in Russia during the last ten years, all make the same assertion. Not only is the Commune of Paris a glorious and inspiring episode in the history of the proletarian movement, not only did it supply socialist revolutionaries with invaluable lessons in revolutionary tactics, but it laid down the foundation of a form of proletarian government which was to receive its full development in communist Russia.

The revolution of March 18th as a source of inspiration to Russian communism is a continuously popular oratorical theme. The 5th Congress of the Komintern devoted a day to the celebration of the Paris Commune. The speech of Antipov expresses the sense of the gathering. "For us, the workers of Russia, the example of the Paris Commune has always served as a torch, guiding us in the darkness of imperial despotism and capitalistic oppression. The example of the Paris Commune has been the source of energy for our fighters. In 1905 we were conquered but this defeat gave us strength for victory in October. And, finally, in those severe days which followed the victory, when we had to defend our conquests, the Paris Commune inspired us to battle. In those grave moments we said: 'Look, workers, at the example of the Paris Communards, and know that if we are defeated, our bourgeoisie will treat us a hundred times worse. The example of the Paris Commune inspired us and we were victorious.' " [2]

The letter addressed by the Moscow sections of the Russian Communist party to the French Communist party

[1] Aleksandr Gambarov, *Parizhskaia Kommuna* (Moscow, 1925), p. 1.
[2] Gambarov, p. 216.

on the occasion of this celebration epitomizes the indebted-
ness of modern communism to the Commune of Paris. "To
us, the proletarian Union of Soviet Socialist Republics, the
idea of the Commune, and its memory, is especially close and
dear; as the first attempt at proletarian government, as the
model of soviet government, as an historical lesson in the
revolutionary struggle which has laid a solid foundation for
the deliverance of the human race from every sort of exploitation and oppression.

"Our revolutions of 1905 and 1917 were strictly continu-
ations of the activity of the Paris Commune." [3]

The communists are inclined to make a sharp division
between the Paris Commune and all previous revolutionary
movements. It stands in a class by itself. No other revolution in the 19th century approaches its importance or significance in the history of the class struggle. The Paris
Commune, the Russian revolution of 1905 and the revolution of 1917 establish themselves as a line of development
in which can be seen emerging the characteristic institutions
and policies of that transition stage to socialism known as
the dictatorship of the proletariat.

"The revolutions of 1830 and 1848, the *coup d'état* of
Napoleon, the 4th of September," says the author of one of
the more notable recent histories of the Commune in Russia,
"were all mere transferals of power within the governing
and possessing class.

"But the Paris Commune was entirely different. Even if
it did not understand itself, the employing class, seeing before it the armed proletariat, at once realized that the Commune was, in the last analysis, the negation of property." [4]

---

[3] Gambarov, pp. 219-220.
[4] I. Stepanov, *Parizhskaia Kommuna 1871 goda i voprosy taktiki v pro-
letarskoi revoliutsii* (1921), p. 93. Another recent historian (Molok, *Parizhskaia Kommuna*, p. 122) expresses the same idea. "In distinction to the great
revolution of the end of the 18th century, the July revolution of 1830, and
the German revolutions of 1848 and 1849, in which the proletariat, stepping
forward to do its part, fought the battles of the bourgeoisie and was not
separated from it, in distinction to the French Revolution of 1848, in which

But the full significance of the Commune, its unique position in the history of the proletariat, did not become evident
until 1917. It was only when face to face with the problem
of their own revolution that the communists were able to
appreciate the experiences and to understand the lessons of
1871. And, conversely, a study of the Commune of Paris is
now of invaluable assistance in comprehending the direction
and purpose of events in Russia. As Stepanov puts it, "The
Russian revolution has given us an understanding of those
things in the Paris Commune for which, earlier, our eyes
were not sharpened. And, conversely, a deepened understanding of the contemporary world proletarian revolution,
to which the Russian revolution appears merely as a prelude,
demands a comparison with the Paris Commune.

"Thus it is that every contemporary work on the Paris
Commune must inevitably become in this or some other manner, a treatise on the tactics of the proletarian revolution." [5]

Every communist history, every communist interpretation
of the Commune, accepts as its explicitly recognized starting
point the *Civil War in France* of Karl Marx. Marx was
alone among contemporaries in his grasp of the essential significance of the events of 1871. It is only because of and by
means of the revolutions of 1905 and 1917 that lesser minds
can appreciate and evaluate the Commune. "Marx gave to
it an exposition of genius. But only the birth of the world
proletarian revolution discovered the whole depth of this
exposition, the prediction in the 19th century of the

the proletariat, taking the leadership of the movement, appeared as a distinct
class and opposed to the bourgeoisie its own demands, to realize which it was,
however, impotent . . . the Paris Commune was the first revolution made
by the proletariat, for the proletariat. The great historical significance of
the Commune . . . as the first attempt at 'a government of the working class'
(Marx), as the first historical 'dictatorship of the proletariat' (Engels) . . .
was its beginning of the destruction of bourgeois government and the foundation of a new proletarian one, which was to receive its full development
and final form in the soviets . . . that child of the three Russian revolutions
and the organ of the proletarian dictatorship of the S.S.S.R."

[5] Stepanov, p. 5 (Introduction).

conditions of the proletarian revolution of the 20th century." [6]

The second fundamental source utilized by communist commentators is Lenin. It was Lenin who compared and contrasted the Russian Revolution of 1905 with the Commune, who drew continually on the revolution of 1871 for illustrations applicable to the political problems of the Russian proletariat, who seized upon the similarity of the relation between the Commune and the Franco-Prussian War on the one hand, and the relation of the Russian Revolution to the "imperialist" war, on the other, who continually throughout his writings and speeches interpreted and reinterpreted the meaning of the Commune in the history of the class struggle, to the Russian Social-Democratic party. It is Lenin's representation of Marx's views on the *Civil War in France* which directs and shapes the account of the Commune presented by contemporary communists. Marx, at the hands of Lenin, becomes the great expositor of the policy of revolution, of terrorism, of anti-parliamentarianism and of the forceful dictatorship of the proletariat. And his great pronunciamento on these questions is the *Civil War in France*.

The communist legend of the revolution of 1871, outlined in its fundamentals by Marx and Lenin, expanded and elaborated by a very large number of Marxian historians in Russia since 1917, has become a fact of very real importance in a variety of ways. It is the purpose of this chapter to consider the nature of this legend and the uses to which it has been put. There can be little doubt that this Commune of the communists was of some influence in the formulation and execution of revolutionary policies during 1917 and 1918, and it is possible that its effect might be discovered in certain institutions of communist Russia. However, it is not our purpose to determine this historical influence, a task

[6] *Ibid.,* p. 175.

most certainly beset with serious difficulties and uncertainties. Rather are we concerned with the position of the Commune in the communist theory of the class struggle, a fact to be discovered from the writings of the communists and not from an examination of historical events and the institutions of contemporary Russia.

The uses to which this legend of the revolution of 1871 have been put may be conveniently considered under three main heads: (1) As a source of instruction in revolutionary strategy and tactics. Whatever may have been the actual importance of the influence of the Commune on events in revolutionary Russia, communist leaders and communist historians have evidently believed it to be considerable. The example of the Commune was continually evoked both in support of bolshevist revolutionary principles and in the condemnation of opposed "opportunistic" or "reformist" principles. In that period, transitional to socialism, which the communists know as the "dictatorship of the proletariat," the Commune has been considered both by politicians and historians as contributing lessons of inestimable importance. (2) As a focal point in the conflict with the 2nd International. The 2nd and the 3rd Internationals, as is well known, divided sharply on the issue which may be roughly expressed as "parliamentarianism against revolution." The bolshevists have repeatedly used the example of the Paris Commune in support of their position, and have utilized Marx's writings on the Commune to demonstrate the purity of their Marxianism. (3) As communist propaganda. The iniquities of the bourgeoisie and of the régime of capitalism, the beauties of socialism, foreseen in its "first pale dawn," the cruelties of a white terror, are all amply demonstrated in the propagandist pamphlets on the Commune of Paris, disseminated by communist agencies. The Russian Communist Party is a past master in the art of propaganda and the Commune of Paris has been extensively used as a primary source of material.

The importance of Lenin in the Russian revolutionary movement and of his views on the Commune in the formation of the communist theory and practice of the class struggle, would seem to warrant a separate consideration at the outset.

LENIN AND THE COMMUNE OF PARIS

Lenin's writings on the Commune have been collected in a slim volume of a hundred pages.[7] But his interest in the revolution of 1871 appeared as early almost as his interest in socialism, and from the division of the Russian Social-Democratic party into a majority and minority group, in 1903, until his death in 1924, he was accustomed to refer on important questions of party tactics to its example. A very fair understanding of the crises and problems faced by the Bolshevist party during this period could be gathered from Lenin's remarks on the Paris Commune. As Zinoviev stated on the occasion of the celebration of the memory of the Commune by the Komintern in 1924, "On not one of the movements of the foreign proletariat did Vladimir Il'ich lavish such attention, such love and such learning as on the Paris Commune; of not one of the movements of the foreign proletariat did Vladimir Il'ich speak with such respect as of the movement of the Paris workers."[8]

Marxians are accustomed to refer to the *Civil War in France* as an example of Marx's practical interest in history, of his habit of drawing from the course of events lessons applicable to the future of the socialist movement. On the question of the Commune, this is much more true of Lenin than of Marx. The Bolshevist leader never wrote or spoke on this subject without applying his interpretation to problems immediately facing the party. His all-devouring interest was the practical politics of the class struggle, and his

[7] Entitled *Parizhskaia Kommuna* (Moscow, 2nd Ed., 1925).
[8] Gambarov, *op. cit.*, p. 218.

study of the revolution of 1871 was made to subserve these ends.

The Bolshevist and Menshevist groups of the Russian Social-Democratic party had separated, in 1903, on much the same issue as was later to divide the 2nd and 3rd Internationals. Lenin, as leader of the Bolshevist wing, envisaged the party as a closely knit, revolutionary group, ready and able to use all possible means, including force, necessary to achieve power. His conception of the "dictatorship of the proletariat" was authoritarian and revolutionary as opposed to the Menshevist leanings toward democracy and parliamentarianism. In order to draw to his policy the support of history Lenin turned, in this struggle against the Menshevists and Martovists, to the example of the Paris Commune.[9] The Commune was lost because it did not act decisively, because it did not crush the reaction, because it compromised and reconciled.

In the summer of 1905 he concluded an article in the "Proletariat" on "The Paris Commune and the Problems of a Democratic Dictatorship" with the statement, "This inquiry should make us understand, finally, that, extracting for ourselves the lessons of the Paris Commune, we must imitate, not its mistakes (the refusal to seize the Bank of France, the failure to march on Versailles, the lack of a clear-cut program, etc.), but its practical, successful steps, illuminating the true way." [10]

The great strength of the Commune was its own existence as a revolutionary workers' government; its great weakness was its timidity toward the reaction, its observance of the forms of bourgeois government.

The failure of the Russian revolution of 1905 caused something of a reaction in Social-Democratic circles against

[9] Slutskii, *Parizhskaia Kommuna* (Moscow, 1925), p. 137. Communist writers recognize, of course, the importance of the Commune in Lenin's thought. Slutskii has a chapter entitled "V. I. Lenin and the Paris Commune," to which I am much indebted.
[10] *Parizhskaia Kommuna*, p. 8. From "Proletarii," No. 8, July 4, 1905.

the policy of revolution. The Menshevists were inclined to regard the event as a confirmation of their own more pacific policies, and Plekhanov in particular excited Lenin with his remark, "You should not have resorted to arms."

Lenin took violent issue with this attitude and, in his introduction to the Russian edition of Marx's letters to Kugelmann, 1907, contrasted Marx's relation to the Commune with Plekhanov's relation to the revolution of 1905, to the great discredit of the latter. Before the event Marx had been inclined to warn the Paris proletariat against the resort to arms. The well-known letter of September 6, 1870, to this same Kugelmann attests the fact. Nevertheless, when the revolution had been initiated, Marx acclaimed the deed, accepted it as a glorious attempt. He described it, as Lenin repeats again and again, as a "storming of heaven."

"Marx, without concealing from the Proletariat a single mistake of the Commune, has honored this deed with a pamphlet which to this day remains the best guide to a 'struggle for heaven.'—They [the Menshevists] ought to learn from the theorist—the leader of the Proletariat—that faith in revolution, that ability to stir the laboring class to a last-ditch defense of its immediate revolutionary aims, that firmness of spirit which excludes any pusillanimous whimpering over the temporary insuccess of revolution." [11]

The next year, in 1908, Lenin took the occasion of the anniversary of the Commune to apply the lessons of 1871 to the existing situation of the socialist party.[12] Contemporary socialism was in grave danger, in his opinion, of inundation by nationalistic, patriotic, chauvinistic ideas and policies. This was one of the great weaknesses of the Commune, a mistake expiated by the lives of its workers. "In the union of these contradictory aims—patriotism and socialism—was the fateful mistake of the French socialists." [13]

[11] *Parizhskaia Kommuna*, p. 11. From "Proletarii," No. 8, July 4, 1905.
[12] *Uroki Kommuny* (Lessons of the Commune). A speech delivered at an Internationalist meeting in Geneva.
[13] *Parizhskaia Kommuna*, p. 18.

He contrasted the Commune with the Russian revolution of 1905 with the purpose of demonstrating that the advance of the latter over the former consisted in the avoidance of just such patriotic and chauvinistic mistakes. In the words of his commentator, "The lessons of the Commune were exploited by the Russian proletariat in the December uprising. And the chief lesson which the Russian proletariat mastered consisted in this, that, under the leadership of V. I. Lenin, it freed itself from nationalistic and patriotic delusions and resorted to a higher form of the class struggle, to mass action and to civil war." [14]

Lenin again, in these "Lessons of the Commune," reverted to that leniency and moderation which cost the workers their victory and their lives. "The Commune made two mistakes: (1) It was satisfied with half measures—instead of 'expropriating the expropriators,' it acted 'moderately' and 'justly' as in the case, e.g., of the Bank of France. (2) It was possessed of a superfluous magnanimity. Instead of marching immediately on Versailles and crushing its enemies, it preferred to act more 'leniently.'. . . But, in spite of all the mistakes of the Commune, it is the true model for the great proletarian movement of the 19th century." [15]

Revolution is necessary and it is the glory of the Paris proletariat that it did not shrink from this necessity. "Remembering its lessons [the Proletariat] knows that it must not neglect the peaceful means of struggle which serve its everyday interests and are necessary during the period of preparation for revolution, but the Proletariat should never forget the fact that, under certain conditions, the class struggle takes the form of military action and civil war; there are moments when the interests of the Proletariat demand a merciless extermination of its enemies in open battle. The French proletariat was the first to show this in the

[14] Slutskii, *op. cit.*, p. 140.
[15] *Parizhskaia Kommuna*, p. 19.

days of the Commune, and the Russian proletariat has gloriously proved it during the December uprising." [16]

The years from 1908 until the outbreak of the war were years during which the advocates of peaceful measures in the class struggle rapidly gained strength. The revisionism of Bernstein made headway not only in Germany but in the whole socialist movement. Socialist parliamentary successes fortified the faith in the ultimate attainment of socialism by means of nothing more forceful than the vote. "Catastrophic socialism" appeared particularly passé.

But Lenin battled valiantly for his declining cause and the example of the Commune, as a weapon, came frequently to hand. In a newspaper article of 1911, *Memories of the Commune,* he recites its revolutionary successes and makes it clear in precisely what respects the Commune constituted a socialist revolution. "In spite of these unfavorable conditions, in spite of the shortness of its existence, the Commune was able to carry through a few measures sufficiently characteristic of its true thought and aims. The Commune abolished the standing army, that blind instrument in the hands of the governing class, and decreed the general arming of the people; it carried out the separation of church and state, suppressed the religious budget (i.e., the state payment of priests), gave to the people an educational system of a distinctly secular character, and by this struck a hard blow at those gendarmes in cassocks. In the matter of social legislation, it succeeded in doing little, but this little, nevertheless, indicates its character as a popular workers' government. There was the abolition of night work for bakers; the abolition of the system of fines, that ordinance for robbing the workers; finally the publication of the significant decree by virtue of which all factories, mills and workshops, abandoned or unoperated by employers, passed into the hands of workers' associations to be reestablished for productive purposes. . . . All these measures sufficiently indicate

[16] *Parizhskaia Kommuna,* p. 20.

this: that the Commune constituted a death threat to the old world, built up on slavery and exploitation." [17]

The outbreak of the World War immediately awakened in Lenin speculation as to the possibility of an outcome similar to that of the Franco-Prussian war, but this time on a European scale. The Commune was a revolution made by an undeveloped proletarian party, in the disordered situation caused by war. In the event of the juxtaposition of the greater disorder of a more considerable war and an organized and disciplined proletarian party, what might the outcome be? While the socialist parties of Europe made peace with their respective governments, Lenin awaited the outbreak of civil war. In the manifesto of the Central Committee of the Russian Social-Democratic party (Bolshevists), published on November 1, 1914, he writes, "The transformation of the present imperialist war into a civil war is the only effective slogan of the proletariat, indicated by the experience of the Paris Commune, laid down in the Basel resolutions (1912), and the obvious result of all the conditions of an imperialistic war between highly developed countries." [18]

Lenin's most considerable presentation of his own revolutionary political theory was developed during these war years and published August, 1917. Translated into English under the title of *State and Revolution*, this volume presents a forceful argument for revolutionary methods. Lenin supports his case by an examination of revolutionary history and by an elaborate Marxian exegesis. The Paris Commune and Marx's treatment of the Commune form important links in his chain of argument.

"The accumulation of opportunist elements during the decades of comparatively peaceful development." says Lenin in his introduction, "has created a predominance of socialist

[17] *Parizhskaia Kommuna*, pp. 15-16. (*Pamiati Kommuny.*)
[18] See Slutskii, p. 143.

chauvinism in the official socialist parties of the whole world."

The leaders of these official socialist parties have been deluded with the idea that it is possible for a proletarian party to utilize the framework, the institutions of bourgeois government.

But it is in precisely the reverse of this, as Marx himself explicitly recognizes, that the main lesson of the Commune lies. The great accomplishment of the Commune, its contribution to proletarian socialism, was its demonstration that the proper technique involves the breaking up of the existing machinery of the state and the substitution of a new political form adapted to government through the dictatorship of the proletariat.

Lenin takes as the text of his remarks on the Commune the letter of Marx to Kugelmann, written April 12, 1871.

"If you look at the last chapter of my *Eighteenth Brumaire*, you will see that I declare the next attempt of the French revolution to be: not merely to hand over, from one set of hands to another, the bureaucratic and military machine—as has occurred hitherto—but to *shatter* it; and it is that which is the preliminary condition of any real people's revolution on the continent. It is exactly this that constitutes the attempt of our heroic Parisian comrades.

"The Commune attempted simultaneously the two great tasks which confront the revolutionary proletariat in Russia at the present moment [1917]; the destructive task of dissolving the repressive organization of the bourgeois state and the constructive task of building the institutions of a proletarian democracy.

"To destroy officialism immediately, everywhere, completely—of this there can be no question. That is a utopia. But to *break up* at once the old bureaucratic machine and to start immediately the construction of a new one, enabling us gradually to abolish bureaucracy—this is not a utopia, it is the experience of the Commune, it is the direct task of the revolutionary proletariat." [19]

Lenin had no doubt that the Commune was a new form of government, that it was the legitimate forbear of the Russian soviet and that it is the form of government with which proletarian socialism must work in the transition stage between capitalism and socialism. He finds the essence of the Commune described in Marx's statement, "The Commune was to have been not a parliamentary but a working corporation, legislative and executive at the same time."

This union of legislative and executive functions is a fact of primary importance. In the hands of the proletariat it makes possible the achievement of those ends which bourgeois democracy everywhere proclaims but everywhere avoids. "For the mercenary and corrupt parliamentarianism of capitalist society, the Commune substitutes institutions in which freedom of opinion and discussion does not become a mere delusion, for the representatives must themselves work, must themselves execute their own laws, must themselves verify their results in actual practice, must themselves be directly responsible to the electorate." [20]

Proletarian democracy, let it be clearly understood, is quite a different thing from bourgeois democracy, a fact which the experience of the Commune makes clear. The fundamental prerequisite of proletarian democracy is economic and social equality. "In this connection the special measures adopted by the Commune and emphasized by Marx are particularly noteworthy: the abolition of all representative allowances, and of all special salaries in the case of officials; and the lowering of the payment of *all* servants of the state to the level of *workmen's wages*.[21] Here is shown, more clearly than anywhere else, the *break* from a

[19] *State and Revolution*, p. 155.
[20] *Ibid.*, p. 154.
[21] This is hardly accurate. The official rates of pay in the Commune's army, for example, ranged from 1 fr. 50 c. per day to 16 fr. 50 c.

bourgeois democracy to a proletarian democracy; from the democracy of the oppressors to the democracy of the oppressed, from the domination of a 'special force' for the suppression of a given class to the suppression of the oppressors by the whole force of the majority of the nation— the proletariat and the peasants." [22]

During the period of the Russian Revolution in 1917 and 1918 and the months which preceded it, Lenin wrote and spoke continuously. He turned to the example of the Commune to enforce his opinion on the revolutionary problem confronting him. When his followers seemed timidly to abstain from the violation of legal forms he turned to the Commune to demonstrate that the cause of the proletariat flourished on the violation of "bourgeois" law. On the question of whether the situation was ripe for revolution, he turned again to the Commune. When the Menshevists taxed him with the advocacy of a Blanquist or anarchist policy, he pointed out that the Soviets of Workers and Peasants were direct descendants of the Commune of Paris, which Marx himself had acclaimed as the future governmental form of proletarian socialism.

The existing situation called for a form of revolutionary government of the type of the Paris Commune. Lenin proceeds to analyze the essential characteristics of this type of government. "The fundamental characteristics of this type are: (1) the source of power is not law, previously discussed and enacted by parliament, but the initiative springing straight from the underlying mass of the people, on the spot, a straight 'seizure' according to the current phrase; (2) it involves a replacement of the police and the army, which are separated from the people and opposed to it, by the direct arming of the whole nation: peace and order are maintained under such government by the armed laborers and peasants themselves, by the armed nation; (3) the bureaucracy is either cashiered in favor of representa-

[22] *State and Revolution,* p. 149.

tives of the people or held strictly under popular control." [23]

His *Letters on Tactics,* which belong to the same period, express the same idea. The political form of the dictatorship of the proletariat has already been discovered; it is the soviet of workers and peasants, a form laid down by the Commune of Paris. The situation is ripe for revolution and the workers must realize that conformity to bourgeois legal forms is not in the Marxian tradition. To seize and destroy the instrumentalities of bourgeois government is not to violate this tradition or to relapse into the puerilities of anarchism or Blanquism.

"Whoever wishes to think about it cannot help but understand that Blanquism is a seizure of power by the minority, and that the Soviets of Workers and Deputies are consciously and immediately an organization of the majority of the people. The work of participating in the struggle for influence within the Soviets cannot, therefore, be lost in the swamp of Blanquism. And it cannot fall into the morass of anarchism, for anarchism is the negation of the necessities of government and governmental power for the period of the transition from the government of the bourgeoisie to the government of the proletariat. But I, with the exclusion of every possibility of misunderstanding my meaning, assert the necessities of government for that period, in perfect agreement with Marx and the example of the Paris Commune: not customary bourgeois-parliamentary government, but a government without a standing army, without a police antagonistic to the people, without the erection of a bureaucracy over the people." [24]

In the victory of the Soviets of Workers and Soldiers' Delegates in the October revolution, Lenin saw the development and perfection of a form of government patterned upon the model of the Paris Commune and adapted to the

[23] O. Dvoevlastii, *Parizhskaia Kommuna* (1917), p. 21.
[24] *Ibid.,* p. 29.

needs of the revolutionary proletariat. He defended this form of government in a series of articles repelling the attacks of the socialists of the 2nd International, who persisted in clinging to the outworn governmental forms of the bourgeoisie. The task of the Russian proletariat is "to consolidate and develop further the Federated Republic of Soviets, as immeasurably a greater and more progressive form of democracy than bourgeois parliamentarianism, and as the only type of government conforming in its fundamentals to the experience of the Paris Commune of 1871, and to the experience of the Russian revolutions of 1905 and 1917-18, for the transition period between capitalism and socialism, that is, the period of the Dictatorship of the Proletariat." [25]

In an address to the first congress of the Communist International he again reverted to the example of the Paris Commune which attempted to replace the bourgeois governmental apparatus "by the self-governing organizations of the mass of workers without separation of the powers of legislation and administration. All the bourgeois-democratic republics of our time, among them the German, which, in mockery of the truth, social traitors call proletarian, are based upon this bourgeois governmental apparatus. All this again is confirmed clearly and absolutely, that lamentations about the protection of democracy in general appear as nothing more than the defense of the bourgeoisie and of privileged exploitation." [26]

Lenin's opinion of the tremendous importance of the Paris Commune in the history of the class struggle is clearly indicated in one of his last utterances on the subject. "This Soviet government has ceased to be a Russian form of the Dictatorship of the Proletariat. It has become an instrument of the International Proletariat in its struggle for

[25] From *Chernovoi Nabrosok proekta programmy. Parizhskaia Kommuna,* p. 83.
[26] Lenin, *Parizhskaia Kommuna,* p. 85.

power. It is the second great step in the world development
of the socialist revolution. The first step was the Paris
Commune which showed that the road to socialism lies only
through a dictatorship, through the violent repression of
exploiters." [27]

COMMUNIST WRITINGS ON THE COMMUNE IN RELATION TO THE RUSSIAN REVOLUTION

The leaders of Russian communism have treated the
history of the Commune in fragmentary fashion, utilizing
its "lessons" in connection with the contemporary political
situation in Russia. In the hands of Lenin, as we have seen,
its use was continuous and striking: in the hands of Trotski
and Zinoviev, it was only less so.

But, in addition, the history of the revolution of 1871
has been broadcast over Russia in recent years through the
media of a large number of historical studies and an even
larger number of propagandist pamphlets. Reserving the
purely propagandist treatment of the Commune for later
discussion, we shall consider in this section the more serious
works. Although these histories base themselves explicitly
on Marx and Lenin and avoid with care any inconsistency
with or deviation from the accepted interpretation of the
masters, they go considerably further in their analysis of
causes and in their presentation of historical detail. There
is, in these Marxian histories, surprisingly little variation
in the general analysis; so little, in fact, that one may con-
clude that a fairly definitive communist interpretation of
the Commune of Paris has been achieved and is in general
acceptance.

The Russian communist literature has been supplemented
by the translation of a number of French histories and a
fair idea of the Russian attitude toward the Commune can
be obtained from an examination of the French accounts

[27] Lenin, *Works*, Vol. XVI, *On Professional Unions.*

which have received the stamp of approval. *La Commune de Paris* by P. Luquet, and *La Commune de 1871* by C. Talès are both histories written since the World War by French communists and immediately translated into Russian. The latter is prefaced by a long introduction from the pen of Trotski recommending a careful study of the March revolution to Russian communists.

"Every time," he says, "that we study the history of the Commune, we see it in a new light, thanks to experience acquired in later revolutionary struggles and particularly in the latest revolutions, not only in the Russian but in German and Hungarian revolutions. The Franco-Prussian War was a bloody explosion, presaging an immense world-wide butchery, the Commune of Paris a beacon presaging the revolution of the world proletariat." [28]

Another French history, popular in Russia, is the able book by the former permanent Secretary of the French Socialist Party, Louis Dubreuihl.[29] Dubreuihl subscribes to the Marxian view and, in a statement much quoted by Russian commentators, declares of the Commune, "before all, indeed, above all, it was proletarian, and consequently socialist; for the proletariat in action can fight for no other end than socialism." [30]

But the most important influence on communist historians of the Commune in Russia has undoubtedly been, next to the work of Marx and Lenin, the history of the Commune written in Russian by Lavrov in 1878, and recently published in a fourth edition.[31] Lavrov, one of the early Russian disciples of Marx, placed a careful and informed account of the Commune in the setting of the materialist interpretation of history. He foresaw, in consequence, that "meaning"

[28] Introduction, dated February 4, 1921.
[29] Translated into Russian by N. S. Tiutchev (St. Petersburg, 1920).
[30] *La Commune*, p. 495.
[31] Moscow, 1925. Lavrov lived in Paris in 1871 and participated in the revolution.

and "significance" of the Commune which has in our time become so evident to communist commentators.[32]

This "meaning," this "significance" of the Commune is the contribution of the Marxian interpretation of history. It guides the communist historian in the selection of his data and it draws from the data, once gathered, a conviction of the significance of the Commune of Paris in the history of the class struggle. In conformity with the dictates of their philosophy of history these historians turn at once, in their explanation of the causes of the Commune, to the economic situation in France under the Empire. We find the rapid expansion of large-scale enterprise and the consequent emergence of an industrial proletariat, particularly in Paris. After a somewhat sketchy analysis of employment figures in France, Molok, one of the better communist writers, concludes that, in the midst of a preponderantly artisan population, there existed a section of the proletariat employed in large industry and transport, amounting to a little over one-eighth of the working population of Paris. "This formed a real industrial proletariat of the newest type." [33]

We are led to suppose that this new type of proletariat had something to do with the Commune. The chain of causation in the Marxian interpretation of history runs— the development of capitalism, the emergence of an industrial proletariat, the birth of a socialist party and, finally, the revolution, or some other manifestation of the class struggle between proletariat and bourgeoisie. Therefore the communist historian of the revolution of 1871 must begin his search for causes in the industrial development of France under the Empire.[34] It would be easy to demonstrate

[32] Stepanov, *Parizhskaia Kommuna,* says of this book, "It is necessary to say frankly that, excluding Marx and Engels, not one western socialist has drawn such fruitful deductions from the lessons of the Commune, nor has anyone studied these lessons so profoundly or with such astonishing revolutionary foresight has laid bare the effective revolutionary procedure of the future movement."

[33] *Parizhskaia Kommuna* (Leningrad, 1927), p. 12.

[34] See Stepanov, *Parizhskaia Kommuna,* Ch. 2.

that the bulk of the strength of the 1st International in Paris was drawn from the upper levels of the artisan class, that the leaders of the Commune sprang in the main from Parisian bohemia. On the other hand it would be extraordinarily difficult to show that this new industrial proletariat had anything whatever to do with the revolution; certainly the communist historians make no attempt to show that it had. But, if the Commune of Paris was, in its essence, a proletarian socialist revolution, and all the communist commentators, following Marx, accept this as given, then the economic interpretation of history would immediately lead such investigators to the industrial situation in France.

The Commune was undoubtedly a proletarian and socialist revolution, all our historians agree. Nevertheless, it was a revolution marked and marred by the "immaturity of the working class." [35] In this fact are to be found the fundamental causes of its failure. "The immaturity of the working class"; here is another conception drawn from the Marxian interpretation of history. A proletariat is mature when an economy, and therefore the working class in that economy, has become thoroughly industrialized. At this stage the maturity of the proletariat is indicated by the fact that it is organized into a closely knit socialist party professing the Marxian brand of socialism. In 1871 the party was by no means well organized, and the immaturity of the workers was further demonstrated by the fact that Blanqui and Proudhon were the favorite socialist leaders.

The Commune was a proletarian socialist revolution but the Communards themselves were unable to realize its true significance. "They wrote with their blood an indelible page in the history of humanity, but they themselves could not decipher this page." [36] Not being acquainted with the economic interpretation of history or blessed with an understanding of scientific socialism they were not in a position

[35] Almost all the communist historians use this phrase and this explanation.
[36] Stepanov, *op. cit.*, p. 175.

to comprehend the historical significance of their acts. "They fought and died. Not a few of those who were left alive endeavored to think out for themselves and explain to others what it was for which they fought, in the name of which their comrades fell under the bullets of Thiers' executioners." [37] But a clear understanding of the significance of their sacrifices was not made clear to ordinary minds until the Russian Revolution.

The Commune was a proletarian socialist revolution, but not at the outset. All the communist historians are agreed on this point. For the first few weeks of its existence the revolution was supported by an important petit-bourgeois element, fighting for its own economic interests in Paris, for a greater measure of local autonomy, and for the preservation of the Republic. However, military reverses and a dawning appreciation of the aims of the Commune rapidly caused this element to withdraw its cooperation. The Commune was reduced to a purely proletarian and revolutionary movement and as such its essential socialist characteristics made their appearance. At the outset patriotic and largely petit-bourgeois, the revolution became toward the end internationalist and proletarian.

The Commune was a proletarian socialist revolution but it was this because of the "logic of the situation," and for no other reason. Its leaders were Blanquists and Proudhonists, its policies were moderate and timid, it had no socialist program and whatever aims it professed were vague and ill defined. Nevertheless it was socialist because "the Proletariat can fight for no other cause than Socialism." Although the principles of scientific socialism had not permeated the minds of the makers of the Commune they could act in no other way but in accordance with these principles for their acts were ultimately conditioned by their economic environment. This, again, was the logic of the situation.

[37] *Ibid.*

The communist interpreters of the Commune, after having explained its "historic world significance," after having described the manner in which a confused and unorganized movement, shot through with patriotic and petit-bourgeois elements, the product of many and conflicting causes, became a proletarian socialist revolution, turn to the problems raised by its failure. Burrowing much further into the question than either Marx or Lenin, they emerge with a series of judgments which are not only presented as an adequate historical explanation of the defeat of the Communards, but which are destined to serve as object lessons to the proletariat in Russia and elsewhere on the problems of political organization and revolutionary tactics. Here again there is little variation in the opinions of communist interpreters. Here again there is constant comparison between the Commune and the Russian Revolution of 1917-18.

While the communist historians frequently, in fact usually, recognize that the leaders of the Commune, at least at the outset, were not attempting to make a socialist revolution, they tend to criticize them on the assumption that this was their explicit intention. The Commune was defeated because the Communards failed to act militantly, to take proper precautions, to do this and that, as if these same Communards were actuated by clearly realized socialist motives or were striving for the same ends which beckoned to the Russian revolutionaries of 1917. Again, it is clear, these commentators on the revolution of 1871 are dominated by their interpretation of history. Having read into the Communal uprising its "true" meaning and significance, it is difficult to refrain from criticizing the Communards for having failed to attain what now appears as their "real" historical objective. To do so, however, is to assign to human initiative, to free will, an importance quite inconsistent with the determinism of the economic interpretation of history.

Although the leaders of the Commune made the supreme
mistake of not recognizing in it a proletarian and socialist
revolution and consequently fell into a series of errors, these
errors were the result of an ignorance which is historically
understandable and, therefore, forgivable. Such is not true
of the self-same errors being made by the present leaders
of the 2nd International with full knowledge of the experience of the Commune. This is a willful delusion of the
proletariat which demands attack and rectification. Thus
it is that the Russian historians of the Commune construct
their accounts with an eye to several purposes. They lay
bare the mistakes of the Communards of 1871, which at the
same time must serve as lessons to the contemporary world
proletariat; in so doing, they attack the 2nd International
for non-observance of these lessons; and, finally, by demonstrating that the Russian Communist Party (Bolshevist
group) has followed these lessons, and, in consequence, has
achieved success in the revolution of 1917 and 1918, they
defend and applaud the program of their own party.

The fundamental and fatal weakness of the revolution
of 1871, all communists agree, was the lack of an organized
and disciplined party and, what comes to the same thing,
of a clear-cut revolutionary program. This weakness had
been emphasized by Lavrov in 1878, and on this as on so
many other points, his post-revolution followers find him
sound. The socialist-revolutionaries in France were not
prepared. "They were not prepared when on the 4th of
September the battle of Sedan brought down the Empire,
although it would seem that at the time of the Mexican
expedition, the wide dissemination of the 'Propos de
Labiénus,' in the speeches which were given after the re-
establishment of the right of public assembly, in the clear-
cut articles of 'La Marseillaise' and 'Le Réveil,' it was not
difficult to discern the approaching collapse of the power of
Napoleon III. The socialists were not prepared on the 31st
of October when circumstances gave them the opportunity

to paralyze the opposition. They were not even prepared on the 18th of March." [38]

The Commune was a "proletarian revolution without a proletarian party," says Molok.[39] Its great weakness was the absence of that clear-cut purpose which only an acceptance of the Marxian theory of class struggle could give,[40] and the same point is reiterated in all the communist histories.[41]

Zinoviev, early in 1917, drew a lesson from the unpreparedness of the Communards applicable to the existing situation in Russia. In an article entitled "What We Have to Do," he warned the proletariat of Leningrad against a line of attack which, in their state of disorganization, might lead to the same results as befell Paris in 1871.

"It is necessary to face the truth. In Leningrad there are now many conditions favoring the rise of a rebellion of the type of the Paris Commune. In many important characteristics our present situation resembles that of 1871, resembles it to such an extent that the comparison becomes self-evident. But the misfortune is, that (in so far as the human mind can foresee) such a rebellion at the present moment is apt to end as the rebellion of the Paris workmen ended—by a defeat." [42]

The contrast between the disorganization of the Paris revolutionaries and their consequent defeat, and the disciplined organization of the St. Petersburg revolutionaries and their consequent victory, is, naturally, one likely to impress communist observers. They make a great deal of it and draw from it lessons too obvious to require statement.[43]

[38] *Parizhskaia Kommuna 18 Marta 1871 goda.* 4th ed. (Leningrad, 1925), p. 212.
[39] *Ibid.,* p. 57.   [40] *Ibid.,* p. 45.
[41] E.g., Stepanov, *op. cit.,* p. 176, "The struggle came—there were groups and orders, factions and factors, schools and sects—but there was not one party of which, completely and with justice, it could be said, that alone it represented the party of the proletariat, behind which a proletarian could march in a determined attack on capitalism."
[42] Zinoviev, *Works,* Vol. VIII.
[43] E. G. Talès, *La Commune de 1871.* From the preface by Trotski, XIV.

The second great mistake of the Commune was its exaggerated respect for legal forms and bourgeois "rights." Marx had suggested this point, Lenin emphasized it and Trotski, in his writings on the 18th of March, can think of very little else. The flock of Russian historians of the Commune faithfully follows these shepherds. This unfortunate weakness is largely to be attributed to the influence of Proudhon who "without perceiving the basic evils of capitalist society, superficially wrestled with its symptoms and looked upon the social problem with the eyes of a petty bourgeois." [44]

Molok, in concluding his survey of the causes of the revolution's failure, remarks, "The exaggerated esteem of the Commune for the principle of private property, a characteristic of all its activities, leading the revolution to eschew all attempts at confiscation, including that even of large scale capital, finds its explanation equally in the strong Proudhonistic ideology and in the tactical situation, which made it necessary not to estrange from this proletarian revolution the broad layers of petty and middle bourgeoisie (which were, as a matter of fact, very quickly estranged.)" [45]

The glaring example of this timidity toward private interests was, of course, the Commune's attitude toward the Bank of France. Zinoviev, in a speech to the 3rd All-Russian Congress of Soviets, contrasts it unfavorably with the confiscation by the Bolsheviks of the banks and private industrial enterprises and their forceful measures against bourgeois sabotage. [46] On this question the communists quote with approval the dictum of Engels, expressed in the 3rd German edition of the *Civil War in France*, that the confiscation of the bank would have been worth 10,000 men to the Commune. [47]

[44] Slutskii, *op. cit.*, p. 14.   [45] Molok, *op. cit.*, p. 81.
[46] *Works*, VII. He is arguing here, against the Martovists, that such measures involve nothing but a strict application of Marxianism.
[47] See Lukin, *Parizhskaia Kommuna*, pp. 298-300.

"The second mistake of the Commune," says Braslovskii, "was its excessively cautious attitude toward private property. This policy of 'reverence' before property was especially evident in the activity of such important commissions as that of 'Finances' and of 'Labor and Exchange.' " [48]

The weakness of the Commune for bourgeois legal formalism stands out clearly enough in its attitude toward the elections. Even after Thiers had attacked Paris, in the midst of civil war, the Commune persisted in the attempt to justify itself by a resort to bourgeois electoral formalities. The elections of April 16th constituted a severe check to the revolution by reason of the smallness of the vote; instead of relying on such antiquated procedure the Commune should have taken its leaders where it found them and by any measures available. [49]

"In the course of a Socialist revolution," says Stepanov, "the Proletariat must seize all material sources of strength. . . . If the Paris revolution had been conscious of its true nature as a revolution of the working class, this very fact would have meant the recognition *that only those who were ready to accept the new social order, who came directly and sincerely under the banner of the Socialist republic, should have here the rights of citizenship. The claims of equality made by the enemies of the laboring class would then appear as ridiculous and foolish.*" [50]

Closely allied to this mistaken regard for law was the third great weakness of the Commune, its failure to resort to terroristic means, to oppose to the white terror of the Bourgeoisie the red terror of the Proletariat. Trotski, in his *Defense of Terrorism,* devotes twenty pages to expounding this weakness of the Commune and again the communist historians are in perfect agreement. As a matter

[48] *Istoriia Parizhskaia Kommuny,* p. 131.
[49] See Lukin, *op. cit.,* pp. 298-300.
[50] Stepanov, *Parizhskaia Kommuna,* p. 80.

of fact, says Trotski, the Commune pursued a terroristic policy but it did not pursue it far enough or with sufficient determination.

"Driven by the logic of the situation, it took its stand in principle on the path of intimidation. The creation of the Committee of Public Safety was dictated, in the case of many of its supporters, by the idea of the Red Terror. The committee was appointed 'to cut off the heads of traitors,' ('Journal Officiel,' No. 123) 'to avenge treachery' (No. 124). Under the head of 'intimidatory' decrees we must class the order to seize the property of Thiers and his ministers, to destroy Thiers' house, to destroy the Vendôme Column, and especially the decree of the hostages. For every captured Communard, or sympathizer with the Commune, shot by the Versaillese, three hostages were to be shot. The activity of the Prefecture of Police controlled by Raoul Rigault had a purely terroristic though not always useful purpose.

"The effect of all these measures of intimidation was paralyzed by the helpless opportunism of the guiding elements in the Commune, by their striving to reconcile the bourgeoisie with the *fait accompli* by the help of pitiful phrases, by their vacillation between the fiction of democracy and the reality of dictatorship." [51]

The Central Committee, instead of repressing violently and effectively the enemies of the proletariat when the situation was favorable, preferred to lose precious days in attempts at compromise and conciliation. "It continued to hope: 'When our enemies know us better . . . and understand the legality of our claims, they will come to us of their own accord.' . . . Instead of extirpating the rising counter-revolution at the root, the Central Committee declares, 'we have treated with disdain all their abuses.' " [52]

Even after April 2nd, when Paris and Versailles had joined

[51] *Defence of Terrorism*, p. 71.
[52] Slutskii, *op. cit.*, p. 51.

issue in civil war, the Commune refused to use terroristic means. "The third mistake of the Commune," says Braslovskii, "was its refusal to utilize the terror, that most important revolutionary measure, arising from the very nature of the class struggle. . . . Political timidity, the desire to escape from such a responsibility by sentimental declarations—the fear of bourgeois opinion, became the inheritance of the Commune Assembly. . . . Tenderness, excessive humanitarianism, political timidity and indecisiveness . . . are qualities which are irreconcilable with revolution." [53]

Bourgeois propagandists sowed treason in the ranks of the proletarian army and among the citizenry; spies from Versailles ferreted out the secrets of the defense of Paris; enemy organizations spouted lies and calumny; and the Commune permitted all from a mistaken allegiance to bourgeois rights of freedom of speech. The weakness of the terroristic machinery of the revolution is obvious in its treatment of the press. The Central Committee suppressed only two newspapers; and although the Communal Assembly suppressed twenty-odd, its chief activity came toward the end of the revolution. Even then these necessary acts of the Commune were bitterly opposed by the opportunist minority. The realization of the necessity of terrorism and, in particular, of the effective repression of personal liberty in various forms came late; but, at the end, "The same inflexible logic of events, which forced the Commune to infringe the freedom of the press, was leading it also to the infringement of freedom of assembly, personal liberty, etc." [54]

Unfortunately, it was too late.[55]

[53] *Istoriia Parizhskaia Kommuny 1871 goda* (Moscow, 1925), p. 131. See also *op. cit.*, p. 243.
[54] Lukin, *op. cit.*, p. 240.
[55] All the terroristic measures favored by the communists were, of course, a part of the political theory and practice of Blanqui and his followers. These were also a part of Jacobinism. It is natural that the leaders of the

These mistakes of the Commune which we have already discussed, the failure to organize the party and provide a program, a weakness for bourgeois "law and order," and an inexcusable timidity before the necessary means of terrorism, are largely attributed by communist historians to the "immaturity of the working class." The industrial proletariat formed a small part of the working population in Paris, and this working population had not yet assimilated the Marxian theory of the class struggle. This is, however, but a partial explanation of certain other serious mistakes which the communists include as causes of the fall of the Commune.

The revolution of 1871 was not represented by an adequate army. Despite the very large supplies of military equipment in Paris and the previous organization of 200,-000 men in the ranks of the National Guard, the Commune, by the middle of April, was defended by barely 30,000 men, and at the end by not over 10,000. For this there were a number of reasons. The Russian commentators discuss them in detail with many comparisons between 1871 and 1917. At the outset the Commune failed to realize the importance of an army in the class struggle, being deluded by hopes of reconciliation. Then, too, the "anarchist tendencies of the revolution deprived it of the strong, disciplined and organized masses required for an army." [56]

The communists are quite willing to recognize, in fact they insist, that revolutionary élan is not a sufficient quality to bring success to the banner of the proletariat. The indiscipline and disorganization of the ranks of the Commune was a fact too patent to be dismissed and Lavrov, who

2nd International should have seen a close resemblance between the ideas and practices of Lenin and Blanqui and have criticized Bolshevism as merely a renovated Blanquism. , But the communists, while esteeming the revolutionary character of Blanqui, see a very great difference. Blanqui, says Slutskii, had no real connection with the labor movement. He was a political conspirator, and an able one, but had not yet absorbed the principles of proletarian socialism. (*Op. cit.,* pp. 14-21.)

[56] Molok, *op. cit.,* p. 110.

fought in these same ranks, has given a picture of it which has impressed the communist historians.[57]

The military weakness of the Commune excited the attention of Trotski, in particular, the organizer of the Red Army. "For a fighting army there must be, first of all," he says, "a centralized and accurate apparatus of administration. Of this the Commune had not even a trace." [58]

On the other hand, "The Russian workers have shown that they are capable of wielding the instrument of war as well [as the instruments of peace]. We see here a gigantic step forward in comparison with the Commune. It is not a renunciation of the Commune—for the traditions of the Commune consist not at all in its helplessness—but the continuation of its work. The Commune was weak. To complete its work we have become strong. We are inflicting blow after blow on the executioners of the Commune. We are taking vengeance for the Commune and we shall avenge it."

The Soviet writers on the Commune are content to take Trotski's opinion of the importance of a military force to a proletarian revolution, and, consequently, his judgment on the army of the Commune.[59]

The Commune possessed trained and able military leaders but it did not know how properly to use their services. The only proper method, according to these writers, is indicated by the communists' treatment of "experts." In placing such men in the highest military positions without special control, the Communards only damaged their cause.

"It is evident," says Braslovskii, "that Rossel was not connected with the Commune. He could be utilized only as a valuable military specialist. Being a stranger to the true aims of the proletarian revolution of March 18th, Rossel

[57] Trotski quotes Lavrov at length on this matter.
[58] *Terrorism and Communism*, pp. 89-90.
[59] E.g., see Slutskii, *op. cit.*, p. 91.

was unable to understand the spirit of a revolutionary army." [60]

A fifth mistake of the Commune, to which the Soviet historians are inclined to attach considerable importance, was the failure of Paris to establish connections with the peasantry. Even after allowance has been made for the conditions of a siege, the severing of telegraph wires, the stoppage of the postal service, etc., these observers feel that the Commune could have done far more. "The Commune failed to agitate in the country districts in any adequate way. Two proclamations to the peasantry, issued too late and insufficiently distributed, could hardly be called adequate. No attempts were made to establish contacts with the peasants by the proper machinery of organization." [61]

As a matter of fact the Communards failed to understand the importance of such connections.[62] Here again the striking contrast between 1871 and 1917 impresses one at first glance. "The Paris Commune of 1871, this first proletarian revolution, failed because it was unable to enlist the support of the peasantry, this peasantry which permitted and even assisted the bourgeoisie to strangle the revolting city." [63]

How different was the Russian handling of this problem, remark the Russian historians. "The problem of the association of the laborers in city and in village," says Molok, "is the greatest problem, not only of the Russian proletarian revolution, but of the whole international struggle of the laboring class against capitalist slavery for the attainment of the future communist society." [64]

It was a problem which the Commune of Paris failed utterly to solve.

The same failure to enlist external assistance is to be

[60] *Ibid.*, p. 102.
[61] Lukin, *op. cit.*, p. 437.
[62] See Slutskii, p. 90.
[63] Molok, *The Paris Commune and the Peasantry in Russia*, p. 5.
[64] *Ibid.*, p. 5.

observed in the Commune's attitude toward the labor movement in other countries. "The Commune," remarks Slutskii, "made no attempt whatever to establish contact with the western European labor movement. Two acts—the destruction of the Vendôme Column, that symbol of militarism, despotism and the oppression of foreign nations; the changing of the name of Place Vendôme to Place Internationale; and the offer of the 15th of May, to hold the next meeting of the International in Paris—both give evidence of the Internationalist aims and the Internationalist character of the Paris Commune. But, as a matter of fact, it made no attempt to find real assistance outside of France." [65]

The Soviet historians criticize the Commune in many other details. For example they find its methods of propaganda, as one might expect, pitifully inadequate.[66] But the main line of their attack we have already outlined. It pretty much all boils down to the failure of the revolutionaries of 1871 to apply those fundamental principles of the "dictatorship of the proletariat" which met with such success in the Russian revolution of 1917-18.

THE COMMUNE AND THE COMMUNIST ATTACK ON THE 2ND INTERNATIONAL

Inextricably intermingled with the communists' account of the Commune of Paris and its relation to the revolution of 1917, is their attack on the principles and practice of the 2nd International. At times the primary purpose of an historical description of the revolution of 1871 is forgotten and the Commune becomes merely a convenient arsenal for weapons useful in the contemporary struggle. This is the use to which Trotski explicitly puts the March revolution in his *Terrorism and Communism*. And since the cleavage between the 2nd and 3rd International is most sharply

[65] Slutskii, *op. cit.*, p. 90.
[66] See Slutskii, p. 61.

outlined in the Trotski-Kautsky controversy, it is convenient
to discuss its relation to the Commune in terms of this controversy. For the Soviet students of the Commune have
followed Trotski to a man.

Both Kautsky and Trotski have written accounts of the
Commune.[67] Kautsky applauds its adherence to democratic
and parliamentary forms, its abstention from the terror,
and in general discovers it to have been actuated by generous
and humanitarian motives; in every sense it was "a noble
experiment." Since Marx approved of the Commune it is
evident to Kautsky that he approved of its institutions. The
Commune was a 'dictatorship of the proletariat' but this
merely means to Kautsky, and, according to him it meant to
Marx, government by democratic forms.[68]

"The Second Commune [1871] was torn asunder by violent opposition. We have seen this in the enmity of the two
parties engaged in the last struggle. But never did one of
these parties ever oppose the other by terrorist means. The
Maximalists—and the Minimalists—[Bolsheviks and Men-
sheviks] fought together, in spite of all, to the bitter end;
and so all factions of socialism in the Commune foresaw the
necessity of common representation of the whole of the
fighting proletariat. In recognizing this they combined the
views of Marx and Bakunin, Lasalle and Eisenach. The
first government of the proletariat has engraved itself deep
in the hearts of those who crave for the emancipation of
humanity. The powerful effect of this 'dictatorship of the
proletariat' on the fight for emancipation in all countries
was due not a little to the fact that it was inspired throughout with a spirit of humanity, which animated the working
classes of the 19th century."[69]

[67] Kautsky, *Terrorism and Communism*. Chapter 6 is devoted to the
Commune. Trotski, *Terrorism and Communism*, devotes 20 pages to the
Commune. See also his long introduction to Talès, *La Commune de 1871*.
[68] See on the interpretation of the Marxian "dictatorship of the proletariat" Bober, *Karl Marx's Interpretation of History*, p. 254.
[69] Kautsky, *op. cit.*, pp. 19-20.

Trotski, of course, envisages the Commune in quite a different manner, and his reading of Marx's interpretation is correspondingly opposed. We are not interested in the relative historical accuracy of the accounts of Kautsky and Trotski or in the adequacy of their Marxian exegesis.[70] What concerns us here is the antithesis between two conceptions of the theory and practice of the class struggle and the manner in which the Commune of Paris is utilized in this controversy, particularly by Trotski.

The Commune was not democratic, as Kautsky tries to make out, but it should have been less so: it employed the terror, contrary again to Kautsky, but it should have been more forceful in its application. That is the essence of Trotski's case.

"The bourgeoisie that remained in Paris, in spite of all its impudence, was still afraid of the revolutionary battalions, and the elections took place under the auspices of that fear, which was the forerunner of what in the future would have been inevitable—namely, of the Red Terror. But to console oneself with the thought that the Central Committee of the National Guard, under the dictatorship of which—unfortunately a very feeble and formalist dictatorship—the elections to the Commune were held, did not infringe the principle of universal suffrage, is truly to sweep with the shadow of a broom." [71]

The situation in Leningrad in 1917, was, Trotski insists, in every way similar to that in the Paris of 1871. If the Bolshevists had pursued the democratic and humanitarian policies which Kautsky apparently approves, the results of these revolutionary movements would also have been similar.

"In what, however," Trotski asks, "lies the difference between them? First of all, in the fact that Thiers' criminal

[70] As a matter of fact, the participants in this controversy are historically ill-equipped. Both owe their documentation to inferior secondary sources on the Commune and, as history, their accounts are pathetically feeble.
[71] *Terrorism and Communism,* p. 75.

plans succeeded: Paris was throttled by him, and tens of thousands of workers were destroyed. Miliukov, on the other hand, had a complete fiasco. . . . For this difference we were to a considerable extent responsible—and we are ready to bear the responsibility. There is a capital difference also in the fact—and this told more than once in the further course of events—that, while the Communards began mainly with considerations of patriotism, we were invariably guided by the point of view of the international revolution. The defeat of the Commune led to the practical collapse of the First International. The victory of the Soviet power has led to the creation of the Third International." [72]

The way of revolution, of dictatorship and of terrorism is swift and successful, and because it is swift it is truly humanitarian. "In the revolution, in the highest degree of energy is the highest degree of humanity." Trotski takes his stand here on a quotation from Lavrov's *Paris Commune*:

"Just the men who hold human life and human blood dear must strive to organize the possibility for a swift and decisive victory, and then to act with the greatest swiftness and energy, in order to crush the enemy. For only in this way can we achieve the minimum of inevitable sacrifice and the minimum of bloodshed." [73]

The communists are inclined to explain the principles of Kautsky and the 2nd International as an outcome of the separation of the proletariat into a "higher" and a "lower" class. The "higher" class adopted bourgeois political forms: the old ideas of proletarian revolutionary theory—revolution, seizure of power, dictatorship of the proletariat, etc., passed into the discard and a reform policy took its place. This development of an aristocracy of the proletariat inaugurated an era of Marxian "criticism"; parliamentarianism, the conception of progress by slow stages, took the place of Marxian catastrophic and revolutionary socialism.

[72] *Op. cit.,* p. 72.
[73] *Ibid.,* pp. 74, 75.

"And, naturally," says Slutskii, "from the Paris Commune, from its methods, it works and its struggle, they reacted negatively. The Commune was for them a product of the 'Blanquist' revolutionary method and it therefore drew their reproof." [74]

But the victory of Russian communism has caused the Commune to be reborn and with it the true principles of revolutionary Marxianism.

THE COMMUNE AND COMMUNIST PROPAGANDA

The revolution of 1871 has had, as we have seen, a certain amount of influence on the formulation of the theory of class struggle applied with such striking results by the leaders of Russian communism. By means of the elaborately organized machinery of communist propaganda its "lessons" have also been brought in forcible fashion to the attention of the masses. In 1917 and 1918 the walls of Leningrad, Moscow and other cities and villages of Russia were plastered with posters depicting the scenes of the Commune, in particular the executions of Bloody Week, and pointing its moral. Leaflets and proclamations dealing with the same subject were distributed on a large scale.

The years which have followed have seen a continuous series of pamphlets and brochures broadcast by various agencies of communist propaganda, by the Communist International, by the Moscow Committee of the Russian Communist Party, by the Komsomol (the organization of Communist Youth) by various local political bureaus of the Komintern, by the Political Bureau of the Military District of Kiev, and by many other agencies. [75]

Collections of readings on the Commune have been pre-

---

[74] *Op cit.*, p. 119.

[75] Bystrianskii, V., *Otets narodnichestva o rabochei revoliutsii*. Communist International, No. 4.

Akty y dokumenty. Épizod krovavoi nedeli. (Intro. by Zinoviev.) Communist International, 1920.

La Commune de Paris. A pamphlet of the Communist International translated into French in 1920.

The White Terror, Communist International, No. 10.

pared for workers' clubs, and programs on this subject have been devised for evenings of entertainment.[76] Handbooks for agitators contain a selection of materials on the revolution of 1871.[77] Poems and plays in great numbers take their themes from various incidents in the Commune, and are apparently staged or recited on occasions commemorative of this "glorious struggle." [78]

There is a difference between these propagandist publications and the communist histories considered in the last section. According to a communist bibliographer, the recent works of Stepanov and Lukin, for example, are written in a "thoroughly scientific, Marxist, fashion." [79] While to a bourgeois historian such a declaration is equivalent, practically, to describing these works as propaganda, it is clear that it was the intention of the authors to write a history of the events of 1871. Such intention is absent, or at least kept well in the background, in the materials now under consideration. These works are described by the communists as "educational"; i.e., as propagandist.

The introduction to a recent collection of literature on the Commune indicates very clearly the nature of these materials and the uses to which they are put.[80] "The present collection has been prepared for the mass of workers in the city workmen's clubs for the anniversary day of the Paris Commune.

"As to the contents of the collection, it has been the aim to present materials for the presentation of lectures, orations, dialogues, readings, artistic presentations, and finally for the staging of 'illustrative evenings' and evenings of 'recollections' having to do with the 18th of March, 1871.

"There is included at the end of the collection, biblio-

[76] See Gambarov, *op. cit.*
[77] Murin and Aronov. *Parizhskaia Kommuna; posobie dlia massovoi raboty v klubye.*
[78] Gambarov gives the names of eight plays on the Commune in Russian. For a collection of poems, see Murin and Aronov, *op. cit.*
[79] Gambarov, *op. cit.*, p. 4.
[80] Murin and Aronov, *op. cit.*, Introduction.

graphical information for the use of workers' libraries in securing books for exhibition and for speakers, agitators and propagandists, that they may more effectively familiarize themselves with the heroic history of the Paris Commune."

The speakers at meetings of this sort are often inexperienced or unfamiliar with their subject matter. Consequently the authors find it desirable to give certain directions on the handling of the Paris Commune.

"The aim of the work of agitation is this: the explanation of the rôle and significance of the Paris Commune for the revolutionary struggle of the world proletariat, for the October revolution and the existing S.S.S.R. . . .

"Of all revolutionary events celebrated in literature, it is recognized on all sides that the Paris Commune is foremost. On the Paris Commune we have the works of Marx, Lenin, etc. . . ."[81]

The authors go on to give advice on the presentation of lectures, the exhibition of maps, drawings, and other things.

The agencies for the dissemination of educational material on the Commune are naturally very careful in their selections. Nothing which does not follow the strict Marxian pattern is permitted. Thus the reminiscences on the Commune published in 1926 by M. T. Sazhin (Armand

[81] Murin and Aronov, *op. cit.,* p. 4.

The authors outline several programs designed to yield a pleasant and profitable evening. E.g., p. 5.

PART I

"Short talk entitled 'The History and Significance of the Paris Commune.'

PART II

" 'Diary of the Commune'—scenes from different episodes in the history of the Paris Commune. For an evening of unusual animation have singing with music and collective declamation. Materials may be had from good literature.

PART III

"On the theme 'Zavezskim Delo'—the beginning of the Paris Commune. To be entirely successful the evening concludes with a *tableau vivant* and the singing of the 'International'."

Ross) a friend of Bakunin, are introduced by a warning from the editors.

"In our century, the century of the realization of the dictatorship of the proletariat, when the standard of the Commune has been already erected over one-sixth of the world, all the mistakes of the Commune have become perfectly clear to the workers and peasants. It is necessary to organize the proletariat for victory, not leaving to class enemies the power and the means of their defense (weapons, materials, economic resources, banks, etc.).

"Anarchist ideas, dominant at the time of the Paris Commune, laid the foundation for many of its mistakes.

"The author of this appreciation, the Anarchist-Bakunist M. P. Sazhin, is certainly, it is obvious, not free from these mistakes. However, his account, as a point of view, does not lack interest, and so the government press has permitted its publication in spite of its variance in many points with established authors."

Not only is any variation from the established formula carefully noted, and accompanied by the proper rectification, but the formula itself is set forth in such elementary and specific detail as to make misconception impossible. This is strikingly illustrated by the following direction to lecturers: [82]

"For worker's groups and for mass gatherings, the plan of the lecture must include the following fundamental points.

"(1) The socio-economic characteristics of the background of the Paris Commune. Here should be treated the industrial situation in France (1852-1870), connected with the great technical advance in France, England, Germany and the United States. At the same time, mention should be made of the crimes of the bourgeoisie manifested in the policy of working-class oppression, the importance of the

[82] Murin and Aronov, *op. cit.,* p. 425.

revolutionary movement, the International and its three factions. Then deal with the Franco-Prussian War.

"(2) The 4th of September, 1870.

"(3) March 18, 1871. History and activity of the Commune. Fundamental mistakes and causes of the failure of the Commune. Significance of the Commune for the world revolutionary movement.

"(4) The October revolution and its continuation of the activity begun by the Paris Communards.

"(5) Contemporary struggle of the bourgeoisie with the forces of the universal social revolution. Significance and rôle of the M.O.P.R.

"(6) The fate of the movement generated by the Paris Commune is in charge of strong arms. Under the leadership of the Komintern, under the standard of Leninism, we shall win."

The purpose of propaganda of this sort, and of socialist and communist propaganda in general, is three-fold: (1) to portray the evils and iniquity of bourgeois society; (2) to describe the advantages and perfection of a socialist society; (3) to strengthen the faith of believers and to increase their ardor in the defense of the cause.[83] The communist interpretation of the revolution of 1871 is made to serve these ends admirably.

(1) The injustice, the cruelty, the oppression and the decay of bourgeois society is demonstrated in the communist accounts of the 2nd Empire. All the epithets which Marx so lavishly applied to Thiers, Favre, Napoleon and Gallifet are borrowed and added to. The suffering of the proletariat during a war made by capitalists and monarchists for the sake of private interest is clearly depicted.[84]

But, naturally, the events of Bloody Week furnish the

---

[83] See Sombart, *Proletarische Sozialismus.* II, ch. 7.
[84] See K. Grinevich, *Ocherki po Istorii Klassovoi boriby* (Leningrad, 1925), p. 88.

most effective material. The pamphlet published under the auspices of the Communist International in 1918, at the beginning of civil war in Russia, describes these horrors most vividly, if not accurately.

"The prisoners were shot down in hundreds and thousands; when it became tiresome to kill by rifle shot, crowds were swept away by grapeshot. . . . Gangs of chained prisoners were driven, tortured and killed on the way to Versailles, where they were received by groups of 'respectable' people; by the *jeunesse dorée*, noblemen, officers and their wives, virtuous concubines, courtisans of various kinds and allure. All this crowd fell upon the 'bandits,' the 'murderers,' the 'incendiaries,' spitting in the faces of the martyrs, jeering at and insulting them. Officers' 'ladies' probed the wounds of injured Communards with their umbrellas; bloody shreds of uniform were torn away from the dead. The cause of 'civilization' was triumphant." [85]

The Soviet propagandists take care to point out that the conduct of the bourgeoisie in 1871 is not unique. Such cruelty and depravity is not limited to France—it is a characteristic of the class.

"The third Bourgeois Republic was founded on the slaughter directed by the butcher Gallifet, as the second was founded in 1848 on the piles of corpses heaped in the workers' quarters by the executioner Cavaignac.

"Such are the noble origins of bourgeois republics." [86]

(2) The history of the Commune shows as clearly the excellence of a socialist republic. The perfection of such a society is not merely the product of theoretical speculation, it is demonstrated by experience.

"Bright and happy days were the lot of the population of Paris," says the 1918 pamphlet of the Komintern, "unfortunately they did not last for long; they were followed

---

[85] Maryek Konkol, *Kommuna, 1871 goda,* pp. 19-21.
[86] *La Commune de Paris.* Translation of a pamphlet of the 3rd International, p. 60.

by a dark and bloody night. . . . Before the catastrophe
Paris breathed with full lungs the pure fresh air and enjoyed her conquered happiness. . . . The Commune of
Paris justified all expectations. . . . It abolished governmental oppression. . . . The highest offices were occupied
by working men and poor citizens. . . . And the 'simple-
tons' taken by the revolution from manual labor, ruled
Paris in abler fashion than any of their predecessors. Paris
never slept so quietly; never had such perfect order reigned
before. For the second time [the first was the February
revolution] all thefts, holdups and robberies were at an end;
it seemed that all thieves and lawbreakers had left for Versailles together with their respectable and highly-paid
colleagues. The other characteristics of a bourgeois society
disappeared with miraculous swiftness. The prostitutes, so
numerous in capitalist Paris, went to join the émigré defenders of the Fatherland; i.e., the defenders, in the first
place, of private property. The laboring class, conquering
its own liberty, liberated the whole of Paris society. Just so,
in times to come, the proletariat, having achieved dictatorship, will become the leader and savior of humanity." [87]

(3) The propagandist literature on the Commune
attempts to stimulate revolutionary enthusiasm in a number
of ways. It is intended that its readers be stirred to pity,
horror and indignation by the picture of the cruelty of the
White Terror; that they should realize their probable similar fate in the event of defeat by the bourgeoisie; that they
should be moved to admiration by the contemplation of the
promise of a socialist society. The reader is asked to admire
the heroism of the Paris proletariat and to remember that
these heroes were fighting not only for the cause of the
Commune but for the cause of the world proletariat. Their
defeat and their suffering cries out for vengeance.

The lack of great revolutionary figures in the Commune
is turned to advantage. It is the mass of the proletariat,

[87] Konkol, *op. cit.*, pp. 15, 16.

the blind crowd of unknown, nameless men, which compels admiration and awakens adoration. This worship of nameless men, the vast, inchoate mass of the proletariat engaged in revolution, is but a variant on the cult of the "Unknown Soldier."

"The Proletariat honors its heroes. It dedicates to them its memorials. But its heroes are not striking personalities blinding our eyes with their radiance, not particular individuals, but a nameless man—the driving force of revolution. That is why the Proletariat attaches such importance to the Paris Commune of 1871." [88]

The dramatic episodes of the revolution of 1871 are already catalogued in the annals of revolutionary heroism.[89] The 18th of March has taken its place among the holy days in the proletarian calendar and the ritual of its celebration is in the full process of development. The cult of the Commune holds a cherished corner in the hearts of the communist faithful.

[88] Slutskii, *op. cit.,* p. 5.
[89] See *Geroizm revoliutsii* (Revolutionary Heroism), 2 vols., edited by L. N. Voimolovskii (Moscow, 1925). The Commune occupies 80 pages in the 2nd volume.

CONCLUSION

THE status of socialism for at least two decades after 1871 was seriously influenced by the Commune of Paris. Both socialists and their opponents persisted in interpreting the movement in the light of the revolution. To conservatives the eccentricities, stupidities and excesses of the Commune served as a sufficient illumination and adequate condemnation of the nature and aims of socialism. To socialists themselves the revolution of 1871 represented an affirmation and consecration of the faith.

Historians have rectified this mistake. But, reacting from both the terrified apprehension of contemporary conservatives and the uncritical enthusiasm of contemporary revolutionaries, they have proceeded too far in the opposite direction and have tended to envisage the Commune merely as an episode in the history of France. In so doing they have oftentimes neglected not only its undeniable relation to the socialism of the period but also its very real effect upon the European socialist movement.

The Commune of Paris had undoubtedly a strong socialist element. This was not, however, in any sense the result of its proletarian origin or character. The working-class membership of the Communal Assembly and the working-class element outside the Assembly imbibed its ideas from the same source as and acted in a way indistinguishable from the bourgeois and petit-bourgeois elements. Indeed one can go further and say that the ideas and policies which Russian communism finds so distinctively socialist or communist in the revolution were nothing other than recrudescence of the bourgeois Jacobin terrorism of 1793. The real socialists of the Commune were, in almost every instance, in

369

opposition to these ideas and policies. And both Jacobin terrorists and socialist reconstructionists in 1871 were fairly evenly divided between the proletariat and the bourgeoisie.

The socialism of 1871 was not in any sense conspicuously proletarian. Nevertheless, it exerted a strong influence on the development of the revolution. The economic egalitarianism of contemporary Jacobinism, the extensive organization and permeation of the first International in Paris, and the antagonistic but effective influence of Blanqui and Proudhon, implanted a variegated and confused impress upon the acts and policies of the Commune. It is not necessary to demonstrate again that influence. It is visible in the proclamations, the propaganda and the acts of the Commune.

But, for all that, the Commune was not essentially a socialist movement. At the outset it recruited its adherents from another milieu and, although at the end its strength had simmered down to a revolutionary group pretty thoroughly imbued with socialism, its impetus and *raison d'être* are to be found in causes which lie outside the domain of socialism. The war with Germany, the events of the siege, disgust with a strongly centralized and incompetent government, were of more decisive significance.

Whatever the historical reality, however, a legend of the Commune has been developed in socialist and communist circles which finds the meaning of the revolution in its socialism. And, as I have attempted to demonstrate, this legend has been and is of more importance in the molding of history than the historical reality itself. The Commune in the hands of Marx and his disciples has become a living and active force. The legend is more vital than the fact. Socialism has taken the Commune from the history of France and has made of it a battle cry for the proletariat of the world.

INDEX

THE FOLLOWING ABBREVIATIONS ARE EMPLOYED

CC20A Central Committee of the Twenty Arrondissements.
CCNG Central Committee of the National Guard.
CLIT Commission of Labor, Industry and Trade.
CPS Committee of Public Safety.
CA Commune Assembly.
GND Government of the National Defense.
INT International.
NA National Assembly.
NG National Guard.

INDEX

160; on encouragement of industry, 245-246; exceeds municipal
functions, 163, 165, 189-191; financial administration, 202-206, 225;
adheres to Geneva Convention,
179n; seizes hostages, 179-180; incompetence, 192, 233; influence of
1793 on, 69, 241, 243; leaders, 61,
73, 182, 345, 367-368; legend of,
ix-x, 282, 330, 367-368, 370; military administration, 173-174, 208-
235, and *see also* NG; partisans a
minority, 141; mistakes, 145n, 161,
172-173, 227, 332, 334, 347-357, 359,
364-365; and NA, 161, 164-166;
order under, 195-196, 367; origins,
x-xi, 58, 96, 99, 119, 168-170, 344-
345, 364, 370; pensions, 200; becomes political, 171; press criticism
of, 234; proclamations, 163, 175,
255-258; program, 255-258, 332,
348-349, 354; and provinces, 161;
takes over public services, 186;
salaries under, 245; sequestrates
property of NA leaders, 187; social legislation, 246-254, 335; relation to socialism, 3, 118, 172, 254,
256. *See also* CA.
"La Commune," 154, 223, 235.
Commune Assembly (CA), 164-165,
199, 220, 229, 255, 318, 353; conflict with CCNG, 222, 226, 230-233;
Delescluze chides, 219, 226, disintegration, 273, 278; dissensions, 3,
221-235; election and installation,
147, 162; membership, 45, 66n,
182-186; proclamations, 188, 256-
258; resignations, 184, 236; weakness, 184, 186, 283. *See also* Commune.
Communism, Blanqui on, 21, 24; in
the Commune, 118, 137; Russian,
325-369.
Communist Manifesto, 1, 50, 306n,
308, 317, 322, 323.
Communists, on the Commune, 19,
137, 145n, 161, 196, 202n, 226, 303,
327; Russian, chief sources, 328-
329, 342; use of Commune history
as propaganda material, *see*
Propaganda.
Conscience, freedom of, 173, 189,
258.

Conscription, abolished, 163, 189,
190, 213.
Conseils de Légion, 183, 207.
Conservatives, 11, 46, 47, 60, 62,
120, 126, 136, 141, 145.
Considérant, Victor, 1.
Contract system, 249.
Coöperation, 28, 42, 50, 55, 249n.
Corbon, 45n, 294.
"La Corderie," 64, 118, 136.
Courbet, 229n, 237, 286.
Courbevoie, encounter at, 173, 210.
Cournet, 184, 197, 259.
Courts martial, 211, 285-294.
Crémieux, 82; Gaston, 101.
Cresson, 77n, 79, 82n, 85.
Creusot, revolts in, 164.
"Le Cri du Peuple," 66n, 106n, 113,
151, 238, 264, 272.
Cults, Ministry of, 193.
Customs revenues, 204.
Cyrille, 72n, 106.

Da Costa, G., 20n, 198, 205, 227n,
243, 275, 279.
Daïs, Gen. Leroy de, 289.
Danton, 11, 173.
Darboy, Archbishop, 179, 266, 267.
Dauthier, 52n.
Debtors, relief of, 103, 134, 143, 188,
227n, 250-253.
Decentralization, 40, 303, 309-310,
370; views on, in Communal revolution, 190, 257, 258, 260, 263. *See
also* Centralization, Federalism.
Declaration of Rights, *1791*, 14.
Defeat as cause of the Commune,
x, 96, 116, 170, 303, 370.
Defenders of the Republic, 108.
Deguerry, 267.
Delahaye, 52n.
Delescluze, 16-18, 67, 72-74, 77, 118,
220, 241, 259, 260n, 297, 302, 313;
age, 186; attacks Favre and Gambetta, 63; calls for battle of the
barricades, 274; Baudin memorial
subscription, 6; chides CA, 219,
226; in CPS, 228; in CA, 184,
219, 226; death, 279; at funeral
of Victor Noir, 8; supports GND
at first, 63; mayor, 79; as military
leader, 220-221; in NA, 101, 102,
167; praises Commune of *1792-3*,

INDEX 377

Salaries under the Commune, 245, 338.
Sapia, 68, 87, 97, 118.
Say, J. B., and son, 22.
Sazhin, 363-364.
Schoelcher, 72n, 143-144, 155n.
Schools, 190. *See also* Education.
Secession of Paris, 111.
Sedan, 58, 59, 88, 96, 348.
Seine, bodies thrown into, 293; poisoning suggested, 81.
Senior, Nassau, 122.
Separation of powers, 338.
Sérizier, 97, 277n.
Serrailler, 229n, 237n, 270n.
"Le Siècle," 6n, 179n, 181n, 276.
Siege of Paris, 16, 65, 86, 89, 92, 94-95, 98-99, 313; as cause of the Commune, x, 3, 157, 170; debts deferred during, 103-104; rationing, 84, 93; schemes for raising, 80-81, 91.
Simon, Jules, 4, 50, 63, 77n, 96, 102n, 152, 186n, 187, 312.
Slutskii, 332n, 334n, 354n, 357, 361.
Socialism, in the clubs, 83; relation to the Commune, 3, 47, 118, 137, 155-170, 172, 254-266, 335, 369-370; dissensions within, 9, 10, 19, 31-32, 48, 227; in France, 1-5, 8, 54, 266, 348; relation to INT, 44, 48, 50; and Jacobins, 9-10; Mutualists on, 39-41, 43; as a relative term, 244; Thiers on, 122-123.
Socialist clubs, statements, 159.
Socialists, on the Commune, 127n, 196, 202, 262, 282, 297; in CA, 159, 184, 227; German, 262, 300, 317, 322.
Société Républicaine Centrale, 29.
Sociétés d'Alimentation, 249n.
"Le Soir," 223.
"La Solidarité," 299.
Sombart, 26.
Sortie torrentielle, 91.
Soviets, viii, 338-339.
Standing army, abolition of, 109, 114, 119, 127, 160, 318, 335, 339-340.
State, withering away of the, 309-311.
Stekloff, 49n.
Stepanov, 328, 344n, 362.
Stone cutters, 158, 248.

Street fighting, *see* Barricades.
Strikes, 7, 28, 52, 56.
Students as revolutionaries, 5.
Suffrage, 100, 151, 323-324.
Supplies, Commission of, 194n.
Susbielle, Gen., 124.
Switzerland, Communards escape to, 278-279, 299, 301.

Taine, 11, 14.
Talès, *La Commune de 1871*, 343.
Tamisier, 77n, 78.
Taschereau document, 30.
Taxation under the Commune, 204-205.
Telegraphs, 140, 190, 206n, 356.
"Le Temps," 223n.
Ténot, 6.
Terrorism, 2, 9, 12, 198, 226, 351-354, 358-360, 369.
Theatres, closed, 80.
Theisz, 43, 56, 185n, 206n, 229n, 245.
Thiers, 11, 102, 104, 106, 130, 157, 186, 187, 262, 279, 294, 365; appeal to provinces, 188; armistice negotiations, 70, 313; army, 128, 139, 169, 209, 210; attacks Paris, 351; Blanqui a prisoner of, 183, 267; character and views, 60, 122-123, 129, 133; chief executive, 101; on the Commune, 146, 150, 154, 289, 293; compromise offers merely to gain time, 144-146, 169; on Courbevoie engagement, 174n; March 18, 121-129, 133, 138, 140-141, 146, 177, 314-315; Marx on, 312-315; in NA, 101; opposition to, 82, 152n; property seized, 234, 240-241, 352; repressive policy, 122-123, 178-179, 223, 287.
Thiéry, 183n.
Thieves, death penalty for, 134.
Thomas, A., *Le Second Empire*, 41; Gen. Clément, 78, 99n, 100, 125, 130, 167, 316.
Tibaldi, 87, 90, 118.
Tinguy, Marquis de, 235.
Tirard, 144, 150, 165, 183n.
Tivoli-Vauxhall, meetings at, 108, 109, 112, 122.
Tolain, 7, 45n, 50, 51, 52, 53, 167n.
Toleration, religious, 266.
Toulouse, Commune at, 164, 168.